AF606088

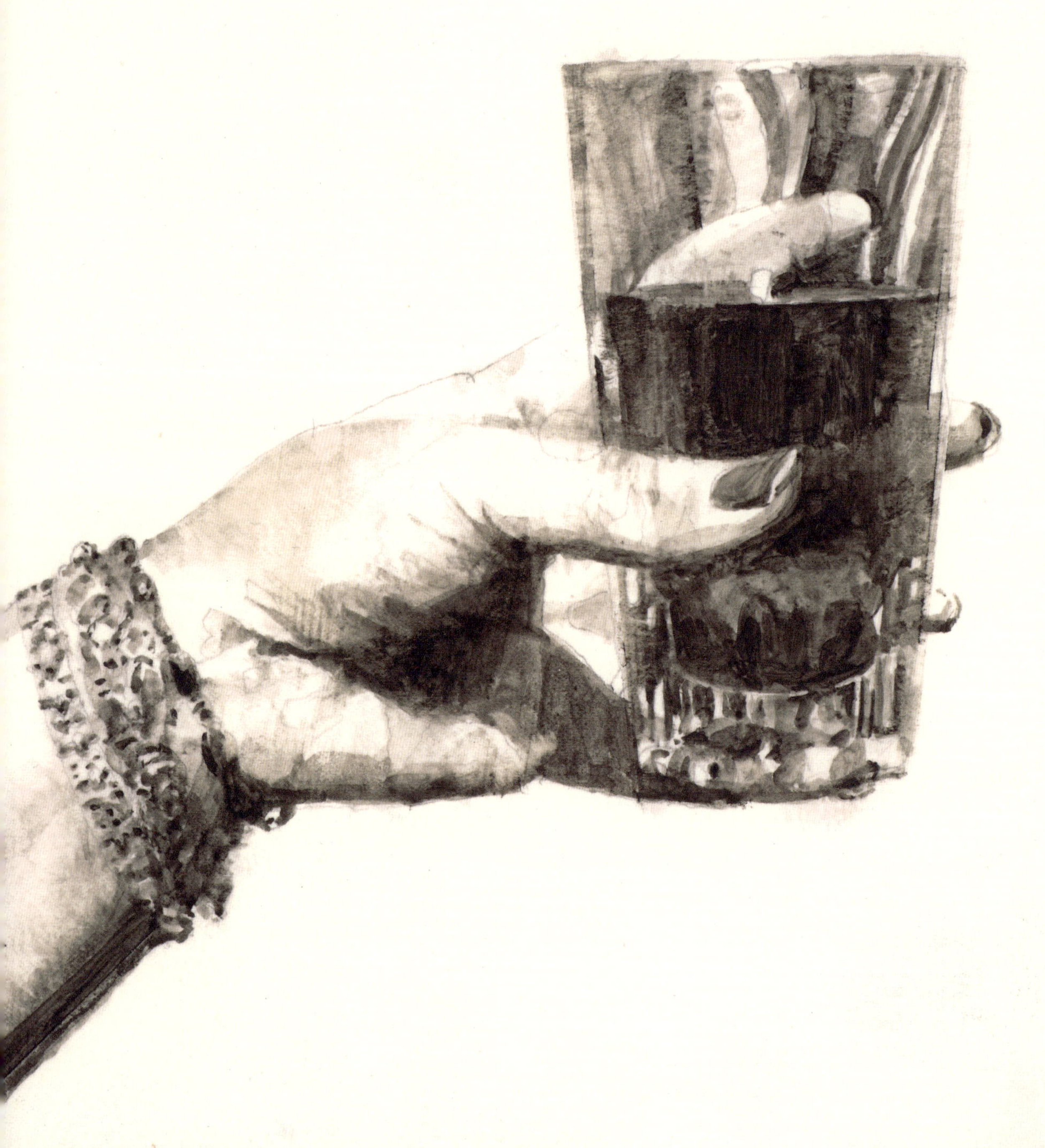

COCKTAILS *with a* CURATOR

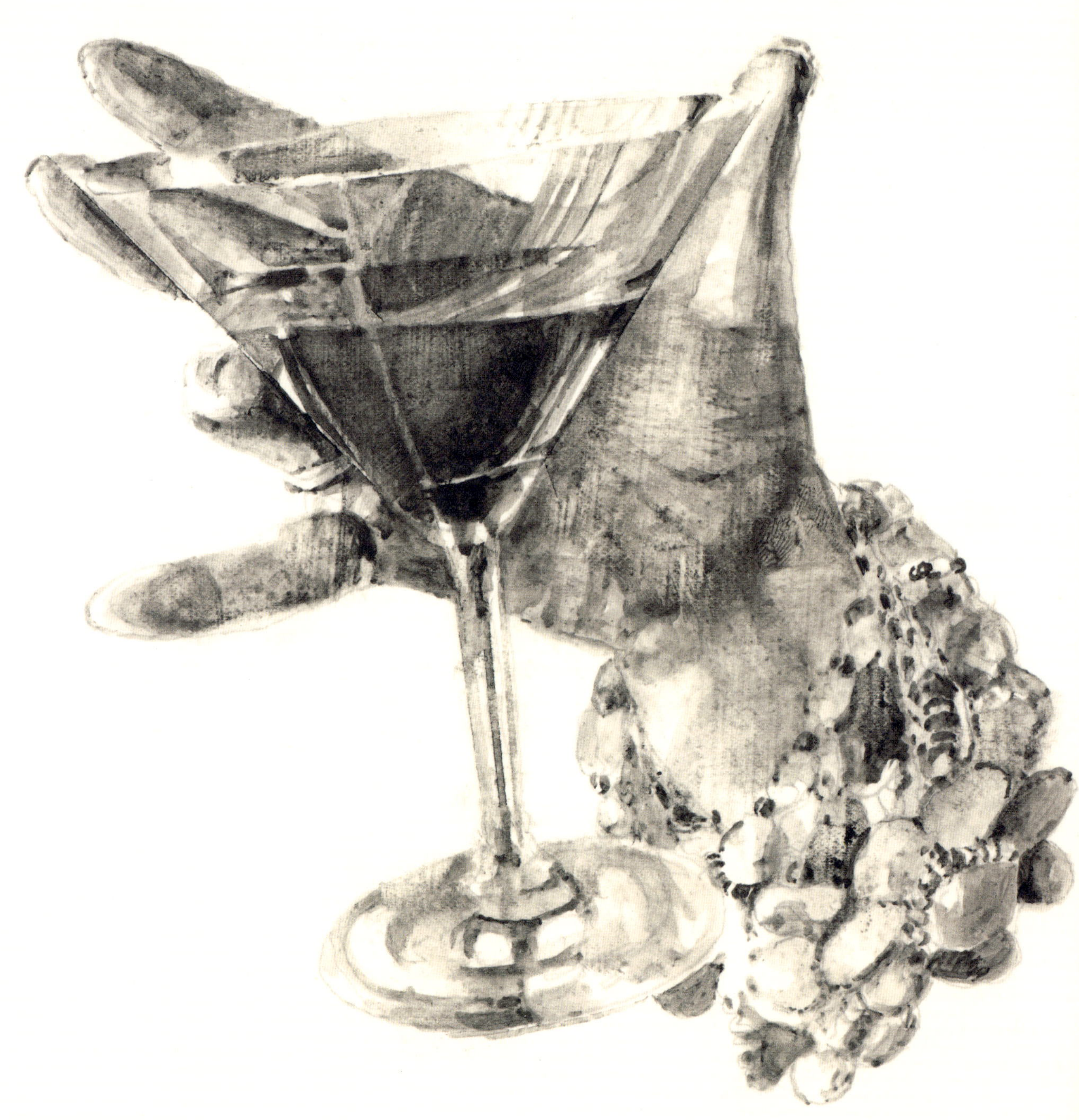

COCKTAILS *with a* CURATOR

THE FRICK COLLECTION

Foreword by

SIMON SCHAMA

XAVIER F. SALOMON
with AIMEE NG *and* GIULIO DALVIT

Drawings by

LUIS SERRANO

RIZZOLI ELECTA
NEW YORK

CONTENTS

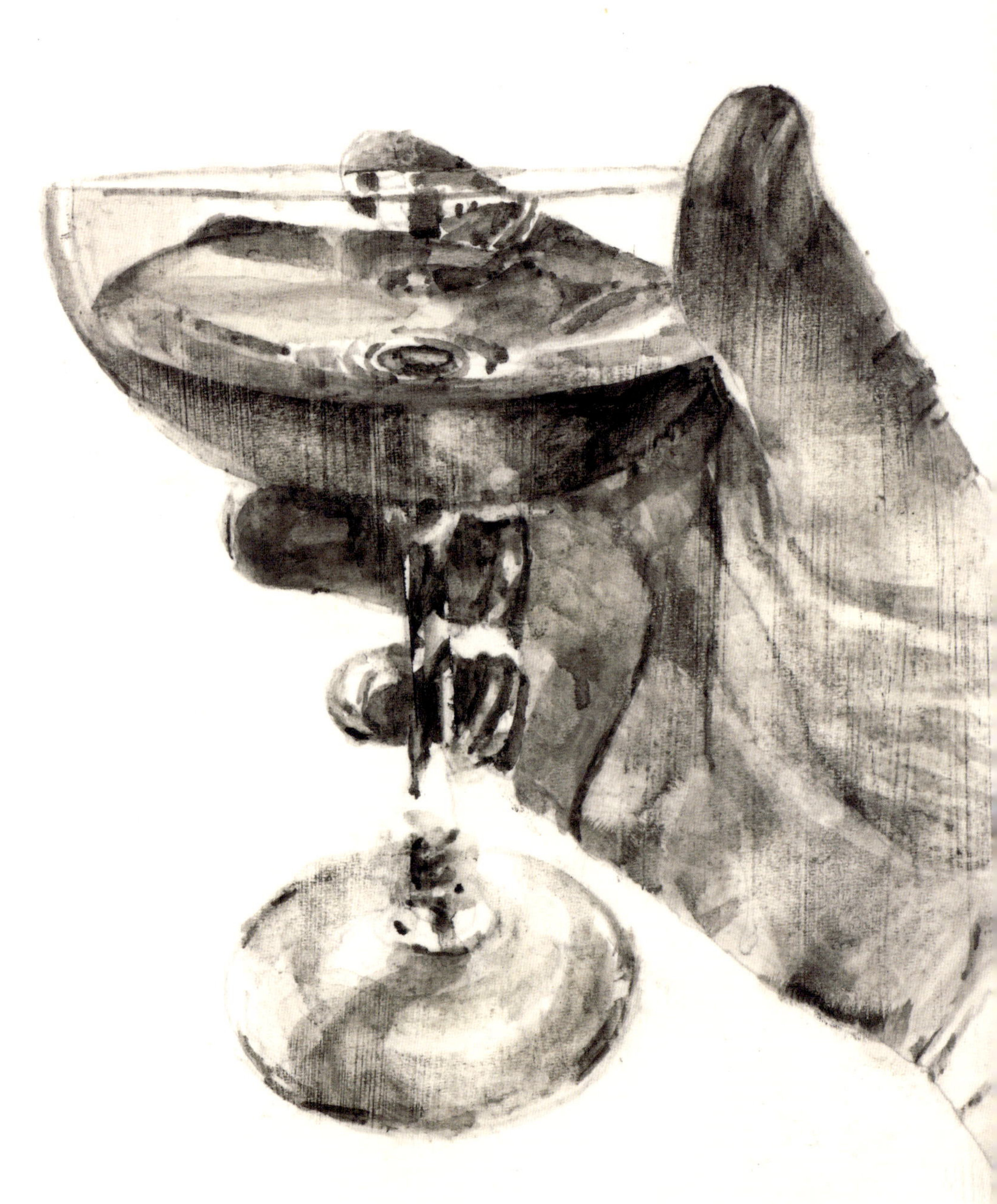

FOREWORD
Simon Schama

Only a Frick curator, in this case, the wise Xavier Salomon, would know that the right drink for looking at, and thinking about, a Giovanni Bellini masterpiece ought not to be a Bellini. The radiance that washes over St. Francis, standing before his cave lodging, is anything but peachy, though it does have a springtime-spritzy brilliance. That velvety-mouthfeel cocktail should go instead to his pupil and successor in Venetian sensuousness, Titian, whom I have no trouble at all imagining occupying a corner of Harry's Bar, eyeballing the talent, together with Aretino (the subject of his great Frick portrait)—one minute grandly high-minded, the next, low and lubricious. The Manhattan matched with Bellini's *St. Francis* is an homage to the Frick's location rather than the Venetian master's luminous marriage of the sacred and the sensuous. All the same, mixologically speaking, I'd replace the bourbon with rye so as to cut Giovanni Bellini's saturated oil-based colors (all hail the maraschino cherry, assuming it's Luxardo) with an edge of the astringent piety that lit his chiseled heads and the most sublime of his sacred histories.

Quibble quibble. But there's no arguing with the whole spirited (in every sense) project of the *Cocktails with a Curator* video series. In the depths of the COVID lockdown, for about half an hour each week, Xavier, Aimee Ng, and Giulio Dalvit—the most engaging, as well as the most deeply learned, of barkeep curators—brought beauty, thought, provocation, and scholarly meditation into our intolerably cramped lives. The lockdown held us prisoner. The three curators got us packing our imaginative bags and heading for Rembrandt's Amsterdam (Polish bison grass vodka); Vermeer's Delft (genever, but then he lived over a tavern); Dieppe, where Turner is sketching (Widow's Kiss cocktail); Hradčany Castle in Prague, where the emperor Rudolf II displays Veronese's two astounding allegories of *Wisdom and Strength* (Negroni? And how.) and the *Choice Between Virtue and Vice* (Negroni Sbagliato). One of the showpiece objects is itself a bibulous accomplice: an eighteenth-century Viennese porcelain wine pourer in the shape (albeit anatomically elasticated) of a white elephant.

Thus the Frick repositioned the space-time continuum, bent out of shape by the fiendish contagion. As long as we were all locked in our pockets of isolation, time folded in on itself, our temporal moorings unpinned. The rhythm of the working week lost meaning; Fridays became just another arbitrary twenty-four-hour calendrical unit, until, that is, *Cocktails* came along and turned Friday at five into a genuinely Happy Hour. I would make my dutiful constitutional trudge up and down suburban hills and roads, but with me—courtesy of the phone, never smarter—came Turner (a vigorous drinker), Jacques-Louis David (not so much), Paolo Veronese, and Diego Velázquez, along with the gripping commentaries of Aimee, Xavier, and Giulio, at once conversational and scholarly. The pieces are all so beautifully written and so imprinted with personal engagement that they sometimes seem to be sketching out a new genre: the art historical true short story. Characters exit their two-dimensional frames to take on a poetic richness, often shot through with tragic irony. Sir John Suckling—the cavalier poet, inventor of cribbage, and compulsive gambler—gets the full Van Dyck treatment set against a glowing Arcadian landscape holding an enormous folio edition. But the man who was not above ordering a pack of marked cards made the wrong gamble in the English Civil War—swallowed up by the defeats of Charles I, indicted as a traitor by Parliament, and committing suicide by poison in his Parisian exile rather than collapse into destitution.

Grace Dalrymple Elliott, the Regency beauty who cut through men like a silver knife through breakfast butter, ended up—after a close relationship with the former Duc d'Orléans, whose Republican name, Philippe Égalité, failed to save him from the Jacobin guillotine—in a French revolutionary prison. There, as she claimed in her memoir, the treatment of the inmates was so unsparing that all their teeth fell out. Ng remembers this when she thinks of Grace's cherry lips, just barely parted, in the sensually charged Gainsborough portrait, one of the greatest things at the Frick. The picture itself is a painterly tour de force—those generous, arched eyebrows framing an intently arresting gaze; a heavy blue and silver locket, suspended by a green ribbon hanging between her creamy breasts; the décolleté bodice described with Gainsborough's most playfully liberated brushwork. All this makes Ng ask, in the style of an intrigued detective, "Who commissioned this intimate, sensuous painting?" And for that matter, "How much of her journal account is true? And what or whom, if anything, did she keep in that blue locket? One gets a sense from her portrait that she held her secrets close."

Warren Hastings, the East India Company's governor general of Bengal, painted by George Stubbs, is rightly characterized by Salomon as "a great intellectual," who spoke "several Indian languages, could read and write in Sanskrit . . . studied Persian . . . and supported the first translation of the Bhagavad Gita." None-theless, Hastings was made the fall guy for the depredations and military insatiability of "John Company." Impeached in the House of Commons—a trial lasting seven years—for crimes and misdemeanors of the Company, Hastings became target practice for the rhetorical artillery of Edmund Burke. His career and life destroyed, he was nonetheless acquitted, and a grand portrait of him, mounted on his favorite Arabian, was presumably meant as a kind of defiant self-vindication. But the Frick's Stubbs—a watercolor study of the head alone—is something else entirely: the features gaunt and haunted; the eyes sunk in stoic melancholy, it is much more memorable than the full equestrian picture.

Don't be fooled, though, by the literary thoughtfulness of the tone. *Cocktails with a Curator,* the book, while preserving the conversational friendliness of the spoken voice of the three curators, is, on almost every page, superlative, hardcore art history. Each essay is not just a fresh reading of the Frick's treasures, generated from concentrated looking and reflection. Each is also an account of the milieu in which the object was created; the point in the artist's career that led him or her to that moment of invention; the grammar of iconography; and sometimes, most interestingly, the journey that object took, from leaving the artist's studio or workshop to arriving (sometimes via the collection of J. P. Morgan!) into the possession of Henry Clay Frick. Thus, *The White Horse,* Constable's spectacular "six-footer," was the work that, in 1819—after many long years of demoralizing indifference—got the artist elected as an Associate of the Royal Academy. (Outrageously, it would be another decade before he became a full Academician.) The archdeacon who bought it and changed its name from the artist's more generic *Scene on the River Stour* fell on times so hard that he implored Constable to buy it back. Once the work was returned at the original price, Constable never let it out of his studio. But before it came into the hands of the collection, it belonged to Henry Clay Frick's rival in both finance and art appetite, J. P. Morgan, as did Rembrandt's brilliant portrait of Nicolaes Ruts. Even then, *The White Horse* stayed unseen, hidden for the duration of the war. New Yorkers getting to see it in 1945 has to be one of the most delectable fruits of victory.

The personal and the painterly are so often woven together, never more longingly than in Whistler's full-length portrait of Frances Leyland, dressed in rosy silk, her face and body turned away from the artist, who, if London talk was to be believed (and in Whistler's case, why not?), coveted her, attaching himself to her sister as a next-best romantic surrogate. For Frances was unavailable, married to the shipowner Frederick Leyland, one of Whistler's major patrons. Thus the result is breathy with sexual yearning. Brilliant, then, for Xavier to have paired it with a sake highball, for Whistler was a devotee of japonaiserie, and the drink cuts the somnolent richness of sake with a spritz of cool reckoning.

As a bit of a shaker myself, I'm bound to have some differences with our hosts and guides. Tokaji (the white elephant pourer) should *never* be chilled; the "seasonal fruits" in Pimm's No. 1 should be replaced by mandoline-shaved slices of cucumber, and you may feel that the scary concoction called Widow's Kiss—combining Yellow Chartreuse, Bénédictine, and Calvados—that goes with Turner's *Harbor of Dieppe,* while definitely Norman and monastic, is, like the painting itself, A Bit Too Much. What can't be disputed, though, is that *Cocktails with a Curator* delivers a procession of illuminations so exhilarating that it confirms what any visitor to The Frick Collection already knows: that great art delivers its own unsurpassable hit of intoxication.

DIRECTOR'S PREFACE

For many, looking at art in museums is a great pleasure and sometimes a source of solace. The March 2020 closing of cultural institutions due to the pandemic abruptly withdrew this activity from the public realm. Two years later, keeping our galleries open remains a challenge. Among the few compensations of this period has been the widespread adoption of virtual means of communication and the creative uses of video on the internet. Many may have been taken aback at the segue to the virtual for an institution like the Frick. What distinguishes this museum above all is the integration of a superlative collection of Old Master art into the fabric of a great Gilded Age mansion. In order to experience the Frick, one has to be present, physically present, in the galleries.

The Frick has long had a robust website. Our first virtual tour was developed nearly twenty-five years ago, and a decade ago, we initiated the practice of live-streaming and archiving most of our lectures. All the information associated with our exhibitions is available on our website, and thanks to Bloomberg Connects, the Frick has developed its second app, replacing audio tours with updated narratives. The Frick Art Reference Library is a leader in digital art history and in making its photo archive accessible internationally. *Cocktails with a Curator* was not conceived in a vacuum but rather in the context of these technical innovations.

What none of us anticipated was the global reception that *Cocktails* would receive, with more than 1.8 million views of the episodes. There are several reasons for this success, which Xavier F. Salomon explores in his introduction. Essentially, I think, the program filled a need that many have to share the experience of looking at and thinking about a work of art, an activity that was unavailable in museums at the beginning of the pandemic. The Frick is a repository not only of masterpieces but of first-rate expertise; the curators presented the art conversationally and without pretension. This turned out to be a winning formula. In the long term, museums must respond to the public's desire to complement the actual experience of art with digital approaches. For the moment, this book celebrates a much-loved digital program by means of a traditional paper volume. We hope that you will enjoy it, perhaps be inspired to rewatch the videos, and visit us in person.

IAN WARDROPPER
Anna-Maria and Stephen Kellen Director
The Frick Collection

ACKNOWLEDGMENTS

Conceived during the extremely difficult time of the COVID-19 pandemic, *Cocktails with a Curator* has been a labor of love on the part of a large group of people. The three of us are enormously grateful to our colleagues and friends at the Frick. Without them we could not have accomplished any of this. We would like to particularly acknowledge the hard work and attention to detail of our digital team: Lisa Goble, David Morneau, and Sean Troxell. In communications, Alexis Light, Patricia Kilbride, and Heidi Rosenau worked on each of the episodes and its promotion. Curatorial assistants Rebecca Leonard and Gemma McElroy were essential in helping us with research material and images and with transcribing the texts of each episode. Michaelyn Mitchell oversaw the production of this book and with Christopher Snow Hopkins beautifully edited the text. We would also like to thank Sally Brazil, Rebecca Brooke, Angie Calderwood, Joseph Coscia Jr., Elizabeth Daly, Julia Day, Joseph Godla, Caitlin Henningsen, Bailey Keiger, George Koelle, Julie Ludwig, Rowan Moody, Gianna Puzzo, and Carolyn Thomas. The support of the Frick's director, Ian Wardropper, was, as always, vital for this project.

Luis Serrano's gorgeous illustrations bring this book to life in a very different way from the video series, and we are very grateful to him. We want to thank Simon Schama for the warmth, generosity, and eloquence of his foreword. We are also indebted to literary agent Zoë Pagnamenta for securing our copublishing arrangements with Rizzoli, and at Rizzoli, we would like to acknowledge Philip Reeser.

Others to whom thanks are due include John Berwald, Piero Boccardo, Christine von Brühl, Emma Capron, Jacek Dehnel, Mathieu Deldicque, Matteo Lafranconi, Simon Lewis, Mee-seen Loong, Hugues Morisse, Michał Przygoda, Neville Rowley, Pat Rubin, Charlotte Vignon, and Francesco Zaffarano.

We are extremely grateful to Virginia and Randall Barbato for their very generous funding of this book.

Finally, we would like to thank all those from around the world who tuned in to the video series and who wrote in not only with support and gratitude for the program but also with additional historical information that has furthered our research.

GIULIO DALVIT, AIMEE NG, and XAVIER F. SALOMON
New York City
April 2022

INTRODUCTION
Xavier F. Salomon

When the New York museums started closing in mid-March of 2020, we did not know the degree to which the COVID-19 pandemic was to upend our lives. Now, two years later, the world is still grappling with the global crisis—its tragic losses and its far-ranging repercussions. During this time, many people questioned and reconsidered the role of cultural institutions. As we closed the Frick, uncertain as to how long it would remain shut, Aimee Ng and I, along with a number of other colleagues, asked ourselves, "What is the role of our museum? And how can a museum, especially a small one devoted to collecting and studying European art from the late thirteenth through nineteenth centuries, remain an important reference point for its audience during a period of turmoil?" The living organism of a museum cannot exist without its collections being accessible to the public. Without an audience, a museum is nothing more than art storage.

As the doors of the museum closed, my mind went to two programs implemented in the 1940s by the National Gallery in London, a museum that has occupied a central role in my art education. Between 1940 and 1941, the National Gallery's collection was moved to the quarry of Manod, in Wales, for safekeeping. Beginning in 1942, however—in the middle of the London bombing campaign known as the Blitz—the gallery inaugurated its Picture of the Month program. Each month, beginning with Rembrandt's *Margaretha de Geer,* they brought a painting back from Wales to the museum in Trafalgar Square, exhibiting it in splendid isolation, free of charge, to the public. Each painting was on view during the day and brought into subterranean storage every night. For forty-three months, masterpieces by Titian, Bellini, El Greco, and Velázquez, among many others, brightened the lives of Londoners amid the terror of war. At the same time, the pianist Myra Hess organized daily lunchtime concerts at the museum. These were held between 1939 and 1946. Sandwiches were provided, and the public lined up outside the gallery every day. Long after the concerts ended, Hess said, "If I had died the day peace was declared, I would have felt my life's work was complete." These extraordinary programs about which I had long heard—including from my English family, which was in London during the war—and the vision of Myra Hess and of the then director of the gallery, Kenneth Clark, were in my mind as the doors of 1 East 70th Street were bolted.

I did not know then that our beloved Frick Collection would remain closed for a full year—between March 2020 and March 2021—and that it would reopen (for reasons unrelated to the pandemic but linked to an extensive restoration of its historic building) in its temporary incarnation in the Marcel Breuer–designed building on Madison Avenue that we call Frick Madison. Beginning on April 10, 2020, and drawing to a close more than sixty-five weeks later, on July 16, 2021, the staff of the Frick embarked on a project that was born of the desire to make our museum a beacon for our public at a time of disaster and need. In the early days of April 2020, Aimee and I met with our communications and digital teams to brainstorm ideas on how the internet could be used to connect us to our audiences, sheltered in their homes. Barely a week passed between that meeting and the airing online of the first episode of *Cocktails with a Curator.* Looking back on that first episode, I cannot help but reflect on how little I knew about what I was embarking on or—frankly—what I was doing. I still think about the inaugural episode on Giovanni Bellini's *St. Francis in the Desert* with a good deal of embarrassment.

There is a small book that has held a vital role for me ever since my youth growing up in Rome. I do not recall how the book entered my life. It may have belonged to my paternal grandmother. I grew up in the house that my great-grandfather purchased after escaping from Mexico at the time of the revolution, in the late 1910s, and where my grandmother had grown up. So much of my interest in the world around me and in what the past has left us is due to the influences of my paternal grandmother, Guadalupe Boari Salomon, and my maternal grandfather, Cecco Baschieri Salvadori. By the time I was a teenager, the treasured book had lost its cover and was in a state of disrepair. In my twenties, I had it rebound in a little shop on the Janiculum Hill. The book, *Pietre, figure, storie e storielle della vecchia Roma* (Stones, Figures, Stories, and Little Stories of the Old Rome), was written and illustrated by Daria Borghese—a member of the illustrious Roman family—and published in 1954. In more than one hundred and forty chapters, each one or two pages long and accompanied by an elegant black-and-white drawing, Borghese narrates engaging stories about sites, monuments, and artworks in Rome from antiquity to the nineteenth century. To a large degree, I still look at my birthplace, and more generally at art, through the lens of this book. Narrative has always been central for me. I think about the past as a series of stories that reach us in the present and can shape our future. I never looked at Trajan's Column, the Protestant Cemetery, or the Trevi Fountain or thought about Poussin, Angelica Kauffmann, Byron, or Francesco Borromini without returning to the Borghese book. As I grew up, the narrative structure of the book—developed and enlarged by many other sources—shaped my interests and life. From the time, at age seven or eight, that I spoke to my class about the Sistine Chapel—at the prompting of my primary school teacher, Suor

Ludovica—to the times, as a teenager, when (I am still not quite sure how!) I convinced my friends to skip school to go and see the exhibitions on Domenichino or other equally elusive baroque painters, I realized that the most meaningful moments were those in which I shared art with the people around me.

Borghese's book was certainly in my head when *Cocktails with a Curator* first emerged as an idea. Could we tell stories about the masterpieces at the Frick online? Could we keep the stories short (fifteen to twenty minutes)? Could we tell them weekly, at the same time? And could we talk about how these extraordinary objects from the past shaped the world we live in, or help us, at least, in trying to understand it? The conversation with Aimee and our other colleagues quickly turned to the details. It was clear that the talks should be informal and fairly spontaneous, not scholarly lectures but more akin to a stroll through the Frick galleries with a friend. What would the timing of the episodes be? What would we wear? How could they be recorded? The plan swiftly emerged. Friday evening, at five p.m., a time when people often gather to celebrate the end of the working week, often in bars or over dinner. We thought of bringing the audience into our homes and accompanying each episode with a drink. Why not the most New York–like way to celebrate the beginning of an evening, with a cocktail? We felt that I should opt for something more informal than the suit and tie in which I spend so much of my life, and the idea of the dressing gown emerged. As old-fashioned as this garment may be, I still have a fondness for it. As the few episodes we originally planned took on a life of their own and brought us into uncharted territory, my limited collection of dressing gowns had to give way to more exotic garments that I never thought I was going to use: a few kimonos bought on a trip to Japan, the ikat coats acquired during an early trip to Turkey, and even the gorgeous replica of Gustav Klimt's blue robe (a much treasured gift from the director of the Neue Galerie in New York).

When the first episode aired, none of us had any idea how many of them we might produce or what the next episode would be. Bellini was followed by Rembrandt and then by Van Dyck, Constable, and Turner. Each episode was born quickly, almost impulsively, as we kept asking, "What will we do next week? What is the cocktail?" The series—soon complemented by two other online series, twenty episodes of *Travels with a Curator* and eight of *Frick Five*—was an instant success. Much to our surprise, we realized that we were reaching an international audience. The live airing of each episode, every Friday, started to be accompanied by comments such as "hello from California," "good evening from Vermont," "greetings from New Mexico," "good morning from New Zealand," and "ciao da Venezia." Thanks to the potential of online platforms, we were reaching audiences we never suspected had an interest in The Frick Collection and, as we often discovered, had never even visited New York.

Sixty-five episodes of *Cocktails with a Curator* created a virtual community: regular followers we started to feel we knew. During the past two years, a great many people have written to the Frick to thank us for this program, telling us how it "helped them through the most difficult period in their lives" or even "saved their lives." I am incredibly proud of this achievement and often wonder at how it is that such a simple idea had such an impact on so many people's experiences of the pandemic. At the same time, *Cocktails with a Curator* kept us going as well. Aimee and I, later joined by our incoming Assistant Curator of Sculpture, Giulio Dalvit, soldiered through the pandemic, physically based in New York, Warsaw, and Milan, following the rhythm of *Cocktails*. It deeply shaped our experience of this dramatic period.

Each episode was recorded in our respective homes in New York (while Giulio was stuck in Milan) and with an interruption during my summer stay in Poland. *Cocktails with a Curator* was filmed in our homes and researched there as well, since the public libraries were closed at the time. I have never been more thankful for having an extensive personal library. Each week, books came down from the shelves so I could delve into the next week's story. Inevitably, the fast pace of the research and recording, and the weekly occurrence of the series, meant that episodes were often not as exhaustive as we would have liked. Each recording was done in a single filming session with no interruptions, and with very minimal editing. Each episode was unscripted—there was no text to follow. On a number of occasions, members of the public and scholars wrote in with comments and corrections. The three of us were very grateful for this and in the process also learned a lot and considered issues we had not previously explored.

This book presents all sixty-five episodes of *Cocktails with a Curator*—transcribed, shortened, and edited—in the order in which they aired. And each episode is accompanied by a related cocktail, as presented online. Following the model of Daria Borghese's book, which, in so many ways, inspired this enterprise, the book includes wonderful black-and-white illustrations, each based on one of the sixty-five works of art examined. These were created by Luis Serrano, who produced these delightful works of art in Rome as the series was approaching its end. Together with Aimee and Giulio, Luis has been involved in this project all along. Apart from its international audience, *Cocktails* has also been an international enterprise, across the Atlantic, with Aimee and me in New York and Giulio and Luis in Italy.

I hope this book provides something of the pleasure that the online series delivered. In a written and published form, the episodes certainly assume a different format, but the intention is to maintain the informality and freshness of the originals.

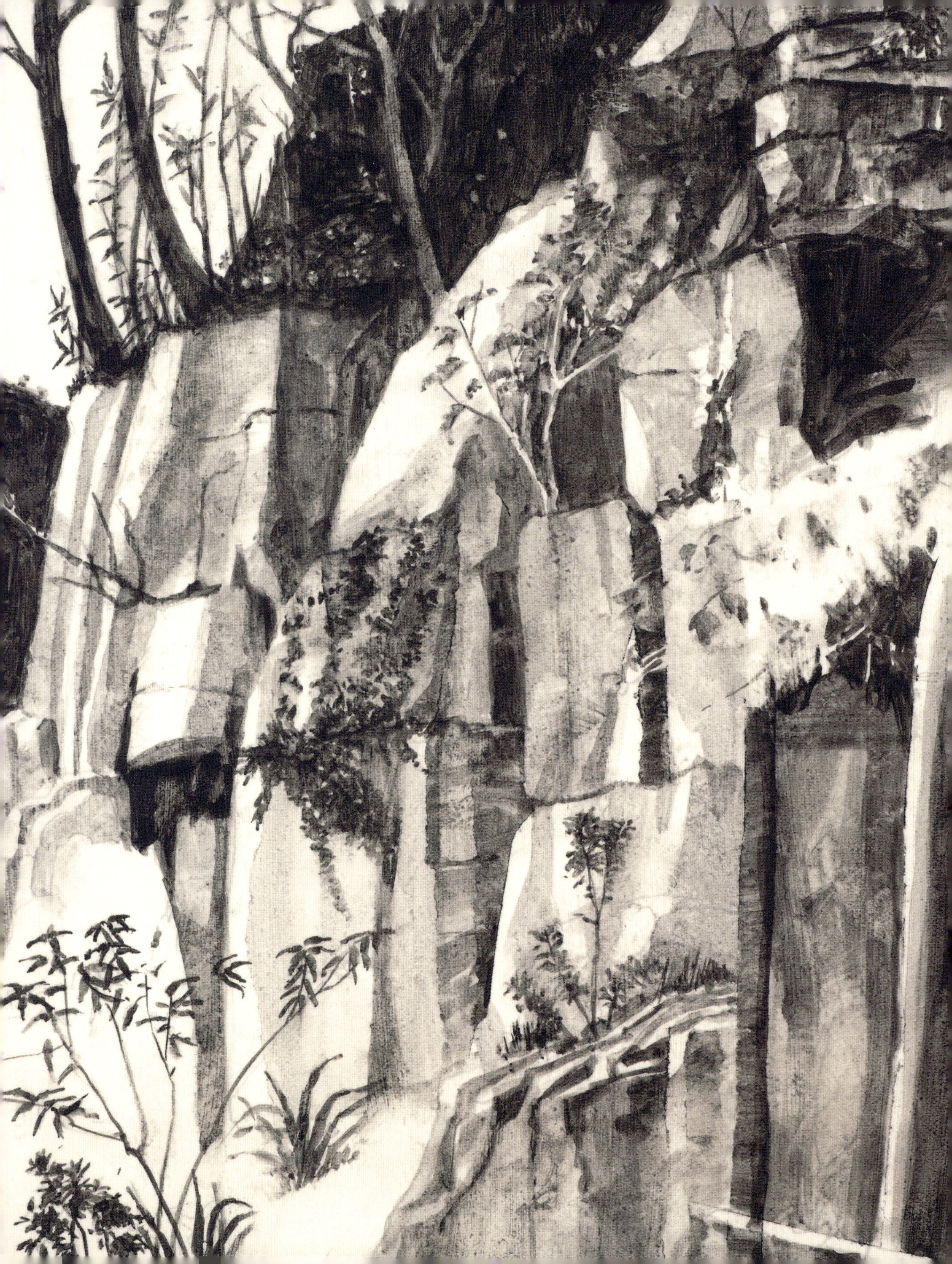

GIOVANNI BELLINI

St. Francis in the Desert

CA. 1476–78

Manhattan

2 OZ. BOURBON

¾ OZ. SWEET RED VERMOUTH

DASH OF ANGOSTURA BITTERS

Serve chilled in a cocktail glass and
garnish with a maraschino cherry

A Manhattan, one of my favorite drinks, celebrates the island of Manhattan and the city of New York. The treasures of The Frick Collection are among the highlights of this wondrous city.

Since 1915, when Henry Clay Frick acquired this extraordinary painting from a private collection in England, it has hung on the same wall at the Frick—in the Living Hall, at the heart of the museum, with portraits by Titian on either side. *St. Francis in the Desert* is a rather mysterious masterpiece. We do not know for whom it was painted or why. We do not know its exact date. And, although many theories have been put forward, we do not know what it represents.

The painting was first referenced in 1525, when Marcantonio Michiel wrote a description of various private collections in Venice. Michiel cited the *St. Francis in the Desert* as being in the house of Taddeo Contarini, near the church of Santa Fosca. According to him, the canvas was painted not for Contarini but for Zuan Michiel, a Venetian of whom we know little. We do not know why Zuan Michiel commissioned the painting. Was this a private devotional work, an altarpiece for a private chapel, or was it for a church in Venice? One theory has it that Michiel intended the painting for San Francesco del Deserto, a Franciscan monastery on a small island in the Venetian lagoon—to this day a very secluded place. If it was meant for, and installed in, that church, it did not stay there for long, because by 1525 the picture was in the collection of Contarini.

St. Francis was born in 1182 in the town of Assisi, in central Italy, where he died in 1226. Francis was the son of a prominent merchant from Assisi who had a lot of business with France; hence his name—in Italian, Francesco—which derives from the word *Francia*. After a vision in the church of San Damiano in Assisi, Francis renounced his family's wealth for a life of poverty, chastity, and obedience. He created his own religious order, which was approved by the pope during his lifetime and named the Franciscan Order after him.

In 1224, Francis went to the mountain retreat of La Verna, a desolate location in the Apennines, the mountains in the Tuscan province of Arezzo. While meditating and praying there, Francis received a miraculous vision that bestowed on him the wounds Christ had received during his Passion, thereby sharing his suffering with Christ. This scene was often depicted in the Middle Ages and the Renaissance, but Bellini (1424/35–1516) represented it in a very different way. With his hands open and his arms outstretched, Francis stands in a rocky area that reminds us of La Verna. On the right, you can see the cave in which Francis presumably lived, with a lectern, a skull, a cross. On the left is a beautiful landscape, very different from the rugged landscape of La Verna. The vision that Francis is experiencing is in his own mind. Divine light comes through the laurel tree at the top left, but apart from that, we neither see nor experience what Francis is feeling. This painting is very much about the power of light; at the same time, it is about the role of man in nature.

Francis has left his clogs to one side, next to a small fig tree and some small flowers. Everything about the painting is about spring, about the flowering and the budding of trees. You can also see some human habitation: in the background is a town—a walled, medieval town of the type that still exists in the Veneto. Above that, in the mountains against a beautiful sky, is a fortress. You can almost feel the wind and the rustling through the trees, trees that are coming back to life after the harsh winter. There are just a few signs of human life—a shepherd bringing his flock along a river, next to the city, far away from Francis. Several animals are among the beautiful details: the donkey, standing alone in a meadow; the gray heron, looking into the distance from this rocky outcrop; and to the side of Francis, just under his right arm, a rabbit coming out of a crevice in the rocks. My favorite detail, in the left-hand corner and rather difficult to make out, is a little kingfisher drinking water from a small waterfall. On a small trompe l'oeil piece of paper—a *cartellino* in Italian—in the lower left corner of the panel, which was probably painted in the mid-1470s, Bellini proudly signed the picture.

Francis was a saint, a thinker, and a philosopher. To this day one of the great heroes of the natural world, he believed nature was a creation of God. In many ways, the painting reflects his beautiful poem *The Canticle of Creatures,* in which he writes not only about his Christian beliefs but also about the sun, the moon, the stars, the air, the water, the various components of the earth, the flowers, the animals. He writes about life and death, and he considers our central role as stewards of this planet. One of the many things this painting does is inspire us to think about who we are and how we inhabit the earth. Hopefully, it can teach us all something about how to take better care of the world around us.

—X.S.

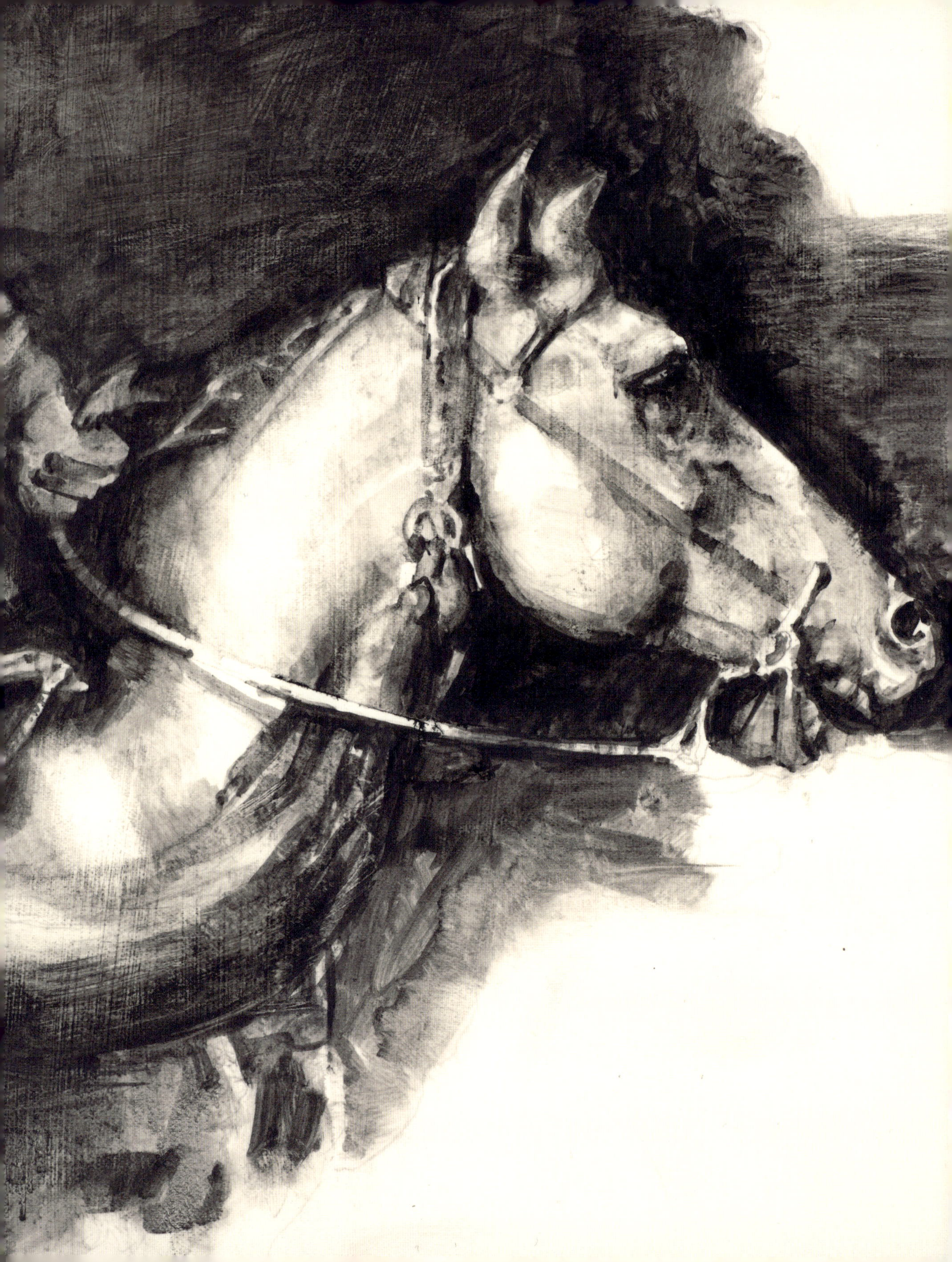

REMBRANDT HARMENSZ. VAN RIJN

The Polish Rider

CA. 1655

Szarlotka

POLISH BISON GRASS VODKA

UNFILTERED APPLE JUICE

Serve on the rocks in a tumbler and garnish with a pinch of cinnamon

Szarlotka *is Polish for "apple pie," but it also refers to this simple drink with just two essential ingredients. One is a type of Polish vodka that has bison grass in it. The only surviving European bison live in Białowieża, the last primeval forest in Europe, on the border between Poland and Belarus. You also have to use freshly pressed apple juice.*

Rembrandt's haunting *The Polish Rider* was described by the great British art historian Kenneth Clark as "one of the great poems" of painting. Set in an indeterminate landscape at an indeterminate time of day is a young man on horseback. Behind him is a series of buildings, a town; there is a domed building at the top of the hill. There is a tower below; a body of water, maybe a river or lake; a little group of figures you can barely make out near a fire in the very far distance. The man is resolutely riding across the painting, across the landscape toward the right. As he does so, he pauses, looking not quite back but past us, out of the frame, in a very puzzling way.

The hat and jacket—a *żupan*—worn by the rider are typical of seventeenth-century Polish clothing. He is armed with a bow and arrow, of a design influenced by Eastern prototypes that was used in Poland in the period. On each side, he has a saber of a type known in Polish as a *karabela*. In his right hand, he holds a *nadziak*, also known as a horseman's pick or war hammer, a weapon used by the Polish military.

Rembrandt (1606–1669) probably painted this about 1655–56. By the 1650s, he was well known in Amsterdam, a wealthy artist with a large workshop and a grand house. He is known to have collected costumes, weapons, shells, and various exotic objects. He was not, however, very good at managing his money, and in 1656, he went bankrupt. His house was sold, and everything in it went to auction. It was around this time, just before or after, that *The Polish Rider* was painted. I think some of the doubt expressed by the figure in the painting may somehow reflect Rembrandt's own situation in those years.

We do not know for whom Rembrandt painted the picture or what he meant for it to represent. The Polish connection started in 1791, when a Polish aristocrat, Michał Kazimierz Ogiński, traveled to the Netherlands, brought back with him *The Polish Rider*, and then offered it for sale to the last king of Poland, Stanisław August Poniatowski. The king had invited to his court a number of foreign artists—among them, Marcello Bacciarelli from Rome and Bernardo Bellotto from Venice—and started to create an important art collection in Warsaw at the Royal Castle and his other residences. He was also a great collector of plants and orange trees. Ogiński offered the painting, curiously, in exchange for orange trees, because he was building a country house outside Warsaw at that time.

Stanisław August displayed *The Polish Rider*—together with other paintings in his collection, including other Rembrandts—at his favorite residence, the Łazienki Palace on the outskirts of Warsaw. Enlarged and decorated by him, the palace is in the middle of a lake, connected to the land by bridges. Stanisław kept *The Polish Rider* in the anteroom to his private apartments on the upper floor of the house, very close to his study and his bedroom. The painting remained there for four years. These were very turbulent times for Poland, and in 1795, Poland effectively ceased to exist. It was partitioned among Austria, Prussia, and Russia. The king abdicated and moved to Russia, where he died three years later, in 1798. The Rembrandt remained in the house, but it was then sold to another family. In her diaries, Waleria Tarnowska described the painting in 1811, when she saw it at the Łazienki Palace and fell in love with it. Her father eventually purchased the painting. When he died, it passed on to Waleria and her husband, Jan Feliks Tarnowski. The Tarnowski family kept the painting for four generations at Dzików, their ancestral home in Galicia, in southeastern Poland.

Waleria's great-grandson, Zdzisław Tarnowski, sold the painting in 1910 to Henry Clay Frick, who bought it on the advice of the art historian and critic Roger Fry. Tarnowski sold it because at that point the area of Galicia was under Austrian rule, and many Polish aristocrats were heroically trying to buy back land from the Austrians to keep as much Polish land as they could in Polish hands. With the two world wars, much of this land would be lost to them, but it is interesting to think that *The Polish Rider*, so deeply connected to Poland and to the image of a new nation that did not exist at that time, actually was in Poland through a century when Poland did not exist on the map.

Who is this man riding across this mysterious landscape? Is this a portrait of someone? A Polish man? If so, the format would be somewhat strange. Is it meant to represent a specific historical character? A specific biblical episode? The names of King David and Nimrod have been put forward, among many others. Is he a theatrical figure? Is he related to certain plays that were being performed in Amsterdam in the 1650s and that Rembrandt may have responded to? It has even been argued that the rider is not actually a man but a woman dressed as a man. And did Rembrandt even think of it as a specific figure? Is this just a fancy picture? Is this just showing a beautiful youth dressed in an exotic outfit going forward toward the unknown? Many theories have been proposed.

What I love about this picture is the sense of mystery and of facing the unknown. I often feel like *The Polish Rider*, going forward and yet looking back, stopping and pausing and puzzling as to what the future holds. Julius Held wrote a beautiful article on this painting in 1944, toward the end of World War II. He was thinking about this picture at a time of great changes and great tragedy in human history. One of the things that Held writes about this painting is a description of it, an ideal description: "the shining youth who himself seems to be in search of something distant, unmindful of things close and familiar, still withholds from us, like another Lohengrin, the secret of his name."

—X.S.

ANTHONY VAN DYCK

Sir John Suckling

CA. 1638

Pink Gin

DRY GIN

A COUPLE DROPS OF ANGOSTURA BITTERS

Serve on the rocks in a cocktail glass

Invented in the late eighteenth century in the Royal Navy, this drink owes its creation to bitters being considered medicinal and useful against all sorts of illnesses. To make the bitters palatable, why not add gin? A popular drink in Malaysia, it is also known as Gin Pahit, pahit *being the Malay word for "bitter." Pink Gin appears in a number of short stories by William Somerset Maugham, many of which are set in Malaysia.*

Born in Antwerp in 1599, Anthony van Dyck traveled to England as a young man and later to Italy, where he lived in Genoa for many years. He traveled to Sicily between 1624 and 1625, just as the plague hit, at which point the island was quarantined and Van Dyck was not able to leave for more than a year. Quarantines were very much a reality of that time; it was probably the plague that

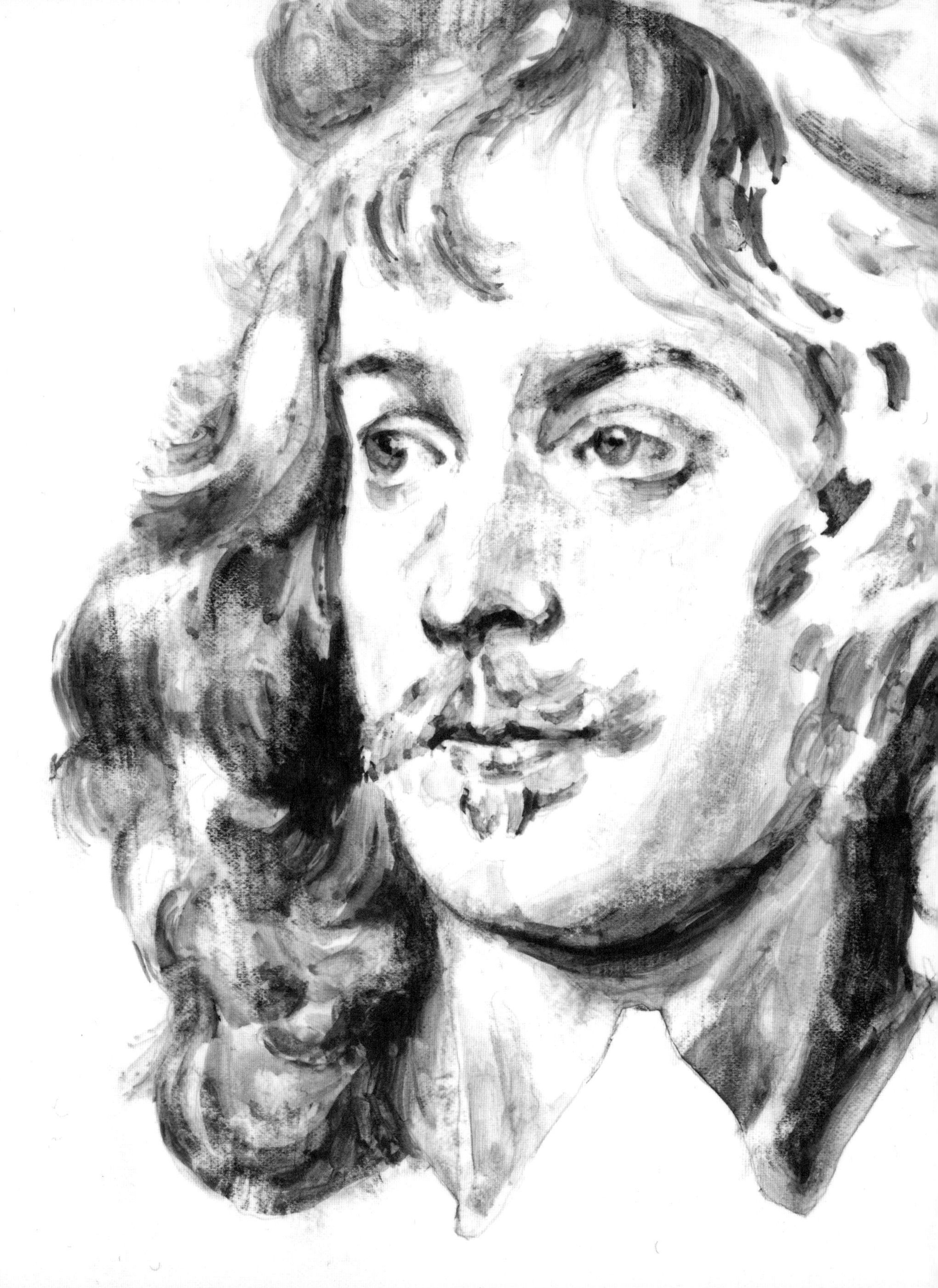

took Van Dyck's life in 1641. He left Sicily unscathed in 1625 and in 1632 moved to England, where he became well known for his portraits of courtiers and aristocrats at the court of King Charles I, the portrait of Sir John Suckling being one of them.

Van Dyck painted *Sir John Suckling* about 1638, toward the end of the artist's life. A wealthy English aristocrat, Suckling owned land in Suffolk, Lincolnshire, and Middlesex. His father had been Secretary of State and was in the Privy Council, and his uncle was Lord Treasurer. After studying at Cambridge, he fought in the army in Germany, in the Low Countries, and on the Scottish border. He traveled extensively and visited the continent. Suckling was described by John Aubrey in his *Brief Lives* as being "of middle stature and slight strength, brisk 'round the eye, reddish faced and red nose, ill liver. His head not very big, his hair a kind of sand color, his beard turned up naturally, so that he had a brisk and graceful look." The description corresponds to what we see in the Van Dyck portrait. Suckling was a notorious philanderer, as well as a gambler and lavish spender. He was also a published poet who wrote poems such as "I Prithee, Send Me Back My Heart" and "Why So Pale and Wan, Fond Lover?" In 1638, at the time when he was sitting for this portrait, his play *Aglaura,* which is set in Persia, was first performed in London. The portrait is likely related to this theatrical success.

Suckling is set among strange rock formations that give way to a beautiful landscape of mountains, a few shrubs, trees, and plants. His attire—an indigo tunic, covered with a red mantle, along with his unusual boots—is not like anything he would have worn at court and is no doubt associated with the theater, probably his play *Aglaura.* We know the costumes for the play, which Suckling paid for, were costly and glamorous and of a style associated with Arcadia, the mythical land in Greece linked to poetry and solitude. Many poets at the court of Charles I refer to this Arcadian idea. The portrait includes a Latin inscription on the rock, which reads NE TE QUÆSIVERIS EXTRA (Do not look outside yourself).

In the 1630s, Van Dyck painted at least two other portraits of English aristocrats in a similar fashion. The earliest of the three represents Philip Baron Wharton (National Gallery of Art, Washington) and was painted in 1632. In an Arcadian costume, he stands against a rocky background and holds a *houlette,* or a shepherd's crook, an instrument that was a typical attribute of shepherds at the time. The third of these portraits (National Portrait Gallery, London) shows George Stuart, the Seigneur d'Aubigny, who was depicted about 1638, at the same time as John Suckling. D'Aubigny, the brother of the Duke of Richmond, was also an admirer of poetry. He is set in a landscape with a little waterfall, roses, and rocks. There is also an inscription on the rock—ME FIRMIOR AMOR

(Love is stronger than I am)—which probably refers to his recent secret marriage to the daughter of the Earl of Suffolk.

In composition, the three portraits are very similar. Here are three gentlemen of the 1630s, all with a love of poetry, all involved in the theater, all wearing costumes understood at the time to refer to contemporaneous ideas. But there is a significant difference among them: Suckling is the only one holding a book. The volume is identifiable because even though the writing on it is just sketched in and you cannot read the lettering on the pages, there is a piece of paper projecting out of the book that has on it the name "Shakespeare," and at the top of the page it says "Hamlet." This is, as far as we know, the very first painted depiction of Shakespeare's First Folio. The volume was published in 1623 in London and includes, for the first time, all of Shakespeare's plays—the fourteen comedies, the twelve tragedies, and the ten history plays—except *Edward III*. It is telling that Suckling, a poet and playwright himself, holds the works of Shakespeare and especially that he shows them open to *The Tragedy of Hamlet*. It is extraordinary for an aristocrat to have asked to be portrayed with what was presumably his favorite play. It is equally remarkable that this is the very first time we see this great masterpiece of literature appearing in visual art. This portrait combines the art of Van Dyck, his great portrait skills, with the idea of literature and poetry and their importance at the time.

These three men found themselves on different sides in the early 1640s during the English Civil War. Wharton joined the Parliamentary forces against the king, and he fought in several battles. He survived the war, but with the Restoration, he had to flee the country and went into exile. Stuart and Suckling joined the royal party, and they both fought for the king. Stuart died at the Battle of Edgehill, at age twenty-four. Part of a plot to bring the king back into power, Suckling was tried for high treason in 1641. He fled the country for France, where he was separated from all his connections and in debt. His sad ending is recounted by John Aubrey: "Being come to the bottom of his funds, reflecting on the miserable and despicable condition he was reduced to, he took poison." He committed suicide, at age thirty-three, in Paris. These wonderful portraits present the very tragic story of these youths who died fighting or defending the king, people whose lives were heavily transformed by the English Civil War.

—X.S.

JOHN CONSTABLE

The White Horse

1819

Gin and Dubonnet

1 OZ. LONDON DRY GIN

2 OZ. DUBONNET ROUGE

SQUEEZE OF LEMON

Stir and strain into a tumbler over ice
and garnish with a lemon wedge

Containing quinine (derived from the cinchona tree native to Peru), which is still taken today as a treatment for malaria, the French aperitif Dubonnet was invented in the 1840s as a medicinal drink. Constable may not have been fond of French things (he wrote, "I hope to never go to Paris, as long as I live"), but the French loved him. The great French romantic painter Eugène Delacroix proclaimed him "the father of French landscape painting." In this drink, rumored to be Queen Elizabeth II's favorite pre-lunch tipple, the British and the French unite.

Described by Constable as one of his "happiest efforts," this painting is more than six feet wide. One can get lost in it, as if it were a portal connecting the viewer to the artist's beloved English countryside. Constable was born in Suffolk, England, in 1776, the year the American colonies declared independence from Britain. His father owned mills and a transport business that brought agricultural goods to London, and Constable was pressured to take

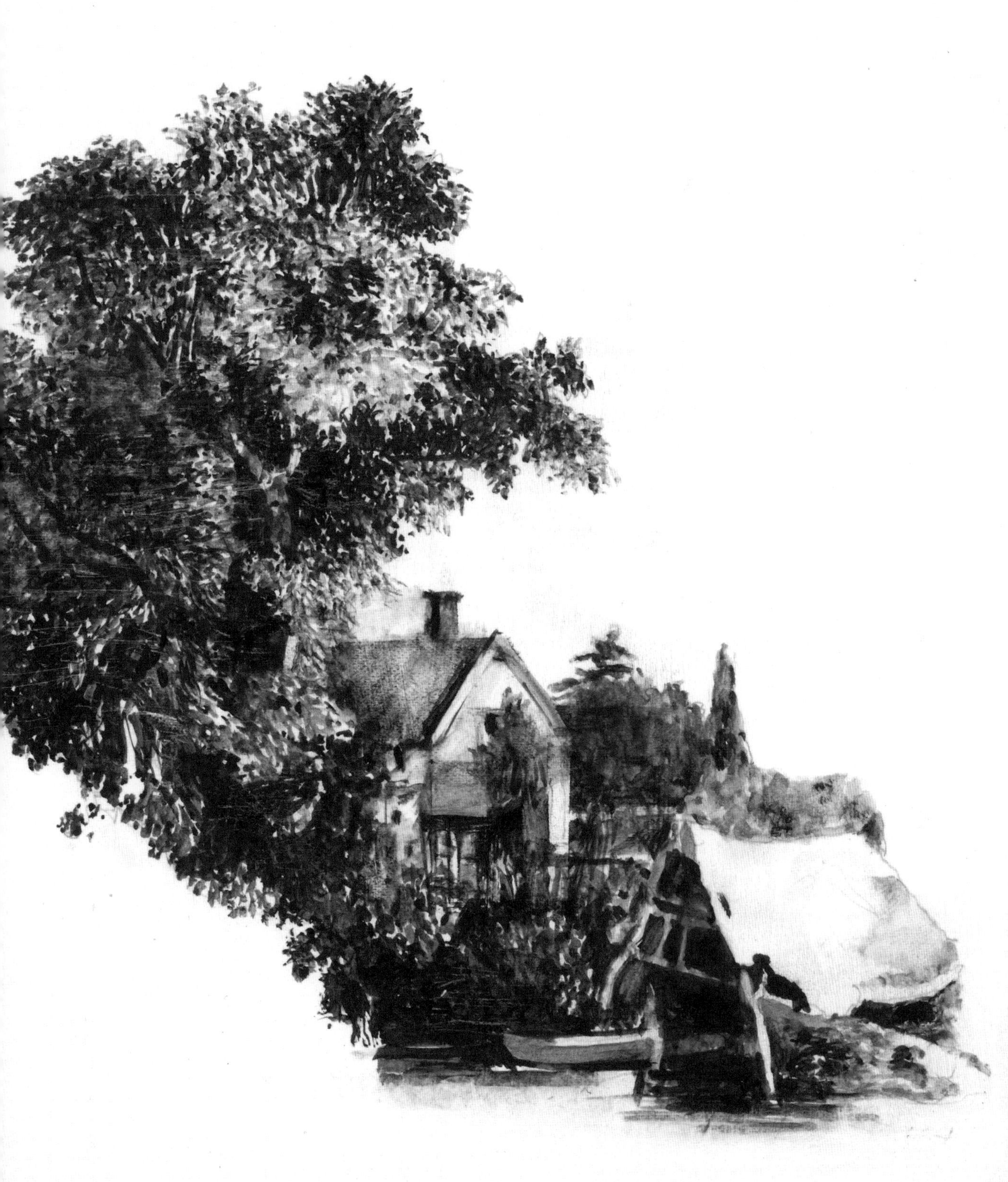

over the family business. But he wanted to be a painter, to elevate the English countryside as a subject for high art.

The White Horse represents a major turning point in Constable's career and life. It was only after he exhibited it at the Royal Academy in 1819 that he was finally, after nearly twenty years of effort, elected an associate member of the academy. (His great rival, Turner, just a year older, had already achieved this milestone at age twenty-four.) This was a big deal for the middle-aged Constable and for *The White Horse.* Inspired by this critical success, he produced five more of these monumental paintings of scenes of life along the River Stour, collectively known as the "six-footers."

In order to achieve in paint the effects of billowing clouds, dewy trees, and rippling reflections in the water for *The White Horse,* Constable took the costly and time-consuming preparatory step of making a full-scale oil sketch on canvas, essentially painting the composition at full scale twice, a practice he repeated for each of the six-footers and one that nearly bankrupted him. The full-size sketch—which is in the National Gallery of Art, Washington—is similar to the painting at the Frick in terms of its composition, but in it the handling is looser and the details are different. He could only exhibit and sell the "finished" one.

The painting depicts an identifiable spot along the river, looking toward the village of Flatford, with a view of a white structure known as Willy Lott's Cottage (named after the farmer who lived there during Constable's time), which still stands today. On the lower left is a leafy island called the Spong. Behind the trees in the back, past the rustic boathouse in the center, is Gibbonsgate Farm. In its yard, three cows wade in the water. This part of Constable's native Suffolk, where he spent many years sketching and which was made famous by his paintings, is known today, as it was in his lifetime, as Constable Country.

Though he seems to capture this region exactly as it was, Constable was also to some degree inventing, editing, and embellishing. He moved trees, changed the shape of buildings and their location, widened rivers, and added details such as the barge with the white horse. Since his father owned a horse-towed barge transport business, the artist knew the industry well. A horse would walk along a towpath at the river's edge and pull the barge, also called a lighter, along the river. At various points, the towpath would, for whatever reason, switch over to the other side of the river. The horse would have to jump into the barge, be ferried to the other side, and then jump back out to continue towing. In *The White Horse,* Constable pictures the moment at which a horse is propelled across the water by laboring bargemen like those his family would have employed. In the painting, he gives them an anonymity, as if they are part of the landscape.

The painting's present title was given to it by its first owner. When Constable first exhibited it in 1819, it was called *Scene on the River Stour.* He referred to it as "a placid representation of a serene grey morning." That may describe what viewers experience when they stand in front of the picture, but there is much more to it than that. Constable was painting during a major economic depression. The end of the Napoleonic Wars in 1815 brought back to Britain, and especially to the countryside, thousands of veteran soldiers—many of them injured—to severe unemployment. The opening of British borders to Europe caused the price of produce in the countryside to plummet. Businesses, including that of Constable's family, were failing. He wrote about the disastrous state of his home region—the crime, poverty, and suffering. This was a moment of great migration out of Britain to other countries in the hopes of a better life. *The White Horse* is something of a memory, inspired by Constable's childhood experiences and based on sketches he'd made on-site years earlier.

Constable signed it at the bottom—*John Constable, ARA* [Associate Member of the Royal Academy] / *London f*[ecit] *1819*—naming London as the place where it was painted, in his studio. In doing so, he acknowledged the distance in time and place between where he made the painting and what it represented. It is a nostalgic memory, one so convincing that it's as if he had been standing on the right bank when he painted it.

How did Constable's *White Horse*, an ode to preindustrial England, end up at the Frick? It was purchased almost immediately after its exhibition by Constable's friend Archdeacon John Fisher. Ten years later, Fisher was struggling financially and begged Constable to buy the painting back from him. Constable bought it at the original purchase price and kept it for the rest of his life. When the contents of his studio were sold in 1838, the year after his death, *The White Horse* fetched the highest price. The man who purchased it, Lancelot Archer Burton, was married to a cousin of Constable's and was appointed co-guardian of the artist's seven children, who were left orphaned at the artist's death. Constable's wife, Maria, had died from tuberculosis years earlier, just months after the birth of their last child.

Eventually, *The White Horse* made its way into the collection of the American financier and collector John Pierpont Morgan, in London. It stayed in the Morgan family's collection—eventually moving to America—until 1943, when The Frick Collection acquired it. Since it was the height of World War II, the painting was not put on public view but was stored in the museum's vault, where the most valuable objects in the Frick's collection were kept for safekeeping during the war. In 1945, the museum's collection was reinstalled in the galleries, and Constable's *White Horse* was presented to the public for the first time at the Frick, inviting its visitors to be transported to the dreamy English countryside that Constable loved so much.

—A.N.

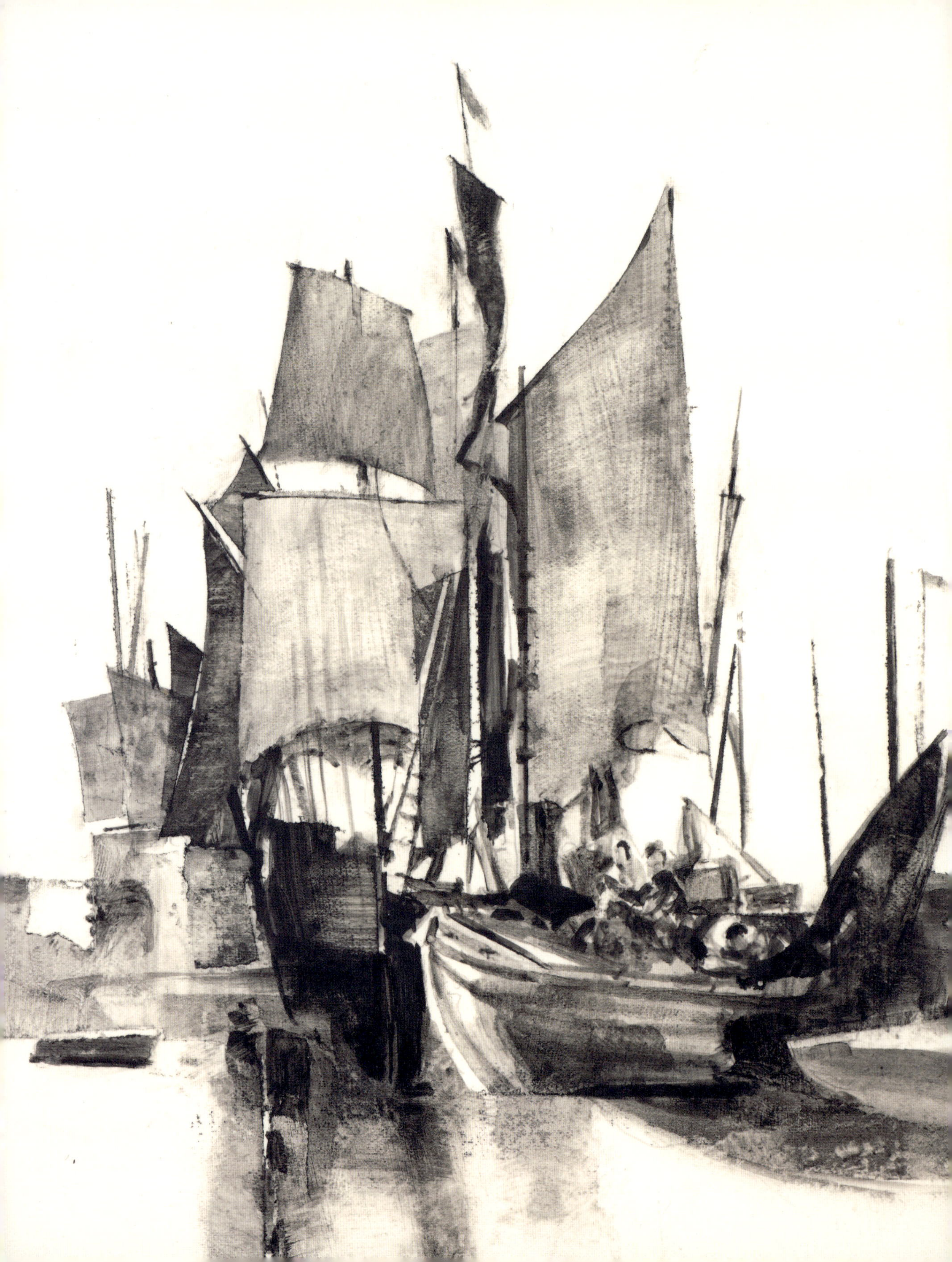

JOSEPH MALLORD WILLIAM TURNER

Harbor of Dieppe: Changement de Domicile

1826

Widow's Kiss

1½ OZ. CALVADOS

¾ OZ. YELLOW CHARTREUSE

¾ OZ. BÉNÉDICTINE

2 DASHES OF ANGOSTURA BITTERS

Serve chilled in a coupe glass
and garnish with mint leaves

This very strong drink was allegedly given to women who had lost their husbands at sea. A French liqueur produced in Normandy, very close to Dieppe, Bénédictine is thought to be based on a sixteenth-century recipe created by Benedictine monks and was made out of various herbs from a monastery garden.

Of the Frick's five Turner paintings—acquired by Henry Clay Frick between 1901 and 1914—the two grandest represent the harbors of Dieppe in France and Cologne in Germany. During Frick's lifetime, *Cologne* was in the South Hall and *Dieppe* was in the North Hall. In 1942, both were moved to the much larger West Gallery, where they have been ever since.

I associate the Dieppe canvas with travel, and not just because the painting is filled with boats and people coming and going. When I was a child in the 1980s, my family would travel every summer from Rome, where I grew up, to England to visit my grandmother. We traveled by car, and after stops in Switzerland and France, we would take the ferry in Dieppe to cross the Channel to Newhaven.

William Turner was born in 1775 in Covent Garden, in the heart of London. His father was a barber. In contrast to his rival, John Constable—who grew up outside of London and whose life was marked by successive attempts to get into the Royal Academy—Turner studied at the academy as a teenager, became its youngest-ever member, and spent all his life publicly showing there. Turner loved to travel. Almost every year from the middle of his life onward, he explored and made sketches in various places in France, Switzerland, the Netherlands, Germany, and Italy. People in the early nineteenth century traveled by horse, carriage, and boat. It was not until the mid-nineteenth century that tourism developed in ways we can recognize today. Steamboats were introduced, as were, of course, the railways. Between the late 1790s and 1815, however, during the Napoleonic Wars, when Britain was at war with France, the borders were closed. For twenty years, British citizens were not allowed to cross the Channel. There was a brief period in 1802, around the Peace of Amiens, when these restrictions were eased, and Turner traveled to Europe at that point. But it was really not until after 1815 that the British could easily travel to Europe. From 1817 onward, Turner went on a yearly pilgrimage to Europe. He visited many places and became particularly interested in harbor scenes.

Exhibited at the Royal Academy in 1825, *Dieppe* depicts the harbor of the French town in Normandy, looking south along the Quai Henri IV. Dieppe was founded in the eleventh century, and its name—from the ancient word for "deep"—supposedly derives from the fact that it has a particularly deep harbor. It began as a fishing town, and when Turner visited in the 1820s, it was still a vibrant fishing community. But the city was starting to change around this time. Dieppe was heavily bombed in 1694, and the Anglo-Dutch attack left the city in ruins. It was rebuilt in the eighteenth century, and that is the city that Turner would have known and that we mostly see today. As you look at the buildings in the painting along the *quai*, or dock, you see a tobacconist and some shops, as well as a number of buildings, some of them still there today. The classical structure with a tympanum is the Hotel d'Anvers, one of the architectural highlights of the city. In the background is the bell tower and the dome of the medieval church of Saint Jacques, one of the few monuments that survived the 1694 bombing. Turner went to Dieppe a couple of times. He started producing small drawings of the city in his little sketchbooks, and he also produced watercolors. Afterward, in his studio, he created this large canvas based on the works he had made in situ.

When Turner exhibited this painting at the Royal Academy, he entitled it *Dieppe: Changement de Domicile* (Change of Address). One idea for the origin of this title is that the boat on the right with paintings and various baskets full of objects might be carrying the belongings of someone moving house from one side of the harbor to the other. However, when you examine the painting, you become aware of many details, among them, a little flea market. And I wonder if the boat has more to do with the flea market than with someone moving their household effects. There is also a fish market. In the early nineteenth century, Dieppe was still a site where fishermen were active. English painters particularly loved Dieppe because of its old-fashioned, picturesque feel.

The life of Dieppe was directly connected to the life of the city directly across the Channel: Brighton. In the nineteenth century, Brighton was becoming fashionable. The Prince Regent had built his Indian folly, the Royal Pavilion, there, and it had become a holiday destination for the aristocracy of England. Because of its crucial connection to Brighton, Dieppe also started to be developed. Between the 1820s and 1840s, Dieppe became more of a tourist destination and less and less of a fishing town.

Turner's *Dieppe* is still one of the most iconic views of the city. But to me, it is also about the effects of light, reflection, and atmosphere that Turner captures so beautifully and dramatically. When you look at the painting, you realize that you are looking straight at the sun. This is probably late morning, around midday, and you are looking south. And you see the sun as a white disc and this wonderful clear sky with a few clouds, and you also see its reflection in the water of the harbor. It is such an extraordinary depiction of the elements. So, *Dieppe* is not just a portrait of a city, not just about travel. It is also about the power of nature and the power of the elements. That is something that Turner was always interested in. When he died in 1851 in Chelsea, in London, of cholera, his dying words allegedly were, "The sun is God."

—X.S.

FRANÇOIS BOUCHER

A Lady on Her Day Bed

1743

French 75

2 OZ. LONDON DRY GIN

¾ OZ. FRESH LEMON JUICE

¾ OZ. SIMPLE SYRUP

2 OZ. CHAMPAGNE

Serve chilled in a flute glass
and garnish with a lemon peel

Known simply as a 75 in France and a French 75 everywhere else, this drink is named after the powerful 75mm field gun used in World War I. The cocktail was invented in France in the early twentieth century, apparently when a lack of tonic for the makings of a Gin and Tonic led to the replacement of tonic with champagne.

We are inside an elegant boudoir, probably in a Parisian home of the mid-eighteenth century, where a woman is lying on a daybed. A fairly new invention in the eighteenth century, a daybed was a combination of a bed and a sofa. Inspired largely by pieces from Ottoman Turkey, it was probably brought to Europe in

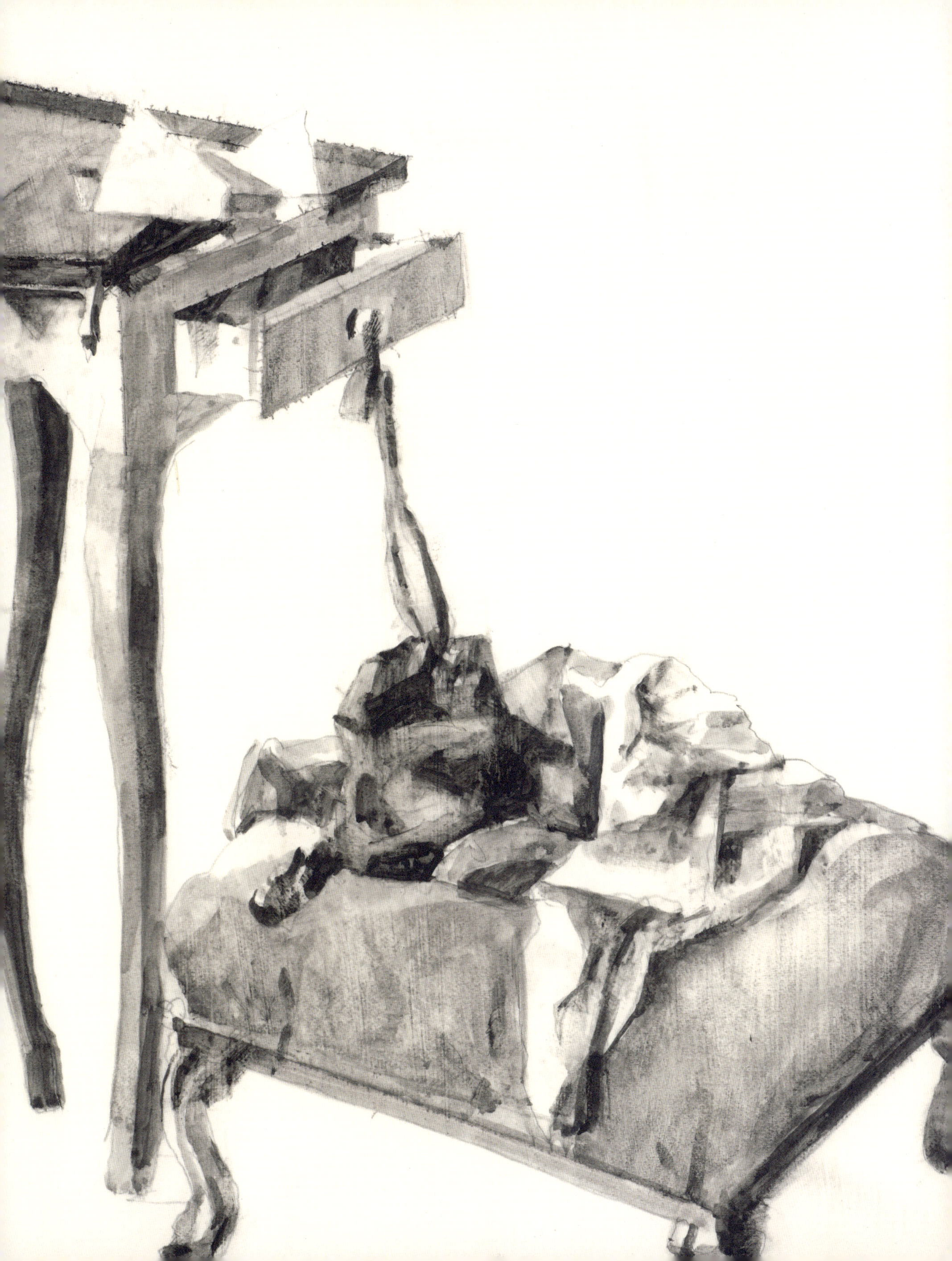

the seventeenth century. Its various names—sofa, ottoman, divan—all come from the Muslim world. By the eighteenth century, sofas were part of every fashionable home throughout Europe.

On the floor, to the right, we see Boucher's prominent signature and the date 1743. Looking around the room, we focus first on the elegantly dressed beautiful woman who looks out at us rather provocatively. She is set against a yellow wall fabric with a bold and decorative pattern and surrounded by a number of objects. Let's take a tour of her room. To her left is a watch attached to the wall. Next to her is a small table, and on it are a book and a letter. Maybe she has just finished reading the book, maybe she is about to pick it up, or maybe she has just put it down. The open drawer suggests that the letter may have either just come out of that drawer or is about to go into it. Who is the letter from? On the floor are her tools for embroidery. There is a string that goes all the way down to the floor. An unusual screen on the right seems to be a foreign import, possibly from China. Such things were quite fashionable at the time. On the wall is an étagère, a kind of hanging bookshelf with a little cupboard below it. On it, you see a magot, a type of Chinese porcelain figure that was hugely popular in eighteenth-century France. Below it, a teapot and cups. These days, we think of a teapot as a common object, but in the eighteenth century, it was quite unusual. Porcelain from China was very valuable, and tea, as much as coffee and chocolate, was a new and very exotic beverage. There is another piece of paper on that étagère, and if you look at it carefully, you can see that it has Boucher's name on it. Boucher has effectively signed this picture twice.

François Boucher was born in Paris in 1703 and died there in 1770, living through most of the eighteenth century. The apex of his success was in 1765, when he was appointed First Painter to the King. In 1733, he married Marie-Jeanne Buzeau, who was seventeen years old at the time. This was a love match; the two had a very happy marriage. Marie-Jeanne was a great collaborator of her husband's as well as an accomplished artist in her own right. She supposedly modeled for him a number of times. She also made miniatures—copying some of her husband's paintings—and etchings, which she signed.

When this painting was acquired by the Frick in 1937, it was titled *Portrait of Madame Boucher*. However, even though Marie-Jeanne may have sat for the painting, it is clearly not meant to be a portrait but is instead more of a genre scene. We think of Boucher as the great painter of voluptuous mythological scenes. These allowed him to represent more directly erotic visions. Some of the paintings without mythological subjects—Boucher's so-called *Odalisques*—became purely erotic depictions. Some are simply private pictures showing beautiful women in overtly erotic poses, and this is what male patrons of Boucher loved at that time. The so-called *Madame Boucher* at the Frick sits within a tradition of pictures by Boucher with more or less veiled erotic undertones.

Writing about Boucher, the Goncourt brothers concluded that for them he was "one of those men who represent the taste of a century, who express, personify, and embody it." Boucher is the epitome, in many ways, of eighteenth-century French art.

—X.S.

DIEGO RODRÍGUEZ DE SILVA Y VELÁZQUEZ

King Philip IV of Spain

1644

Fitifiti
(or Fifty-fifty)

EQUAL PARTS OF:

FINO (DRY SHERRY)

PEDRO XIMÉNEZ (SWEET SHERRY)

Serve chilled in a cocktail glass

Popular in southern Spain, the birthplace of Velázquez, who was born in Seville in 1599, this refreshing cocktail is perfect for warm Spanish summers.

Personally, I think Velázquez (1599–1660) is the greatest painter who ever lived. He is certainly unsurpassed, in terms of painting technique, by any other artist in Western art. Looking closely at this portrait, one cannot fail to see the painter's incredible technique. Apart from the way the flesh is rendered and the different textures of the hair, beard, and mustache, the real tour de force is the clothing. The king is wearing a red coat adorned with extraordinary silver embroidery—a type of surcoat called a *sobraveste*—over a yellow outfit. The colors of yellow and red represent the heraldic colors of Aragon, one of the regions of Spain. Velázquez quickly and assertively placed white and gray paint over the red. The shimmering effect of the textiles that you see as you walk away from the portrait is a miracle of painting, as is the depiction of the *sobraveste* against the softness of the white *valona* collar. The king is shown with many of the tools of his trade, symbols of command and of power: a sword at his side, a baton in his right hand, and a large felt sombrero in his left hand.

In 1623, Velázquez moved from his native Seville to the court of Madrid, where he spent the rest of his life working for King Philip IV, who had been crowned just two years earlier. Their lives and careers would be deeply intertwined. Velázquez portrayed the king more often than any other sitter. The king also appears in *Las Meninas,* Velázquez's most celebrated work of art. It depicts the artist himself at work on a large canvas that portrays a royal princess (an infanta) with her court in the foreground. But in the background is a mirror, in which can be seen the reflections of the king and queen. The painting captures the moment at which the infanta and the court are bowing, welcoming the king and queen as they enter a room of the Alcázar—the royal palace—in Madrid. Though this is not a straightforward portrait of the king, he does appear in it. Velázquez would continue to portray the king until the end of his life.

Also known as the "Fraga Philip," indicating the town of Fraga where it was painted, the Frick's painting lies in the middle of the chronological trajectory of the king's portraits. It is the most militaristic depiction of Philip and the one most directly related to a historic event. The king's reign was enlightened in terms of art and culture, but when it came to military history and politics, it was a disaster. Most of Philip's life was spent fighting the French: the Franco-Spanish War, which lasted from 1635 to 1659, occupied all of his reign. In the spring of 1644, the king and part of the court traveled with an army to Catalonia, where they planned to take the French-controlled city of Lleida. The Siege of Lleida, during which the king traveled through Aragon and into Catalonia, lasted from the late spring through the early summer of 1644 and was one of the king's rare victories. Contemporaneous records tell us that on at least two occasions during this campaign, the king paraded the army while wearing an outfit of red and silver, most likely the one shown in the portrait. During this time, the king and the court took as their headquarters the small town of Fraga, on the border between Aragon and Catalonia, not far away from Lleida. Velázquez was with the king. Records survive for many payments relating to the painter's stay in the Aragonese village. Velázquez was given a small studio in a house in Fraga; he asked builders to open up a window to get some light so that he could paint properly, and a carpenter built an easel for him and eventually crates for the transportation of paintings.

The "Fraga Philip" shows the king as the victorious ruler of the Siege of Lleida. Painted in three sittings in June of 1644, it was created so that an image of the king could be swiftly sent to the court in Madrid. Soon after the siege, the king had the portrait shipped to Madrid, and the Catalonian community in Madrid exhibited the painting in the church of San Martin, in the center of the city. There, under a baldachin, the king presided in effigy over a sermon and a mass to celebrate his victory. The portrait essentially took the place of the king during this mass. It was written at the time that the king's "costume and bearing were copied from most handsome Mars in the royal portrait depicting the living Sun as he presented himself during the campaign; displayed under the richest canopy, he revived the court, inspiring respect, love, and renewed allegiance in all those who saw it in admiration, not without tears, and witnessed the tenderness that the Spaniards feel for their monarchs."

—X.S.

JEAN BARBET

Angel

1475

Angel Face

EQUAL PARTS OF:

DRY GIN

CALVADOS

APRICOT BRANDY

Serve straight up in a cocktail glass
and garnish with an apple slice

Given its name, the drink seems a suitable companion for the sculpture at the Frick. Invented in the 1930s, this cocktail, however, is thought to have been inspired by the famous American gangster Abe Kaminsky, also known as Angel Face.

The fifteenth-century bronze *Angel* is one of the most important pieces of sculpture at the Frick. A single bronze figure, with a tall column-like shape, it is adorned with fluted drapery. The angel's right hand points toward the distance. His left hand may have originally held a cross. His beautiful long wings have an extraordinarily elegant texture.

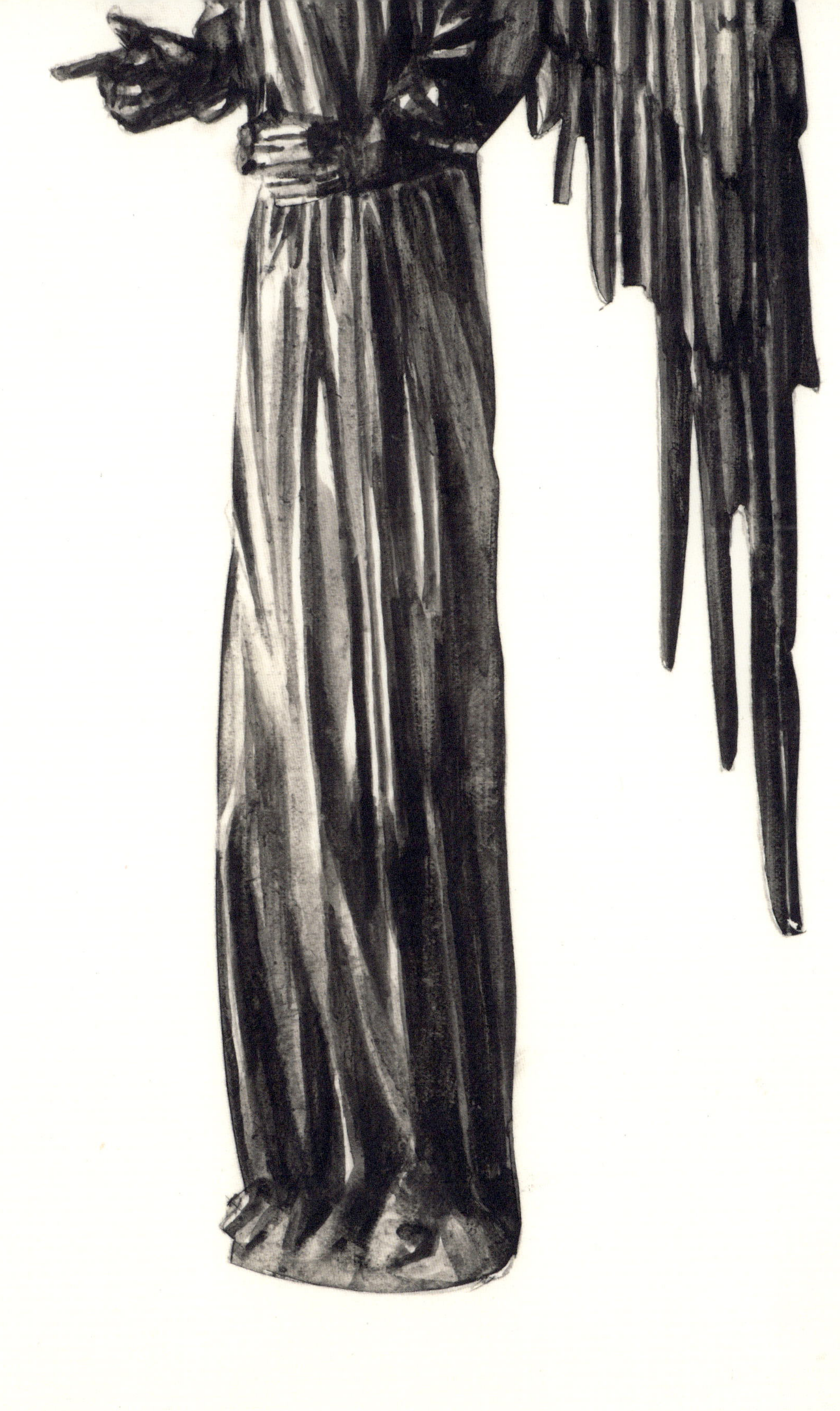

The origins of the winged creatures we know as angels go back to antiquity and to biblical times. The word comes from the Greek *angelos* (ἄγγελος), which means "messenger." In the Old Testament, angels are mostly messengers of God. In the Judeo-Christian tradition, angels of different types were described and a hierarchy was created. Later, the concept of a guardian angel—an angel that guards the soul of a particular human being—was developed. This is found not only in Christianity but in other religions as well. In the Islamic world, for example, every individual has two guardian angels—one always in front, the other behind—protecting them at all times. It is unclear if Barbet's *Angel* was meant to be recognizable, like, for example, the Archangel Gabriel of the Annunciation.

Most of the information we have about the Barbet *Angel* appears on the object itself. On the inside of the left wing is an inscription that tells us, in French, that "on the 27th day of the month of March of the year 1475, Jean Barbet from Lyon made this angel." March 27, 1475, was actually Easter Monday. Beyond the information conveyed by the inscription, we know that the *Angel* is first documented in the nineteenth century as belonging to the Marquis de Talhouet at the Château du Lude, in the Sarthe area of France. It stood at the bottom of the chateau's grand staircase and its left hand held a cross, which had been added to the sculpture at a later date. In 1867, the *Angel* was lent to the International Exposition in Paris. It was subsequently sold and then went through a number of dealers before entering the collection of John Pierpont Morgan in 1906, and eventually reaching the United States. The Frick purchased it in 1943, after the death of Morgan's son, together with a number of other works of art.

It is unlikely that the *Angel* was originally made for the Château du Lude. It has been argued that it may have been created for another location, for example, the Cathedral of Le Mans, not far from the chateau. In the nineteenth century, an intriguing suggestion was put forward. A family tradition at Lude recorded that the *Angel* came from the Sainte-Chapelle in Paris, one of the most important Gothic monuments in France. Created between the 1230s and '40s for King Louis IX of France, it was designed to hold the most important Christian relics that the king owned, including Christ's Crown of Thorns. With its extraordinary screen of stained glass, the interior of the chapel is one of the most striking buildings of the Gothic period. The chapel was refurbished a number of times. It was drastically restored in the 1460s, badly damaged during the French Revolution, and repaired and partially redesigned by the architect Viollet-le-Duc in the nineteenth century. There is no visual evidence that Barbet's *Angel* came from inside or outside the chapel, but it is not impossible that the sculpture was removed from the building at some point during one of its significant refurbishments.

Recent studies on the *Angel* have provided interesting new information. Jean Barbet, who signed the sculpture, is documented as a cannon maker in Lyon. Known as Jean Barbet or Jean from Lyon, he is first documented in 1491. In 1493 and 1495, he appears as the *canonnier du roi* (cannon maker of the king). He is documented a number of times, sometimes with his brother, Valentin, all the way until his death, about 1514. He was involved with a number of military commissions. He cast cannons, cleaned the rust off them, and worked on the fortifications of Lyon and other sites. The signature by Jean Barbet does not mean that Barbet was the designer of this angel. Instead, it means that he cast the object. At this time in Europe, objects were often signed by the caster rather than the artist who designed them. The *Angel* must have been based on a clay or wooden model, on drawings, but the name of the person who designed it, who envisioned it, eludes us. So this beautiful object, one of the Frick's most beautiful sculptures, is still an orphan in a way. What is curious and puzzling is that the Jean Barbet who is mentioned in the documents appears from 1491 to 1514, which is a little later than 1475, when the *Angel* was signed. Is it indeed the same artist? Or could we have two artists with the same name? A father and son, maybe.

Nothing else quite like the *Angel* survives from that period. Bronzes of this size from France are unbelievably rare because the French Revolution saw the melting down of metalwork and the substantial destruction of works of art. This utterly unique sculpture cannot be compared with anything else we have. For a long time, it was rumored that it might be a nineteenth-century forgery, but recent analysis of the sculpture has shown that the *Angel* was cast in the way that cannons were made in the fifteenth century in France, proving that it cannot be a later fake. No one in the nineteenth century would have known how cannons were made in the fifteenth century. It is fascinating to think that this beautifully elegant angel and a weapon of destruction like a cannon are intrinsically connected.

—X.S.

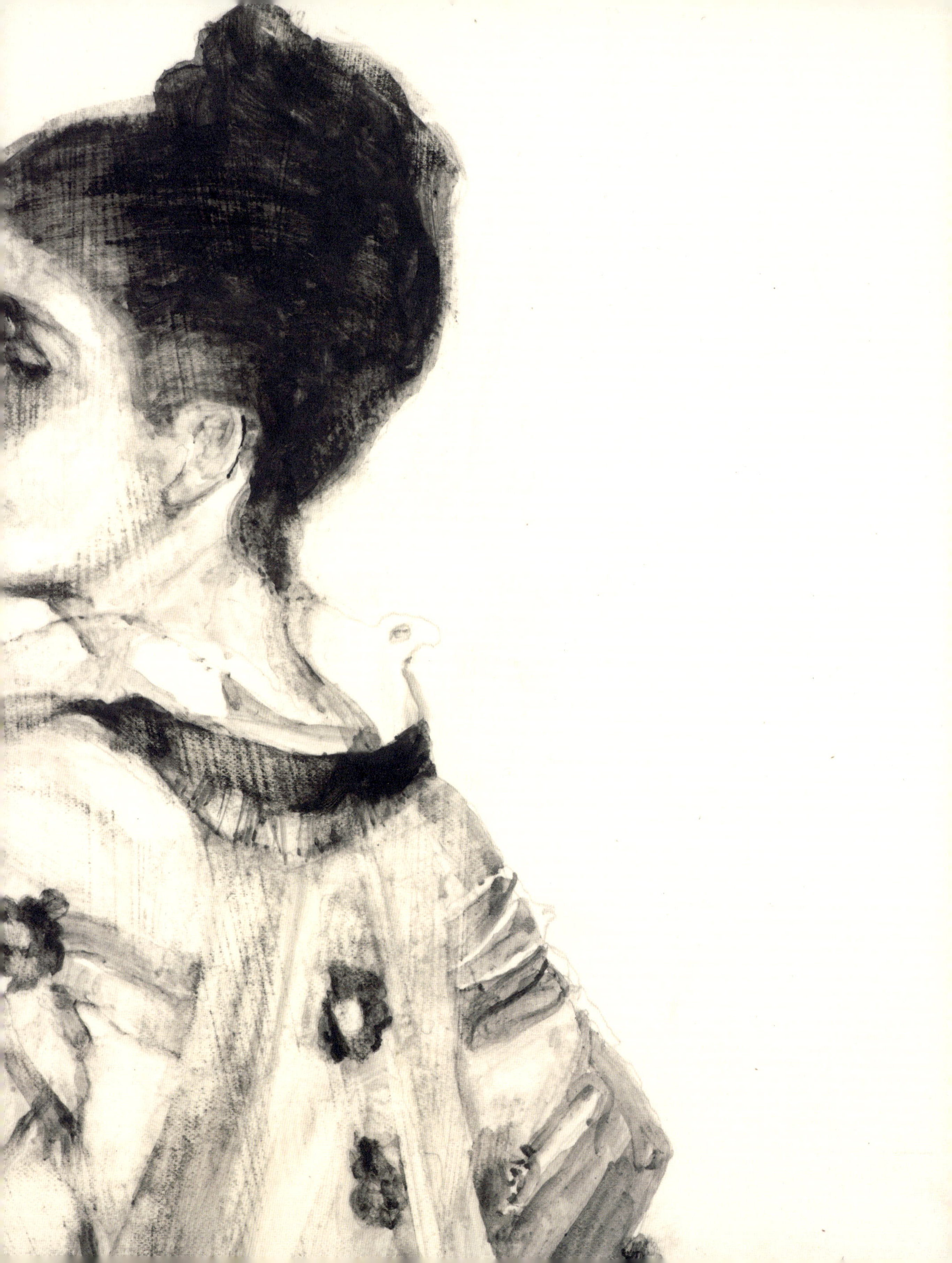

JAMES McNEILL WHISTLER

Symphony in Flesh Colour and Pink: Portrait of Mrs. Frances Leyland

1871–74

Sake Highball

SAKE

MIXED WITH AS MUCH (OR AS LITTLE)
CLUB SODA AS DESIRED

Serve on the rocks in a highball glass

One of the most beautiful details from this portrait is the blossoming branch of an almond tree, coming in from the left. Whistler was often inspired directly by Japanese models, as evident in details like this. This simple cocktail is a twist on one of the best-known Japanese drinks.

The Frick's five paintings, three pastels, and twelve etchings by Whistler (1834–1903) make him the artist best represented in the collection. Henry Clay Frick acquired them all toward the end of his life, between 1914 and 1919. Most of Whistler's portraits in the collection originally hung in Frick's private office, a room that was demolished and replaced with the Oval Room. A great proponent of

Art for Art's Sake, Whistler is probably the most important painter of what we now know as the Aesthetic Movement. He was born in in Lowell, Massachusetts, but as a young man moved to Europe, where he spent the rest of his life between Paris and London.

Frances Leyland was the wife of Frederick Richards Leyland, one of Whistler's greatest patrons in the 1870s. A shipowner from Liverpool, Frederick became extraordinarily wealthy and later in life owned as many as twenty-five steamships. A great patron of the arts, he was particularly fond of Pre-Raphaelite paintings and commissioned a number of works by Dante Gabriel Rossetti and Edward Burne-Jones. Leyland was so close to Burne-Jones that the artist designed the patron's grave in the Brompton Cemetery in London.

In 1855, Frederick Leyland married Frances Dawson. The couple had homes in London at Princes Gate and near Liverpool in a large Tudor country residence at Speke Hall. They commissioned a number of portraits. In the 1870s, Whistler created a portrait of his patron: *Arrangement in Black: Portrait of Frederick Richards Leyland*. About the same time, Leyland's wife served as a model for Rossetti, for a painting entitled *Monna Rosa* (The Lady of the Roses). After his own portrait, Leyland commissioned one of his wife from Whistler. Entitled *Symphony in Flesh Colour and Pink*, the portrait of Frances was commissioned in 1871 and painted up to about 1874, when it was exhibited in the first solo show of Whistler's work, an exhibition largely sponsored by Leyland. When Rossetti saw the painting, he said, "I cannot see that it is at all a likeness." He realized that Whistler's portraits are much more than a simple likeness. Whistler was not entirely happy with the painting and never considered it finished. Frances is shown in a statuesque pose from the back, her face in profile. Whistler made a series of sketches showing details of this portrait and portraying Frances from different angles. He also designed the frame for it. His paintings at the Frick are among the very few works in the museum that still have their original frames.

Frances Leyland joked later in life that she had wanted to be portrayed in a beautiful, elegant black dress that she owned but that Whistler insisted that she wear a dress that he designed himself. She and Whistler were very close. Although the painter was briefly engaged to her younger sister, Elizabeth—their breakup was apparently quite amicable—it was widely believed in London at the time that Whistler and Frances were romantically linked. This is evidenced in a series of letters. In August 1871, for example, Whistler was in London and wrote to Frances, who was out of town: "What shall I tell you of this dreary waste they call London? You seem to have carried away with you not only the life and joy of the place, but even the sun, too."

Whistler's relationship with the Leylands broke down over the creation of one of the artist's most famous works, the so-called Peacock Room. Originally entitled *Harmony in Blue and Gold*, it was designed to decorate the Leylands' dining room at Princes Gate. Whistler's ambitious vision for the project took over, and what was originally imagined as a fairly minor intervention in the space became a dramatic transformation of the room into one entirely decorated with images of peacocks. The room, which was meant to display the Leylands' collection of blue-and-white porcelain, became the breaking point between patron and artist. Whistler eventually completed the Peacock Room in 1877, but it marked the end of the relationship between the two. As a final touch, Whistler painted two fighting peacocks on the end wall of the room, with the idea that the one on the left is Whistler himself and the one on the right, covered in gold coins and with gold coins on the floor, is Frederick Leyland.

The relationship soured so badly that in the late 1870s Whistler painted a caricature of Frederick Leyland called *The Gold Scab: Eruption in Frilthy Lucre*. (Leyland was well known for his frilly shirts, and Whistler expected money from Leyland that he never received.) In 1879, Whistler went bankrupt, and that same year the Leylands separated. Eventually, Frances Leyland inherited the house, and she was the one who then sold the Peacock Room to Charles Lang Freer, in America, who reinstalled the room first in Detroit and then at the Freer Gallery of Art in Washington, DC, where it is today.

—X.S.

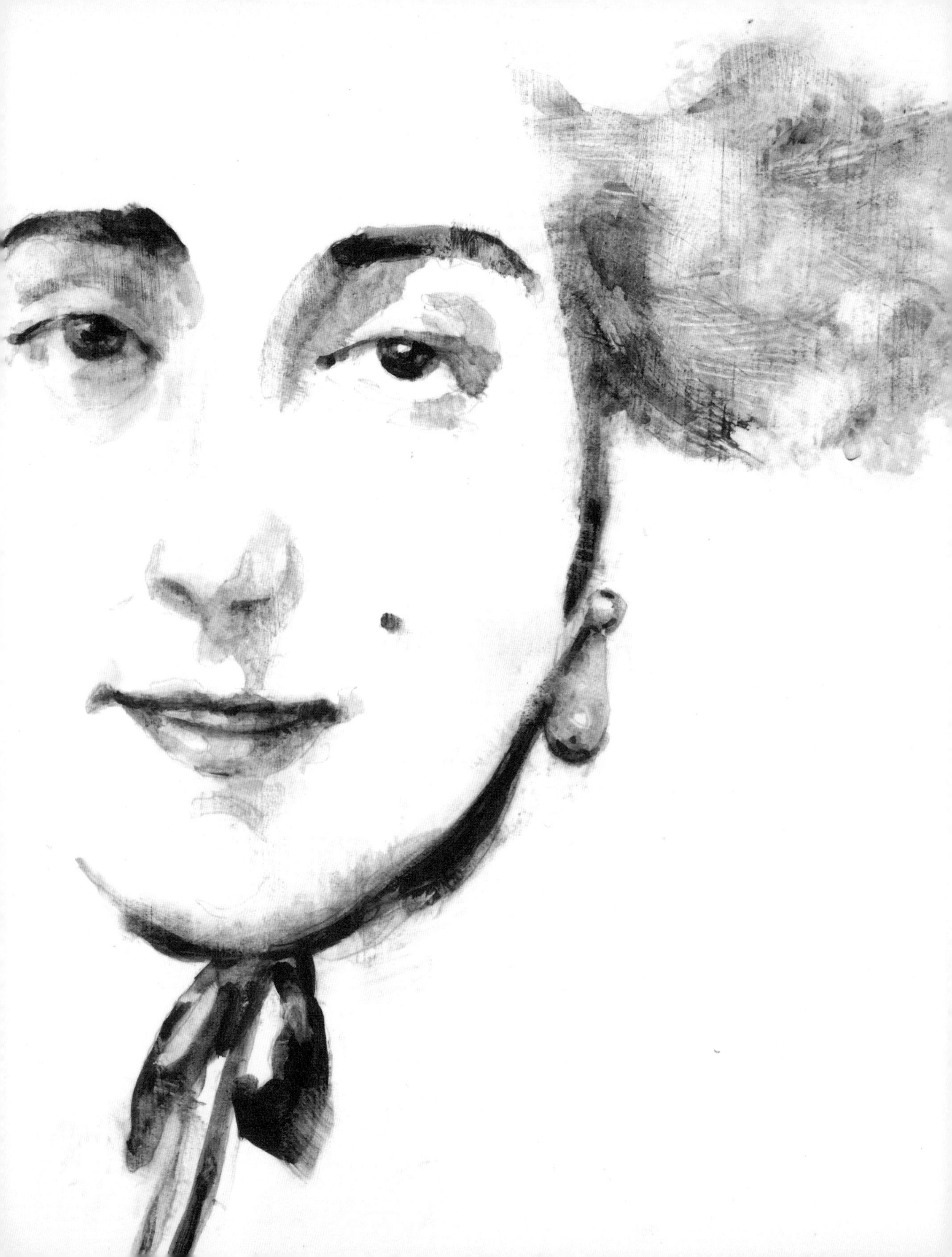

THOMAS GAINSBOROUGH
Grace Dalrymple Elliott

CA. 1782

Pimm's Cup

1½ OZ. PIMM'S NO. 1 ON ICE

ADD SPARKLING LEMONADE
OR GINGER ALE TO TASTE

Serve in a tumbler and garnish with a slice of lemon and other seasonal fruits

This is a typical summer drink in the United Kingdom, where it's called a Pimm's or a Pimm's No. 1. Pimm's is a liqueur invented in the 1820s by a London oyster bar owner, James Pimms, and, like many British drinks, it was touted as a medicinal concoction; it's supposed to aid digestion.

As a portraitist in Britain, Thomas Gainsborough (1727–1788) had a clientele that ranged from wealthy merchants to royalty. He was patronized by King George III and Queen Charlotte and was one of the founding members of the Royal Academy of Arts. The academy's annual summer exhibitions were the most important venue for artists in Britain or affiliated with Britain to show their art to the public and to critics. When Gainsborough showed this portrait of Grace Dalrymple Elliott at the summer exhibition of 1782, it was met with criticism; however, this had less to do with any perceived inability on Gainsborough's part than with his having captured his subject a little too well. According to one commentator, the eyes, as painted by Gainsborough, were too revealing of the sitter's vocation.

Born in Edinburgh about 1754, Grace Dalrymple Elliott was a great beauty reputed to have had affairs with prominent members of British and French society. Her father, Hugh Dalrymple, a barrister, was appointed attorney general of Grenada. This connection to Grenada reminds us that the British Empire's colonization, and all of its attendant atrocities, is in the background of so many works of art produced in Britain in the eighteenth century. When Grace was a young girl, her mother passed away, at which point Grace was sent to France to be educated in a convent. When she was a teenager, her father returned from his post in Grenada, and she moved back in with him in England. At her father's home, she met John Elliott, a wealthy physician about twenty years her senior. Immediately enamored with the seventeen-year-old girl, Elliott proposed marriage and Grace said yes. Only a couple of years later, he filed suit for adultery and was awarded a hefty monetary settlement. Five years after their marriage, in 1776, he filed for divorce.

One of the prominent men with whom Grace had a relationship was George, the 4th Earl of Cholmondeley, later the 1st Marquess of Cholmondeley. She also was associated for a short time with the Prince of Wales, who would eventually become the king of England as George IV.

When this portrait was shown at the Royal Academy in 1782, it drew a lot of attention to Grace. Just as the exhibition opened, she gave birth to her first and only child—Georgiana Augusta Frederica, who took the surname Seymour. The father was reputed to be the Prince of Wales, but Georgiana was raised in the household of Cholmondeley. One has to wonder to what degree Gainsborough anticipated—and took advantage of—the notoriety and attention his sitter would attract at the Royal Academy exhibition.

The attention it received was not just a matter of who he painted but also how he portrayed her. This is a very intimate portrait; look at how close we are to her. She looks languidly out at the viewer, in an open, encouraging way, provocative and familiar. Her expressive, dark eyebrows contrast with her white skin and powdered hair. Whiteness in skin was a complex, complicated part of ideal feminine beauty in this culture and is especially exaggerated in portraits like this one, in which a white European woman exaggerated her whiteness through the application of makeup. Very often, women's makeup included deadly lead white. In addition to the white skin, a generous application of red on her cheeks creates a sense of flush. Her rosy cheeks are matched with ripe red lips, which part to show a hint of teeth.

One of my favorite details is the touch of black paint to mark the beauty spot on her left cheek, which was fashionable at the time.

From afar, one might see a lot of browns and whites in the portrait, along with a smattering of a few other hues, but if you look closely, the painting presents a play of subtle hues of white on white. The diaphanous silk of her neckline spills open to reveal and frame the creamy expanse of her chest and ample breasts, all of this exaggerated by a dark ribbon falling between her breasts and attached to a bright blue locket. That blue probably would have been even more pronounced in the eighteenth century, surrounded by diamonds and nestled in the sumptuous pink ribbon.

In 1786, Grace Elliott left England for France, where she spent the rest of her life. She arrived just a few years before the tumultuous years of the French Revolution would change her life and the history of France and beyond. Among the men with whom she had relationships in France, perhaps the most famous was the Duc d'Orléans, a proponent of constitutional monarchy who, despite being a noble, was active in fomenting the revolution. He changed his name from the Duc d'Orléans to Philippe Égalité (meaning equality). Regardless, he was executed in the Terror of 1793.

Grace was there through it all. She recorded the events of the revolution in her diary, the sensational contents of which were published posthumously as *Journal of My Life during the French Revolution*. We don't know how much of it is true. For instance, she names four prisons in which she was held prisoner, but her name has not been found on any of those prison lists. There are deeply human descriptions in the diary. In one description of her incarceration, she recounts that every night she would beg from the jailer who locked up at the end of the day a drop of brandy in order to clean her teeth. She credits those drops of brandy for being able to keep her teeth. All her cellmates, she wrote, lost theirs. This anecdote comes to mind when I think of her parted lips in this portrait.

The portrait seems to have remained in Gainsborough's studio until his death. A mysterious bill, written by Gainsborough's widow, was addressed to the Prince of Wales for the "head of Mrs. Elliott," referring to a painted head, at a price of 31 pounds and 10 shillings. It's unclear if this bill was ever paid. The portrait does not appear to have entered the Prince of Wales's collection when he was the royal heir or, later on, when he was George IV. One theory posits that it was inherited by her daughter, Georgiana, who sadly died ten years before her mother, at the age of thirty-one, but this has not been substantiated.

Who commissioned this intimate, sensuous painting? How much of her journal account is true? And what or whom, if anything, did she keep in that blue locket? One gets a sense from her portrait that she held her secrets close.

—A.N.

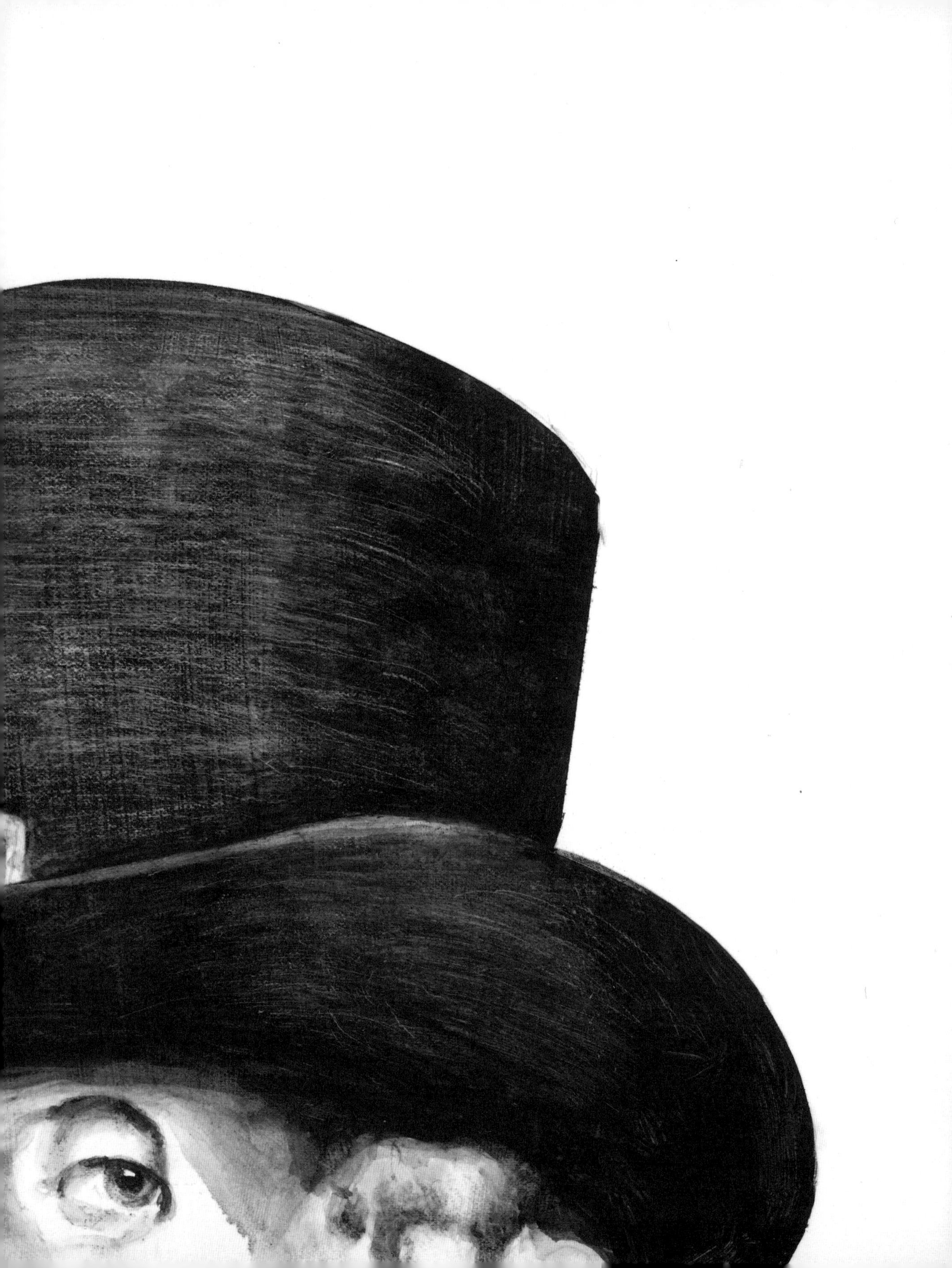

GEORGE STUBBS

Warren Hastings

CA. 1791

Gin and Tonic

2 OZ. BOMBAY GIN

4 OZ. TONIC WATER

Serve on the rocks in a tumbler
and garnish with a lime wedge

A Gin and Tonic is a quintessential British drink. Bombay gin takes its name from the city of Bombay, today known as Mumbai, one of the first cities belonging to the English crown in India. In 1661, the new queen of England, Catherine of Braganza, who was the daughter of the king of Portugal, brought the island of Bombay as part of her dowry to her new husband, Charles II, the king of England.

The history of how the East India Company took over the Indian subcontinent and effectively ran it on behalf of the English government is a complex and horrific tale. Established in the late sixteenth century, the company reached its apex of power in the eighteenth century. This tiny Stubbs watercolor, slightly more than five inches high, painted about 1791, portrays one of the most interesting figures linked to the British colonization of India.

The watercolor came to the Frick fairly recently, in 2010, as part of the bequest of Charles Ryskamp. After having taught at Princeton and been the director of the Morgan Library & Museum in New York, Ryskamp became the director of the Frick in 1987, serving in that position until 1997. He was a great collector of books and works on paper, especially of drawings by central European and Scandinavian painters and by English artists from the romantic period. The Stubbs portrait of Warren Hastings is one of a group of about ten works of art that he bequeathed to the Frick.

George Stubbs (1724–1806) was celebrated for his sporting pictures—paintings of horses and horse races and portraits of people on horseback. A contemporary of Stubbs, Warren Hastings (1732–1818) was just slightly younger. As a young man, he joined the East India Company, traveled to India, and quickly rose to the top of the company. A number of portraits were made of him, one of the grandest painted about 1766–68 by Sir Joshua Reynolds. In 1772, the year before Hastings became the first governor general of Bengal, the British portraitist Tilly Kettle traveled to India and painted his portrait.

A great intellectual, Hastings was also among the few in the East India Company who understood, respected, and was interested in the Indian subcontinent's culture. He wrote about how he loved India more than his homeland. He spoke several Indian languages, could read and write in Sanskrit, and studied Persian. He also supported the first translation of the Indian epic poem the Bhagavad Gita from Sanskrit into English. He lived in a grand house in Calcutta, on the eastern coast of India, where the headquarters of the East India Company was located at that time.

Hastings's career suffered a swift downfall. In 1785, when he returned to England from India, he was accused of a number of crimes. The resulting trial, the longest trial in British history, took place in Westminster Hall, next to the Houses of Parliament, and lasted from the mid-1780s all the way to 1795. The trial brought to light the East India Company's criminal behavior in India, unfortunately blaming, in many ways, the wrong person. Of all those who had run the East India Company and had been active in India on Britain's behalf, Hastings was perhaps the least culpable. In the end, he would receive a full acquittal, but by then his career was ruined by ten years of vicious slander and bad publicity. He retired to private life after the trial and lived for another twenty years, never returning to his beloved India. Painted around this time, the watercolor by Stubbs was probably a preparatory work for a full-length portrait of Hastings on horseback, which Stubbs painted at that same time, and for an engraving that was created by Stubbs's son based on his father's drawing. This may have been linked to an effort to publicize the image of Warren Hastings after his acquittal as the print was published in 1795 at the end of the trial.

After the trial, Hastings took refuge at Daylesford, a country house that had belonged to the Hastings family but had later been sold by them, only to be repurchased by Hastings when he was in India. When Hastings died, most of the contents of the house were sold. He was buried at Daylesford in a very elegant tomb, just outside a medieval church that he had helped restore.

This portrait is one of the very few watercolors of people painted by Stubbs and one of his very few portraits of a well-known personality of the time that survives. What I find interesting is that it brings to us one of the main characters of this complicated, bloody, and tragic history of the relationship between Britain and India in the eighteenth century. But it also focuses on one of the people in that history who really deserves to be better known and better appreciated.

—X.S.

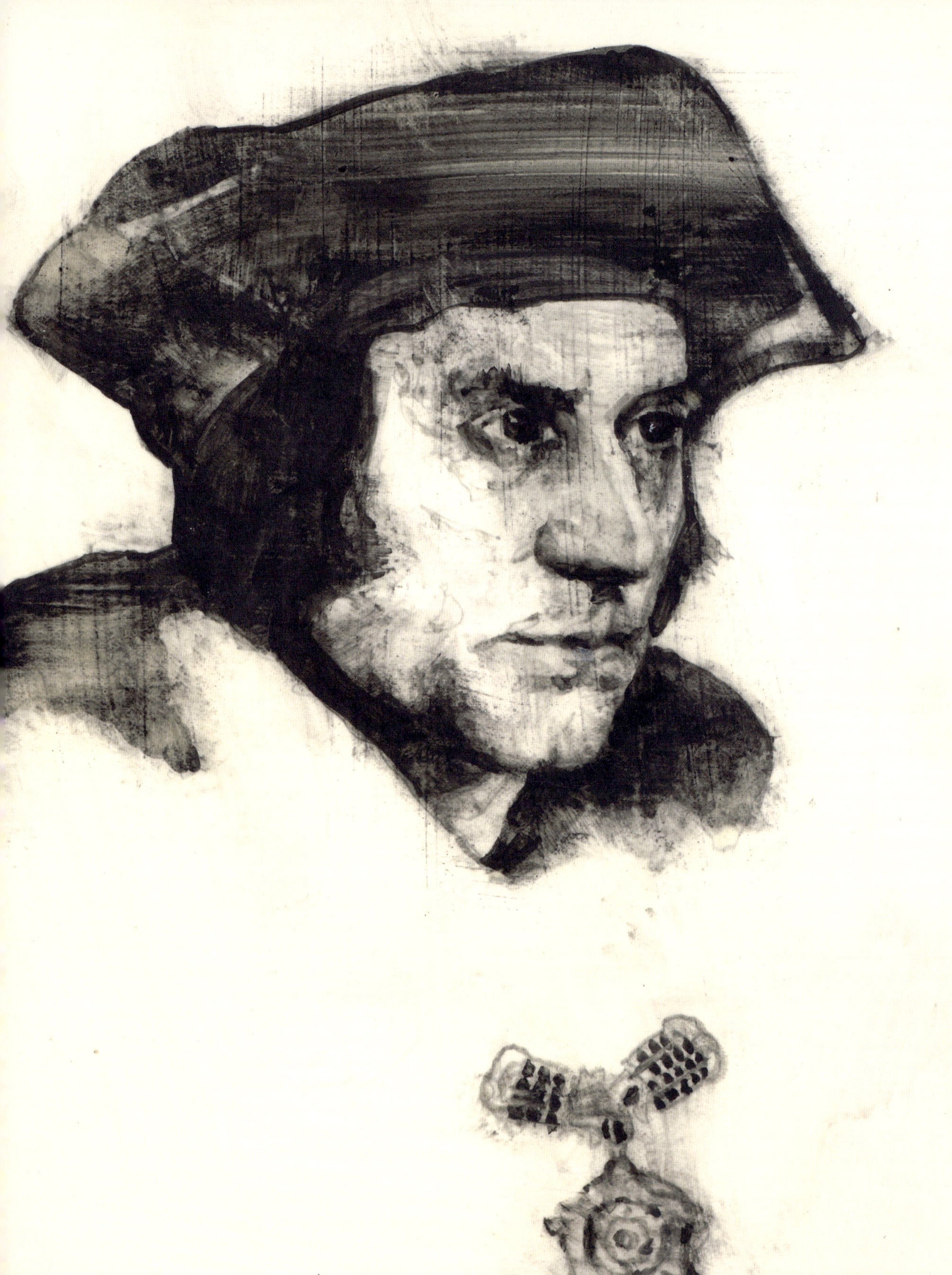

HANS HOLBEIN THE YOUNGER

Sir Thomas More

1527

Bloody Mary

1½ OZ. VODKA

3 OZ. TOMATO JUICE

½ OZ. LEMON JUICE

2 DASHES OF WORCESTERSHIRE SAUCE

2 DROPS OF TABASCO

SALT AND PEPPER

Serve on the rocks in a tall glass
and garnish with a celery stalk

Invented in Paris in the 1920s, the Bloody Mary is named after Mary I, who was Henry VIII's daughter with Catherine of Aragon and whom Thomas More knew as a princess. As Mary was the last Catholic queen regnant of England, this seems an appropriate cocktail for the topic of the Reformation in England.

In the fifteenth century, the Italian architect and art theorist Leon Battista Alberti wrote, "The painter possesses the truly divine power in that not only does he make what is absent present, as they say of friendship, but he also represents the dead to the living many centuries later." At a time when we are so accustomed to our smartphones and other technology making possible the virtual presence of friends and loved ones, it is interesting to think about how in earlier times people had to rely on portraits to make those absent present.

Holbein's portrait of Sir Thomas More is one of the most beloved paintings at the Frick. More is probably best known for his tragic downfall in the 1530s, after having been Lord Chancellor of England. His refusal to acknowledge the divorce of Henry VIII and Catherine of Aragon and to recognize Anne Boleyn as the king's new wife was his fatal mistake. In 1534, he was imprisoned in the Tower of London, where he spent the better part of a year, and on July 6, 1535, he was beheaded on Tower Hill. In 1935, about four hundred years after his death, he was canonized by the Catholic Church.

Henry Clay Frick's relationship with Holbein predates the acquisition of *Sir Thomas More*. In England, in 1909, he acquired Holbein's full-length portrait of Christina of Denmark, Duchess of Milan, who had been considered a potential new wife for Henry VIII. Frick was keen to purchase the painting and was waiting for an export license to bring it from the United Kingdom to the United States. But the portrait was at the center of a large public debate, and it was saved for the nation at the last minute, when an anonymous donor stepped in and provided the funds necessary for the National Gallery in London to secure the painting. Frick was very disappointed about losing it, and a few years later, in January 1912, he consoled himself with the acquisition of *Sir Thomas More*, which was followed a few years later by the purchase of a portrait of More's great rival, Thomas Cromwell. By the time the Frick family moved into the house at 1 East 70th Street in 1914, the two canvases had taken up their positions on either side of the mantelpiece in the Living Hall, where they have remained ever since (apart from a brief stay at Frick Madison). It is one of the great displays at the Frick.

The details in this extraordinary portrait are what made Holbein a renowned artist, first in Basel and then in England, beginning in the late 1520s. This kind of attention to detail is what is so celebrated in northern European painters. Set against a bright green curtain, More holds a letter and wears a black cap and a chain around his neck. This is not the chain of the Lord Chancellor since the painting was done several years before More became chancellor. It is either a chain the king gave him when he joined the king's council in 1516 or when he was knighted in 1521. More always wore the chain, refusing to take it off even when he was in his cell at the Tower. At the bottom left, you can see the inscribed date of 1527. His face, of course, is incredible—the detail of every hair of his eyebrows, the five o'clock shadow on his chin and cheeks, the hair emerging from underneath his cap. A truly miraculous painting.

Holbein (ca. 1497/98–1543) was born in Augsburg and as a young man moved to Basel, where he worked within humanist circles. Basel at that time was an important intellectual center in Europe, its great star the philosopher Desiderius Erasmus, the author of *The Praise of Folly*. Erasmus was a good friend of Holbein's and was portrayed by him a number of times. Erasmus was also a very good friend of Thomas More's. The two frequently exchanged letters, and Erasmus stayed with Thomas More in London. We have a tender image of this written by Erasmus himself: "We talk of letters, 'till we fall asleep, our dreams are dreams of letters, and literature awakens us to begin the new day."

Erasmus suggested that Holbein visit London and stay with Thomas More, and sometime between the end of 1526 and 1528, Holbein moved to London and spent time with More in his house in Chelsea. At this time, Holbein began producing a series of beautiful drawings of Thomas More and his family. Most of these were done in preparation for a very large painting, which showed the family of Thomas More with life-size figures, probably made in 1527 as a present for More on his fiftieth birthday. Unfortunately, this painting only survived until 1752, when it was destroyed in a fire in a castle in Moravia.

The relationship between the Frick portrait and the large family portrait, painted the same year, is unclear. Was the *More* also painted for Thomas More? Did he give it to a friend? We have no trace of the portrait until around the end of the sixteenth century, when the portrait appears for the first time in Rome. All the way to the mid-nineteenth century, the painting was in the Crescenzi family collection in their palazzo next to the Pantheon. It traveled to England in the mid-nineteenth century, and Frick acquired it from an English collector in 1912.

When I look at Thomas More in this portrait, I think of something he wrote in his famous book *Utopia*. In the introduction, More describes the sorts of activities that would have occupied him around the time Holbein painted him:

> *Most of my day is taken up by legal affairs, so at one moment I'm pleading a case, at another I'm hearing one, then I'm settling a dispute, and at another handing down a judgment. At the same time visits must be paid to somebody out of official obligation and to someone else on business matters; almost the whole day I'm out dealing with others, and what's left I devote to my family, which leaves just nothing for myself—that is, for writing. Naturally when I get home I have to talk with my wife and chatter with the children, as well as speak to the servants. All this activity I count as part of my duty since it has to be done (and so it does unless you want to be a stranger in your own house). . . . Between all these activities that I've described, the days, the months and the years slip by.*

—X.S.

JEAN-HENRI RIESENER

Commode and *Secretaire*

CA. 1780 AND CA. 1790

Kir Royal

⅓ OZ. CRÈME DE CASSIS

3 OZ. CHAMPAGNE

Serve chilled in a flute glass and garnish with a blackberry

This cocktail was invented in the twentieth century by Félix Kir, a Catholic priest who was part of the French Resistance and later mayor of the town of Dijon in Burgundy. With its royal name and red color, it seems in keeping with works of art related to Queen Marie-Antoinette.

Commodes and secretaires were typically created as pairs for the rooms of the aristocracy in France. These specific pieces have a royal provenance, as they were made for the queen of France, Marie-Antoinette, daughter of Empress Maria Theresa and wife of Louis XVI. The designer, Jean-Henri Riesener, was a German

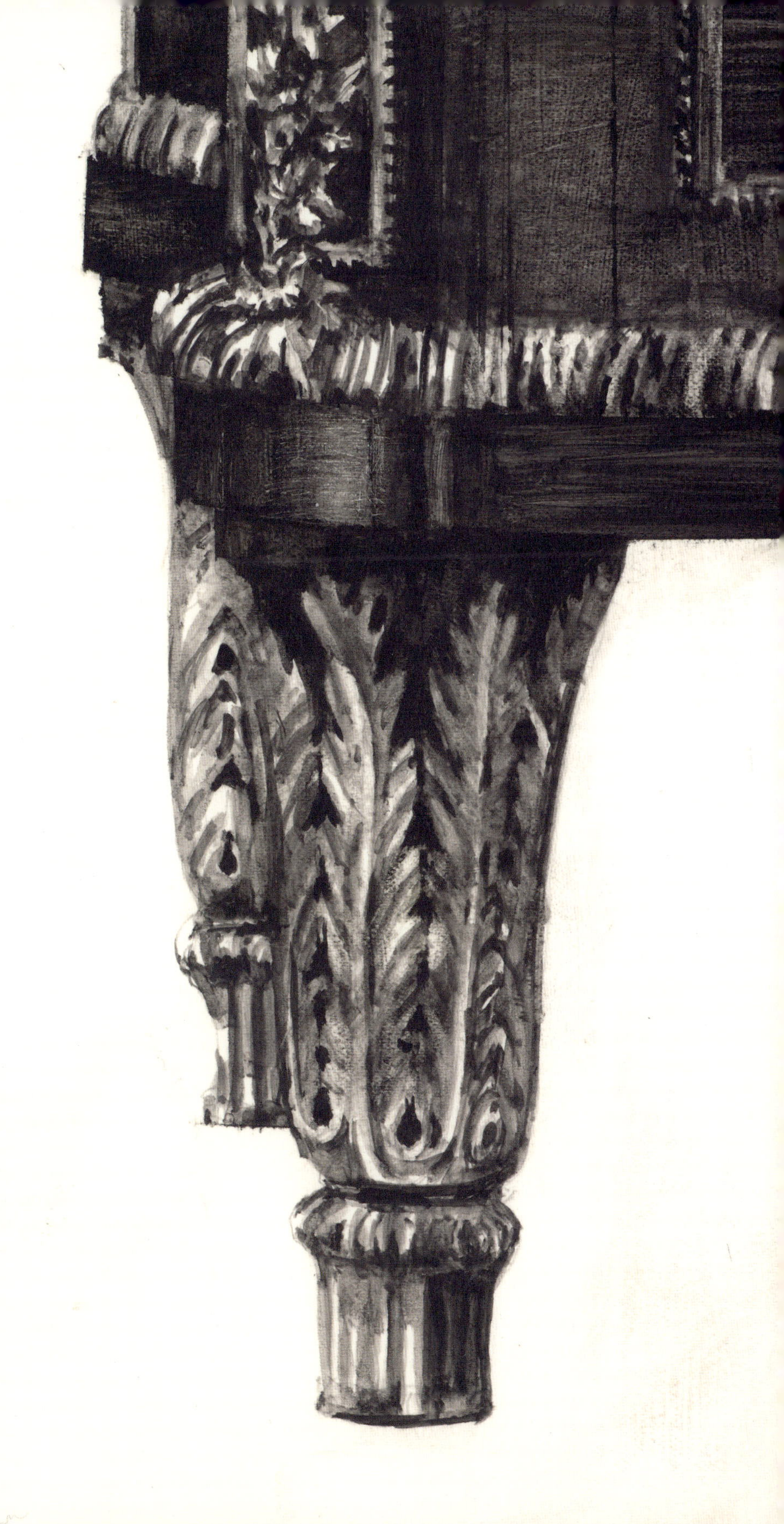

cabinetmaker active in France. Born Johann Heinrich Riesener in the town of Gladbeck in Westphalia, he moved as a young man to France, where he worked with one of the makers of royal furniture, Jean-François Oeben, who was also German. When Oeben died in 1768, Riesener married his widow. A few years later, in 1774, he was made the *ébéniste du roi,* the royal furniture maker.

The Frick has five pieces by Riesener, of which these two are the most important because of their royal patronage. Basically a chest of drawers, with two central drawers, the commode is adorned with a number of inlaid precious woods in a technique known as marquetry and topped by a slab of marble known as Breche d'Alep. The rest of the piece is decorated with gilt-bronze mounts. In the central part is a medallion with two doves and Cupid's bow and arrows. All around the piece, the inlaid-wood decoration provides depictions of garlands of flowers and beautiful geometrical patterns.

The companion piece is the secretaire, which, as the name suggests, has secret compartments. While it looks monolithic from the outside, the top part opens so that the secretaire can be used as a writing desk, and there are various drawers and small compartments above and below. It is a complex piece of furniture in the way it was made. In the plaques of the marquetry are wonderful details of flowers in vases and various scientific instruments and books, as well as a number of plaques with little birds flying between the flowers. This piece looks to us today as if it was made with different woods and different colors, but in fact, only a limited range of colors survives. When new, French marquetry furniture was very brightly colored. The exotic woods would provide the brightness—the red, the pink, the green, and the blue—that gave a colorful look to the piece of furniture. The bright colors that one often sees in porcelain pieces are what was achieved with marquetry. Unfortunately, these colors are not stable, and soon after a piece of furniture was made, the wood would start changing color. And so today when you look at a great Riesener piece, you have to imagine it with the color that has unfortunately been lost.

These two pieces were made for Marie-Antoinette, probably in the mid-1780s, for the Château de Saint-Cloud, a few miles west of Paris on the Seine. Formerly the residence of the Duc d'Orléans, the chateau was purchased by the king and given to Marie-Antoinette, for whom it became a refuge. Decorating Saint-Cloud became one of her favorite pastimes in the mid-1780s, and the chateau remained one of her most beloved residences. Unfortunately, it was destroyed in the early 1870s during the Franco-Prussian War.

At the beginning of the French Revolution, after the taking of the Bastille, the crowd stormed Versailles, and the king and queen were moved to Paris to the Tuileries Palace, another royal palace that no longer exists, having been destroyed in 1871. The king and queen were brought there as prisoners in the 1790s, and this was their last residence. Marie-Antoinette redecorated her apartments on the ground and first floors of the Tuileries, toward the garden, with pieces she brought from Versailles. The commode and the secretaire that Riesener had made for Saint-Cloud were actually sent to the Tuileries. An inventory of 1793 lists them both and explains that the marble top of the commode had been damaged and was broken. This probably happened when the Tuileries Palace was stormed in 1792.

Both pieces of furniture at the Frick are signed and dated. Even though they were made in the 1780s, the secretaire is dated 1790 and the commode 1791. The Riesener signatures and dates actually mark the substantial restoration of the two pieces. They were altered, probably simplified, for the queen's new apartments. They were probably deemed to be too lavish, and so the queen herself asked for them to be altered by Riesener.

These are among the last pieces of furniture that the king and queen lived with. With the storming of the Tuileries and the murder of the royal guard, both king and queen were imprisoned and put on trial, and in 1793 both were beheaded—the king on January 21, the queen on October 16. The furniture was removed from the Tuileries and put up for sale. It eventually reached the collection of the Dukes of Hamilton, from whom John Pierpont Morgan acquired them. After Morgan's death, the art dealer Joseph Duveen sold them to Henry Clay Frick, in 1915.

—X.S.

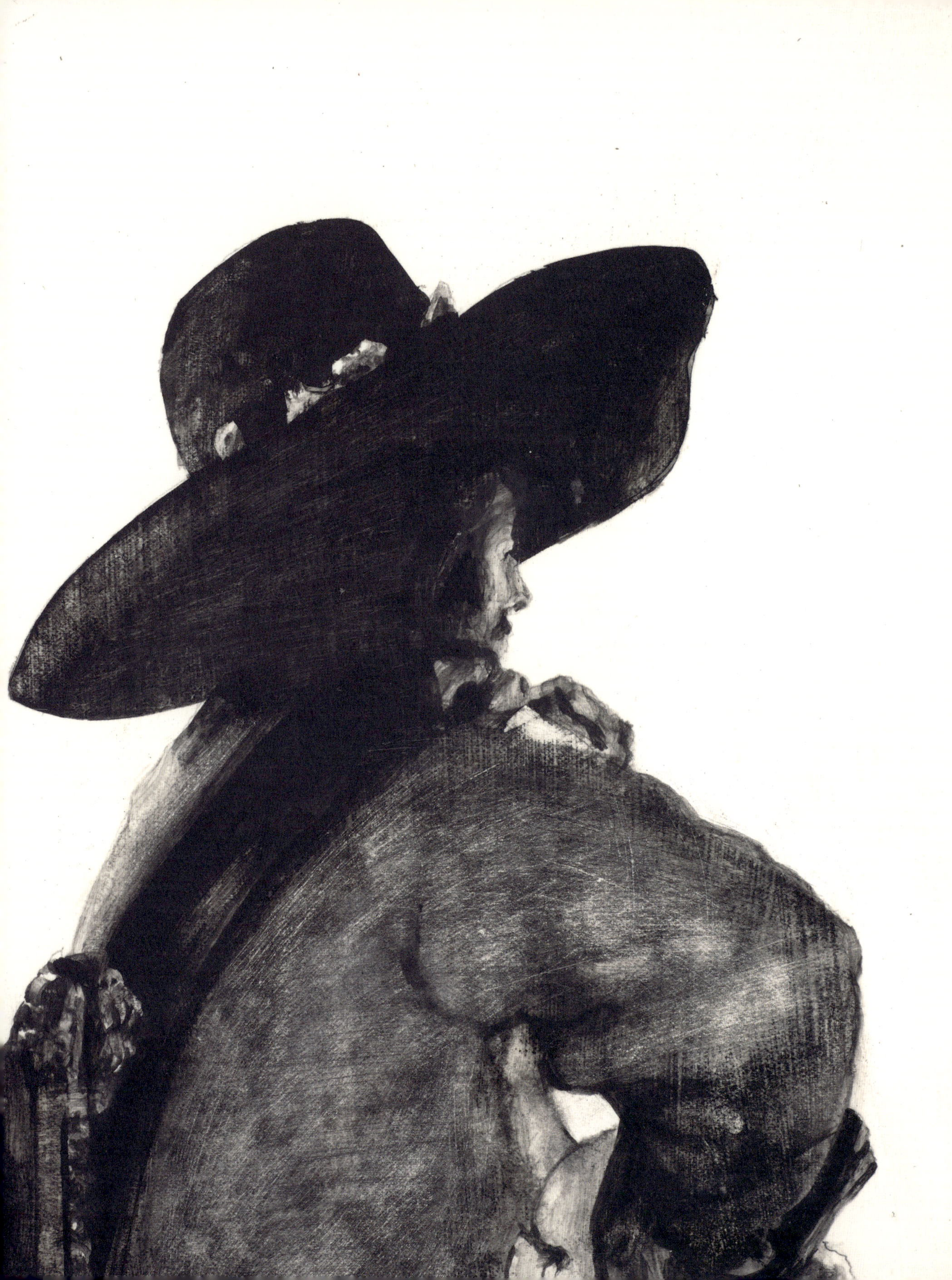

JOHANNES VERMEER

Officer and Laughing Girl

CA. 1657

Kopstootje

1 OZ. GENEVER

Follow with a pint of Dutch lager in a beer glass

*Genever is a Dutch liquor made of malt wine and other flavors, including juniper (*genever *in Dutch). In the late sixteenth century, English soldiers encountered Dutch soldiers drinking genever before going into battle, and this is purportedly the origin of the term "Dutch courage." The drink became so popular in England that English distillers began to make their own version, which they called gin. Drinking genever followed by a beer is called a Kopstootje, a "little head-butt." Like a little glass of genever, the woman in this painting is, as the Dutch saying goes, "kort maar krachtig" (short but powerful).*

Though now one of the best-known European artists of the early modern period, Vermeer (1632–1675) was all but unknown during the two centuries following his death, with paintings by him bearing erroneous attributions. This painting—its title dating from the late seventeenth century—carried the false signature of Vermeer's contemporary Pieter de Hooch, who also painted genre scenes like this and who had greater market value than Vermeer in the centuries after his death. Only in 1866 did the French art historian and critic Théophile Thoré-Bürger "rediscover" Vermeer and assemble what he believed to be the artist's true corpus. Since then, Vermeer's popularity has not waned. Today, thirty-four paintings are universally accepted as by Vermeer, three of them in The Frick Collection.

In *Officer and Laughing Girl*, a seated man courts a woman seated across from him at a table, a typical scene in Dutch genre painting. In her right hand, the woman holds a glass that is usually used to drink white wine. Her opened left hand rests on the table. Some art historians have taken these details to indicate that she is a prostitute, that the officer will be paying her for her company. To me, however, there is a sense of innocence and sweetness in the room bathed in light.

Vermeer is renowned for his mastery of the effects of light on surfaces. The light from the window is picked up by the gold thread in the woman's dress, by the reflections in glass, and on her face. Because he is so successful at creating the illusion of reality, some have argued that Vermeer used optical devices such as the camera obscura. Frankly, I don't think it would take away from the quality of these paintings if he had used devices. To me, it is the magic of dabs of paint on a canvas that creates the effect. There is an eloquence to the way just a few small shapes and forms convey so much. We barely see anything of the man's profile, not even a quarter of his face, and yet one senses his absolute focus on the woman.

Vermeer is unusual in his copious use of ultramarine, an extremely expensive pigment made from lapis lazuli mined, then as now, in Afghanistan. Over the centuries, painters almost always used ultramarine for areas of great significance, such as the Virgin Mary's dress in Christian paintings. Pigment analyses of Vermeer paintings have found it in unexpected places, blended into walls, included in a map. It begs the question of how Vermeer afforded it and has led some to suggest that he had a patron who fronted the money to acquire the pigments and also commissioned the paintings. The name Pieter van Ruijven has come up as someone in Delft who may have been this patron.

The room in the painting appears in many other paintings by Vermeer and is believed to be the second-floor room in the artist's home in Delft, at the front of the house. The woman may be the same one who appears in many of his paintings—his wife, Catharina Bolnes. It is not unusual for an artist's wife to be the frequent model for his paintings.

For Vermeer, an artist who seems never to have left his home country, one wonders how much he thought about the greater world as he painted upstairs in a second-floor room, possibly with his wife, his young children downstairs; yet the wider world makes its way into the painting in a number of ways. The hat worn by the officer, for instance, is almost certainly made of beaver. As the historian Timothy Brook has written in *Vermeer's Hat,* beaver was the optimal choice for making hats like this in the sixteenth and seventeenth centuries because of its color retention, water repellency, and sturdiness in keeping its shape. In fact, its popularity as a material for hats led to overhunting, which made beavers nearly extinct in northern Europe. The vast majority of beaver pelts in the seventeenth century came from what was then New France, now Canada, through indigenous trade with Europeans, and as Brook points out, this was at no small cost in human life. The indigenous population in what is now North America paid dearly for these luxury objects to be made and sold in Europe.

With a west-up orientation (rather than north-up), the wall map in the room depicts the provinces of Holland and West-Friesland. Another disorienting factor is that the land appears blue. This could be due to the maze of bright blue arteries denoting waterways but is probably the result of a fugitive yellow pigment; the land was probably green originally. The map painted so meticulously here has been identified; rare examples of it are conserved at the Westfries Museum in Hoorn and the University of Leiden, dated about 1621, by the mapmaker Van Berckenrode and the publisher Blaeu.

Seventeenth-century Dutch mapmaking went hand in hand with an explosion in travel, trade, wealth, and colonies, conducted particularly by the Dutch East India Company. Though long referred to as the Dutch Golden Age, this period was by no means a golden age for the thousands of Africans forced into slavery and the indigenous populations in North America and Asia. There are always two sides to a story of great wealth.

The year 1672, when the Dutch War started, was called the "Disaster Year." Among other things, there was a severe economic crisis, and it was apparently from extreme stress due to financial struggles that Vermeer died in 1675, at the age of forty-three. About eighteen months later, his wife, Catharina Bolnes, who had been left with eleven underage children, filed for bankruptcy. Catharina had given birth to some fifteen children in her life, four of whom did not survive infancy. She raised the surviving eleven on her own, and, from what we can gather from historical documents, at least seven survived into adulthood.

We don't know if the woman in this picture is Catharina. Her smile is not an easy expression for a model to hold. I suspect this is a face that was familiar to the artist, one he could visualize smiling. I would like to think that it is his wife, maybe some twenty years before the struggles at the end of his life.

She is made to look diminutive by the wall map behind her and the swashbuckling officer, yet her radiant face is the focus of this painting. She is, as the Dutch saying goes, "kort maar krachtig"—short but powerful, small but strong.

—A.N.

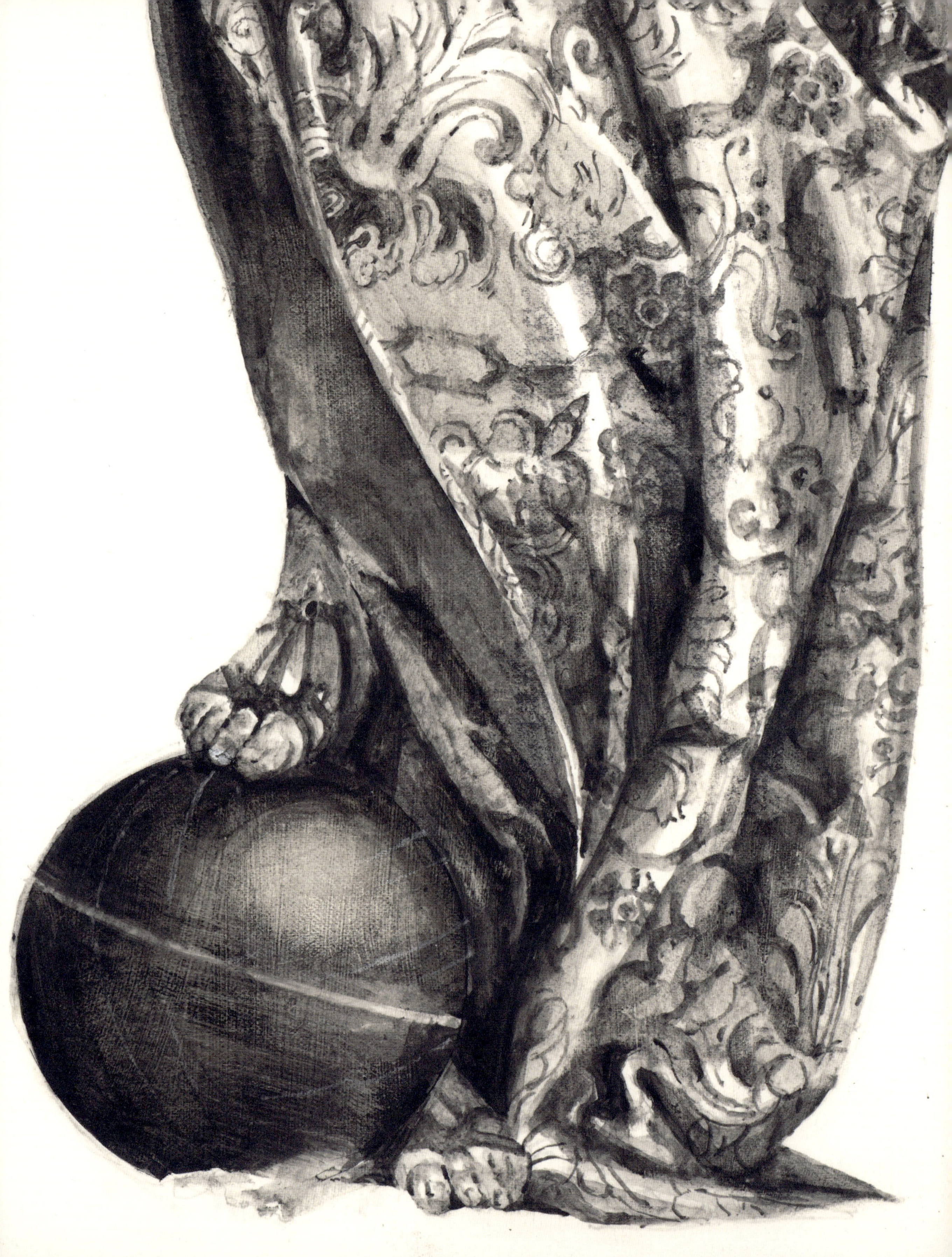

PAOLO VERONESE

Wisdom and Strength

CA. 1565

Negroni

1 OZ. CAMPARI

1 OZ. GIN

1 OZ. SWEET RED VERMOUTH

Serve on the rocks in a tumbler
and garnish with an orange peel

One of the best-known Italian cocktails, the Negroni was invented in Florence in 1919. Count Camillo Negroni went to his favorite bar and asked that his customary drink, an Americano, be strengthened by substituting gin for club soda.

For more than a century, two grand allegories by Paolo Veronese (1528–1588) have presided over the Frick's West Gallery. They are probably my favorite paintings in the museum. They were acquired by Henry Clay Frick in 1912 and brought to New York to decorate the grand picture gallery he was building in his house.

These two paintings have a most prestigious provenance, having belonged to some of the most famous art collectors in Europe. They first appear in the seventeenth century in the inventories of Emperor Rudolf II, as part of a group of paintings by Veronese that were displayed in his castle in Prague. When Swedish troops sacked Prague in 1648, they brought Rudolph's art collection to Sweden, where it became part of the royal collection. Later in the seventeenth century, when Queen Christina of Sweden abdicated and converted from Protestantism to Catholicism, she moved to Rome, bringing the collection of paintings with her. At her death, they were inherited by Cardinal Decio Azzolino and subsequently belonged to the aristocratic Odescalchi family. Later, in the eighteenth century, the Odescalchi sold the collection to the Duc d'Orléans. So after having been in Prague, Stockholm, and Rome, the paintings were moved to Paris, where for most of the eighteenth century they were in the Palais-Royal. With the French Revolution, however, the Duc d'Orléans sold the collection. In what became a legendary London sale, the collection was largely dispersed and acquired by various English aristocrats and collectors. The two Veronese allegories were purchased by the collector Thomas Hope and hung first in his London home and then in Deepdene, his country house in Sussex. It was from Hope's heirs that Frick acquired the paintings in 1912.

The allegories are part of a larger set of works by Veronese that includes two other paintings of about the same size: *Mars and Venus United by Love* (Metropolitan Museum of Art, New York) and *Herse, Aglauros, and Mercury* (Fitzwilliam Museum, Cambridge). Although it was long believed that these four paintings were painted together as a group for Rudolph II, we now know that Veronese painted them at different points in his career—the two Frick canvases in the mid-1560s, the one at the Metropolitan Museum probably in the early 1570s, and the one at the Fitzwilliam in the early 1580s—and probably for different patrons. The origins of these four works are still somewhat mysterious. They reached the collection of Rudolph II through slightly different routes and by the seventeenth century were together in Prague.

Allegorical painting is a way in which the invisible—in this instance, an abstract concept—can be made visible. The first of the two Veronese allegories is set against great marble columns and golden and green drapery, with a landscape that opens on the left. There are three human figures: a woman, a man, and a young boy. By identifying them and unpacking the symbolism in this painting, the message of the canvas is finally revealed. On the right is a bearded man, covered in a lion's skin and resting on a wooden club. This is clearly the image of the ancient hero Hercules. He is slouching, falling down, and this is part of the message of the picture.

Below Hercules is a little boy with wings, another mythological figure—Cupid. Hercules is always interpreted as representing strength; Cupid, as representing love. Cupid is shown sitting on a red flag with gold letters. In his left hand, he holds a scepter that rests upon a royal crown. As you look closely, you pick up on other details. The female figure has her foot firmly placed on a globe. Below it are more scepters and coins and various jewels, as well as the imperial crown. Just above it is the Latin inscription OMNIA VANITAS (All is vanity), which comes from the Old Testament Book of Ecclesiastes: "Vanity of vanities, saith the preacher, vanity of vanities, all is vanity." With this phrase, we begin to understand the rest of the picture, how all is vanity. Strength, love, the kingdoms and empires of the earth, money, nations, wealth—all of this is vanity.

At the center of the painting is a woman—neither a goddess nor a heroine of antiquity—who stands proudly over everything else. She is partly naked, with one of her breasts revealed. The key element of this figure is the shining sun placed over her forehead. She looks up to heaven. She is a representation of Divine Wisdom.

So what is the message of this allegory? It is telling us that all is vanity but that divine wisdom conquers all. In a different passage from Ecclesiastes we can read: "Remember: wisdom is better than strength." And so the message of the painting, what the picture would have told the patrons at the time, is that divine wisdom is the most desirable virtue to pursue and that wisdom, in life, is infinitely better and more important than brute strength, love, and all the power and the wealth people can accumulate in the world. A very interesting picture for an emperor—and for various rulers and members of aristocratic families and even for a man like Frick—to own. I've often wondered how much Frick thought about the message in this painting when he was smoking his evening cigar in the West Gallery.

—X.S.

PAOLO VERONESE

The Choice Between Virtue and Vice

CA. 1565

Negroni Sbagliato

1 OZ. CAMPARI

1 OZ. PROSECCO

1 OZ. SWEET RED VERMOUTH

Serve on the rocks in a tumbler
and garnish with an orange peel

A Negroni Sbagliato—a "wrong" Negroni in that it is made with prosecco rather than gin—is a popular version of the traditional cocktail. It is somewhat lighter and therefore more of a summer drink.

A big question around the Frick's two Veronese allegories is whether or not they were painted as pendants or were, instead, independent pictures that happened to be hung as a pair from the time they reached the imperial collection of Rudolph II in Prague. Technical analysis done in 2006 showed that the pictures were painted on different types of canvas, that their preparation is

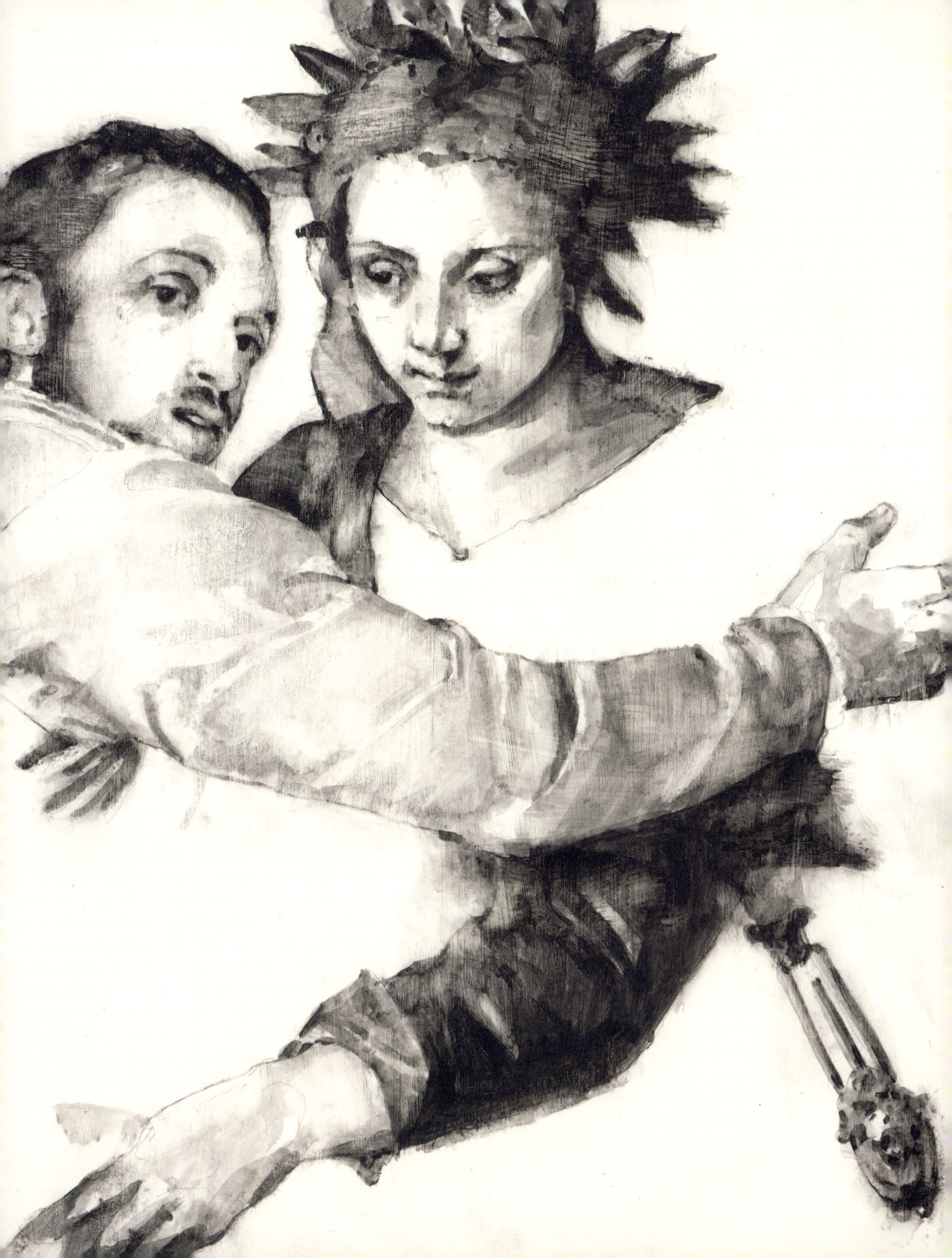

different, and that even the pigments were used in different ways. This certainly suggests that the paintings were not created as a pair. Perhaps one was painted first and the second created later to match it. So, the question persists as to whether the meanings of these two pictures are complementary or have nothing to do with each other.

Veronese was a master of allegorical painting. He painted ceilings with allegories in Venice for the Doge's Palace and the library of St. Mark's and also frescoed allegories at Villa Barbaro at Maser and in other villas in the Veneto. These paintings can be difficult to interpret today as we are much less likely to know what these figures and scenes mean.

This painting centers on an episode from the life of an ancient hero. There is a broad landscape with ruins and a damaged statue at the top left. A man in the center is flanked by two women, and he is moving from one toward the other. This is a play on the so-called Choice of Hercules, or Hercules at the Crossroads, an ancient story in which the young Hercules is offered a choice when he reaches a crossroads. On one side is a lusciously dressed, beautiful young woman who points to a road going downhill, very pleasant to walk along; on the other, an older woman in relatively plain dress who points to a steep path going uphill. The two women offer different life paths—one is a life of pleasure, which eventually leads downhill; the other, a life of virtue, which is more difficult but eventually brings you to the top of the mountain and to glory.

Veronese's painting is not a straightforward Choice of Hercules. The woman on the left is very cleverly depicted. She is richly attired in a beautiful orange and blue dress, which is unfastened at the back. In her hair are cyclamen flowers, which were thought to be used for love potions and were also believed to be poisonous. We cannot see her face. In her left hand, she holds a pack of cards, and she is sitting on the statue of a naked woman with lion paws, which identifies this being as the sphinx, another mythical creature. According to legend, the sphinx presents riddles to travelers, and if the riddle is not answered, she kills the traveler. In this painting, the sphinx, which has a large butcher's knife placed in front of it, signifies danger.

What we see of this woman is not what the protagonist of the painting sees. The man dressed in white sees her face and the front of her dress, which must be opened to reveal her body. He does not see the cards behind her back or the sphinx and the knife. This woman's claws are very sharp, and she has just attacked the man and scratched his leg. She has ripped off part of his hose, and you can see that his flesh is wounded and bleeding. The woman standing opposite is more somberly dressed. She wears a laurel wreath in her hair, to signify glory and military victory. The man is clearly moving toward her and embracing her. At the top is the Latin inscription HONOR ET VIRTUS POST MORTEM FLORET (Honor and virtue will flourish after death).

The painting is clearly a play on the Choice of Hercules. There can be no doubt that the figure on the left represents Vice, as well as lust and danger; behind this figure lies ultimate danger, the sphinx and the knife. The figure of Virtue on the right stands upright and tall in her somber dress. The man is not choosing between the two figures. He has already made his choice and is clearly going toward Virtue and embracing her. The man, however, is not Hercules. He is not dressed in a lion's skin, does not have a club, and does not have the beard that Hercules usually has. So who is he? Various theories have been proposed: he could be the patron of the painting or Veronese himself. He is the only figure in both of the allegories who wears contemporary clothes. If it is a portrait of the person for whom the canvas was painted, the white clothes may suggest that he is being celebrated after an untimely death. White represents purity, and no one in Venice wore fully white garments like this, partly because they were impractical and partly because white was considered an otherworldly color. In some countries, white was the color of mourning.

How—or if—this picture of a man choosing between Virtue and Vice relates to the other Veronese canvas, his allegory about divine wisdom, is unclear. But certainly the message in each case is about virtuous living, exemplifying goodness for the people looking at these paintings. It is worth thinking about them and unpacking all these details to get to their ultimate messages.

—X.S.

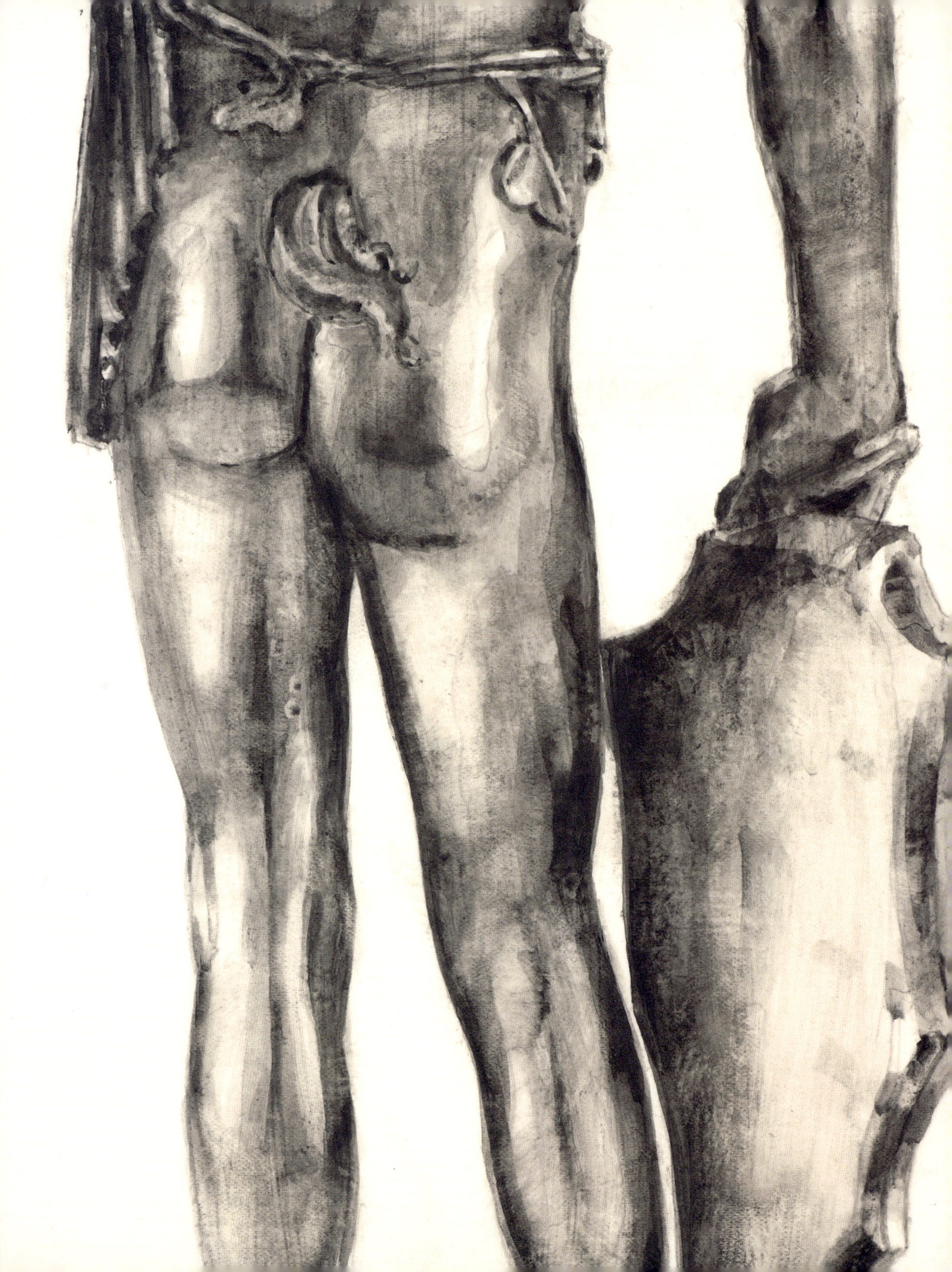

BERTOLDO DI GIOVANNI

Shield Bearer

CA. 1470–80

Daiquiri

1½ OZ. WHITE RUM

1 OZ. LIME JUICE

½ OZ. SIMPLE SYRUP

Serve chilled in a cocktail glass
and garnish with a slice of lime

The Daiquiri was invented in the late nineteenth century in Cuba, near a beach and silver mine called Daiquiri. A similar drink mixing rum and lime or lemon juice was drunk in the eighteenth century on navy ships around the world, as the citrus component was believed to help prevent scurvy.

In 1916, Henry Clay Frick acquired this exquisite small statuette together with a large group of bronze sculptures, from the collection of John Pierpont Morgan. There are only about twenty-five works that are securely attributed to Bertoldo di Giovanni (ca. 1440–1491), and this mysterious statuette is his only known work in an American collection.

This standing figure holds a shield with his right hand, and with his left hand, he clutches a club. The sculpture was originally entirely gilded, and some traces of the gilding can be seen across its surface. Though covered in tendrils and vine leaves, the man is largely naked. Just above his forehead are two tiny, curving horns; above his backside is a little tail. Just under his left arm is a set of panpipes.

Bertoldo's parents were German, but he was born in Florence, where his parents were involved with the textile industry in the area of Oltrarno. As a young man, Bertoldo worked closely with Donatello and quickly came into the orbit of the Medici family. He was also one of Michelangelo's first teachers and collaborated with other artists in the Giardino di San Marco, a garden created by the Medici family for their collection of antiquities and a place where young students could study. Bertoldo acted as a curator of that garden. We know Bertoldo never married, and criminal records tell us that he apparently had a habit of not paying his rent. Over and over again, he appears in documents as being evicted, with the Medici family regularly stepping in to pay his debts. Finally, the Medici took him into their palazzo. Lorenzo il Magnifico was Bertoldo's greatest patron; many of the artist's works were created for Lorenzo or as gifts for Lorenzo to distribute to other rulers. When Bertoldo died, he was living in Lorenzo's favorite villa, in Poggio a Caiano just outside of Florence.

The Frick's *Shield Bearer* is connected to a similar nude in the Princely Collections of Liechtenstein, in Vienna. The figure is a little older and his beard fuller. He also has these vine leaves and tendrils curled around his body and holds a shield and a club. (The shields would originally have had coats of arms, probably colored, made out of enamels inset in them, or maybe in *niello*, which is a typically Florentine type of metal technique.) The main differences between the statuettes, however, are that the Liechtenstein *Shield Bearer* does not have horns, panpipes, and tail. Were the two figures part of a larger ensemble and possibly fixed to something like a piece of furniture or fireplace, or were they portable objects that could be moved around?

So what do these two figures represent? For a long time, they were interpreted as Wild Men, an iconography commonly seen in northern Europe that dates back to the Middle Ages. Heraldic Wild Men are creatures of the forest. They are usually old and bearded, their bodies covered in hair, and they often hold clubs and shields with coats of arms. The Frick and Liechtenstein figures have also been associated with Hercules. Like the mythological hero, they have clubs, but they do not wear the lion skin usually associated with Hercules. Were Bertoldo's figures meant to have a specific identity? Are they heraldic Wild Men from the north that have been classicized in some way? Instead of being the older hairy figures of the medieval German world, they have been made to look more like ancient sculptures. We have to remember that Bertoldo had German origins so likely would have known about the iconography of the Wild Man. Is this a classicizing Italian spin on the more northern iconography of the Wild Man? Or are we looking at identifiable figures? If the Liechtenstein sculpture is Hercules, why isn't he wearing his lion skin? And what about the Frick figure? Is it a faun? Is it a satyr? Is it Pan?

We have to remember that in the 1470s and 1480s, around the time that these sculptures were made, classical antiquity was not well known, and many of these iconographies were not yet codified. The Renaissance was the time when the rediscovery of antiquity was taking place, and scholars were having important debates about how to represent specific gods and goddesses and various heroes from antiquity. Figures like Pan, satyrs, and fauns appear in slightly different guises. For example, satyrs and fauns are often represented with goat's legs, but not always. We still have a lot of questions about how these statuettes were displayed, how they were used, where they were placed. Part of the mystery, the enigmatic nature of these statuettes, is due to their being groundbreaking objects responding to antiquity in the world of Renaissance Italy.

—X.S.

SÈVRES PORCELAIN MANUFACTORY

Vase Japon

1774

Long Island Iced Tea

¾ OZ. GIN

¾ OZ. VODKA

¾ OZ. TEQUILA

¾ OZ. WHITE RUM

¾ OZ. TRIPLE SEC

¾ OZ. LEMON JUICE

¾ OZ. SIMPLE SYRUP

A SPLASH OF COCA-COLA

Serve on the rocks in a tall glass and garnish with a lemon peel

A Long Island Iced Tea has as little to do with iced tea as the Vase Japon *has to do with Japan. The cocktail was invented on Long Island in the 1970s but is likely based on a drink that existed already in America in the 1920s, at the time of Prohibition.*

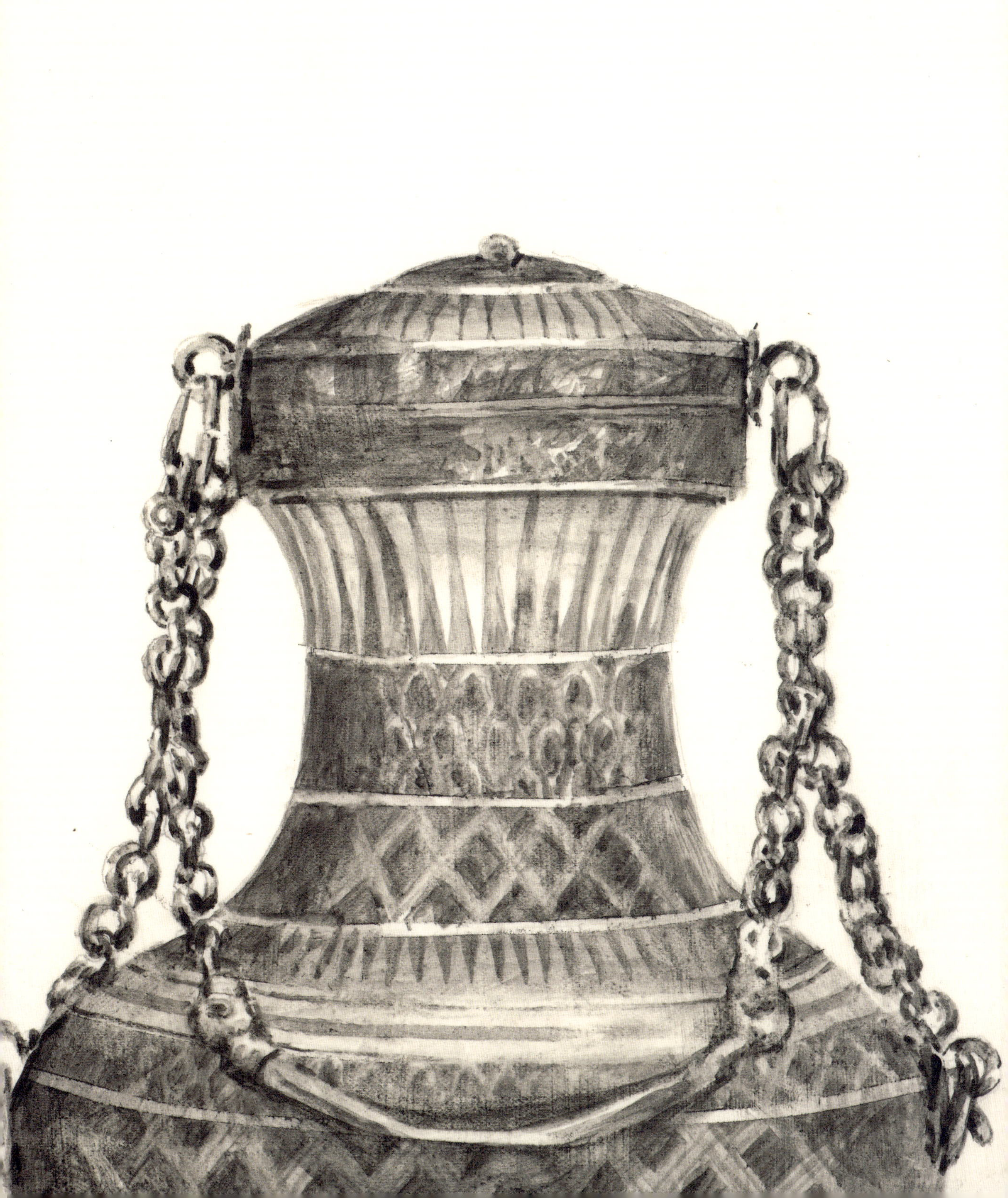

The name of this vase is quite misleading, as the vase follows Chinese rather than Japanese models. This misnomer is indicative of the European confusion when it came to Asian sources. The *Vase Japon* is inextricably linked to the fascinating relationship between the court of Louis XV in France and that of the Qianlong Emperor in China, in the second half of the eighteenth century. The two rulers were more or less exact contemporaries, and each had a long reign.

China closed all its borders to foreigners in the eighteenth century. Nonetheless, some contact remained, mostly through Jesuit priests, who had established missions in China dating back to the origins of the Jesuit Order in the sixteenth century, when St. Francis Xavier himself went to China. The Jesuits were both European clerics living in China and Chinese men who converted, took Christian orders, and became ordained as Jesuit priests.

The relationship between the king of France and the emperor of China was cemented with a series of gifts. Official diplomacy was difficult because of strict gift-giving protocols relating to the status of one ruler versus the other. Neither one could be the first to provide a gift, as that implied a level of inferiority to the other ruler. To get around this, many gifts were transmitted through a series of complicated, semi-diplomatic routes, and the Jesuits were very much part of this exchange.

There were a number of such exchanges between France and China during the reign of Louis XV. The Qianlong Emperor was particularly fond of European art. At the same time that chinoiserie—anything with a Chinese inspiration produced in France, England, Italy, and a number of other countries—was invented in Europe, China was producing objects and architecture with a very strong European influence.

The first of these semi-diplomatic gifts was a series of tapestries with Chinese scenes based on designs by François Boucher. In 1742, Boucher exhibited these models for tapestries at the Salon in Paris. The tapestries were woven at Beauvais and sent to China in the 1760s. After a lengthy series of diplomatic maneuvers, they finally reached the emperor, who loved them so much that he built an entire pavilion, called the Observatory of Distant Oceans, for them at Yuanming Yuan, the Old Summer Palace outside of Beijing, where he lived. The palace was a series of pavilions with an eccentric combination of European and Chinese architecture. Unfortunately, it was destroyed by Europeans during the Second Opium War, when French and English troops demolished the entire palace over a period of a few days.

The person responsible for this gift was Henri-Léonard Bertin, Louis XV's Secretary of State. Bertin was also the *commissaire du roi* for a number of state manufactories—in charge of textile production in Lyon, of the Beauvais factory of tapestries, and of the Sèvres Porcelain Manufactory. Bertin had a passion for China. He never traveled there, but he collected Chinese objects and designs of Chinese objects. He was very interested in how they could provide inspiration for objects created in France, in the same way that he believed that the technology of the weavers in Lyon and at Beauvais, or the porcelain makers at Sèvres, would be of interest to the Chinese public. Even though the borders between the two countries were officially closed, there was an exchange of art. Bertin commissioned drawings of Chinese objects and used them for inspiration for the French manufactories. In 1767, he received a gift of a set of forty volumes of woodcuts that were produced for the Qianlong Emperor, showing all the great objects in the Chinese imperial collection. This was an enterprise that took many years, between 1749 and 1755, and as far as we know Bertin was the only European to own a set of these volumes. In his role as *commissaire du roi* for Sèvres, Bertin used a specific woodcut as inspiration for the vase at the Frick. The vase shown in the woodcut, however, was not a porcelain but was instead a Yu vase, made of bronze and produced during the Han dynasty, between around 206 BC and 220 AD. By all standards, the Yu vase was an ancient object by the eighteenth century.

There are two other vases similar to the Frick's *Vase Japon*, both recently acquired by the Louvre Abu Dhabi. The Abu Dhabi vases were decorated, painted, and gilded by Jean-Armand Fallot (act. 1764–90), who was the gilder and painter at the time at Sèvres, but they do not have the metal chains that the Frick vase has. They were probably intended to have chains, but for some reason, they were never made. The chains on the Frick's vase, which were also part of the original bronze Yu vase, were made by Charles Ouizille, who became the goldsmith of King Louis XVI after 1784.

One of these vases, produced at Sèvres around 1774, was given to the king. In 1785, Bertin commissioned another to give to the Qianlong Emperor. But Sèvres could not produce it in time, the embassy going to China left early, and it was finally decided that the king's own vase would be sent to Beijing, to the emperor. We do not know what happened to this vase. Is it still somewhere in Beijing? Was it lost when Yuanming Yuan was destroyed in 1860? Sèvres continued to produce these vases, but the one at the Frick is unique. We do not know of any other example of this vase existing today with the chains and with this level of quality.

—X.S.

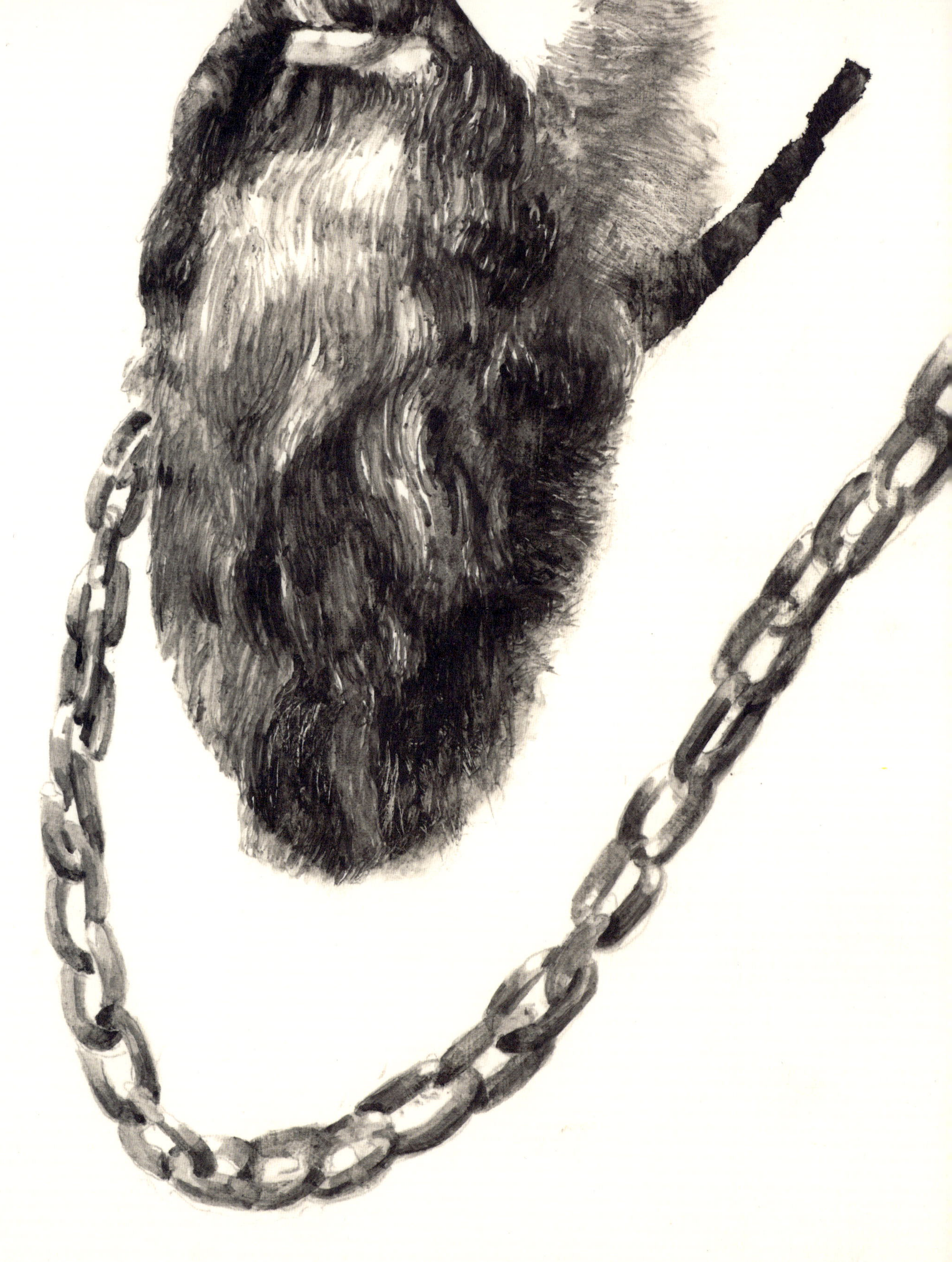

TITIAN

Pietro Aretino

CA. 1537

Bellini

2 OZ. WHITE PEACH PUREE

4 OZ. PROSECCO

Serve chilled in a flute glass

Invented in the 1930s by Giuseppe Cipriani, the founder of Harry's Bar in Venice, this cocktail was called a Bellini because its typical pink color is like that found in paintings by Giovanni Bellini, who was Titian's master. If you use the juice of red Italian grapes, known as uva fragola *(strawberry grapes), instead of peach puree, the cocktail has a dark red color and is called a Tiziano—a Titian.*

This portrait by Titian (1488–1576) is the first Italian Old Master painting acquired by Henry Clay Frick. He bought it from the dealer M. Knoedler & Co. at the end of 1905, when he moved from Pittsburgh to New York, where he rented a house on Fifth Avenue that belonged to the Vanderbilts.

One of the most celebrated literary figures of the Italian Renaissance, Pietro Aretino was renowned for his writings and for his role in the artistic world of Venice. As his surname indicates, he was born in Arezzo, in Tuscany. His father was a shoemaker who abandoned his family very early in Aretino's life. Fortunately for the young Pietro, his mother's close ties—possibly of a romantic nature—with an aristocrat in Arezzo led to Aretino being raised and educated with the children of this gentleman's family. As a young man, he moved to Perugia and then, about 1517, to Rome.

Aretino wrote religious treatises, scurrilous verses, erotic poetry, and plays, moving effortlessly from the serious to the playful. In 1524, a huge scandal erupted in Rome with the publication of a series of prints designed by Giulio Romano and printed by Marcantonio Raimondi known as *I Modi* (The Ways), showing a variety of sexual positions between a man and a woman. Aretino had composed sixteen *Sonetti Lussuriosi* (Lustful Sonnets) to accompany the images. The enterprise was halted by the Inquisition, and all copies were destroyed. Raimondi was imprisoned, and Giulio fled Rome. Aretino had many enemies at the papal court, and less than a year later, in July 1525, he was attacked in the streets of Rome, stabbed, and left for dead. He did recover, however, and a few months later, in October 1525, he left Rome for good.

In March 1527, Aretino moved to Venice, where he spent the rest of his life—first in the beautiful house of Domenico Bolani on the Grand Canal, whose view overlooking the Rialto Bridge and the market he described as the most beautiful in the world; and later, in the 1550s, on the Riva del Carbon on the other side of the Rialto. It was in Venice, where he grew close to many writers and literary figures, that he wrote his best-selling books. One of the most famous of these is the *Ragionamenti,* published in 1535, in which he discusses the three ways in which a woman could lead her life in sixteenth-century Italy: as a wife, a nun, or a courtesan. As two women in the *Ragionamenti* discuss the advantages and disadvantages of each of these paths, they conclude that the most honorable and best one for a woman, providing her with the freedom she needs, is that of a courtesan.

In these years, Aretino became close to Titian, who by the 1530s was a very celebrated painter, working for the emperor, the pope, and a number of kings. As described by Sheila Hale, in her wonderful biography of Titian, "the closest companion of Titian's life was Aretino, his most sensitive critic, as well as his adviser, agent, publicist, debt collector, scribe, and hanger-on. He broadcast Titian's talent to the world in his plays, sonnets, and more than 225 published letters, while using his friend's growing international reputation to gain entrée and gather information for his own journalism."

Titian painted Aretino's portrait on three occasions. Made right after Aretino's arrival in Venice, the first one was for Federico II Gonzaga, Marquess of Mantua. The last one was a gift to Cosimo I, Duke of Florence, and sent to Florence in 1545. Sitting chronologically between these two is the Frick portrait, which was made for Francesco Marcolini, a publisher who was a friend of both Aretino and Titian. Marcolini was probably the same age as Aretino. He had moved from his birthplace of Forlì, in Romagna, to Venice in 1527, the same year that Aretino moved there. Marcolini became the main publisher of Aretino's works in the 1530s and '40s, with an interruption of three years, between 1545 and 1548, when Marcolini fled to Cyprus, probably in financial distress. By the time he returned, his relationship with Aretino had cooled somewhat. He published only a few of Aretino's books after 1548.

From a letter written by Marcolini in 1551, we know that he owned a number of works of art by other artists, by sculptors like Alessandro Vittoria and Jacopo Sansovino, and in this letter he also discusses Titian's portraits of Aretino. He writes that the Frick portrait was painted for him by Titian in three days. This explains why it is painted in such a simple, direct way. The portrait represents Aretino richly dressed, clad in fur and gold fabric. He wears a gold chain, probably given to him by Empress Isabella of Portugal. The portrait is a friendship portrait, very much like the Holbein portrait of Thomas More, which usually hangs directly across from it in the Frick's Living Hall.

—X.S.

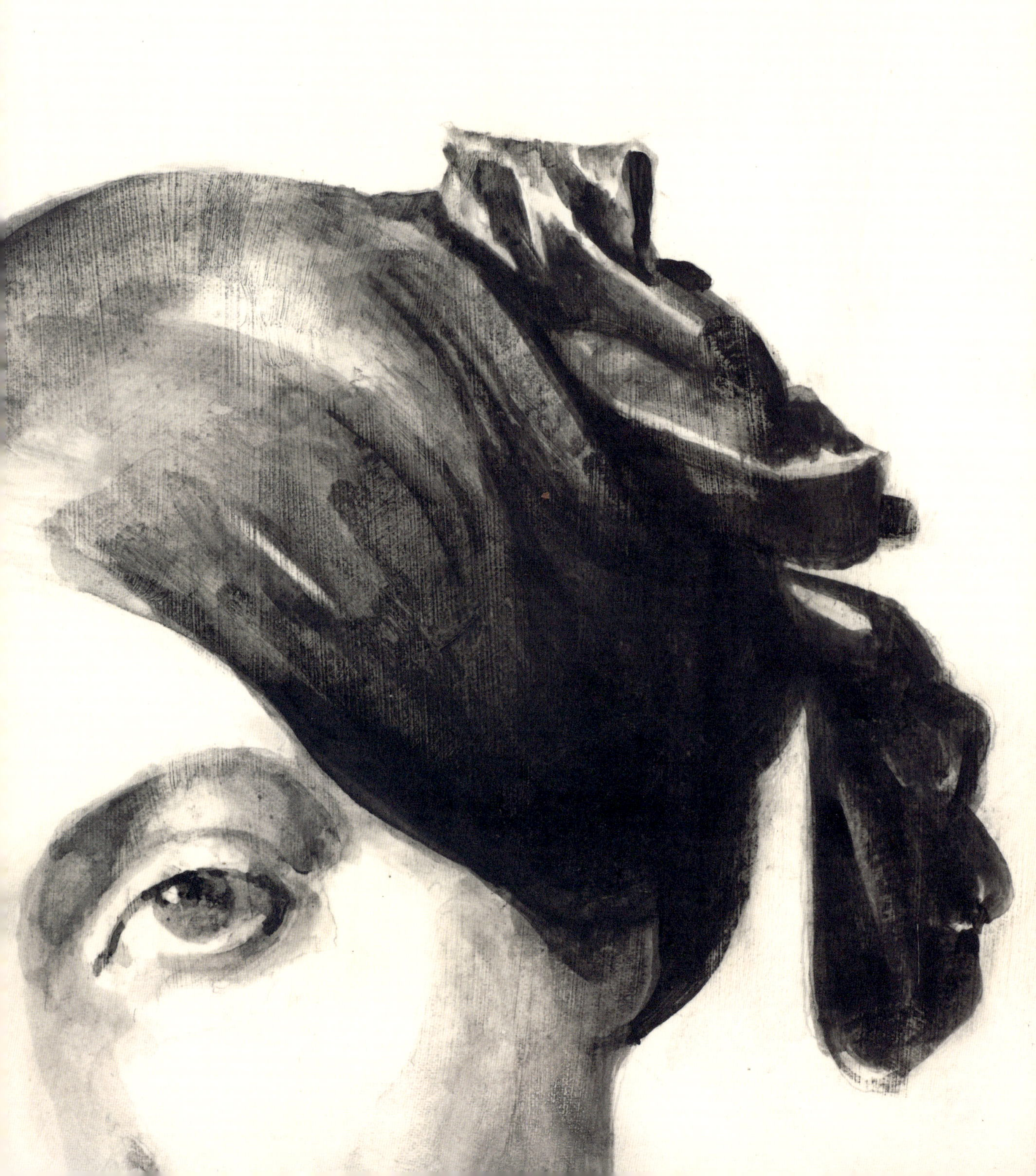

JEAN-AUGUSTE-DOMINIQUE INGRES

Louise, Princesse de Broglie, Later the Comtesse d'Haussonville

1845

Jaded Countess

1 OZ. ABSINTHE

½ OZ. VODKA

½ OZ. FRESH LEMON JUICE

½ OZ. SIMPLE SYRUP

Stir with ice and strain
Top with champagne
Serve in a cocktail glass and garnish with a lemon twist

This cocktail pays tribute to the Swiss origins of the Comtesse d'Haussonville. Its main ingredient, absinthe, was invented in Switzerland in the mid-eighteenth century. It contains wormwood (Artemisia absinthium) *and was thought to cause madness and hallucinations, leading to its prohibition in a number of countries for much of the twentieth century.*

Ingres's portrait of Louise de Broglie (pronounced "de Breuil"), Comtesse d'Haussonville, is one of the most beloved paintings at the Frick. When this portrait was signed, in 1845, Broglie was still a viscountess. One year later, when her father-in-law passed away, she became the Comtesse d'Haussonville. She has been referred to as the "poster girl" of The Frick Collection. The first color photograph of this painting was taken for the cover of a special issue of *Life* magazine in 1937.

Jean-Auguste-Dominique Ingres (1780–1867) was born in the south of France, in Montauban, near Toulouse. He was a pupil of Jacques-Louis David, the leader of the neoclassical school of the late eighteenth and early nineteenth centuries. Ingres too became one of the leaders of the neoclassical school, although he spent much of his career in Italy. He aspired to produce history paintings, large-scale narrative scenes of historical, biblical, and mythological subjects. History paintings topped the customary hierarchy of genres and were considered more prestigious than portraiture and other types of painting. But like many painters, Ingres had to pay his bills by painting portraits, and he was an extremely talented portraitist.

By the time Louise approached Ingres to paint her portrait, he was in his sixties and well established. They met in Rome. He was there as the director of the Académie de France, housed in Villa Medici, and she was there traveling. Her husband was a politician and diplomat, and she lived in a number of cities around Europe. When, in 1840, she walked into Ingres's studio in Rome, he was painting a history painting, *Antiochus and Stratonice*. She fell in love with it and wanted him to paint her portrait. At this point in his career, Ingres was turning down most commissions for portraits, but he agreed to paint hers. Some have said that he gave in to her because of her extraordinary beauty, but it is more likely that he could not turn her down because she was the daughter of the Duc de Broglie, a high-powered patron.

This portrait is animated by a tension between precision and impossible beauty. Ingres produced many drawings to study the details of features such as her blonde eyelashes. In some twenty surviving drawings, made during several sittings, he plays with the composition, turning her from one side to the other. And yet, that precision is paired with imprecise anatomy: her right arm, crossed over her belly, could not possibly have been so low. It was not a mistake. He made these contortions of her body in the interests of an ideal composition.

The portrait is signed and dated, with *1845* and the artist's name inscribed on the side of the chair. The date marks the end of a three-year process, with interruptions caused by his other projects and her travel schedule, as well as by one of her pregnancies and her recovery after giving birth. He constructed the painting so that it seems that she has just returned from the opera. A yellow shawl has been thrown onto the chair next to her. On the mantel, she has dropped her opera glasses, and her blue evening handbag is draped on the gilt bronze–mounted porcelain. Her reflection in the mirror allows us to see her plaited hair held up with a comb, as if it is about to be taken out for the night.

Her gold bracelet and ring are embedded with turquoise (in France, *pierre turque,* "Turkish stone"). Turquoise was brought to France from Egypt or Persia, now Iran. Her snake-form ring was called *á la Cléopâtre* (of Cleopatra), the joke being that Cleopatra was killed by the bite of a snake.

An opera lover, Louise made a number of drawings inspired by opera. She played the piano and had lessons with Frédéric Chopin, a Polish émigré who came to Paris and earned his livelihood giving lessons to wealthy French women like her. She was also a prolific writer, as well as the granddaughter of the celebrated author Madame de Staël, who was exiled under Napoleon and spent most of her time in the family chateau in Switzerland.

Louise published a number of books, most of them biographies, including one of Lord Byron and another of Robert Emmet, the Irish revolutionary who was executed for high treason under the British crown. But she was forced by her husband to publish anonymously to avoid public scrutiny.

One gets a better sense of who she is from her personal journals. She was troubled. She lived under the shadow of her grandmother, a lauded author, and Louise never acquired the same status. She was haunted by the death of her sister at age fourteen. She became preoccupied with death, with the decomposition of bodies. In her will, she specified that she would like to be embalmed or, if cremation was more popular, to be disposed of through cremation because she found that to be a more poetic treatment of her body.

She struggled with her beauty. One passage of her memoir reads: "I was destined to beguile, to attract, to seduce, and in the final reckoning to cause suffering in all those who sought their happiness in me." A description of her by the writer Prosper Mérimée cruelly describes her about twenty years after this painting was made as "quite fat, with hardly any hair left." It's hard to reconcile that description with Ingres's portrait. The same thing happens to Ingres: an account of him at age seventy-five describes him as a "bourgeois little elephant, put together out of misshapen stumps, of an outward vulgarity that contrasts startlingly with the mannered elegance of his works." These descriptions remind us that portraits represent just one moment of a life.

Ingres received great praise for this portrait. One cheeky viewer commented to Louise, "Well, Monsieur Ingres must have been in love with you in order to paint you like that." She loved it. In her will, she included a list of belongings in which this portrait is second only to the chateau in Switzerland. She left both the portrait and the chateau to her daughter, requesting that the portrait remain there, where she was born and buried. The painting stayed there until the death of her youngest child, a son, in 1924, at which point it was sold to the Frick.

—A.N.

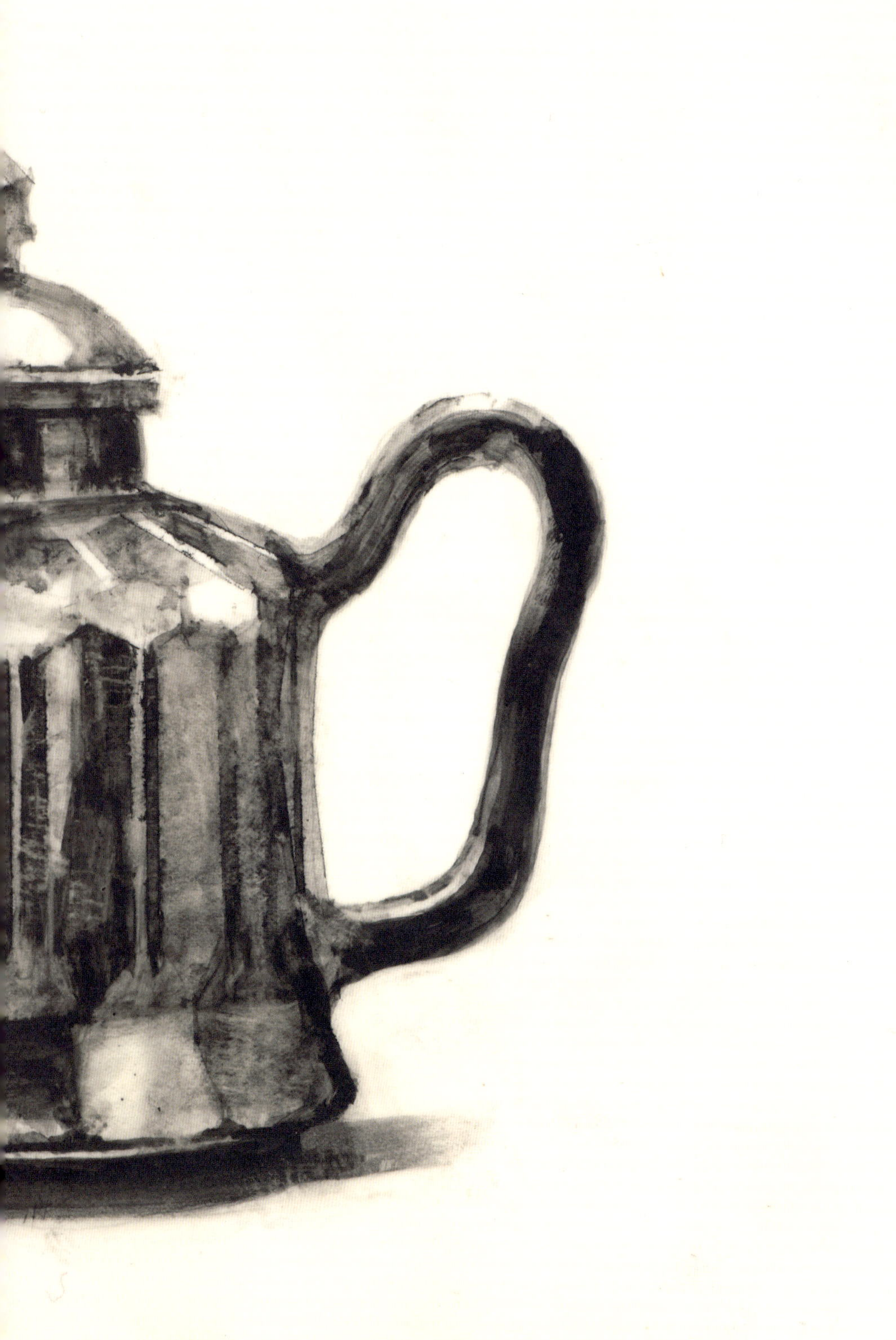

MEISSEN PORCELAIN MANUFACTORY

Teapot

CA. 1710–13

Saxon

1½ OZ. DARK RUM

½ OZ. LIME JUICE

1 TSP. GRENADINE

Serve chilled in a cocktail glass and garnish with an orange peel

It is unclear what the connection is between this cocktail and Saxons. It seems a fitting drink for this episode, however, because European porcelain was invented in the eighteenth century in Dresden, the capital of Saxony in eastern Germany.

A tiny teapot, polished and brown, with geometric details that look almost carved into it—an exquisite work of art. The story behind this teapot and many other objects like it is the story of the discovery of a formula for making porcelain in the early eighteenth century in Germany, in the city of Dresden. A number of wonderful pieces produced at the Meissen Porcelain Manufactory were given to the Frick by the great German collector Henry Arnhold, as part of one of the most significant donations to the museum in its recent history.

The story of Europe's passion for porcelain really begins in the thirteenth century, with the voyage of the Venetian Marco Polo and members of his family. Polo traveled to China and brought back not only Asian objects but also tales of customs and architecture that no one in Europe had heard about before. One of the things he describes is porcelain: "In China, they collect a certain kind of earth, as it were from a mine, and laying it at a great heap, they suffer it to be exposed to the wind, the rain, and the sun, for thirty or forty years, during which time it is never disturbed. By this time, it becomes refined and fit for being wrought into vessels." Until this point, porcelain was unknown in Europe. It was invented in China and then also produced in Japan and was very much a luxury material. Such was the demand in Europe that between 1602 and 1657, the Dutch East India Company, which was one of the main trading companies that brought goods from Asia to Europe, brought into Europe about three million pieces of porcelain. Many in Europe became consumed with finding out how this material was made.

Augustus the Strong, Elector of Saxony and King of Poland until his death in 1733, was a lover of the arts. He transformed Dresden into one of the great European centers of the eighteenth century, assembling an incredible collection of paintings, decorative arts objects, and furniture. He was obsessed with porcelain and amassed a vast collection of Chinese and Japanese pieces. This he mostly displayed in a palace that he had redecorated and which became known as the Japanese Palace because of the Japanese style of its roof. Porcelain was so precious to Augustus that, in the spring of 1717, he organized a diplomatic trade with the king of Prussia, exchanging six hundred Saxon and Polish soldiers for 151 porcelain Chinese vases. The vases in Dresden are still known as the Dragoon vases because of the dragoons that were exchanged for them.

Johann Friedrich Böttger (1682–1719) was born in the small town of Schleiz, where his family worked at the mint. Böttger trained as a chemist and worked briefly at the mint. He became fascinated by what was known at the time as the "arcanum"—the secret for transforming a base metal into gold through a series of chemical processes. Many rulers in Europe were intrigued by this quest because, of course, finding a way to make gold would have made any of them incredibly powerful. Böttger became an alchemist, and a number of people claimed to have witnessed him perform this alchemical miracle. August the Strong imprisoned Böttger—in a fortress in Meissen, about fifteen kilometers northwest of Dresden—in order to control his experiments. The alchemist's many attempts to make gold failed, but in Meissen, he met Ehrenfried Walther von Tschirnhaus, a mathematician who was interested in glass production and mirrors, as well as porcelain.

Böttger and Tschirnhaus made the discovery that porcelain is principally made from a combination of kaolin and feldspar. While imprisoned at the fortress, Böttger managed to produce a reddish material that looked like some Chinese porcelains. He was subsequently moved to another military structure, the Jungfernbastei (the Maiden's Bastion) along the Elbe River in Dresden, and it was there, in January 1708, that Böttger discovered how to make true porcelain. To commemorate that moment, he inscribed over the doors of his cell, "God the creator made a potter from a gold-maker."

What Böttger had discovered was actually red stoneware, which is not porcelain but at the time was known as red porcelain. In March 1709, slightly more than a year after the stoneware discovery, he discovered how to make white porcelain. The first public showing of European porcelain took place in 1710, at which point the factory was moved from the bastion in Dresden to the castle in Meissen. The manufactory remained there from 1710 until 1863, when it was moved to a purpose-built factory in the valley below, which is where Meissen porcelain is made to this day. His important discovery notwithstanding, Böttger had a rather unhappy life, spending most of it imprisoned in Saxony, prone to severe depression and excessive drinking.

This small Böttger teapot also correlates to the arrival in Europe in the late seventeenth and early eighteenth centuries of three types of beverage that had been previously unknown to Europeans: tea, coffee, and chocolate. Imagine life today without any of these. But they all arrived in Europe around this time: coffee from Arabia, chocolate from Mexico, and tea, of course, from China. So rare and expensive were these beverages in Europe that costly vessels—tea, coffee, and chocolate sets—were made for rulers at the time. Some of these objects are small, because the beverages were so expensive. Many of them also look back to Asian models. At first sight, the Böttger teapot may look like a very simple object, but it embodies a rich and complex story that changed the world we live in. Think of it when you next drink tea from your porcelain teapot.

—X.S.

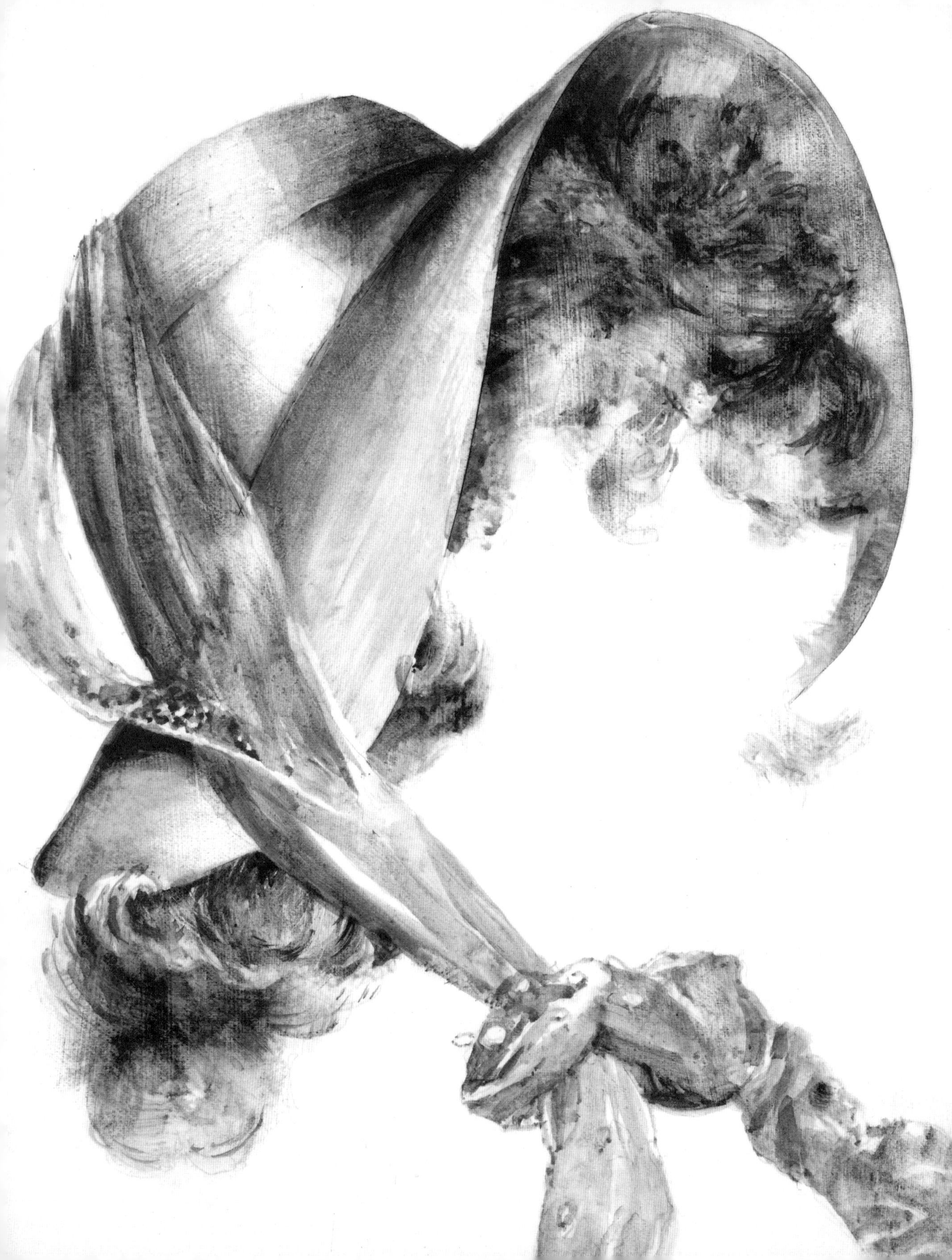

WILLIAM BEECHEY

Elizabeth Sophia Baillie (née de Visme)

1795

Great Maiden's Blush

EQUAL PARTS OF:

GIN

LEMON JUICE

ELDERFLOWER CORDIAL

Top with pink champagne
Serve chilled in a cocktail glass and garnish with a lemon peel

Between the end of the nineteenth century and the beginning of the twentieth, American collectors were very keen on British portraits of female aristocrats. Many such portraits of blushing maidens—by Gainsborough, Reynolds, Romney, Lawrence, Beechey, and Hoppner—made it across the Atlantic and into the dining rooms of American tycoons.

This portrait epitomizes the importance of art historical research. Henry Clay Frick was particularly interested in female British portraits and in April 1899 bought this one from M. Knoedler & Co. The painting had been acquired by the firm's partner, dealer Thomas Agnew, in July 1898, from Moore and Temple estate agents. We do not know who they were or where they got the portrait from. At the time, Frick was still living in Pittsburgh, where he displayed it in the parlor of his house, Clayton, later transferring it to his New York home.

The painting was attributed to John Hoppner (1758–1810), a British portraitist born to a family of German origins in London, where he spent his entire career. Hoppner became a beloved society portraitist, portraying members of the royal family, political figures, aristocratic ladies, and many of the great celebrities of the time. The portrait came with a specific identification of the sitter, who was described as the daughter of Admiral Byng. Subsequent studies in the Frick's catalogues identify this woman as Lucy Elizabeth Byng (1794–1875), the daughter of Vice-Admiral George Byng, who later became the 6th Viscount Torrington. This attribution and identification of the sitter have, however, been dogged by the fact that Hoppner died in 1810, when Lucy Byng was sixteen years old, and the woman in the portrait looks older.

The mystery was solved by one of the Frick's curatorial assistants, Eloise Owens. A private collector had gotten in touch with her about a miniature by Henry Bone he owned that was based on the portrait. Owens found a related drawing by Bone, a copy of the Frick portrait, which was inscribed *Miss de Visme, after Beechey, for Captain Baillie, 1795*. A different artist, a different sitter, and, suddenly, a very different story came to light. So, we now know that the portrait is not by John Hoppner but by William Beechey (1753–1839), a contemporary of Hoppner's, born just five years earlier in Oxfordshire. A pupil of Johan Zoffany, Beechey worked for the royal family and ended his life as the official painter for King William IV. He was well known for his irascible temper but also for the generosity he showed young artists, a number of whom he supported, among them, John Constable. His style is similar to Hoppner's, and he portrayed many of the same sitters.

While a portrait of Lucy Byng by Hoppner is not documented, a portrait of Miss de Visme by Beechey is very well known. Until Owens's discovery, however, it was believed to be lost. Beechey showed the portrait at the Royal Academy in 1795, at which time it was described as being very beautiful for its quality of light and harmony of coloring.

Elizabeth Sophia de Visme (1775–1804) was born and grew up in London, but the De Visme family was, as the name suggests, of French origin—Huguenots who escaped to Britain during the religious wars in the seventeenth century. Her father died when she was fourteen, and when she was painted by Beechey, she was twenty. Her maternal grandfather was Captain Thomas Baillie, the lieutenant-governor of Greenwich Hospital. The drawing by Bone mentions a "Captain Baillie" as the man for whom the portrait was painted. It is likely that he assumed guardianship of Elizabeth when her father died. The portrait may have been commissioned in anticipation of a possible marriage, a common purpose of portraits of this kind.

In 1801, Elizabeth married her first cousin, John Baillie. The two lived together for only three years, until her death, at just twenty-nine years old. We do not know what happened to the portrait after her death. John Baillie must have kept it, but the couple had no children, and where the painting was between Elizabeth's death in 1804 and 1898, when Agnew acquired it, is unknown.

So, the study of art history still brings us new information as we work on the collection at the Frick. The stories in this book are all based on the research done by generations of art historians before myself and my colleagues. Museums are, above all, important research centers where the history of our works of art, of our past, becomes better understood.

—X.S.

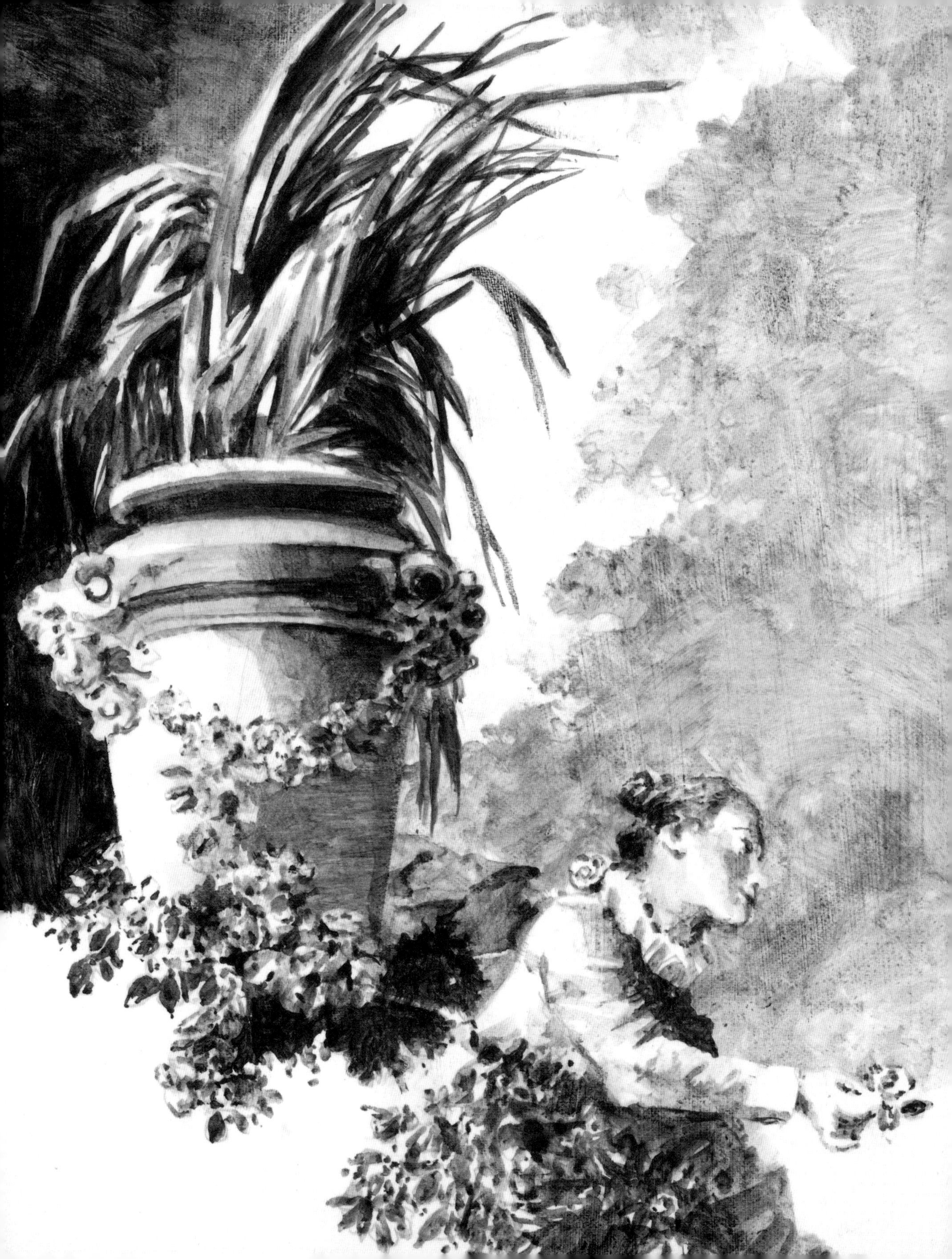

JEAN-HONORÉ FRAGONARD

The Progress of Love—Part I

1771–72

Champagne

Serve chilled in a coupe glass

The story of Fragonard's Progress of Love *is about ancien régime France—about kings, royal mistresses, and a court artist. A glass of chilled champagne seems a perfect accompaniment.*

The story of the great cycle *The Progress of Love*—installed in the Fragonard Room at the Frick—is a complex tale with two main parts. The canvases arrived at 1 East 70th Street in 1915, when Henry Clay Frick purchased them, after the death of John Pierpont Morgan, who had owned them since 1898. They had been painted by one of the most famous artists of eighteenth-century France, Jean-Honoré Fragonard (1732–1806), the son of a glove-maker in the town of Grasse, in Provence. As a young man, Fragonard moved to Paris to study in the workshops of two of the most celebrated painters in Paris: François Boucher and Jean-Siméon Chardin.

Between 1756 and 1761, Fragonard traveled to Rome, where he visited the monuments in the city and in the surrounding countryside. He produced a series of spectacular drawings at Villa d'Este in Tivoli, and it was there that he started to study the park settings and gardens that would become a feature of many of his best-known works.

While Fragonard was working in Paris and becoming known as an artist, he came to the attention of the king's mistress, Madame Du Barry. Born Jeanne Bécu in 1743, the illegitimate daughter of a seamstress and a priest, she spent part of her childhood in abject poverty. As a young woman, she became a prostitute and then the lover of Jean-Baptiste Du Barry, a celebrated libertine. Du Barry extolled the charms of his mistress to a series of prominent men at court with the idea that this might bring her to the attention of the king, and that is indeed what happened. In 1768, when Jeanne was in her mid-twenties, she and King Louis XV began a romantic liaison. She was hurriedly married to Jean-Baptiste Du Barry's brother, the Comte Guillaume Du Barry, so that she could be presented at court. She moved to Versailles and lived with the king for more than five years, until his death in 1774.

Madame Du Barry was a renowned lover of the arts. In 1769, the king gave her a house overlooking the Seine—the chateau of Louveciennes, just west of Paris—for which she decided to commission a music pavilion. For this, she went to Claude-Nicolas Ledoux, one of the great architects of the day. An exquisite but rather small building—one floor with four main rooms—the pavilion had incredibly lavish interior decoration. Du Barry paid a fortune for Pierre Gouthière, the great *ciseleur-doreur du roi* (gilder of the king), to produce gilt bronzes for the fireplaces, doorknobs, and window fixtures. The pavilion was abandoned for a long time, but in the 1930s the perfume maker François Coty bought it and effectively rebuilt it. What you see today is a much-restored building.

Imagine this enchanting small pavilion, surrounded by a huge park, with a view of the river. It was for one of the rooms of this building that Madame Du Barry commissioned Fragonard to paint four large canvases. The designated room at Louveciennes—much smaller than the Fragonard Room at the Frick—was decorated with white fabric on the walls, a fireplace, and three large mirrors. Two windows would have looked out to the park, drawing a connection between the painted gardens by Fragonard and the garden outside. The four scenes represent stages in the love story of a couple. First, a young woman is next to a fountain with two friends, when she is surprised by the arrival of a man who offers her a rose. She is running away but looking back while doing so. In the next painting, the couple—by now lovers—is meeting in secret. The man is climbing a ladder into the garden, and the woman is looking around to make sure they have not been seen. In the third picture, the two lovers are portrayed as being happily together. In the final canvas, the two lovers are reading their love letters. There was a belief in eighteenth-century France that a great love story would become a great friendship once the sexual energy was worn out. The cycle suggests the development of the relationship of a couple, as it was understood in the eighteenth century, from a meeting, to sex, to marriage and long-term friendship.

The canvases were painted between 1771 and 1772. We still do not know why exactly, but Du Barry did not like them, and soon after they were installed at Louveciennes, they were returned to the painter. Fragonard rolled them up in his studio at the Louvre, where he stored them for another twenty years. In the meantime, Madame Du Barry redecorated that same room with four canvases showing more or less the same subjects by the painter Joseph-Marie Vien. These were painted as Greek scenes, much chillier in style.

Madame Du Barry's story was ultimately a tragic one. When the king died, she was sent to a nunnery. When she was allowed to leave, a year later, she went to Louveciennes. She would have new lovers, the main one being the Duc de Brissac, who became her closest companion for the remainder of her life. What was on the horizon, however, was the French Revolution. The bloodiest year of the revolution was 1793, the year Louis XVI and Marie-Antoinette were beheaded. At the end of that year, Du Barry was arrested, put on trial, and, on December 8, guillotined in the same place where the king and queen had been killed. The most tragic account of her death is by the painter Elisabeth Vigée Le Brun, who knew Du Barry well and had painted her a number of times:

> *Madame Du Barry is the only woman among the women who perished in those dreadful days who could not stand the sight of the scaffold. She screamed, she begged for mercy of the horrible crowd that stood around the scaffold. She aroused them to such a point that the executioner grew anxious and hastened to complete his task. This convinced me that if the victims of those terrible times had not been so proud, had not met death with such courage, the Terror would have ended much earlier.*

By the time of her death, Fragonard had just reinstalled *The Progress of Love* in another house, in his birthplace in the south of France.

—X.S.

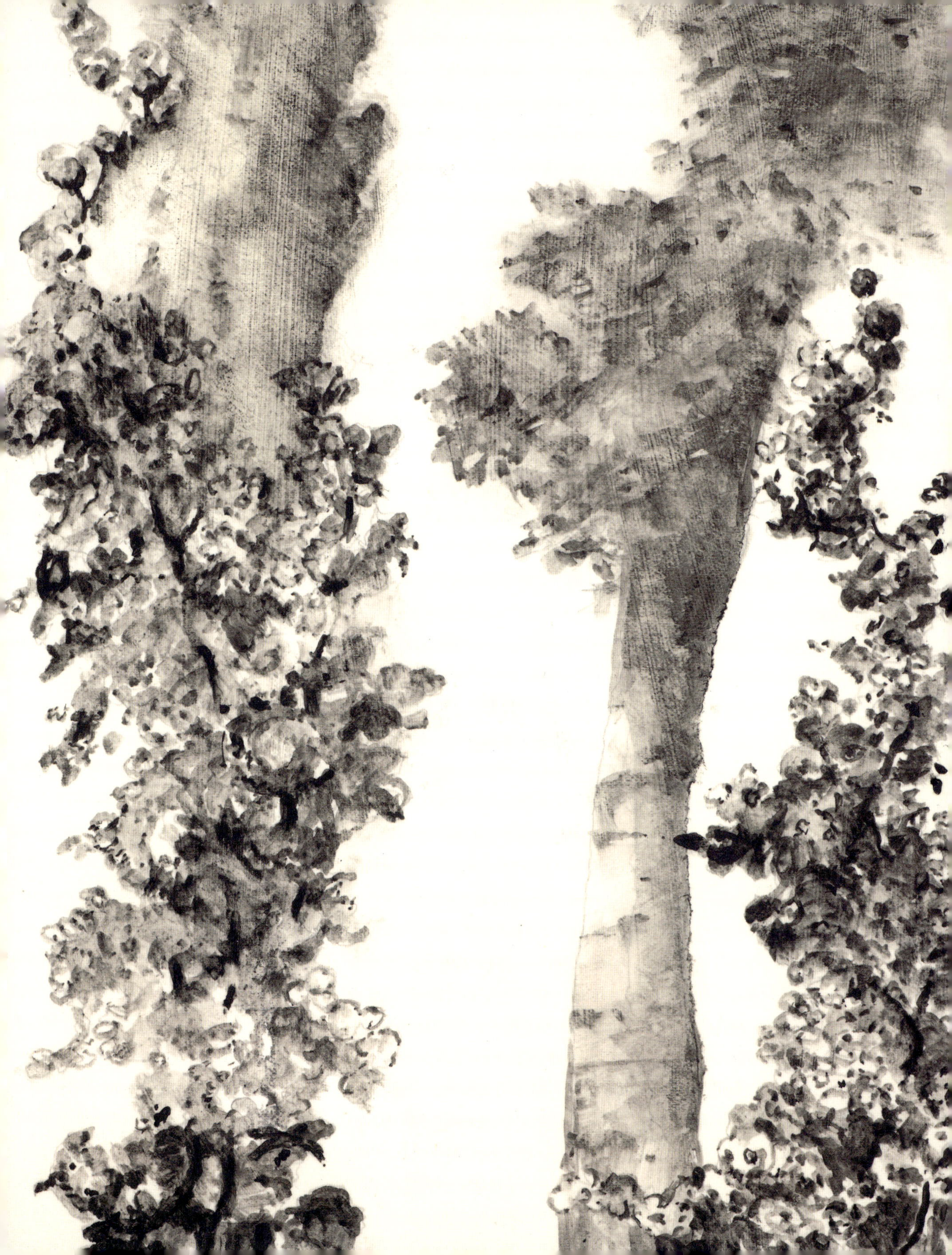

JEAN-HONORÉ FRAGONARD

The Progress of Love—Part 2

CA. 1790–91

Champagne Cocktail

3 OZ. CHAMPAGNE

⅓ OZ. BRANDY

1 SUGAR CUBE

2 DASHES OF ANGOSTURA BITTERS

Serve chilled in a coupe glass and garnish with a maraschino cherry

One of the oldest cocktails, the Champagne Cocktail—sweeter and stronger than a simple glass of champagne—is appropriate for the second part of this story, even if now the ancien régime has given way to a period of revolutionary turmoil.

Twenty years after completing *The Progress of Love*—commissioned and then rejected by Madame Du Barry—Fragonard returned to the four canvases and installed them in a very different setting. Looking at the Frick's Fragonard Room today, we should remember that the room is the result of two different campaigns.

Fragonard must have been particularly stung by the rejection in 1773 of his four canvases, surely one of the most important commissions he had executed by that point in his life. In October of that year, he left France for Italy, where he stayed for at least a year. The last chapter of the artist's career consisted of making small paintings for private patrons, none of them the great altarpieces and historical paintings commissioned from other painters at the time. Fragonard's life was also very much affected by the French Revolution. Many of his patrons had fled France or been killed. In the early months of 1790, he left Paris for Grasse, his birthplace. There, he—along with his wife, son, and sister-in-law, Marguerite Gérard—lived with his first cousin, Honoré Maubert, who with his son, Alexandre, worked in the perfume industry, which was thriving in Grasse, as it is today.

Surrounded by a garden with jasmine, fruit trees, hollyhocks, and numerous other plants and flowers, the beautiful Maubert villa has a view of the valley below Grasse, all the way to the Mediterranean Sea. While Fragonard was living there, he began work on a series of paintings for which we think we may have the receipt: a receipt of March 1791 indicates a payment of 3,600 livres received by Fragonard from "mon cher cousin, Maubert" (my dear cousin, Maubert). Fragonard decorated the villa's staircase, which connects the ground floor with the upper floor, with wall paintings, not true frescoes but painted *a secco*, with oil painting directly on the walls. The cycle features gods and goddesses and figures from antiquity accompanied by all'antica and Masonic symbols. During the revolution, Grasse was a particularly strong republican center; the decoration reflects the new regime that was being instituted in France at the end of the ancien régime.

Fragonard also decorated the villa's central room, where he installed the four canvases painted for Du Barry. Did he travel to Grasse with them? Did he have them shipped to Grasse? Was this part of the reason for Fragonard's return to Grasse, or did the idea come to him while he was redecorating the villa? We do not know. What we do know is that in 1790, almost twenty years after he painted *The Progress of Love*, he reinstalled the canvases in Grasse. In order to accommodate the four canvases—two pairs of slightly different widths—the salon had to be reshaped. Two doors were moved so that the pairs could be installed on opposite walls, each with a door in the middle. While this room, like the salon in Du Barry's pavilion at Louveciennes, was much smaller than the Fragonard Room at the Frick, it still had more space on the walls. For this reason, Fragonard produced ten more canvases for the space so that every inch would be covered.

He added two large canvases, the first of which depicts a solitary woman. In the nineteenth century, this painting was cruelly and somewhat romantically viewed as the finale of the story: at the end of the parable of the love affair, the woman is abandoned by the man. This was viewed as a reference to Du Barry's fate, to the fact that the king had died and she was left alone. We now know, however, that the painting is, in fact, very much in the same erotic mode as the others. A woman is daydreaming about her lover. The little cupid at the top points to midday, which in the eighteenth century was considered an erotically charged time of the day. The girl sits below in reverie. On the opposite wall—originally over a fireplace—the artist depicted the god Hymen, the god of marriage, holding two torches. Around him are cupids kissing. Over each of the four doors at Villa Maubert, Fragonard painted four cupids, each representing a different type of love. They are cupids who pursue, who avenge, who jest, and who encourage secrecy.

Fragonard's style has changed in these canvases. The brushwork is freer, and the colors are warmer, and this is particularly apparent when you see all the canvases together at the Frick.

The four very thin, tall canvases painted for the corners of two walls are my favorite part of this cycle. These beautiful canvases showing hollyhocks are purely decorative and give the viewer a sense of the room in Grasse, of looking out of the window and being surrounded by a garden. They are almost abstract. Each flower is so beautifully painted, with its leaves and white, pinkish petals.

The 1790s were a very difficult period for Fragonard. Once back in Paris, he worked primarily on a series of jobs related to the running of the Louvre museum, effectively giving up painting. The second part of *The Progress of Love* is his great swan song. He died on August 22, 1806, almost forgotten. He was buried in the cemetery of Montmartre, and even his tomb is now lost.

—X.S.

AGNOLO BRONZINO

Lodovico Capponi

CA. 1550–55

Aperol Spritz

3 OZ. APEROL

2 OZ. DRY PROSECCO

A SPLASH OF SPARKLING WATER

Serve over ice in a wine glass and
garnish with an orange or a lemon slice

This Italian drink has its origins in the Veneto region. Aperol is the flavored liqueur invented in 1919 in Padua, by the Barbieri brothers. As for the splash of sparkling water, the story goes that the Austro-Hungarian soldiers who occupied the Veneto after the Napoleonic Wars were in the habit of adding a splash—in German, spritzen*—to the local wines.*

Years before I became a curator at the Frick, I would make sure to stop by and say hello to the Bronzino painting every time I went to the museum. I'm not the only one who did so. In 2004, in a *New York Times* piece titled "My Friend Lodovico," the essayist David Masello wrote about his friendship with this painting. He would visit it whenever he went to the Upper East Side—after a bad breakup, in the days after September 11. This painting is in the hearts of many people who are close to the Frick.

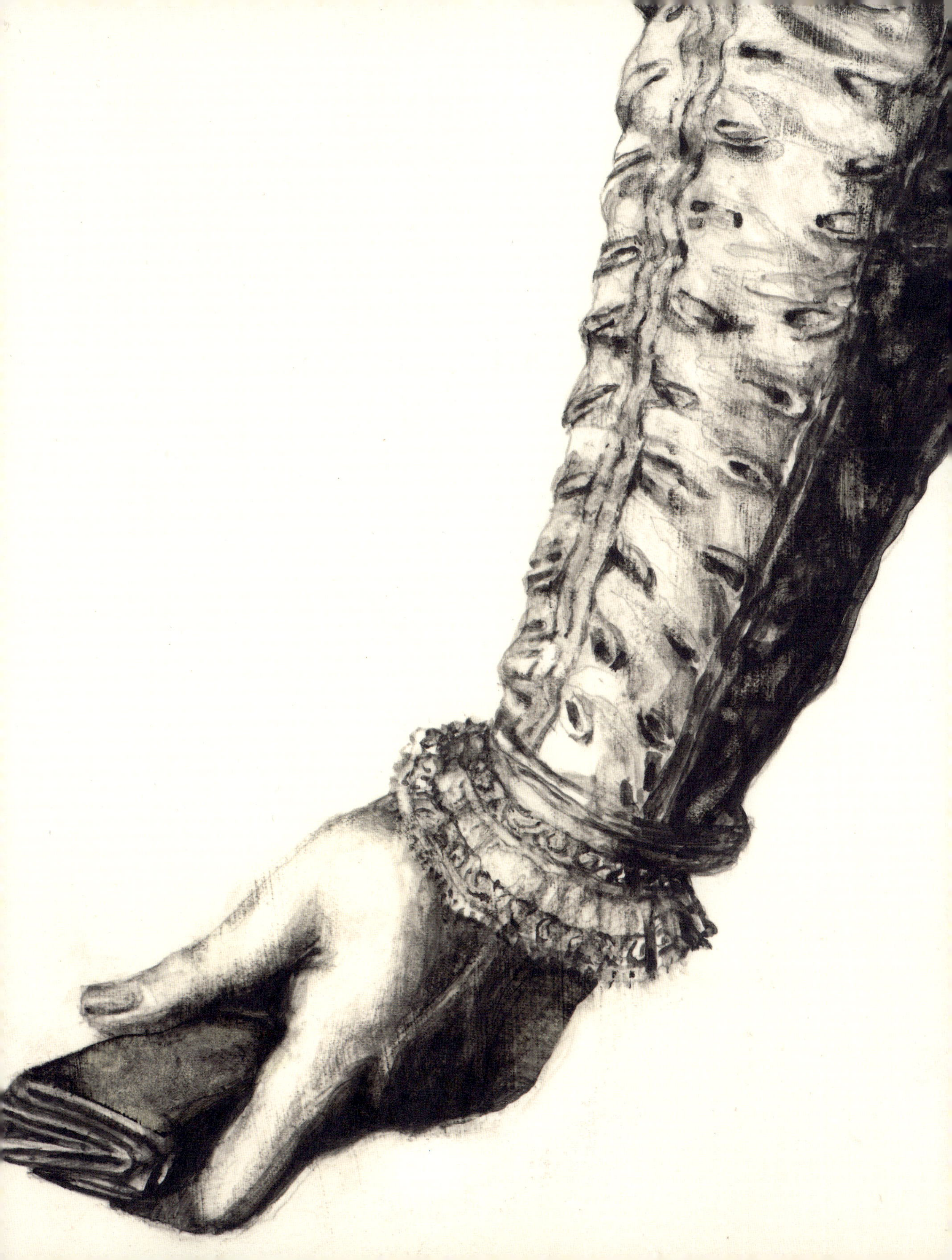

Lodovico has the cold, somewhat impassive face that is a hallmark of Bronzino's portraiture. Bronzino (1503–1572) spent his entire life in Florence, where he was born. His birth name was Agnolo di Cosimo, but he came to be known as Agnolo di Bronzino. Some speculate that this had something to do with his complexion: *bronzino* means "the bronze one."

One can't talk about Bronzino and his career without talking about the Medici family. Bronzino was appointed court painter to Cosimo I, Duke of Florence and later Grand Duke of Tuscany. The best known of Bronzino's portraits is his depiction of Cosimo's wife, Eleonora da Toledo, with their son Giovanni. In all of Bronzino's portraits, one sees his commitment to meticulous detail, particularly in articles of luxurious clothing, like brocaded dresses, silks, velvets, and jewels. The fact that the tailor to the Medici court had about the equivalent salary as the court painter Bronzino tells us how important it was not only to dress sitters in sumptuous clothing but also for them to be painted that way.

The portrait has everything one would expect in a late portrait by Bronzino: extreme refinement, impossibly long fingers, a porcelain face. Lodovico is probably depicted when he is in his late teens or early twenties, at which time he was a page at the Medici court. He has cold gray-blue eyes, a slightly raised eyebrow, the left eye a little bit walleyed. He conveys the self-assurance of someone who is very serious about who he is. And yet he has ruddy, red hair tousled in a way that points to his youth. His clothing—the white sleeves and fitted black doublet—has been associated with the black-and-white Capponi coat of arms. Looking closely, one can see that the simple white sleeves are slashed in tiny strokes to reveal another sumptuous layer beneath. Every thread, every frayed slash, is carefully articulated. Bronzino also renders in fine brushstrokes the meticulous needlework on his cuffs.

In my many discussions of this painting with visitors, particularly younger ones, one thing comes up again and again: the placement of what is often mistaken for Lodovico's sword. I explain that it is a codpiece, an intriguing accessory in the history of European male fashion. It originated as a simple flap of fabric covering the space between a man's pant legs but in time became more ostentatious and suggestively shaped to represent masculine virility and strength—exactly what a sword hilt hanging from the side of a man would signal.

Lodovico holds a pair of brown gloves. For European men and women, from the Renaissance through the nineteenth century and beyond, gloves were a symbol of fashion, luxury, wealth, and, to some degree, of practicality. The fact that Lodovico has removed them—thus exposing his flesh—and is carrying them suggests informality.

In his right hand, with those long and elegant fingers, Lodovico holds a round object largely concealed from our view. It may be a medal or a cameo. On it is a female bust, but all we can see are the top of her head and neckline of her dress, as well as the letters S-O-R-T-E, *sorte,* in Italian, meaning "fate" or "fortune." Some scholars suggest this is just half of the word, that the legend goes all the way around the object to say *consorte,* so "consort" or "wife." The possibilities are enriched by the fact that Bronzino was also a poet. The letters in the painting may be a visual play on words, a game with whomever his viewer was meant to be.

Some have associated the message that one does not know one's fate with the drama of Lodovico's life. He had fallen in love with Maddalena Vettori, a Florentine whom the duke, Cosimo I, had promised to someone else. Lodovico and Maddalena were not allowed to be together, but they conducted a secret relationship for several years. Lodovico even rented a palazzo near hers so he could see her in the streets. Eventually, Florence's duchess, Eleonora da Toledo, intervened and convinced Cosimo to allow them to marry. Cosimo's consent was conditional on their wedding within three days, which they did. The couple went on to have eight, some sources say six, children, and Lodovico lived a very long life, dying at the age of eighty, in 1614.

Some might wonder how we know the sitter is Lodovico Capponi. The identification was made in the 1950s by the scholar Luisa Becherucci, who discovered a key piece of evidence in Palazzo Capponi-Vettori, one of two Capponi palazzi in Florence and now a luxury hotel. In the grand salon, an extensive fresco decoration made in 1585 by Bernardino Poccetti celebrates the history of the Capponi family. For example, one lunette commemorates the great military victory in 1431 of Neri di Gino Capponi. Below this lunette is a small portrait that is unmistakably based on the Bronzino portrait. The sitter is dressed differently, wearing a gorget, a piece of armor that protects the neck, but he has the same features and even the same tousled hair. The inscription on the ceiling attributes the commission of the fresco to Lodovico Capponi, so presumably it is he who is depicted in the portrait, and that is how the sitter in the Frick portrait has been identified. Moreover, on the wall is a portrait that is presumably Maddalena Vettori, as well as two portraits of very young women, probably two of their children. There are also six empty medallions where portraits of their other children would have appeared. The Bronzino portrait clearly meant a lot to Lodovico Capponi for him to have the portrait made of him in 1585, when he was in his fifties, based on a likeness made thirty years earlier.

Mysteries remain. What exactly is Lodovico holding and what is he trying to convey with it? When and why was this portrait made? And what special place did it have in the life of Lodovico that it served as the source for his identity thirty years later in Palazzo Capponi? As with any good friend, no matter how well you know them, there is always more to discover.

—A.N.

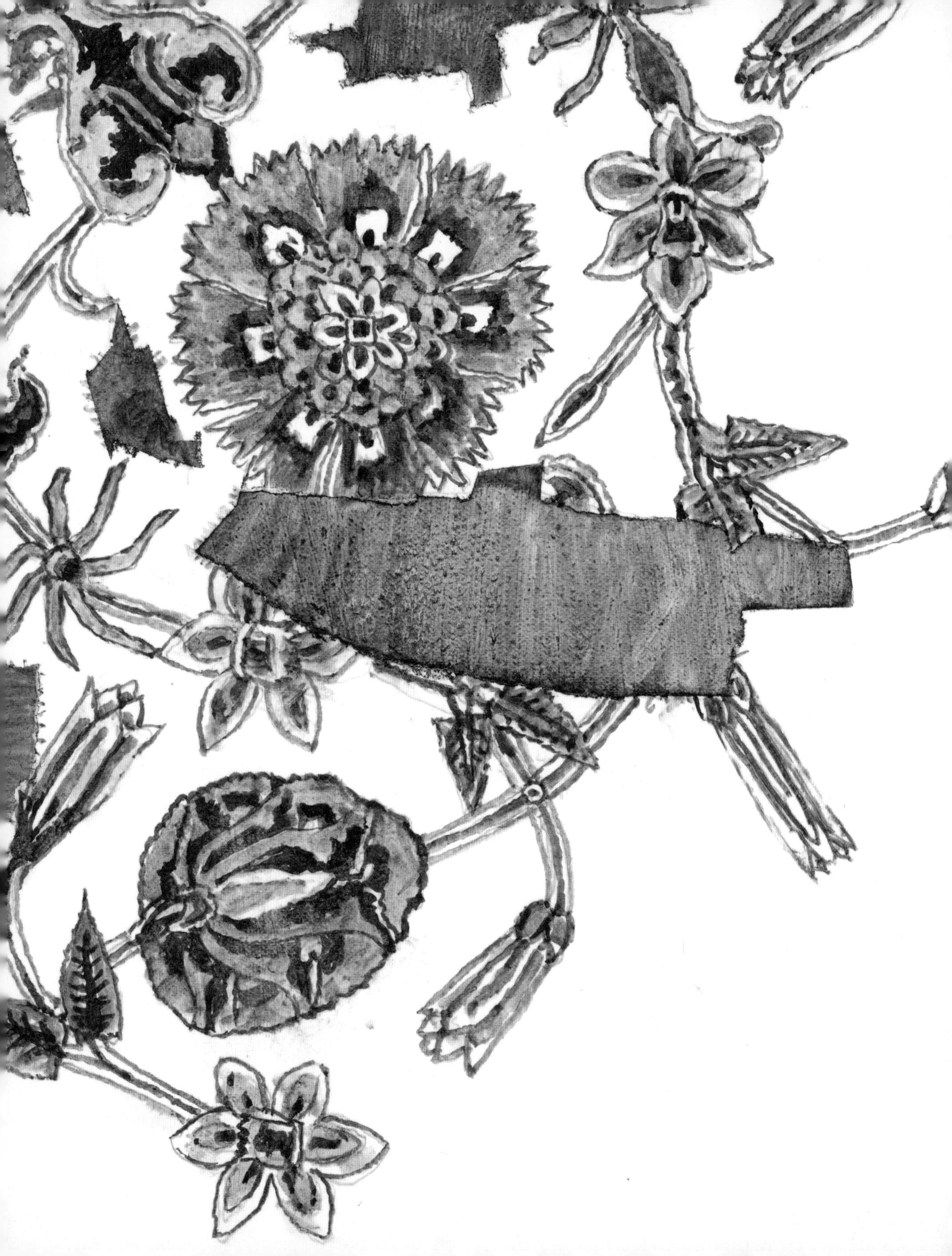

NORTHERN INDIAN

Carpet with Trees

CA. 1630

Carpet with Flowers

CA. 1650

Chai Martini

1 OZ. VODKA

2 OZ. ICED CHAI LATTE

Serve chilled in a martini glass and garnish with cinnamon

This cocktail is based on masala chai, a spiced tea popular in India, where these astonishing carpets were made. It is also very refreshing when iced.

The Frick is generally known as a collection of European art from about 1200 to 1900, but there are some exceptions—a few objects that were made outside of Europe. Among these are two carpets from northern India that were created between the 1630s and 1650s and are made from silk and pashmina wool, which comes from goats in the Himalayas and was used, in particular, to make cashmere shawls. Carpets, especially of this quality, were, of course, expensive to produce.

Both of these carpets were acquired by Henry Clay Frick in early 1918, one destined for the Enamels Room and the other for the Library. For the house at 1 East 70th Street, Frick bought a number of carpets, most of them Persian. Carpets, of course, were made all over Asia, from Turkey to Persia, India, and China, but in the nineteenth and twentieth centuries in America, Persian carpets, especially those dating to the sixteenth century, were considered among the most important. Frick bought a number of carpets from both northern and southern Persia, most of them with designs typically associated with the area around Isfahan. Some of these carpets are still on the floor at the Frick, while others are so fragile that they can be displayed only occasionally.

These two carpets were part of a group of objects—furniture, porcelain, and carpets—that Frick acquired from the dealer Joseph Duveen. Duveen had owned the carpets for quite a while as part of his stock and actually sold them at a slight loss, but this does not mean they were inexpensive. Frick paid more for these two carpets than he did for the Manet and the Renoir in the collection, which he bought around the same time.

One of the two carpets is decorated with depictions of trees against a wonderful dark red background. The trees are not all identifiable. Some are cypresses; some of the others are peach-like and plum-like. And there are some fantastic trees that have leaves that are similar to sycamore leaves but flowers that look like lilies. These are not real plants but were often depicted on Indian carpets. The second carpet is decorated primarily with flowers—lilies, carnations, different types of flowers more or less naturalistically depicted. They are set against a similar red background.

Described as Persian or Indo-Persian when they arrived at the Frick, the carpets were associated with two carpets (now in London and Los Angeles) known as the Ardabil Carpets, large sixteenth-century carpets made in Persia for the shrine of one of the local rulers, Sheikh Safi al-Din, in the town of Ardabil. They reached Europe in the late nineteenth century, and after a number of restorations, one of the carpets was repaired with pieces of the other and became very celebrated. Ardabil as the origin of the Frick tree carpet was first proposed in the early twentieth century, together with the idea that it may have been a gift from one of the Mughal emperors of India to a Persian ruler.

The carpet is actually made out of fragments, and the legend developed at that time that the reason the carpet was in pieces was that pilgrims stole parts of it because it was considered a sacred object in Ardabil. We now know this is not true. The confusion with Ardabil is due to the fact that the two Ardabil Carpets were described in the same volume as this carpet, but there was no mention in the late nineteenth century that this also came from Ardabil. This is clearly an

Indian rug, not a Persian rug, and the fact that it is in fragments is simply due to the wear and tear of the past four hundred years.

Both of these carpets are composed of fragments that came from much larger carpets. They were originally very long and narrow carpets, much larger than survives now. These types of carpets were produced during the Mughal Empire in India, especially in the sixteenth and seventeenth centuries. The Mughal emperors arrived in India in the 1520s. They were of Turkish-Mongolian origins and descended from Timur, the great ruler of central Asia. Babur was the first of the Mughal rulers of the Indian subcontinent. Many of these emperors were great patrons of the arts, like Akbar and his successors. The Mughal emperors ruled India, at least in name, all the way to the 1850s.

These two carpets at the Frick were produced during the reign of Shah Jahan, the emperor from the late 1620s to the late 1650s. Shah Jahan is, of course, remembered today primarily as the builder of the Taj Mahal in Agra. Carpets of this kind, of this size, of these materials, would have only been produced by the state manufactories that worked for the imperial family. We do not, however, know if they were made for a palace or for a religious site. Carpets of this quality were produced in the Mughal Empire for about two hundred years, but only about five hundred of them survive, most of them still in India. It is really wonderful for us to be able to display them and show great works of Indian art to the public.

—X.S.

BERTOLDO DI GIOVANNI

The Pazzi Conspiracy Medal

1478

Cardinale

I OZ. GIN

I OZ. DRY VERMOUTH

I OZ. CAMPARI

Serve on the rocks in a cocktail glass
and garnish with an orange peel

Cardinale *is the Italian word for a cardinal. Named for its dark red, bloody color, this cocktail is particularly appropriate for the events commemorated on this medal.*

We have already spoken about Bertoldo di Giovanni (ca. 1440–1491), one of Lorenzo de' Medici's favorite artists. This extraordinary medal, among his most celebrated works, is from one of the great private collections of medals, that of Stephen K. Scher and his wife, Janie Woo Scher, who have donated a substantial part of their collection to the Frick, making the museum one of the most important repositories of medals in the United States.

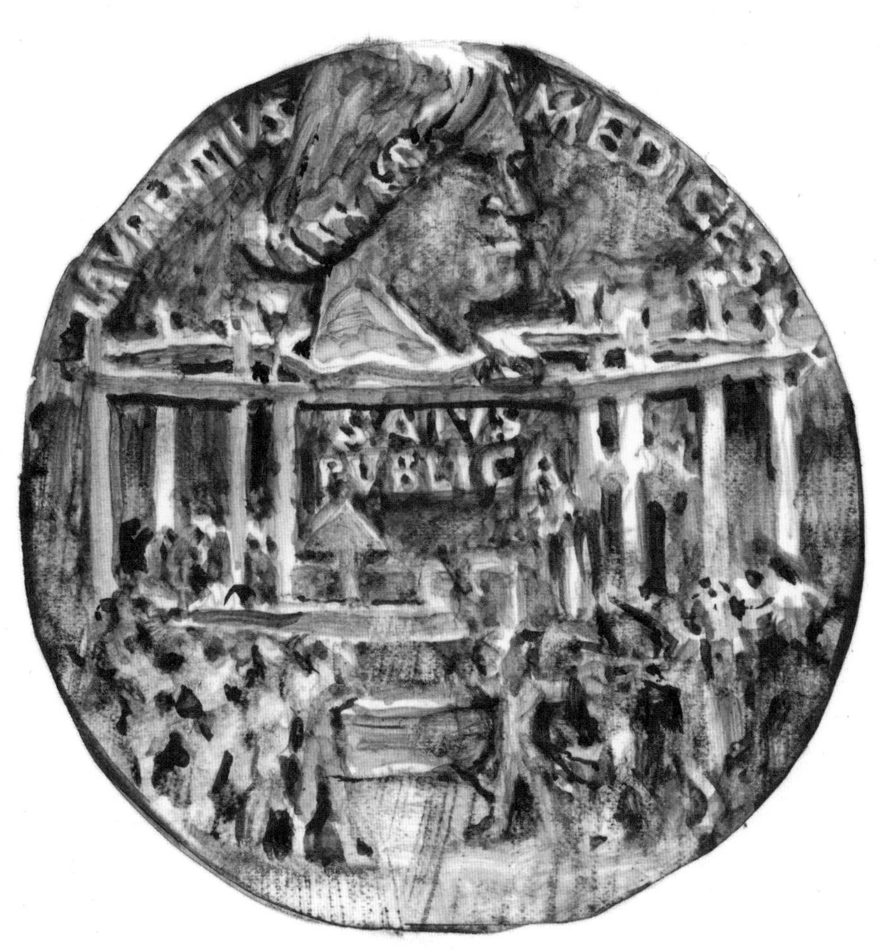
LAVRENTIVS
MEDICES
SALVS
PUBLICA

Medals are often confused with coins, but while Renaissance medals were inspired by ancient coins, there are a number of differences between the two. First of all, a coin has a currency value, while a medal is a commemorative object with no currency value. Medals usually have an obverse and a reverse. The obverse, the front, typically displays a portrait in profile, surrounded by an inscription identifying the sitter. The reverse, the back of the medal, usually depicts a historic scene, an allegorical subject, or heraldic symbols that are connected to the portrait on the obverse.

Bertoldo's medal focuses on what's known as the Pazzi Conspiracy, an event that took place on April 26, 1478, in the cathedral of Santa Maria del Fiore in Florence. Although Florence was, at least in name, a republic at the time, the brothers Lorenzo and Giuliano de' Medici had effectively become its rulers. And they clearly had a number of enemies inside and outside Florence. The conspiracy against them was organized by two other brothers from a Florentine aristocratic family, Jacopo and Francesco Pazzi, and we now know that it was, to a large degree, supported by Pope Sixtus IV in Rome. The Pazzi brothers assembled a group of about nine conspirators from other noble families, like the Salviati and the Baroncelli, as well as two priests. Their plan was to strike in a religious site, and at the time of the mass, on the Sunday before the Feast of the Ascension. The cardinal celebrating the mass, Cardinal Riario, was one of the papal nephews, but he does not seem to have known about the plan.

Both Lorenzo and Giuliano were present in the choir of the cathedral with a large number of people. It is unclear when the conspirators struck. Most likely, it was at the end of the mass, as everyone was leaving, that the Medici brothers were attacked on opposite sides of the choir. The conspirators tried to stab Lorenzo, who was on the right of the altar, and wounded him in the neck, but he was brought safely to the Sagrestia delle Messe, where the Medici supporters locked the door. On the opposite side of the altar, Giuliano was killed, left in a pool of blood at the side of the altar after being struck nineteen times.

Lorenzo's revenge over Giuliano's death was swift. The conspirators had counted on the support of the citizens of Florence, but that support did not materialize. One by one, Lorenzo apprehended all the conspirators. They were put to death and their bodies publicly displayed in Florence for all to see. While this was a traumatic episode for Lorenzo, in many ways it solidified his support among the citizens of Florence.

Bertoldo's medal, cast after the bloody events of April 1478, does not have a straightforward obverse and reverse but rather conflates the two. One side shows a portrait of Giuliano de' Medici, with his name at the top in Latin—IVLIANVS MEDICES. Below the portrait is a representation of the wooden choir of the cathedral in Florence as it looked at the time. Outside the choir is a group of people with daggers inflicting wounds on the body of Giuliano. Below is a second inscription: LVCTVS PVBLICVS (public mourning). The other side of the medal represents Lorenzo de' Medici, LAVRENTIVS MEDICES. He is looking the other way, also floating over the choir of the cathedral. Here, the inscription tells us that this is SALVS PVBLICA (public safety/health). At the bottom, the choir is seen from the opposite side. One of the clever things about this medal is that it projects the viewer into the site where the events occurred. But here you see Lorenzo and a group of people escaping and taking refuge in the sacristy.

The depiction of the events in the choir of the cathedral is particularly pictorial. The portraits are also probably derived from painted portraits; the one of Giuliano is based on a portrait by Botticelli. Bertoldo produced this medal together with a canon in Prato, Andrea di Filippo Guazzalotti. We have a letter of September 11, 1478, in which Guazzalotti sends the first copies of this medal to Lorenzo, writing that Bertoldo was in Prato and together they produced it. Bertoldo clearly designed and probably modeled the medal, while Guazzalotti cast it, we assume in bronze, possibly even in richer materials such as gold and silver. And these examples were then distributed by Lorenzo.

Why was this medal created? It was most likely made for distribution among the Medici supporters. Around the same time, one of the great literary figures of the court of Lorenzo de' Medici, Angelo Poliziano—who was in the cathedral with the Medici brothers and witnessed the events—published a text describing the conspiracy. Maybe Bertoldo himself was also present that day. Lorenzo wanted to record the event because it commemorated his success over the conspirators. But it also represented a moment of deep mourning for his brother. The medal memorializes a loss and celebrates a triumph at the same time.

—X.S.

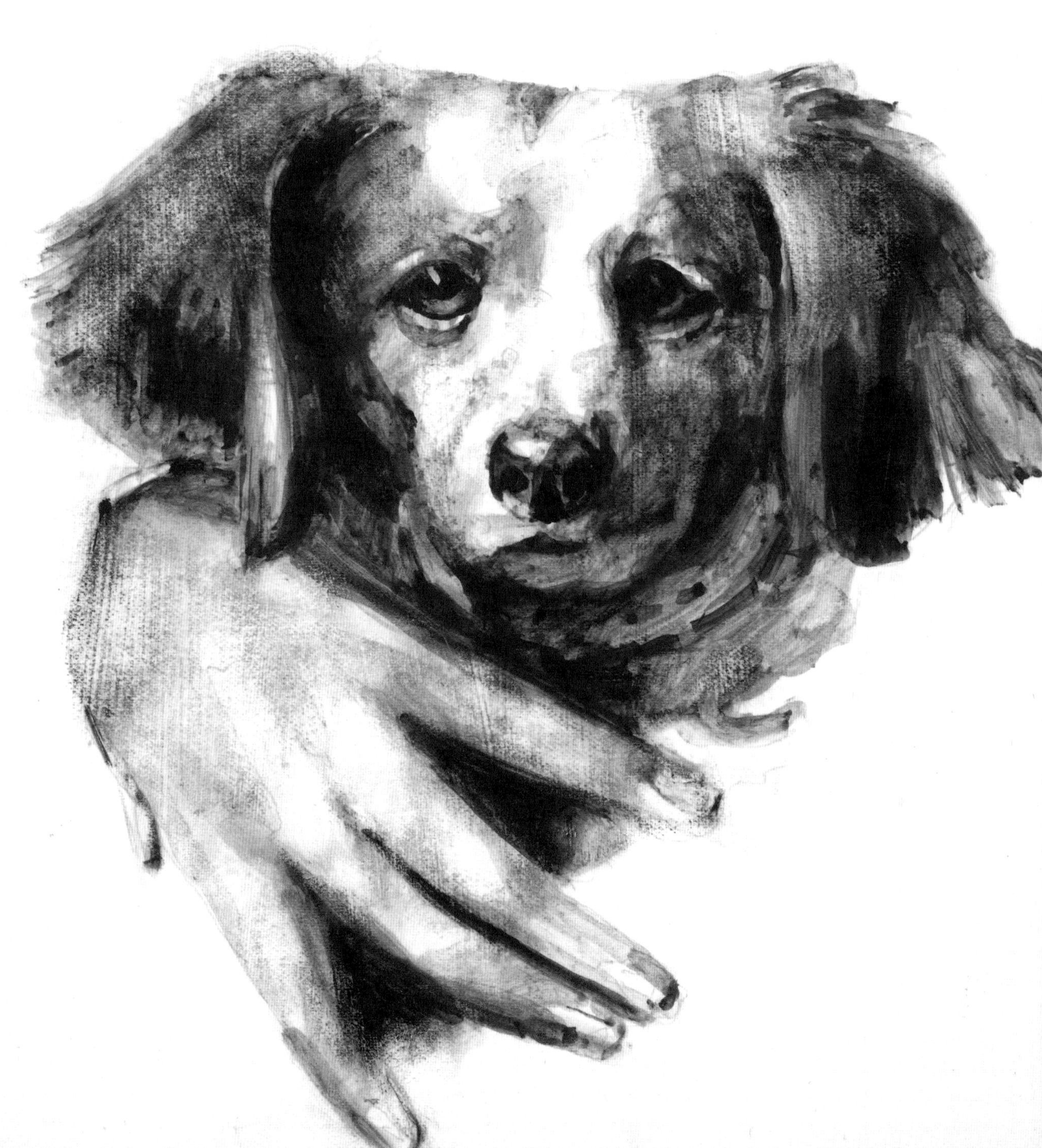

GEORGE ROMNEY

Lady Hamilton as "Nature"

1782

Limoncello Spritz

1 OZ. LIMONCELLO
1 OZ. SPARKLING LEMONADE
TOP WITH PROSECCO

Serve over ice in a wine glass and garnish with mint

A digestif typically served after meals, limoncello is traditionally made from Sorrento lemons grown in southern Italy, where Lady Hamilton spent a significant chapter of her life.

George Romney (1734–1802) was a fashionable eighteenth-century portraitist whose career cannot be discussed without talking about Emma, Lady Hamilton, who was his muse. He was infatuated with her appearance, painting her dozens of times in various guises—with different expressions, gestures, and attitudes; in a wide range of costumes and outfits; and playing mythological and allegorical figures. The very first of these, the one that started it all, was the Frick picture.

Emma was born Amy Lyon or Lyons to a modest family. Her blacksmith father died when she was young, and from the age of twelve, she worked as a maid, cleaning wealthy people's homes to support her mother and grandmother. Throughout her adolescence, she took on other jobs, one of which, working as a hostess at parties, got her into some trouble: she became pregnant with the baby of an aristocrat who wanted nothing more to do with her or the child. A man by the name of Sir Charles Greville came to the rescue. Greville began a relationship with her and agreed to support her on a couple of conditions to which she agreed: one, that she give up the baby, and two, that she change her name. (Apparently, "Amy" was not sophisticated enough for him.) She became Emma Hart and lived with Greville as his mistress. She was seventeen years old at this time.

Knowing that Romney was seeking a new muse, Greville brought Emma to the artist's studio. He commissioned this painting of Emma from Romney, and it stayed with him for some time. But Greville had an ulterior motive in introducing her to the artist: he, like Romney, was interested in a kind of commercial venture in which Emma's image would feature as the subject of a series of works that could be sold on the market. The images would subsequently be made available at a lower cost for a less wealthy clientele as prints. In fact, just a couple of years after Romney made the Frick painting in 1782, he—along with the mezzotint engraver John Raphael Smith—issued a print of it to be disseminated to those who wanted art like this but could not afford paintings.

It is worth noting that Romney's images of Emma are not quite portraits. For example, the names of the printmaker and painter, Smith and Romney, appear on the print after the Frick painting, but the name of the sitter does not. It is not about Emma. Indeed, through the print, the Frick painting took on an allegorical subject, for the print was circulated with text below the image: a poem called "Nature." This is how the Frick picture came to be called *Lady Hamilton as "Nature."* The poem is a celebration of the model's features, of her youth, the sweetness of her blushing lips, the wetness of her eyes; it imagines her heaving chest and wild breath. The vaguely erotic language is masked and legitimized by the adorable and innocent-looking puppy she holds. The juxtaposition of the puppy with her low-cut dress exposing the flesh of her breasts encapsulates that tension between innocence and exploitation; where her bared décolletage ends, the puppy's head begins. Her long, flowing brown hair at once shows off the energy of Romney's brushstrokes and indicates her health, youth, and beauty.

Emma's appearance in the Frick painting contrasts sharply with conventional society portraits painted by Romney and his peers. Portraits of wealthy women typically show them wearing their hair or wigs elaborately tied up and powdered white or gray, as well as white makeup on the face and sharp red blotches of blush on the cheeks—a somewhat artificial, worked elegance. In comparison, the Frick painting of Emma exudes a sense of freedom, a fantasy of youth, perhaps a fantasy of female availability.

Unfortunately for Emma, the man she associated herself with, though titled, lacked sufficient funds to secure his lifestyle. To remedy the situation, Greville sought to marry a wealthy woman and, in order to detach himself from Emma, concocted a ruse whereby Emma was sent to Naples under the belief that he would soon join her for a holiday. In reality, he sent her to become the mistress of his uncle, a man about forty years older than Emma. Recently widowed and well respected, Sir William Hamilton was the British ambassador to the Kingdom of Naples, a volcanologist, and an avid art collector. (Unfortunately, his extraordinary collection was sold off toward the end of his life.) She ended up marrying Hamilton and became Lady Hamilton in 1791.

Emma became very popular in Naples. In the same way that she transformed herself by assuming various guises for Romney's paintings, she developed a sort of theatrical tableau performance called the "Attitudes," which she performed at the court in Naples to great acclaim. She became close friends with Maria Carolina, the queen of Naples and Sicily, who was the sister of Marie-Antoinette.

In Naples, Lady Hamilton also met the British military hero Horatio Nelson. Revered for his naval victories against Napoleon's fleet, most famously in the Battle of the Nile in 1798, Nelson was already married, but he and Emma fell in love. Their affair was scandalous: people disapproved because he was a celebrated military figure, and she was who she was. Curiously, Sir William Hamilton seemed to condone the affair and maintained a strong friendship with Horatio Nelson. In fact, the three of them invented a motto about themselves: "Three in One." It was socially condemned, but it worked for them.

With the French army arriving to conquer Naples, the three escaped to England. In 1802, Sir William Hamilton sold his great art collection—which by then included the Frick painting, Romney's first of Emma—in order to pay debts and possibly for other personal reasons. I wonder what that must have felt like for them, to sell that painting while both of them were still alive to see it go. That same year, Emma gave birth to a daughter with Horatio Nelson, named Horatia. Her husband died the following year.

Just a few years later, Horatio Nelson was mortally wounded in his victorious battle at Trafalgar. It did not end well for Emma. Despite the fact that she received an inheritance from both men, she fell into debt and was imprisoned for not being able to pay off the debts. She died in 1815, destitute, at the age of forty-nine.

There is sadness behind the fantasy of youth and freedom in Romney's painting. Emma's great strength was her ability to transform herself, not just for Romney's paintings or in the theatrical "Attitudes" that made her so popular in Naples, but in the reality of her life. From the blacksmith's daughter Amy Lyons, she became Emma Hart, mistress of Charles Greville, and then Lady Hamilton, darling of the royal court in Naples. She looks out from Romney's painting at the age of seventeen, and to me, it gives a sense of the great strength of a young person who has already been through so much.

—A.N.

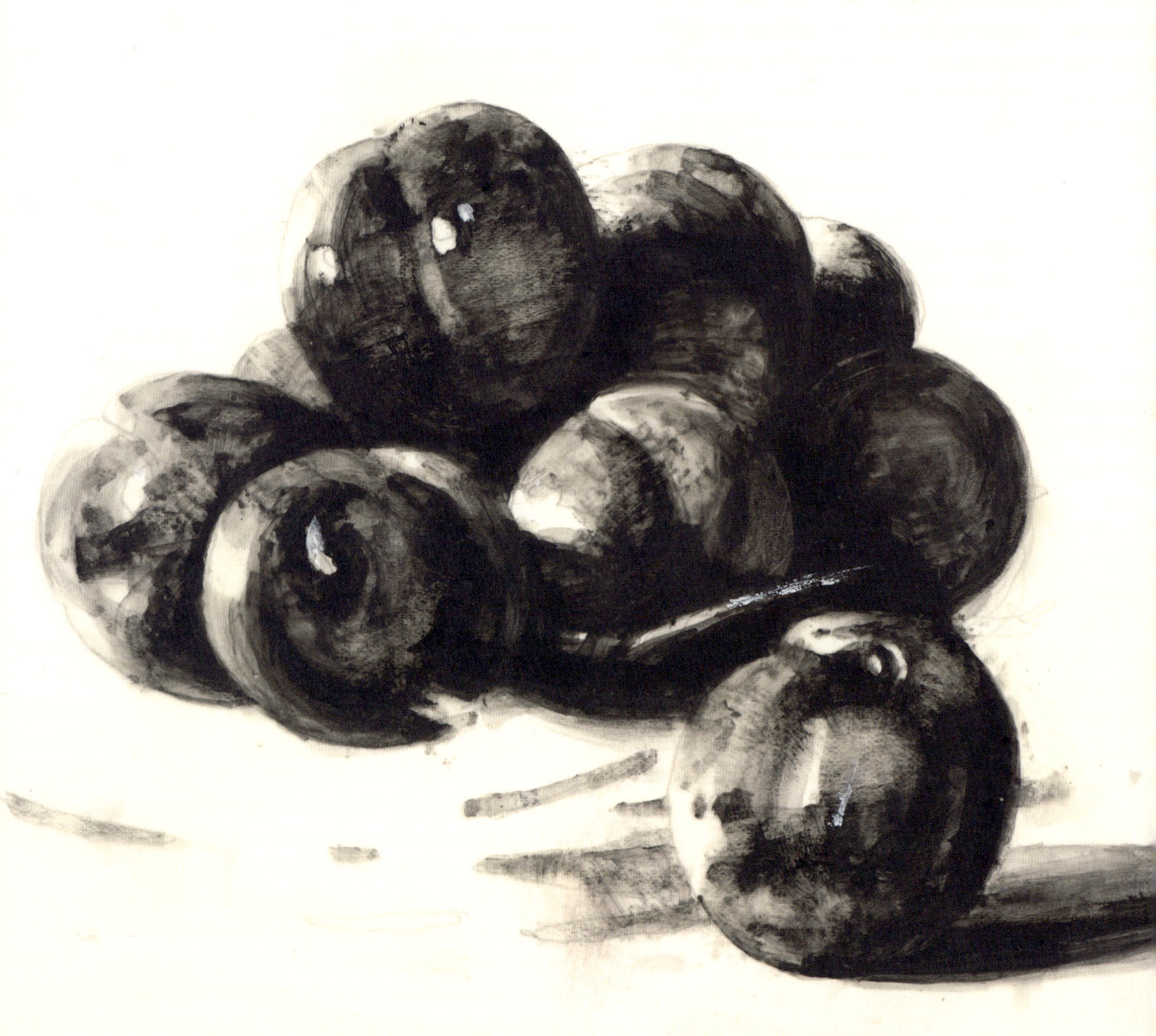

JEAN-SIMÉON CHARDIN

Still Life with Plums

CA. 1730

Gin Martini

3 OZ. GIN

½ OZ. DRY VERMOUTH

Serve chilled in a martini glass
and garnish with a lemon twist

The effortlessness of this beautiful still life is reflected in the simplicity of this classic cocktail. There is more than one way to make a Martini, but I always prefer mine with gin, strong, and with a slight lemon accent. Like this Chardin painting, it is pure bliss.

This very small, seemingly simple painting by Jean-Siméon Chardin is an extraordinary creation. Acquired by the museum many years after Henry Clay Frick's death—arriving in 1945, at the end of World War II—it was the only still life in the collection. Although the very first Old Master painting that we know of Frick buying was Jan van Os's *Still Life with Fruit*, for the most part, he acquired landscapes and portraits. I always wonder about the fact that he was clearly interested in being surrounded by images of people and places. I often imagine him, his family, and the people working in the house amidst all these faces from the past.

Chardin (1699–1779) is generally less known than Watteau, Boucher, Fragonard, and other artists in the pantheon of eighteenth-century French painters. Unlike these colorful personalities, Chardin neither traveled much nor had an exciting life. Most of his career was devoted to painting genre scenes and still lifes, which was unusual. Painting at the time was organized into a hierarchy of types, with religious, history, and mythological paintings at the top of the scale, followed by portraiture and landscapes, and genre scenes and still lifes at the bottom. Most of the great artists of the eighteenth century aspired to become court painters or academicians, and the best path for that was the painting of the genres at the top of the hierarchy so as to attract the attention of the royal family, prominent aristocratic patrons, or the Church. Boucher worked along those lines, and Fragonard started his career that way, while Watteau developed an unusual type of painting—his beautiful *fêtes galantes*. Largely self-taught, unlike his contemporaries, Chardin developed something that other artists were not really pursuing.

Most of Chardin's still lifes depict everyday objects invested with a wonderful plainness and poetic mood. You can feel the textures, the surfaces of the different things, of the glass, the porcelain, the fabric, the wood, the stone. The paintings are usually fairly small. When I visit museums, I always stop in my tracks, enchanted, when I encounter a Chardin still life. His output was relatively small, apparently because he painted very, very slowly. It has been argued that he only painted a couple of hundred paintings in his long career. That would be an average of about four or five paintings a year. His patrons would have been aristocrats, the collectors of the time. We do not know who many of them were, but they were clearly people who had a very refined and unusual taste, not necessarily those who were acquiring grand mythological scenes or portraits.

Chardin is a magician of paint; every single amazing brushstroke reflects his extraordinary technical skill. His still lifes are often composed of a group of objects that do not necessarily go together, often objects from the kitchen. You get the feeling that a dinner has just ended, and someone has put the scraps on a ledge for Chardin's sharp eye to focus on.

In the Frick's still life, there are three groups of objects: a basket with fruit, some vegetables, and, in the middle, a bottle and a glass. The plums in the woven basket have a silver sheen on their skin; you get the feeling they may have just been plucked from a tree. On the right are two large squashes. Each brushstroke—the white, the bright orange, the yellow—gives the painting an almost abstract quality. And then you have a bottle of colored glass and a transparent glass, both of them disclosing their contents through the magic of glass. The glass is half full, and the bottle contains some liquid, probably white wine but possibly water.

Light is reflected, refracted; it bounces off these objects. The transparency of that glass of water is absolutely magical. Here is an artist representing miracles of nature, literally showing prosaic objects in a new light. Light shines off the plums, off the surface of the squash, off the bottle of wine and the glass. Chardin makes us pause and look at these objects very, very carefully. His still lifes were enormously influential for Picasso, Braque, Morandi.

Chardin is supposed to have said, "Who said one paints with colors? One employs colors, but one paints with feeling." Not surprisingly, he was well ahead of his time. His still lifes were tremendously influential, and he was one of Proust's favorite artists. When I think of the celebrated scene in the first volume of Proust's *À la recherche du temps perdu,* when the narrator dips his madeleine in a cup of lime-blossom tea, I imagine Proust making a coy allusion to Chardin. We should all pause for a few minutes to think about some of the marvels of nature, of art, and of life.

—X.S.

GIAMBATTISTA TIEPOLO

Perseus and Andromeda

1730

Milanese Gin and Tonic

EQUAL PARTS OF:

GIN

CAMPARI

TONIC WATER

Combine the gin and Campari in a tumbler filled with ice and add tonic water

In this Milanese twist on a Gin and Tonic, the traditional cocktail is enlivened with Campari. Although Tiepolo is usually associated with Venice, his painting at the Frick was created for a palazzo in Milan.

Henry Clay Frick was not particularly interested in seventeenth- and eighteenth-century Italian paintings. It was not until much later in the twentieth century, well after Frick's death in 1919, that American collectors started buying Baroque paintings. This makes Giambattista Tiepolo's *Perseus and Andromeda* an unusual work at The Frick Collection. The sketch was

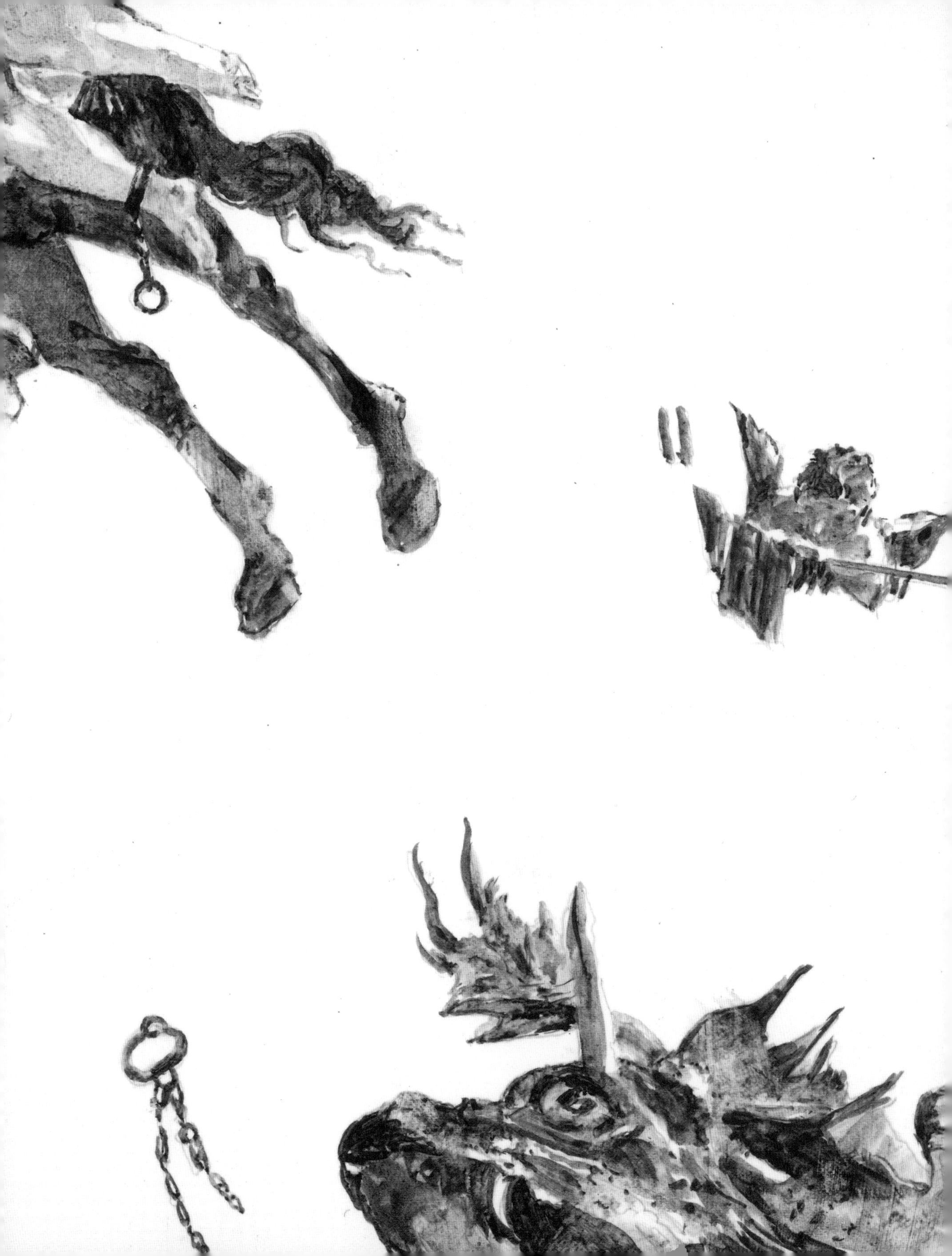

probably acquired for decorative purposes, for the second floor of Frick's house. It used to be in an upstairs corridor, in spaces decorated by Elsie de Wolfe for the Frick family.

One of the greatest painters of the eighteenth century, Tiepolo (1696–1770) worked mostly in his birthplace, Venice, and in the Veneto. But he also traveled around Italy and Europe, decorating buildings at sites in northern Italy and, later in his life, in Germany—at Würzburg—and finally in Madrid, where he died.

The Frick sketch was made for a fresco cycle for the palazzo of the Archintos, a prominent aristocratic family in Milan. Located on Via Olmetto, the palazzo is in the ancient center of the city, where the ruins of the Roman imperial palace are. The head of the Archinto family, Carlo, commissioned the frescoes, which may have been connected to the marriage, in April 1731, of his firstborn son, Filippo Archinto, to Giulia Borromeo, a member of another important family in Milan. Tiepolo worked on the frescoes—his first major commission outside of the Veneto—between 1730 and 1731.

The palazzo still exists, but, unfortunately, the frescoes do not. They were destroyed on the night of August 13, 1943, when the palazzo was bombed by the Allied forces. Milan had been very heavily bombed that year; it is estimated that about sixty-five percent of the artistic and historic monuments of the city were either destroyed or damaged. In the 1950s and '60s, the palazzo was reconstructed, and its exterior today survives in much the same condition as it would have been before the bombing.

Tiepolo painted a number of ceilings for the palazzo. Fortunately, very good black-and-white photographs of all the frescoes were taken, and they give us an idea of what was lost, as do three extant sketches for three of the ceilings, one of which is the Frick sketch. The grandest allegorical fresco in the palazzo was *The Triumph of the Arts and Sciences*, with allegorical figures. This pays tribute to Carlo Archinto, an enlightened patron who was particularly interested in science and the arts. It also alludes to the fact that Palazzo Archinto had one of Milan's most important libraries, and it was open to the public. Another ceiling represented *Phaëton Asking Apollo to Drive the Chariot of the Sun*.

The Frick sketch and the related ceiling represent a mythological scene from the story of Perseus and Andromeda by Ovid. The Ethiopian princess Andromeda was chained to a rock after her mother, Cassiopeia, had boasted that she was more beautiful than some of the sea nymphs, the Nereids. As a punishment, the god Neptune sent a monster—which could only be appeased by human sacrifice—to plague the waters of Ethiopia. Cassiopeia and her husband decided to sacrifice Andromeda, their only daughter. Perseus was flying on the winged horse Pegasus after having slain Medusa, when he saw and fell in love with the beautiful woman chained to a rock. He asked her parents if he could have her hand in marriage if he managed to save her. In the painting, Cassiopeia is praying in front of the god Jupiter, and below, at the center, is Perseus on Pegasus with the naked Andromeda, shackles still attached to her wrists and ankles. And at the very bottom, on the right, is the dead sea monster; the water nymphs on the left are crying for its death. Most of the figures in this painting—Cassiopeia, Perseus, Andromeda, Pegasus—correspond to constellations in the sky—the ceiling of the palazzo echoing the starry sky outside.

It is worth pausing to think about the destruction of monuments and the fragility of so many works of art. Palazzo Archinto is one of the many examples of great works of art that were lost in the last hundred years, not all of them through natural causes, some due to wars and human damage. One of the most touching aspects of the destruction of Palazzo Archinto, for me, is the fact that even though the architectural shell survived, everything in it was destroyed. The one thing that survived was actually a plant. The oldest wisteria in Milan still grows in the courtyard of the building. There is a wonderful sense of hope in this.

—X.S.

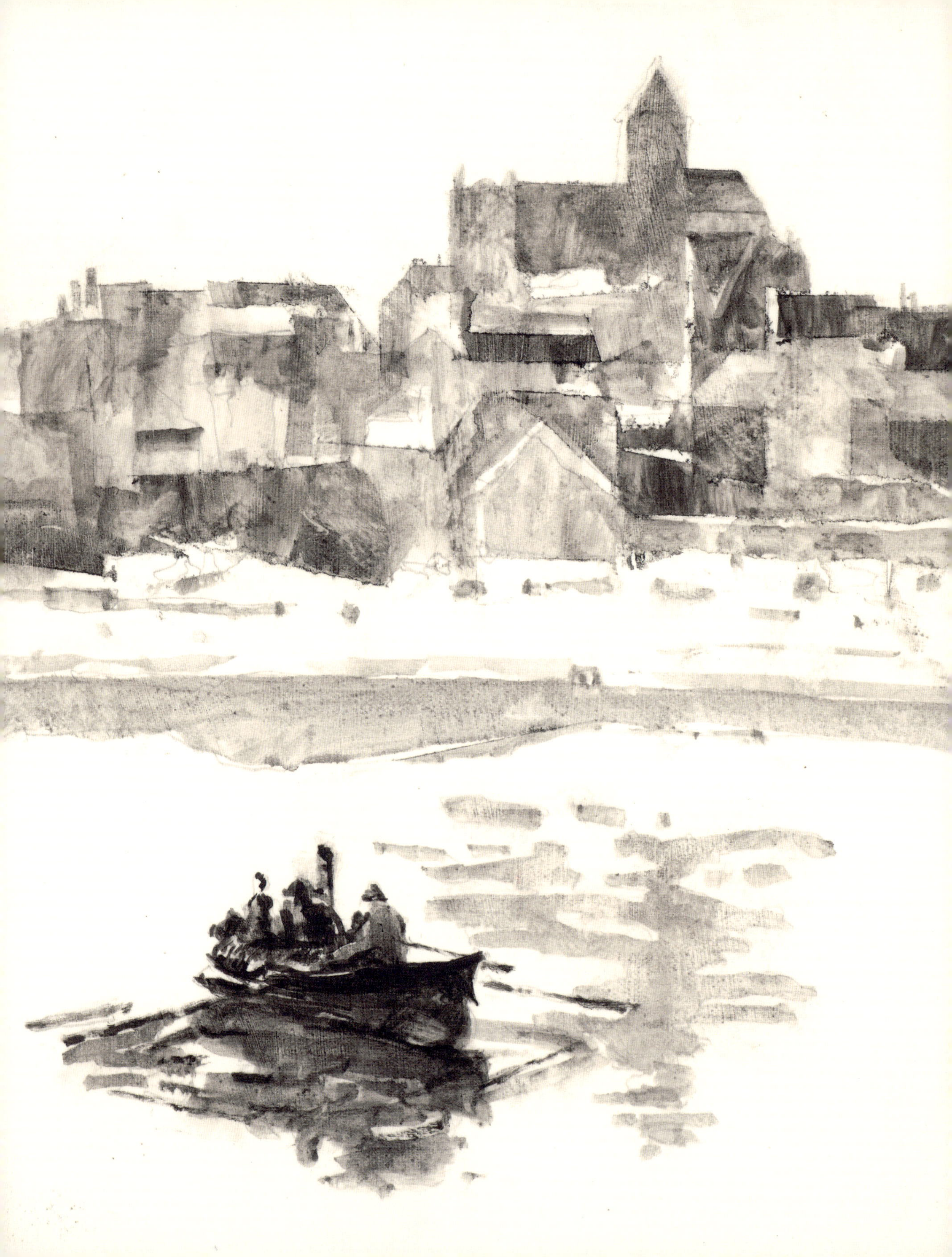

CLAUDE MONET

Vétheuil in Winter

1878–79

Mulled Wine

RED WINE

2 SLICES OF ORANGE

1 CINNAMON STICK

5 WHOLE CLOVES

2 CARDAMOM PODS

1 TBSP. HONEY

Mix in a pot and bring to simmer
Serve in a mug when hot

The perfect antidote for one of the coldest winters on record in France or, for that matter, for any winter!

Henry Clay Frick bought two paintings by Claude Monet (1840–1926) during his lifetime: a view of Argenteuil (which he later swapped for another painting) and *Banks of the Seine at Lavacourt,* which he purchased in 1901 and is now at the Frick Pittsburgh. *Vétheuil in Winter* was acquired after his death—by the Frick in 1942. Lavacourt is the small settlement across the river from Vétheuil; the paintings now in New York and Pittsburgh show opposite sides of the river in different seasons.

Of course, we think of Monet as the painter of the great *Water Lilies*, as the artist based in Giverny who depicted flowers and sites—the Cathedral of Rouen, the haystacks—at different times of day and during different seasons. The Frick is part of this story. The term Impressionism was coined in the spring of 1874, after an exhibition in which Monet showed a painting titled *Impression, soleil levant* (Impression, Sunrise). The exhibition launched the Impressionist movement of which Monet—together with Degas, Pissarro, Sisley, Caillebotte, and Renoir—was a key protagonist.

Born in Le Havre, in the north of France, Monet moved to Paris as a young man. He also spent time in London. In the 1870s, he began to conceive of serial works that would show the same subject in different light conditions. The first such subject was the Gare Saint-Lazare, the train station in Paris from which Monet would travel to Argenteuil, the town on the Seine where he had moved with his wife, Camille Doncieux, and young son. While in Argenteuil, Monet often worked on a studio boat, painting sites along the river.

In September 1878, Monet moved his family farther down the Seine, from Argenteuil to the village of Vétheuil, about thirty-seven miles from Paris. He was to spend three winters there, between 1787 and 1881. Moving with them was his patron, Ernest Hoschedé, along with his wife, Alice, and their six children. Hoschedé was an art collector and owned department stores in Paris. Monet painted Vétheuil at different times of day and during different seasons. The village today is much as it was, retaining a good deal of its rural character.

The Vétheuil years were difficult for both families. Hoschedé, who had gone bankrupt and had to sell many of his Impressionist works, eventually left the country, leaving Alice and the children to live under the same roof as the Monet family. Monet was also having financial difficulties, and Camille was in poor health, suffering from tuberculosis and then cancer. She was in serious decline, and while Monet was painting, Alice Hoschedé looked after her.

The winter of 1878 was particularly cold, and the Frick painting dates from this time. Monet captured Vétheuil covered in snow, with the river frozen. This was a low point for the artist. He wrote to a friend:

> *I am absolutely sickened with and demoralized by this life I have been leading for so long. When you reach my age [he was in his late thirties] there is nothing more to look forward to. Unhappy we are, unhappy we will continue to be. Each day brings its tribulations and each day difficulties arise from which we can never free ourselves. So, I am giving up the struggle once and for all, abandoning all hope of success, and I no longer have the strength to work in such conditions. I hear my friends are preparing another exhibition this year, but I must discount the possibility of participating in it, since I have nothing worth showing.*

This is Monet's midlife crisis. His wife is sick, his patron Hoschedé is bankrupt, and his paintings are not selling.

Camille died in Vétheuil in September 1879 and was buried there at Notre-Dame. The first thing Monet did after she died was to paint her. He produced a heartrending deathbed portrait of her, beautifully described by the art historian John Berger as "a terrible blizzard of loss." The following winter was even harsher, one of the coldest winters on record in France—so cold that it became known as the "Little Ice Age." The river froze, and great chunks of ice—ice floes—drifted down the Seine, thumping against the embankments. There are descriptions of the Monet family waking up in the morning to the thunderous noise of the ice breaking.

Hoschedé died in 1891, and one year later, Alice and Monet were married; together they brought up the eight children. A few years after leaving Vétheuil, the couple moved to Giverny, where they spent the rest of their lives and where Monet continued painting. Caillebotte, among others, helped support him, and from the 1880s onward, he enjoyed a successful career—very different from the challenging years in Vétheuil.

—X.S.

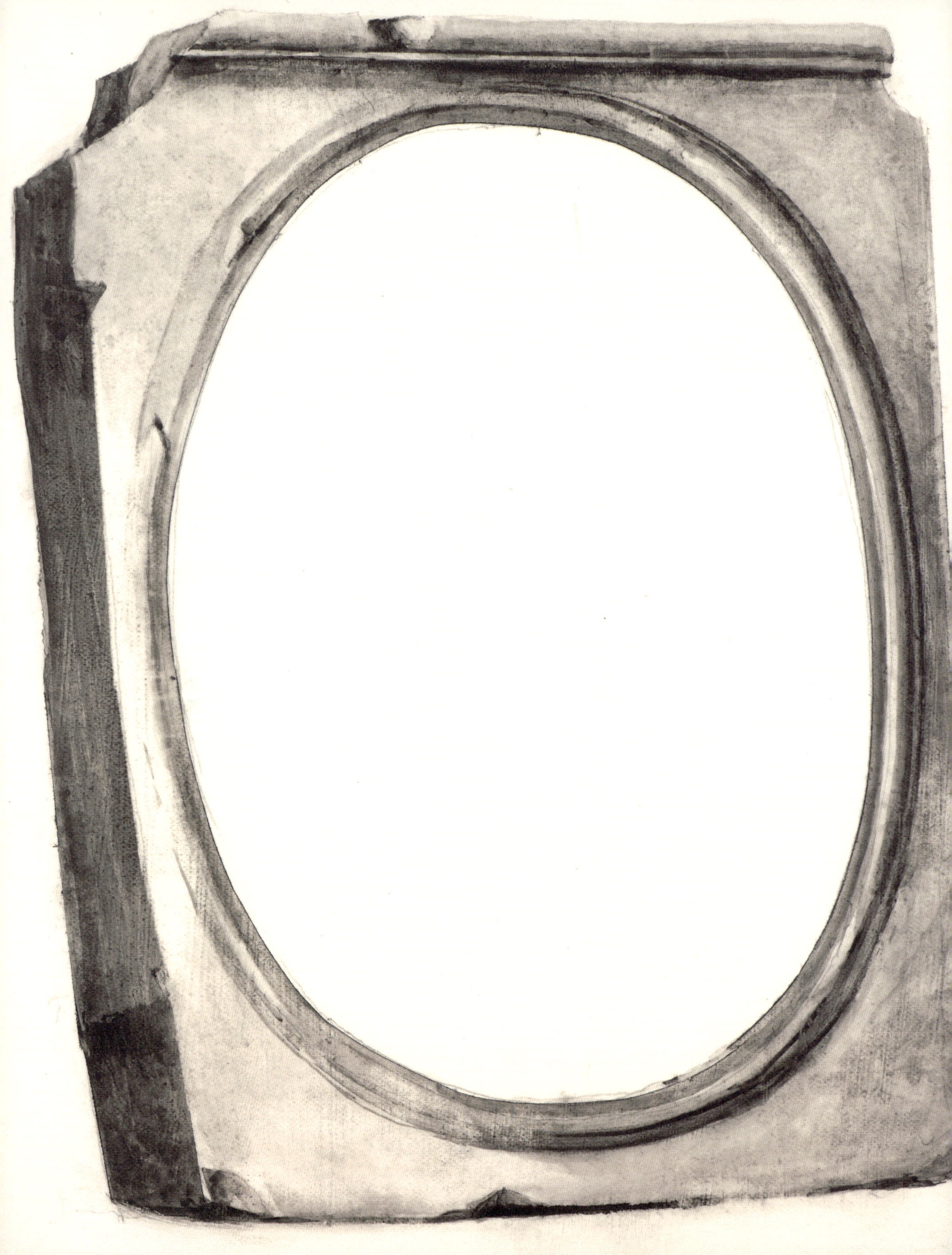

BARTOLOMÉ ESTEBÁN MURILLO

Self-Portrait

CA. 1650–55

Rebujito

1 OZ. FINO (DRY SHERRY)

4 OZ. LEMONADE

½ TSP. SUGAR

Serve on the rocks in a tall glass
and garnish with mint leaves

A Rebujito is typically drunk in the south of Spain, especially in Seville and in Jerez, around the time of the Ferias, the feasts in April and May. It is similar to a Gin and Tonic but made with Manzanilla (fino sherry) mixed with either sparkling lemonade or tonic water and fresh lemon juice, with a bit of sugar.

Of the many portraits at the Frick, only two are self-portraits, and coincidentally, they were painted in the same decade. One, by Rembrandt, was painted in Amsterdam in 1658. The other, by Bartolomé Estebán Murillo, was painted in the first half of the 1650s. The Murillo self-portrait was the first Spanish painting acquired by Henry Clay Frick, in 1904, but it wasn't until 2014 that it entered the collection, as a gift from the Frick family.

Murillo represents himself elegantly dressed in black with the starched linen collar known in Spanish as a *golilla*. His long flowing hair, mustache, and goatee identify him as an upper-class Sevillian. One of only two known self-portraits by the artist, this one was made for Murillo's family. The Latin inscription at the bottom was added after Murillo's death, probably by a later owner, maybe a Murillo family member. It tells us that this is the "true effigy" of Bartolomé Estebán Murillo, who was a famous painter, born in Seville in 1618 and deceased on the third day of the month of April of 1682. A second self-portrait, now in the National Gallery in London, was painted fifteen to twenty years later, about 1670.

Murillo was born in Seville in 1617—not 1618, as the inscription on the Frick self-portrait asserts—and spent his entire life there. The birth date discrepancy is probably due to his being born in very late December of 1617 and baptized in the early days of 1618. Seville had been powerful and wealthy in the sixteenth century, but in Murillo's lifetime, the city was in economic and social decline. The harbor was less active than it had been, with many of the maritime routes from Europe to the New World, Asia, and Africa shifting to other parts of Europe, especially England, the Netherlands, and Portugal.

Murillo became well known for his religious pictures—a popular genre in the seventeenth, eighteenth, and nineteenth centuries—but he also received other types of commissions. He made a series of paintings focusing on the poor children in Seville, as well as pictures of young Sevillian women and men gazing out of windows. He also worked as a portraitist, an aspect of his career that has not been studied much.

The Frick self-portrait has an unusual background. At the bottom is a stony ledge, on top of which is a block of carved stone that is chipped and broken. The portrait is contained within the carved stone, literally set in stone for posterity. This unusual framing device is meant to create a trompe l'oeil effect, fooling the viewer into seeing a parallel reality through the canvas. However, it is an impossible depiction: the man could not physically stand within this block of stone. Originally, the background, which now looks somewhat brownish, was blue, and the stone was set against an open sky.

Ruins appear in many of Murillo's works, even the religious paintings. Unlike Madrid, a city founded in the sixteenth century, Seville originated as an ancient Roman city, Hispalis. Many Roman ruins survive in Seville; one of the houses in which Murillo and his family lived was not far away from beautiful granite columns that were once part of an ancient Roman building. Just a few miles from Seville are the ruins of Italica, one of the largest cities in the Roman Empire and the birthplace of two emperors: Trajan and Hadrian. The ruins of Italica were not discovered and excavated until the nineteenth century, so

Murillo would not have known about them, but Seville had many antiquities that were known in his time. We have a very interesting glimpse of this moment from a document related to Murillo's collection of ancient coins. So, as much as Murillo is thought of as the great religious painter, he also engaged very directly with antiquity, particularly with the past of his own city.

Between 1648 and 1650, Seville was hit by the plague, one of the deadliest epidemics in the history of early modern Spain. A large portion of the population of Seville died. Many people Murillo knew died at that time, but he survived, and it has been argued that this portrait, probably painted in the early 1650s, was made as an ex-voto, an expression of thanks for having been spared.

In the self-portrait, Murillo is looking at Seville's ancient past, here alluded to by the ruined block of stone, and he is also looking ahead to the future. The portrait is intended for posterity, for future generations, for us. People hundreds of years after Murillo's death in 1682 are still looking at him through this portrait.

—X.S.

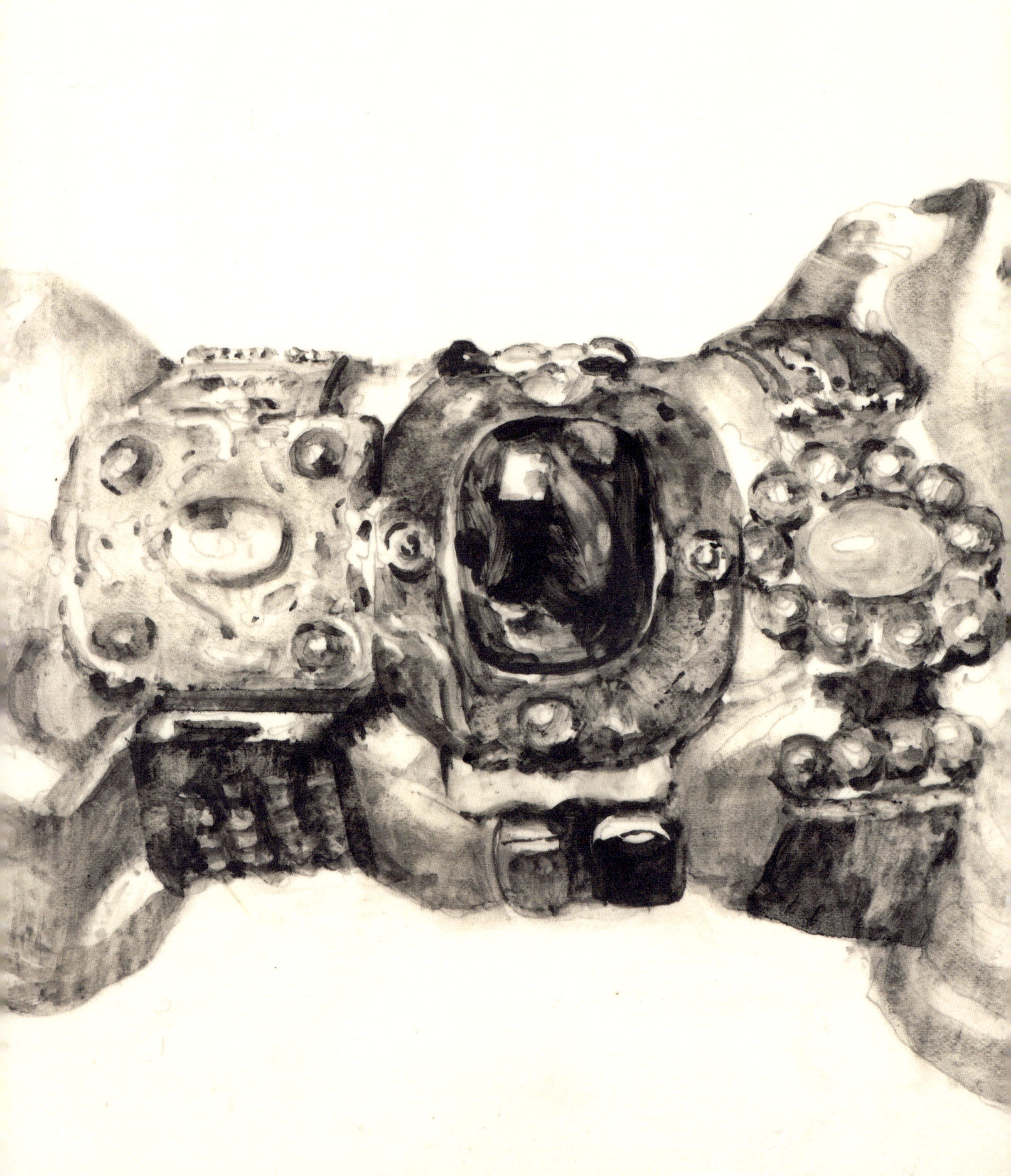

THOMAS LAWRENCE

Julia, Lady Peel

1827

Bijou

1½ OZ. GIN

¾ OZ. GREEN CHARTREUSE

1 OZ. SWEET VERMOUTH

2 DASHES OF ORANGE BITTERS

Stir with ice and strain into a chilled cocktail glass

The Bijou (French for "jewel" or "jewelry") was invented in the nineteenth century by the so-called father of modern bartending, Harry Johnson. It is so named because the three main ingredients—gin, chartreuse, and vermouth—represent the colors of the three precious stones diamonds, emeralds, and rubies. The drink is a fitting celebration of Lady Peel's stacks of bracelets and rings.

Thomas Lawrence (1769–1830) was arguably the most prominent portrait painter in Britain in the late eighteenth and early nineteenth centuries. Like Joshua Reynolds before him, Lawrence served as the Painter in Ordinary to King George III and as the president of the Royal Academy. Though he painted some of the most powerful people of his day in Europe—heads of state, royalty, and other influential people—it was this painting of Lady Peel that was widely thought to be his greatest portrait, perhaps even one of the great works of modern art up to that time. It was made late in his career, in 1827, just three years before his death, and exhibited at the Royal Academy summer exhibition of that year.

The painting's story begins with Lawrence's friendship with Lady Peel's husband, Sir Robert Peel, who served twice as prime minister of the United Kingdom. Peel may be best remembered for having established London's police force, the Metropolitan Police; to this day, a police officer in Britain is referred to as a "bobby" after him. He was also a serious art collector, primarily of Dutch and Flemish paintings; many of his paintings ended up at the National Gallery in London, where he served as a trustee.

After King George IV, Peel was Lawrence's greatest patron, commissioning from him a series of portraits of heads of state who had fought against Napoleon, as well as portraits of himself and his family, including a couple of portraits of his wife. The first, exhibited in 1825 at the Royal Academy, remains in a private collection. Two years later, in 1827, Lawrence painted the one now at the Frick. It garnered attention at its exhibition that year in part because of its connection to a well-known painting that had made its way into Robert Peel's collection just a few years earlier: Peter Paul Rubens's portrait, probably of Susanna Lunden, the sister of Rubens's future second wife, Helena Fourment, known as the *Chapeau de Paille* (now in the National Gallery, London). The painting made headlines when Peel acquired it. There are obvious similarities between the two paintings, made about two hundred years apart: the fact that both figures are set against a stormy sky, for instance, or the bright red accents in the sitters' accessories. But they're very different in character. For example, where the sitter looks out coyly from the shadow cast by the brim of her large hat in the *Chapeau de Paille*, Lady Peel offers instead a confident and dignified authority. Her authority and ease are evident despite what is by any measure an extravagant and flamboyant outfit topped with a cascade of red feathers streaming from her broad hat. She is probably wearing what the British call "fancy dress," meaning a frivolous costume, as opposed to what would be fashionable for women to wear out on the streets of London every day.

When you look closely, you can see the range of paint handling throughout the composition. Each eyebrow hair and eyelash is articulated as if with a casual stroke, just a moment's thought, effortlessly. Peel's earnest eyes belie the labor required to plot the paint on the canvas with such meticulous care; it is as if it all appeared naturally. Elsewhere in the painting, such as where the red feathers meet the fur trim of her mantle, the paint is applied as if at random, abstractedly. At the very right appears just a hint of a landscape in a few strokes.

The portrait became famous, and shortly after it was exhibited in 1827, two prints after it were made and circulated: a line engraving by Charles Heath that served as the cover of a publication and a mezzotint by Samuel Cousins. And along with Lawrence's portrait, Lady Peel herself became well known.

Julia Floyd was born in 1795 in India, in Chennai—then under British rule—where her father worked in the British military. She lived there until the age of five, at which point she, her parents, and her three siblings moved to England. Tragedy struck early in her life. When she was seven, her mother and her eldest sister died of scarlet fever. Her father remarried, and she was well taken care of; but he, too, died before she got married. Thus, by the time she met and married Robert Peel in 1820, at age twenty-five, she had lost both her parents and a sibling. By all accounts, however, the marriage was a very happy one.

There can be a cynical view of women like Lady Peel who are known to history merely as the wives of important men. I would like to look at this differently and honor women—and it is not always women, but it most often is—who support their spouses and their families within the home, either by choice or compelled by circumstance. Julia made it possible for her husband to serve his country twice as prime minister. This is known from the evidence of the letters between them and with other people, which make it clear how much she supported him. She was not a politician herself, but she suffered every anxiety with him as a confidante and counsel. She was recognized for this role by others, for supporting him through his successes and also through his failures. For there were failures: Peel is remembered as a great politician, but his first term as prime minister lasted only four months before his government collapsed. One can imagine the ups and downs and the important role that she played for him then.

She was devastated when Robert Peel died in 1850. Respects were paid to her by a number of heads of state; even Queen Victoria paid her a visit. The queen of France, Maria Amalia, sent notes of condolence. Nicholas I of Russia did too, among others. She was, in a sense, recognized for her place and her loss. She was even offered a peerage. This would have elevated her title and changed her name, but she refused it. She wanted to keep the name her husband had given her, saying that she always wanted to be remembered only as the wife of her husband. That she is.

—A.N.

JOHANNES VERMEER

Mistress and Maid

1666–68

Genever Brûlée

2 OZ. GENEVER

1 TSP. BROWN SUGAR

A FEW DASHES OF CLASSIC BITTERS

A DASH OF ORANGE BITTERS

A SPLASH OF SPARKLING WATER

Serve in a cocktail glass and garnish with a caramelized orange slice

Made with the traditional Dutch liquor genever, which was both a precursor to British gin and the legendary source of the term "Dutch courage," this is the perfect concoction for warming up on a cold winter's day.

Like so many of Vermeer's paintings, this one may have been painted in the second-floor studio of the artist's home in Delft, where he is thought to have spent his entire life. So little is known about Vermeer (1632–1675) that he has been called the "Sphinx of Delft." Though today he is one of the most famous artists of the early modern period in Europe, he struggled financially during his

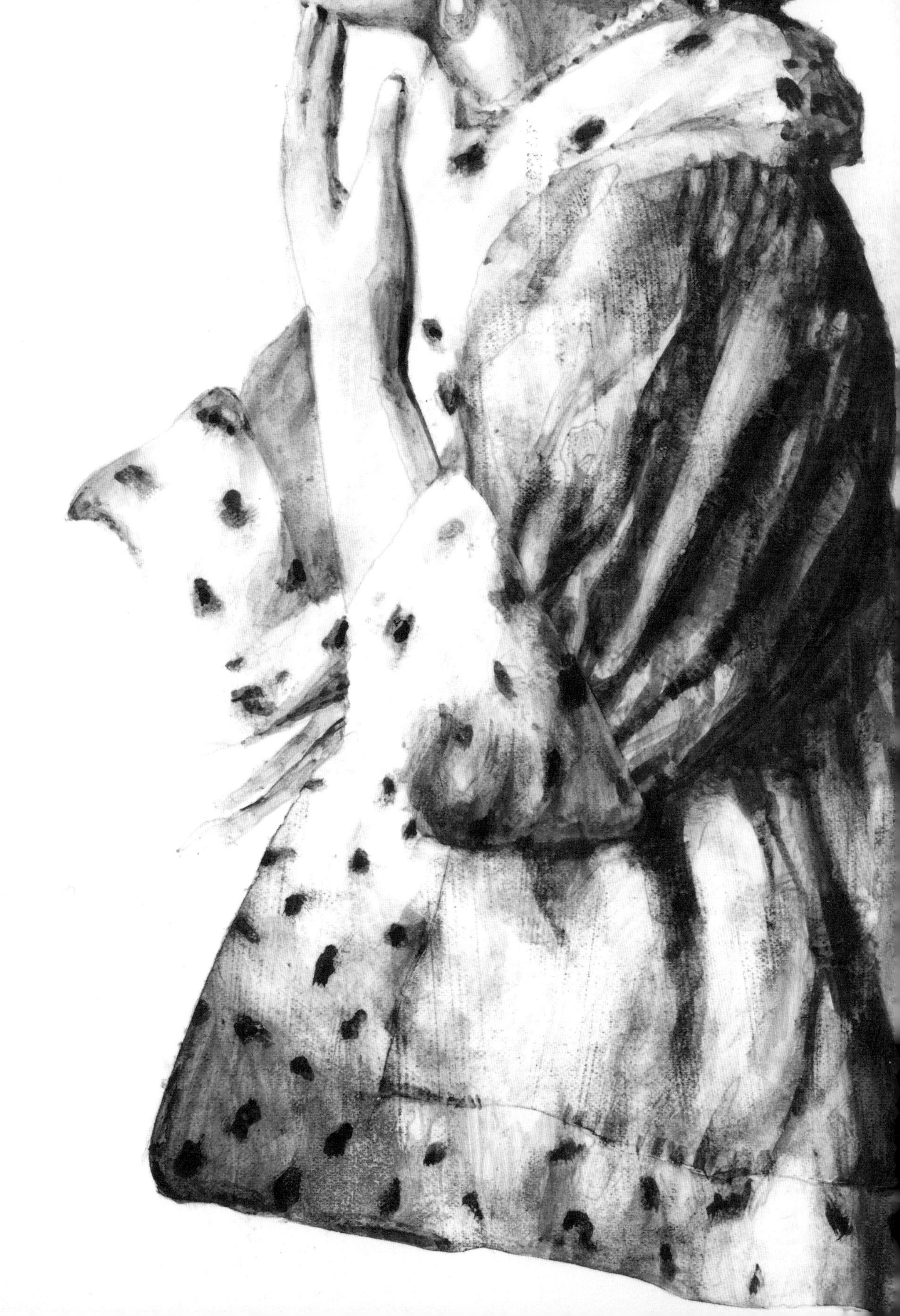

short life, dying nearly bankrupt at the age of forty-three. He is best known for compositions like this, interior scenes of everyday life with remarkable attention paid to the details of objects and the fall of light on figures and on surfaces.

The "mistress and maid" theme was popular in seventeenth-century Dutch genre painting. Vermeer painted two other scenes on this topic: in one, now in the National Gallery of Ireland, the maid waits for a letter to be written by her employer; in the other, now in the Rijksmuseum, the maid seems to sneer as she interrupts her employer to pass her a letter. The paintings are full of intrigue, quiet drama, and mystery. They stir viewers to wonder, what is in the letter? Who is it from? Who is the mistress writing to? Does she have a lover? What is the maid's role in each one of these? Each one tells a slightly different story but is a variation on the theme.

It is not often that a famous work of art made hundreds of years ago can offer new discoveries today, but such is the case with this painting. Of the thirty-four unanimously accepted paintings by Vermeer known today, three are in the Frick's collection, and of these, *Mistress and Maid* is somewhat unusual. It is much larger than the other two Vermeer paintings and than Vermeer's paintings in general. For this reason, it has been suggested that *Mistress and Maid* was commissioned to be installed in a particular place, perhaps above a mantelpiece. Also unusual is the relatively flat and dark background. In his other domestic scenes, Vermeer typically enriches the space with wall maps, paintings, curtains, and tapestries. *Mistress and Maid* instead seems as if it is set on a stage, the dark background forcing the figures into the immediate foreground and heightening the drama between them.

Looking closely, viewers can get a sense of the luxury in the scene, including costly goods imported into Europe through a network of global trade, such as the seated woman's massive hanging pearl earring, probably harvested in the Gulf of Mannar between India and Sri Lanka. Like large pearls that appear in other paintings by Vermeer, this one is so big, and presumably so expensive, that it has been suggested by some scholars that it is a fake, made of polished silver or tin or glass, perhaps exaggerated by the artist in paint. The objects on the table include a glass and silver writing set, and the seated woman has just put down her pen. It has been suggested that the veneered box on the left, possibly holding writing materials or letters, was made in Goa, a Portuguese colony at the time. The rumpled blue tablecloth would itself have been an object of value.

The woman raises her hand to her chin, a gesture that communicates concern or surprise. What has the maid said? What is in the letter she is passing? Some have suggested that the painting seems unfinished because of the lack of detail in areas like that hand to her chin, the ringlets in her hair. But they are not unfinished. Technical examinations show that these are areas of thinly applied paint, in line with Vermeer's later technique, a gentle layering of paints that over the course of centuries have become more and more translucent and, in some cases, altered in color. The evolution of paint over time has also affected the dark background. It is not actually a flat black background: there are ghostly lines that suggest a curtain pulled toward the right. These clues led to an interesting discovery, led by the Frick's former Associate Research Curator Margaret Iacono and conservators at the Metropolitan Museum of Art, with colleagues at the Doerner Institute in Munich.

It has been determined that the dark background was applied by Vermeer and not by a later hand. It was originally much greener in tone, with the curtain drawn to the right. The tablecloth, too, has transformed in color, also due to changes in pigments over the centuries; it was originally green. Intriguingly, a green tablecloth was included in the list of Vermeer's possessions at the end of his life.

The green (now nearly black) curtain was, in effect, Vermeer's Plan B, painted over a discarded first idea. When conservators examined the painting, they discovered a set of figures painted in the background. They are not articulated in detail, but at least four figures were blocked in. Vermeer had originally planned a figural background, perhaps a tapestry hanging behind the figures of the mistress and maid, which would have been in line with his treatment of other paintings. For unknown reasons, he abandoned that idea and painted a curtain over the background figures, changing the composition entirely to focus the drama on the mistress and maid and the power of that letter to cause the woman to drop that pen.

Mistress and Maid holds a special place in the Frick's collection. This was the very last item Henry Clay Frick brought into his collection, in 1919. He had already determined in 1915, shortly after he and his family had moved into the new house at 1 East 70th Street, that the home would one day open as a public museum, after his death and the death of his wife. Months after acquiring *Mistress and Maid,* he fell ill and died, at the age of sixty-nine. This celebrated painting offers a fitting end, on a high note, to Henry Clay Frick's collecting practice.

—A.N.

MALVINA CORNELL HOFFMAN

Henry Clay Frick

1922

Old Fashioned

1½ OZ. BOURBON

1 SUGAR CUBE

2 DASHES OF ANGOSTURA BITTERS

Serve on the rocks in a whiskey glass and garnish with an orange peel and a maraschino cherry

Henry Clay Frick began his career working as an accountant in his maternal grandfather's whiskey company, the Overholt distillery, in western Pennsylvania. An Old Fashioned is an appropriate cocktail for Frick himself but also in some ways for The Frick Collection.

In the Frick's archives, we have an intriguing letter sent to Henry Clay Frick by John Singer Sargent: "I beg to state that if the object of your visit should happen to be a commission for portraiture, I feel bound to inform you that I'm not taking any commissions and not adding any promises to those I have already made for the future." Asking Sargent to paint his portrait may very well

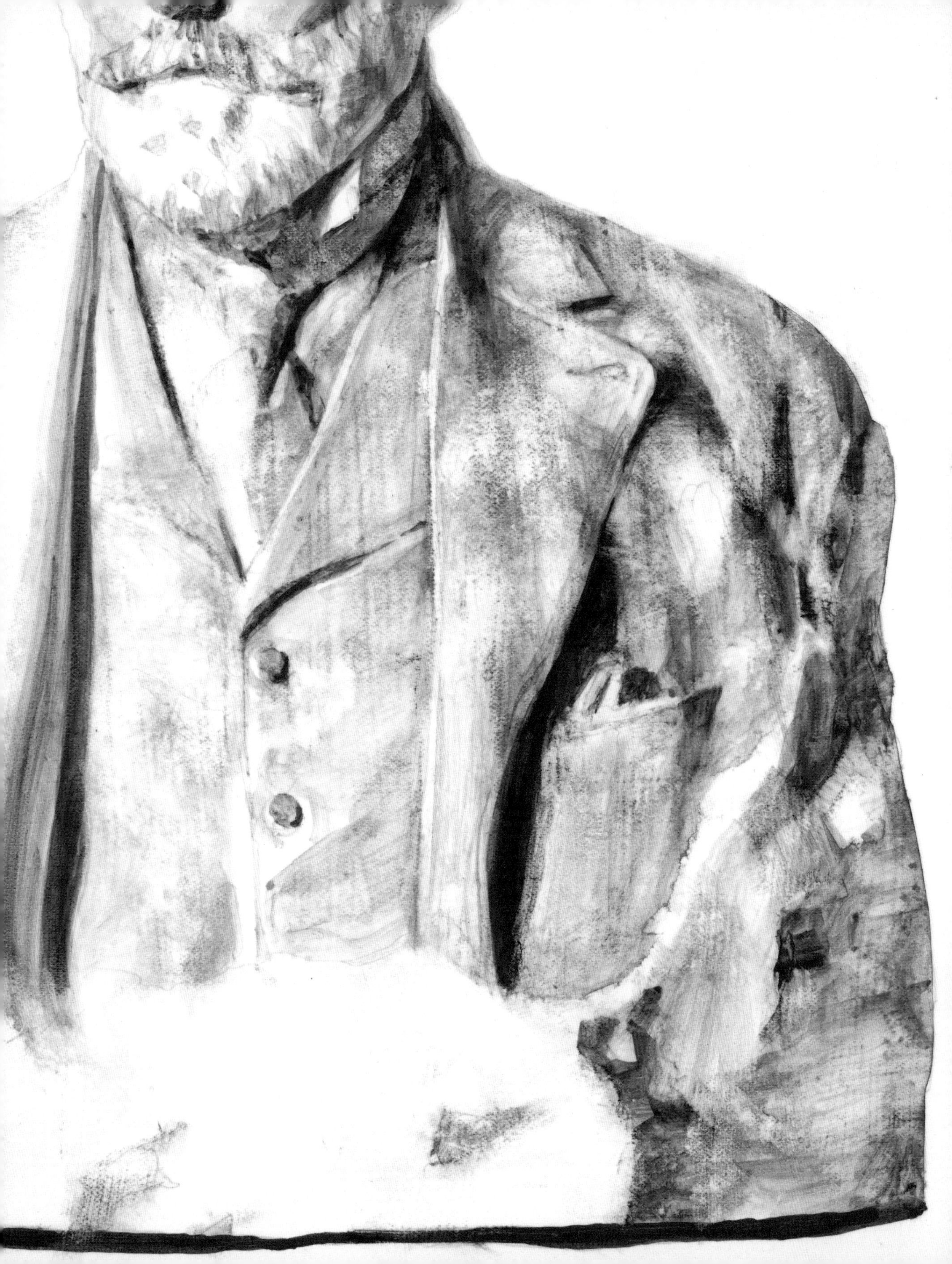

have been the purpose of Frick's proposed visit. Unfortunately for posterity, Sargent never portrayed him. The Frick Collection does, however, have a few portraits of its founder, all of them posthumous and most commissioned by his daughter for the museum. Among these is the life-size marble bust by the American sculptor Malvina Cornell Hoffman (1885–1966).

Ever since the museum opened in 1935, the Hoffman bust—one of the Frick's very few works by a female artist—has been in the Entrance Hall. Most of Hoffman's sculptures are in bronze, some in stone. During the artist's lifetime, she was especially known for sculptures of groups of dancers. She was also celebrated for her portraits. One of her most beautiful works is *Martinique Woman* (now at the Brooklyn Museum), which was carved about 1928 and is made of a lovely polished black stone. Despite its title, it is not known whether the sitter was from Martinique. Even though at that time large stone sculptures were typically commissioned from male artists, Hoffman worked on a number of large-scale projects of this type.

Among her works are two large sculptures that grace the magnificent entrance to Bush House. Built in London in the 1920s as an international trade center, it was one of the most lavish and expensive buildings erected in the British capital at the time. It later became the headquarters of the BBC and now serves a number of different purposes. The Hoffman sculptures are of men holding a flame together and bearing the coats of arms of the United Kingdom and of the United States to represent the friendship between the two countries. There is a wonderful photograph from the 1920s that shows Hoffman putting the finishing touches on the figure representing the United Kingdom as it is placed in situ at Bush House.

Hoffman was famous during her lifetime for a series of more than one hundred life-size sculptures commissioned by the Field Museum in Chicago for a permanent exhibition called *The Hall of Man* or *The Races of Mankind*. To create these sculptures, Hoffman traveled widely and made sketches illustrating the physical variations of people of different races around the world. Controversy over the "types" documented eventually led to the racial exhibition's deinstallation in the 1960s.

Henry Clay Frick commissioned from Hoffman a bust of his beloved daughter Helen Clay, and as soon as the portrait was completed, shortly after Frick's death in 1919, Helen Clay commissioned Hoffman to make a bust of her father. Started in 1920 and completed in 1922, it was based partly on photographs, partly on memory. Hoffman had met Frick while working on the portrait of Helen Clay. The bust was reproduced in a number of versions, in many ways becoming the key image representing Frick. The primary version is the one at the Frick, made for the museum. There is also a plaster version, possibly preparatory and painted as if made in bronze, that Hoffman gave to the New-York Historical Society in the 1960s with a group of other portraits in plaster. Helen Clay commissioned two further marbles of the same size. One was intended for Clayton, the family house in Pittsburgh, which is now part of the Frick Pittsburgh. The second one was displayed in the foyer of the Frick Building in Pittsburgh, the headquarters of the Frick business, built for Henry Clay Frick. A bronze version is at the McKinley Memorial Library, a library in Niles, Ohio, to which Frick had donated some funds.

Hoffman also worked on a portrait of Frick for the Frick Building of the University of Pittsburgh. It was largely sponsored by Helen Clay Frick, who was very interested both in art history and in her father's legacy. She funded the Art History Department at the University of Pittsburgh. At the center of the facade of the building is a portrait of Frick. This was made about 1922, at the same time as the marble bust. A plaster life-size model for it is at the Frick, where you see, almost like a giant medal, the image of Frick in profile with the dates of his birth (1849) and death (1919). This was given to the Frick by the Malvina Hoffman Estate in 1967, a year after she died.

Notwithstanding the fact that Henry Clay Frick was already a controversial figure during his lifetime and also that some of Malvina Hoffman's works are contentious today, the Frick is fortunate to be able to recognize the founder of the museum through the extraordinary work of a woman artist.

—X.S.

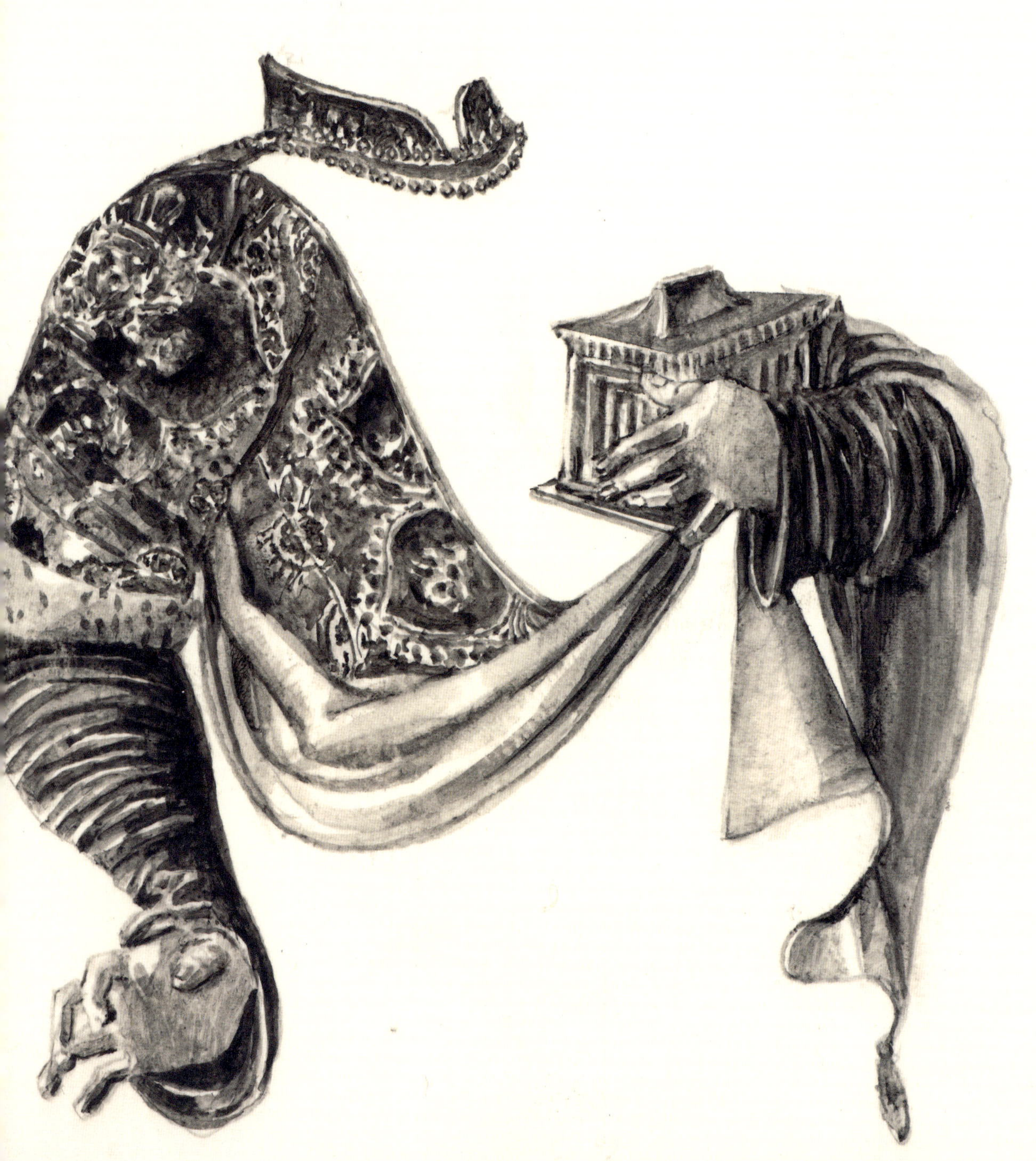

LAZZARO BASTIANI

Adoration of the Magi

1470s

Cranberry Bourbon

EQUAL PARTS:

BOURBON

CRANBERRY JUICE

Serve on the rocks in a whiskey glass and
garnish with a fresh rosemary sprig

With its red color, this drink is particularly fitting for the festive winter season, especially for the holiday period in late December and early January, between Christmas and the Epiphany.

This small painting depicts the Adoration of the Magi, a New Testament episode following the birth of Jesus that is celebrated during the Feast of the Epiphany, on January 6. Traditionally named Melchior, Balthazar, and Gaspar, the Magi are three mythical kings who were alerted to the birth of the Messiah by a star. The kings came from different lands—Africa, Asia, and Europe. Guided by the star, they first went to Jerusalem, where they met with

King Herod, and then to Bethlehem, where they worshipped Jesus and gave him gifts of gold, frankincense, and myrrh. In the Frick painting, the journey of the Magi is depicted in the landscape; from a distant land on the horizon they arrive in Jerusalem and then, in the foreground, in Bethlehem and the stable where Christ was born. A wonderful element in this painting are the angels announcing the birth of Christ. Shown in groups on small clouds that look like flying saucers, they are reading from scrolls and singing. The angels are painted in different colors, each color a symbol of the angel's place in the traditional angelic hierarchy.

The painting was purchased by The Frick Collection in 1935 as a work by Bartolomeo Vivarini, who was a member of a large family of painters, originally from Murano, whose workshop in Venice was the rival of Bellini's. The painting belonged to an English collection in the nineteenth century and then entered the collection of John Pierpont Morgan, from whose heirs the Frick bought it. Even though the traditional attribution to Vivarini was accepted by the celebrated art historian Bernard Berenson, other scholars started questioning it. There had already been alternative authors proposed—for example, Andrea da Murano and Quirizio da Murano. These attributions were superseded by the one to Lazzaro Bastiani, which is now unanimously accepted.

Bastiani is an important Venetian artist of the 1460s and '70s, but we know very little about him. He was probably born in Venice and is documented from at least as early as 1456 until his death in 1512. We do not know where he trained. We know he was active for most of his life in the parish of the Arcangelo Raffaele, an unusual area for artists in Venice, most of whom were in San Lio and Santa Maria Formosa, parishes that were much closer to the center, and Rialto. His brother, Marco, was also a painter.

Bastiani was paid as much for his paintings as were members of the Bellini family. In 1508, he was one of the small group of artists whose judgment was so trusted that he was asked to provide estimates for the works by Giorgione on the facade of the Fondaco dei Tedeschi, the German mercantile headquarters in Venice on the Grand Canal. He was known for portraits, as well as for his large narrative paintings, which were exhibited in *scuole* (headquarters of lay charitable confraternities). Later on, Bastiani was the teacher of Vittore Carpaccio, another great painter of narrative scenes.

The Frick picture is probably a devotional painting. Bastiani painted them for a wide range of patrons, one of whom was Antonio Corradi, who lived in Pera (the European side of the Golden Horn in Istanbul). Corradi wrote to Venice asking for a painting of Christ. He specified that he would like to have this work painted by Lazzaro Bastiani, and if Bastiani could not do it, then he would like to have it painted by Bellini. The priest Giovanni degli

Angeli commissioned from Lazzaro a lunette for the church of San Donato in Murano, signed and dated by the artist in 1484. It shows the Virgin and Child enthroned in a wonderful architectural setting, set in a landscape, with St. John the Baptist on the left and St. Donato, the patron of the church, on the right. Degli Angeli is shown kneeling in this painting. Another important work by Bastiani is his St. Jerome, an almost life-size painting in the Diocesan Museum of Monopoli, in southern Italy. It was painted for the Cathedral of Monopoli, and the man who commissioned it, Saladino Ferro, is portrayed as a donor in it. A doctor of Jewish origins who had converted to Christianity, Ferro sponsored a chapel in the cathedral of his city. The patron of the Frick's *Adoration of the Magi*, unfortunately, remains anonymous.

—X.S.

CLODION and JEAN-BAPTISTE LEPAUTE

The Dance of Time: Three Nymphs Supporting a Clock

1788

Metropolitan

2 OZ. BRANDY

1 OZ. SWEET VERMOUTH

1 TSP. SIMPLE SYRUP

2 DASHES OF ANGOSTURA BITTERS

Serve chilled in a martini glass

This cocktail celebrates life in a city like New York, punctuated by our clocks and watches, as we go about our daily routines.

So much in our lives depends on the measuring of time. We divide the years into seasons and months and weeks and days, and we subdivide the days into hours and minutes and seconds. And to do so we have always relied on instruments—sundials, clocks, watches, and now cell phones. It is not surprising that people

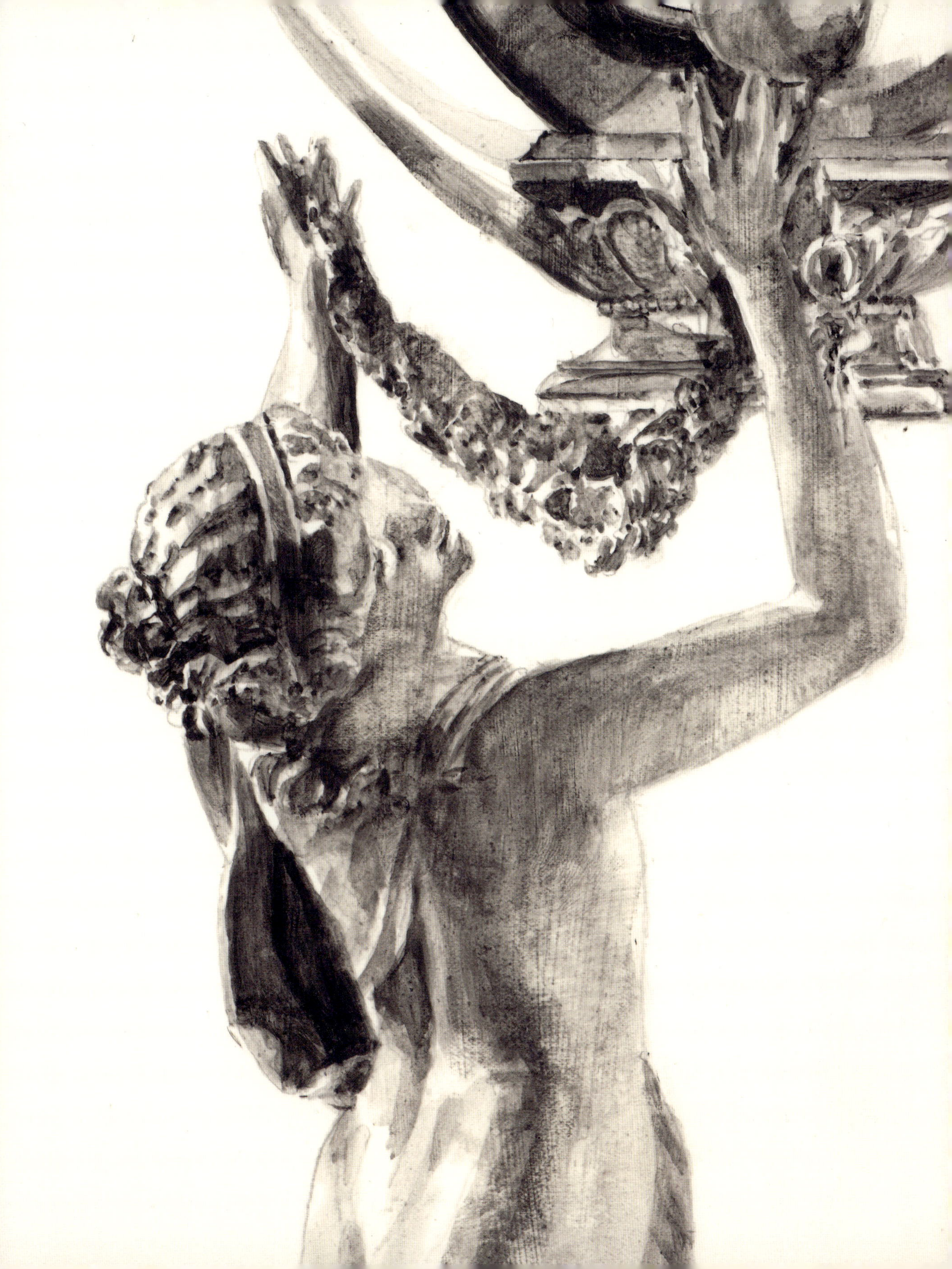

have always collected these instruments. One of these collectors was Winthrop Kellogg Edey (1938–1999), who donated his important collection to the Frick. Edey was a great expert in the field and a New York society figure. He was particularly close to Robert Mapplethorpe and Andy Warhol, for whom he modeled in Warhol's film portraits *Screen Tests,* some of which were filmed in Edey's Upper West Side townhouse. In 1982–83, Edey curated an exhibition of French clocks for the Frick. In addition to donating his significant collection to the museum, he also left funds for subsequent acquisitions in the field, such as this clock, which was purchased in 2006.

Made around 1788, this extraordinary work of art is the result of the collaboration of Jean-Baptiste Lepaute (1727–1802), Louis XV's and Louis XVI's clockmaker, and the wonderful French sculptor Clodion (1738–1814), who created the terracotta structure that holds the clock. One of the most wonderful French sculptors of his time, Clodion was born Claude Michel in Nancy, in northeastern France, into a family of sculptors. His father was a minor sculptor, and his mother was related to another dynasty of sculptors, the Adam family. His life, like those of artists such as David and Fragonard, spanned the period of time from the ancien régime to the French Revolution to the Napoleonic era. In 1755, he moved from Nancy to Paris, where he worked first with his maternal uncle and then with Pigalle, one of the great sculptors of the time. He drew much of his inspiration from antiquity, which he studied between 1762 and 1771, when he was based in Rome. Clodion married Flore, the daughter of another sculptor, Augustin Pajou, but the unhappy marriage ended in divorce. While he worked in metal, stone, and marble, his most famous works remain his terracottas, which were very avidly collected in the United States in the late nineteenth and early twentieth centuries. Clodion died in Paris on the eve of the fall of Napoleon.

I like the fact that this object was made for an architect, Alexandre-Théodore Brongniart. The idea of measuring time, and these beautiful figures dancing around time, is very appropriate for someone engaged in spatial design.

Enclosed in the original glass dome, which would have been difficult to fabricate at the end of the eighteenth century, the Lepaute clock is a great feat of technology. The female figures below the clock are the work of Clodion. We do not know what they represent or who they are, if they are nymphs or if they are Hours, the goddesses of the seasons. The allegory of the Dance of the Hours has a long tradition in the Western world. Clodion's women dancing around the clock allude to the cyclical nature of time, with the change of seasons, and the twenty-four hours of the day.

Poussin's *Dance to the Music of Time* (Wallace Collection, London) is one of the most celebrated representations of this subject. Painted about 1636 for

Cardinal Giulio Rospigliosi, who later became Pope Clement IX, it shows Time as an old man playing an instrument, surrounded by figures dancing to the music of time, just like the Clodion clock. There are four figures in the painting, so they probably represent the four seasons, while in the clock there are only three. At the top of the clock is Apollo, his chariot an allusion to how the hours of the day and the change of day to night are calculated by referring to the course of the sun.

Poussin's celebrated canvas inspired the great twentieth-century British novel *A Dance to the Music of Time* by Anthony Powell, a monumental work divided into four movements and written between 1951 and 1975.

—X.S.

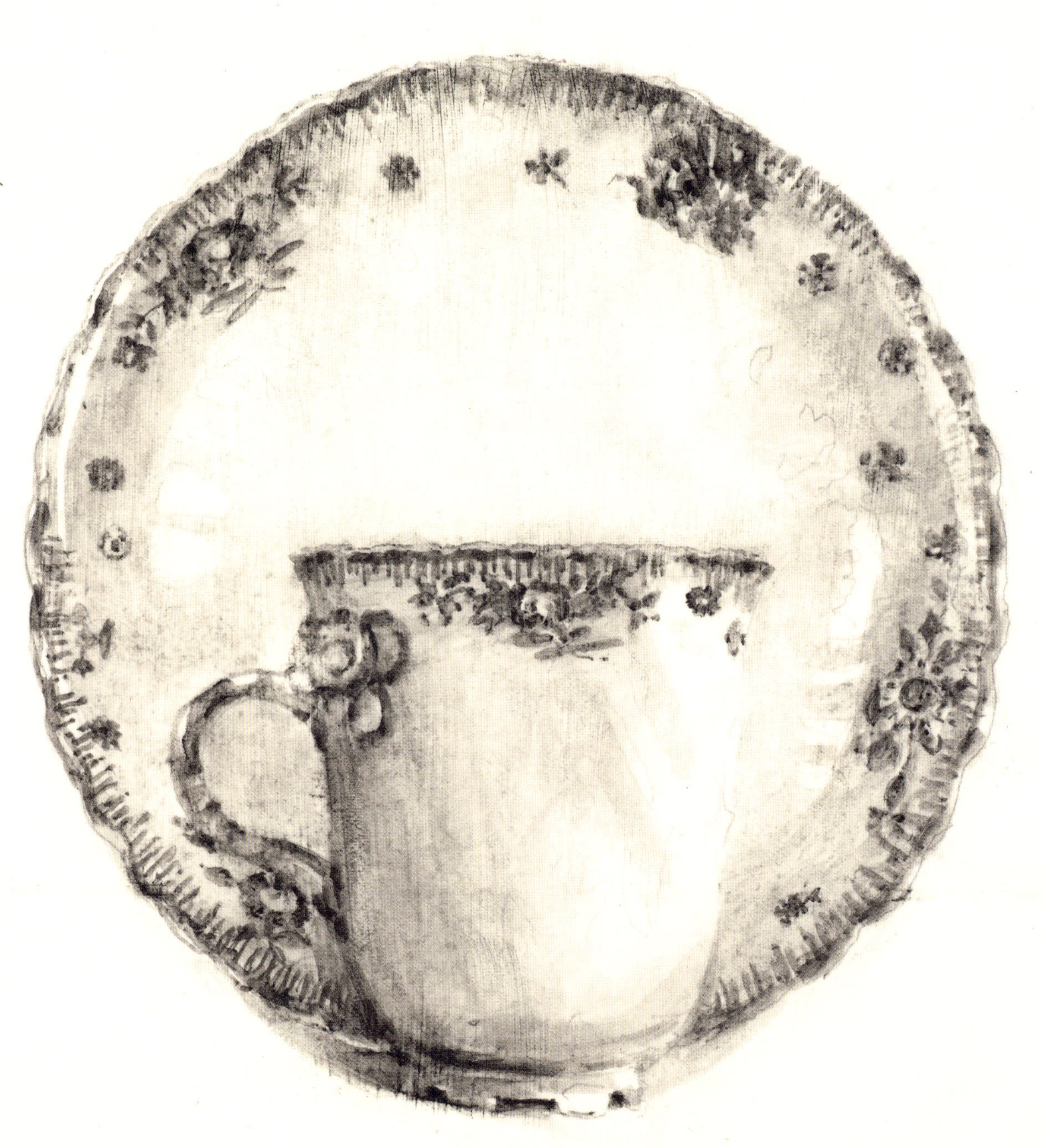

MEISSEN PORCELAIN MANUFACTORY

The "Swan" Service

CA. 1737–40

Spiked Chocolate

HOT CHOCOLATE

DARK RUM

Add dark rum to the chocolate according to taste
Serve in a porcelain cup and garnish with whipped cream

In the eighteenth century, the chocolate, coffee, and tea that had recently come from Mexico, Arabia, and China, respectively, were drunk from porcelain cups. A spiked chocolate can be served with different types of alcohol. I like mine best with dark rum.

A formula for porcelain, invented centuries earlier in China, was devised in Europe under the reign of Augustus II, Elector of Saxony and King of Poland—known as Augustus the Strong—whose son, Augustus III, was also deeply interested in the material. For the grand ceremony that took place in Kraków for the crowning of Augustus III as King of Poland on January 17, 1734, the

Meissen Porcelain Manufactory produced the so-called Coronation Service. Decorated with the arms of the House of Wettin, to which Augustus belonged, quartered with those of the Polish Commonwealth at its center, the service was for display only as the guests at the coronation ate on silver dishes. One of the dishes from the service is at the Frick, given to the museum by the eminent collector Henry H. Arnhold.

An even more splendid service was the "Swan" Service, made for Count Heinrich von Brühl (1700–1763) and one of the most famous porcelain services ever made. The Frick's two pieces—a spicebox and a cup and saucer—were bequeathed to the museum by Henry Arnhold. While the service takes its name from its primary decoration, two herons are also depicted.

Brühl was Augustus III's prime minister and one of the most powerful men in Europe at the time. When Augustus II died in Warsaw, in 1733, it was Brühl who made sure that his most important belongings were sent back to Dresden. He was also an important fundraiser in the election of Augustus III. Under the new king, Brühl swiftly became the most influential man in Saxony and Poland. He spent his life between the two capitals—Dresden and Warsaw—living in palaces that were enlarged and entirely redecorated for him. Unfortunately, neither building exists anymore. The Brühl Palace in Dresden was demolished in 1900. Today, near its site, is Brühl's Terrace, a promenade overlooking the Elbe River. As for the palace in Warsaw, it was destroyed during World War II. There have been discussions in recent years about rebuilding it where it stood, near the so-called Saxon Palace and Garden. The story of Brühl and the "Swan" Service is one of both creation and destruction. Dresden and Warsaw were arguably the two most beautiful cities in Germany and Poland and were altogether destroyed between 1944 and 1945.

Brühl had a very important library and was also a great collector of paintings and drawings and all kinds of luxurious goods. He was something of a compulsive buyer and is known to have had an incredible collection of clothes, shoes, and watches. Many of his paintings and most of his drawings were eventually acquired by Catherine the Great, whose collection became the cornerstone of the Hermitage Museum, which she founded.

Apart from being a politician and art collector, Brühl was also the supervisor of the Meissen Porcelain Manufactory from 1733 and its director from 1739. Supposedly a gift from the king, the "Swan" Service was made for him in the late 1730s, starting around 1736. It was designed by one of the great artists working at the Meissen Porcelain Manufactory, Johann Joachim Kändler, together with Johann Friedrich Eberlein and Johann Gottlieb Eder. Each piece is made of white porcelain and decorated with aquatic iconography, which is a reference to his surname—Brühl—which in German means "marshland." The swans and herons are always shown surrounded by wetlands and amid bulrushes, elements Kändler studied in the natural history collection in Dresden. The service is partly gilt and decorated with what were known as "Indian flowers," small flowers based on Asian designs. The Brühl coat of arms appears on each piece.

The "Swan" Service included more than two thousand pieces for diverse uses—enough for a banquet at the Brühl Palace, which would typically include eighty to a hundred courses. Over time, the service was dispersed, some given away by Brühl's heirs and many pieces destroyed. About a quarter of the service probably survives today in public and private collections. The largest group of objects is at the National Museum in Warsaw, which has almost one hundred pieces.

The Brühl family kept the "Swan" Service at Schloss Pförten, which is now in the Polish town of Brody. The impressive residence survived until 1945, when the Red Army destroyed the building, as well as what was left of the service. According to local reports, some of the pieces were used to feed animals, and some were used as shooting targets. There are accounts of the Russians driving tractors in fields covered with pieces of the "Swan" Service. Even in recent times, people in the area of Brody would find shards in the fields around the castle.

The story of the senseless destruction of the "Swan" Service in Brody (and of the miraculous survival of part of it) reminds me of a poem by the Polish writer Czesław Miłosz. Titled "Song on Porcelain," this beautiful meditation on the fragility of humankind was written in 1947, when Miłosz was in exile in Washington, DC. The poem begins:

Rose-colored cup and saucer,
Flowery demitasses:
You lie beside the river
Where an armored column passes.
Winds from across the meadow
Sprinkle the banks with down;
A torn apple tree's shadow
Falls on the muddy path;
The ground everywhere is strewn
With bits of brittle froth—
Of all things broken and lost
Porcelain troubles me most.

—X.S.

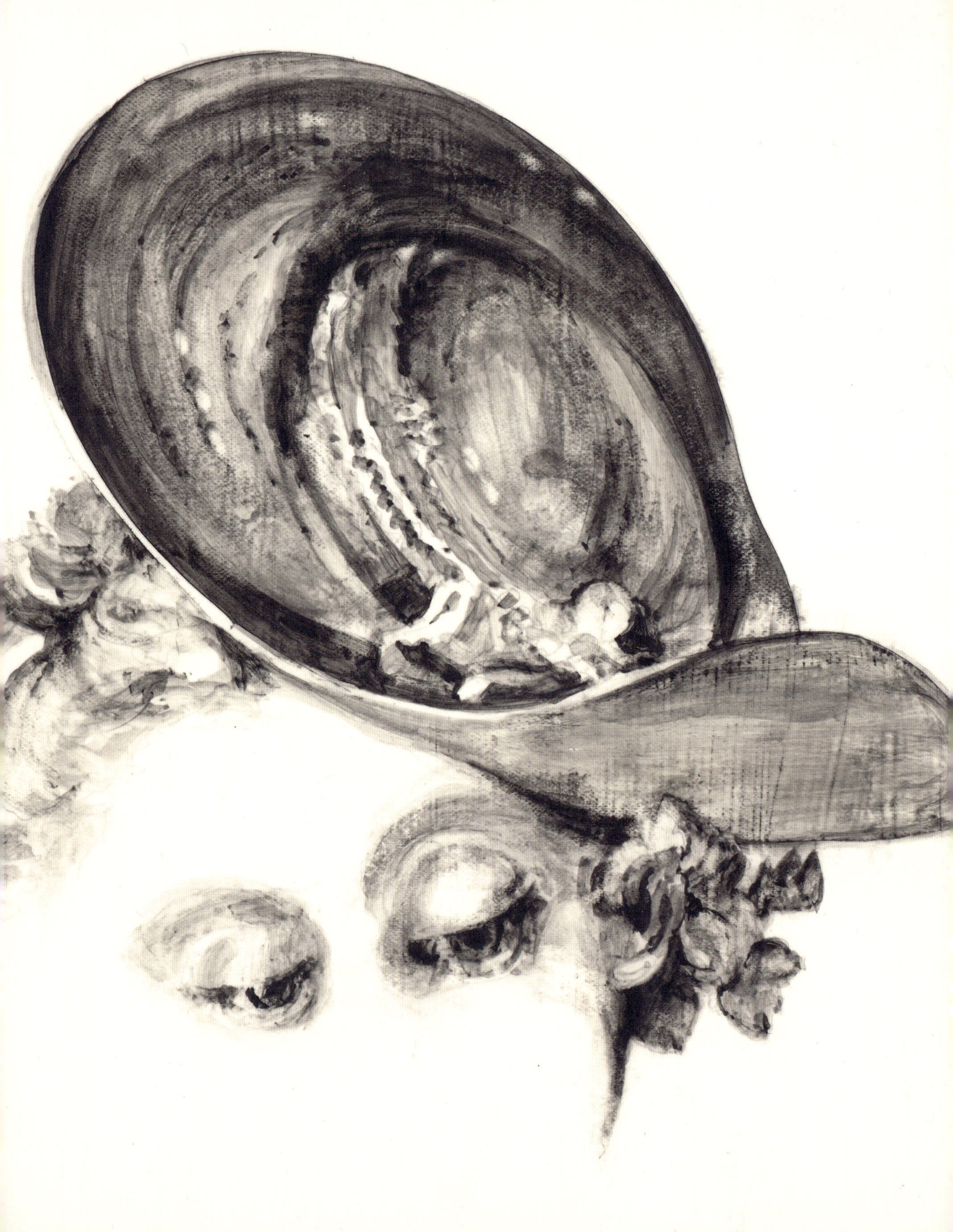

FRANÇOIS BOUCHER

The Four Seasons

1755

Time Regained

2 OZ. SCOTCH WHISKEY

¾ OZ. DRY VERMOUTH

½ OZ. PISCO

¼ OZ. JASMINE TEA SYRUP
(EQUAL PARTS OF COLD JASMINE TEA AND SUGAR)

Serve chilled in a cocktail glass

The four seasons symbolize the cyclical aspect of nature. A Time Regained is, of course, a cocktail in honor of Marcel Proust's masterpiece of the same name—one of the greatest novels ever written—the main subject of which is time.

Eighteenth-century French art—paintings, sculpture, and decorative arts—was an area of collecting in which Henry Clay Frick became interested toward the end of his life. One of these late acquisitions was Boucher's *Four Seasons,* which Frick purchased in 1916, three years before he died. The odd shape of the four canvases suggests that they were probably created as overdoors. They are signed by the artist and dated 1755. Soon after, they were engraved by Jean Daullé, and the prints were dedicated to Madame de Pompadour, which suggests that the canvases were originally painted for her.

Madame de Pompadour was the mistress of King Louis XV for almost twenty years, from 1745 until her death in 1764. Pompadour was a great patron of the arts—of the porcelain made at Sèvres and of painters such as Boucher (1703–1770), who painted her portrait a number of times. She also commissioned paintings by Boucher, such as the monumental *Sunrise* and *Sunset* (Wallace Collection, London).

In a theme that dates back to antiquity, the seasons are usually represented by figurative allegories, accompanied by symbols such as the flowers or vegetables associated with them. Before making the Frick canvases, Boucher had painted a set of seasons in 1753 for the ceiling of the council hall at the Château de Fontainebleau, just outside Paris. He depicted four groups of frolicking putti with attributes for each season. The original location of *The Four Seasons* by Boucher for Madame de Pompadour is unknown. They were made for one of her many properties, but we do not know which one. After her death, in 1764, the canvases appeared in the collection of her brother, the Marquis de Marigny, who inherited many of her belongings.

In each scene, Boucher depicts a man and a woman, not unlike Fragonard's *Progress of Love*. Not particularly keen on landscapes, Boucher is famously recorded as having said about nature: "C'est trop vert et mal éclairé" (It is too green and badly lit). Nonetheless, he often represented nature in a very lyrical way. Here he sets each couple in a landscape. Two of the canvases are pastoral scenes—shepherds and shepherdesses. The canvas for spring portrays a shepherd crowning his mistress with flowers; she holds an amazing basket of them, roses and violets and a number of other beautiful and colorful blossoms. Autumn is represented by a shepherdess with a lover, and they are sharing grapes, the harvest of the season. The young woman is wearing a type of straw hat that was associated with shepherdesses at the time. The grapes in this canvas are extraordinary, each one of them made up of little touches of different shades of purple, blue, white, yellow, and red.

The heat of summer is represented by a group of women bathing under a fountain. The fountain is decorated with a stone sculpture of a dolphin with two putti, an iconography usually associated with love. A similar fountain appears in the first canvas of Fragonard's *Progress of Love* series. This erotic picture, interestingly enough made for a female patron, looks back to a long-standing tradition in Venetian Renaissance art, especially to the work of Titian. Representing winter, the last of the *Seasons* focuses on two extraordinary figures surrounded by snow—an elegant woman in a sleigh with a man pushing it on the ice. In the inventory of the Marquis de Marigny, the man is described as a "Tartar." Cossacks and Tartars, exotic figures from the steppes of Central Asia, were particularly popular in the European imagination in the eighteenth century.

The Four Seasons are described in the prints that were made after them with very specific titles: *The Charms of Spring, The Pleasures of Summer, The Delights of the Autumn,* and *The Amusements of the Winter.* I love the way these titles characterize each season of the year.

—X.S.

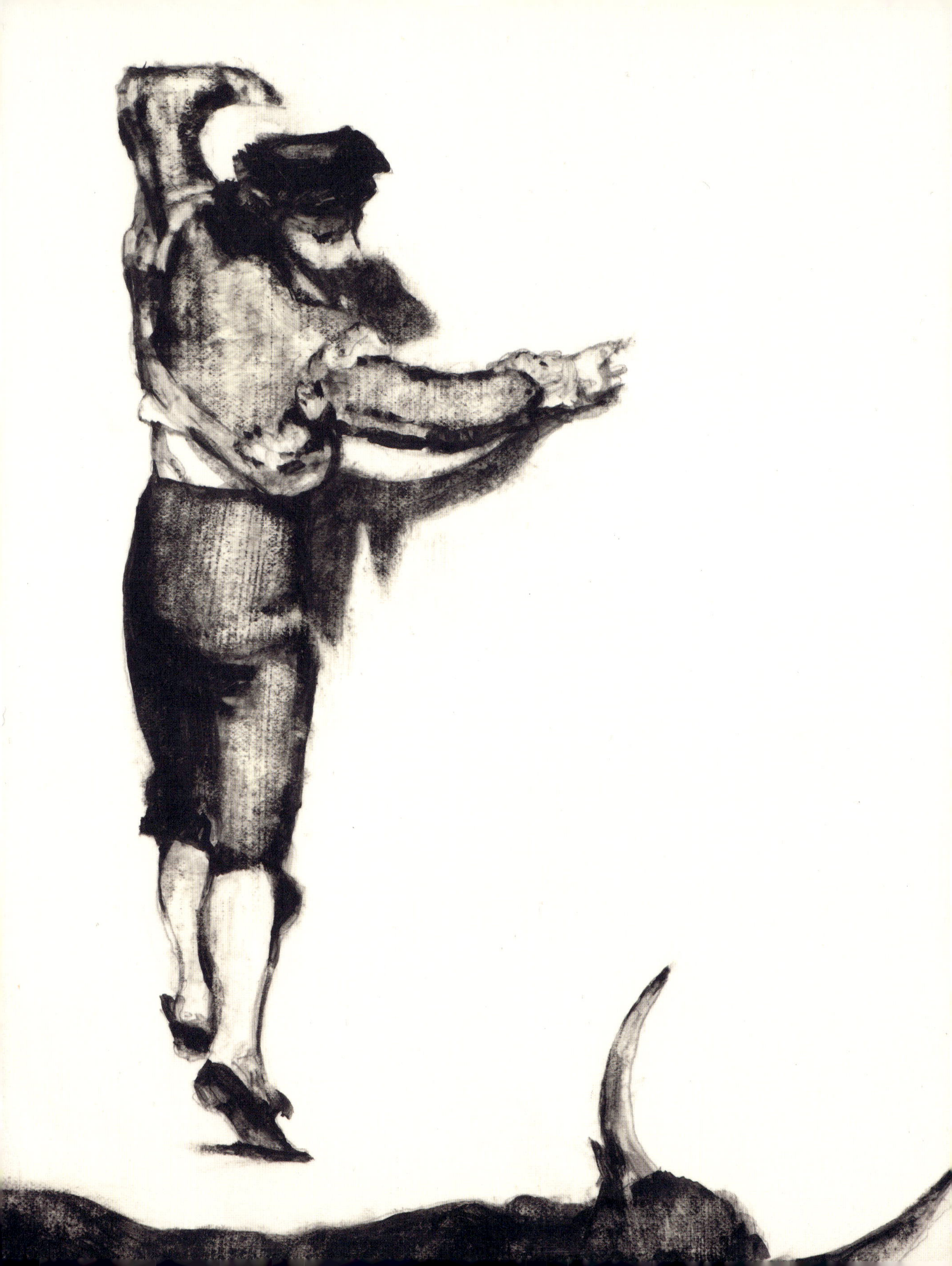

ÉDOUARD MANET

The Bullfight

1864

Toreador

1 OZ. BLANCO TEQUILA

½ OZ. APRICOT BRANDY

½ OZ. FRESH LIME JUICE

1 DASH OF ANGOSTURA BITTERS

Shake with ice and strain into a cocktail glass

This fruity drink is one of many tequila cocktails. Distilled from blue agave, tequila was invented in the early seventeenth century in Mexico, then a Spanish colony.

Manet (1832–1883) is hard to fit into a clear category. He has often been called the "father of Impressionism," a leading light for artists like Monet and Renoir, but he never exhibited with the Impressionists or identified himself as part of this rebellious group of artists. He strived to be accepted by the French Academy, by the jurors and the critics of the Paris Salon, the most important public venue for the display of art in France at the time, but he was never fully embraced by the academy.

It may be hard to imagine a time when Manet, and the Impressionists, were considered rejects outside of the mainstream; these days, their work is extremely popular and fetches high prices on the market. But in the 1860s, paintings by Manet and the artists who would become the Impressionists were considered unacceptable, their paintings an affront to the teachings of the French Academy: too messy, too brushy, unfinished. Rebuffed by the salon, these artists sometimes showed their work at the Salon des Refusés, a sort of exhibition for the rejected. Eventually distinguishing themselves and growing out of this group, they started to organize their own exhibitions, beginning in 1874.

Bullfighting, especially the Spanish *corrida*, which ends with the killing of the bull, is an important part of historic Spanish culture, and it has been a subject of great debate. Though banned by the Catalan Parliament in 2010, the *corrida* recently became legal again throughout Spain. A scene of violence, *The Bullfight* was born of a great struggle on the part of the artist. A version of it was accepted by the Paris Salon for 1864, but it elicited vehement responses from the critics and, in turn, incited Manet to a sort of violence himself, directed toward this very canvas. Close looking at *The Bullfight* reveals the very modes of painting that rubbed Manet's critics the wrong way in so many of his other works—pure colors laid side by side; red applied as if straight out of a tube; unmediated black, white, red, and yellow. Details are fudged over with broad brushstrokes of paint, almost abstracted. Among the spectators in the upper section, one can hardly tell one figure from another.

The Bullfight as it exists today at the Frick was not what Manet exhibited at the Salon of 1864. It is the result of his reworking of this painting after he had taken a knife to the original canvas. We don't have a record from him of what the original canvas looked like, only caricatures made by his critics that show a much larger composition and exaggerate certain elements. One caricature pokes fun at what was considered to be Manet's inept use of color, as if he were just relying on blotches of ink. Another ridicules the perceived woodenness of the figures, picturing each one, including the bull, as wooden toys. Above all, the critics derided the perspective, the bull, for example, considered to be way too small to appear in the foreground. According to one critic, it looked like a "horned rat."

After the explosive criticism of the painting at the 1864 Salon, Manet cut it into smaller parts, disposing of some of the canvas. The lower section that showed the body of a fallen toreador became *The Dead Toreador,* now at the National Gallery of Art in Washington, DC. He signed it at the bottom right, "Manet." The upper portion became the Frick's *Bullfight,* also signed as an independent painting with an *M* at lower left.

Technical examination of *The Dead Toreador* reveals that part of the bull seen at the bottom of the Frick painting had previously been painted at the top of *The Dead Toreador*; this is where the two had fit together before being separated. The examination also shows how much Manet struggled with this composition from the beginning, even before he showed it at the Salon of 1864. He moved several elements around, especially the bull. He struggled with getting this composition right in order to show it, but it seems that he never really succeeded and therefore decided to cut up his work. This act of creative destruction resulted in two very different works, with the Frick's *Bullfight* taking on a long, horizontal format, as if telling just a slice of a larger story.

When he painted *The Incident in the Bullfight*—the title of the original, larger painting he showed at the 1864 Salon—Manet had been neither to a bullfight nor to Spain. He had relied instead on depictions of bullfights, especially prints by Goya. Like many of his contemporaries, he was inspired by Spanish painters, among them, in addition to Goya, Velázquez and El Greco, who was Greek but has long been considered a Spanish artist. His interest in Spanish culture included a fascination with bullfighting, which was not perceived entirely positively by his contemporaries in Paris. It was seen as a sort of barbaric element of the somewhat "exotic" culture of Spain, at least to urban Parisians.

Manet finally went to Spain in 1865. There he made drawings and watercolors of scenes of bullfighting, writing to his friend, the critic Baudelaire, back in Paris, that bullfights were "one of the strangest, most beautiful, and most terrible spectacles that one can see." He continued to paint Spanish subjects after he returned to Paris, and his scenes of bullfights made after the Spanish trip highlight more of the atmosphere, the sense of a crowd gathering under the hot sun to witness the art and violence of the *corrida*.

—A.N.

EL GRECO

Vincenzo Anastagi

CA. 1575

Ouzo Lemonade

2 OZ. OUZO

1½ OZ. LEMON JUICE

3 OZ. WATER

1 TSP. HONEY

Serve on the rocks in a tall glass
and garnish with mint leaves

A uniquely Greek drink, ouzo is an anise-flavored liquor that dates back to the late Middle Ages, when the monks of Mount Athos are said to have consumed something similar. I wonder if El Greco drank something like ouzo in his native Crete.

The El Greco portrait of Vincenzo Anastagi is first documented in 1848, in a private collection in the United Kingdom, where it remained until Henry Clay Frick acquired it in 1913. We have no idea where it was before then or how it reached the United Kingdom. It was painted, however, by a truly

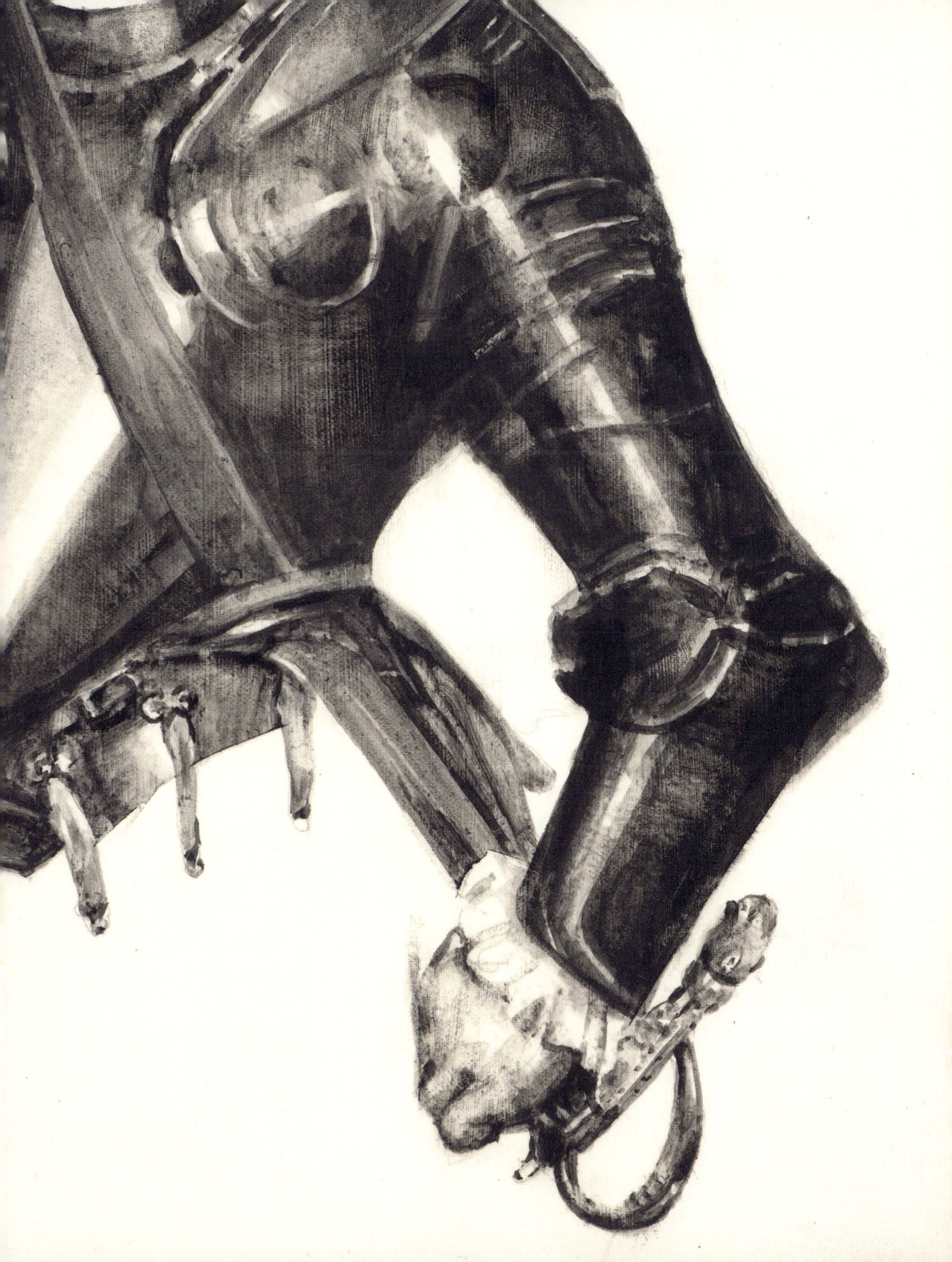

international painter—born in Greece, El Greco trained in Italy and became a celebrated artist in Spain.

Born Doménikos Theotokópoulos on Crete in the town of Candia (now Heraklion), in 1541, El Greco (the Greek man), as he became known, would spend most of his life outside of Greece. In the extraordinary trajectory of his career, he began in Greece as a painter of Byzantine icons and became celebrated in Spain as a painter of incredibly sophisticated, eccentric works. The better part of his career—from 1577 to his death in 1614—was spent in Toledo, where he worked for the local aristocracy and church. His most celebrated paintings—*El Expolio* in the sacristy of the Cathedral of Toledo and *The Burial of the Count of Orgaz* in the church of Santo Tomé—are among the city's most important artistic treasures.

The portrait of Vincenzo Anastagi was painted in Italy and therefore falls between El Greco's years in Greece and his years in Spain. At the time of his birth, the island of Crete was under Venetian rule; in 1567, the artist moved to Venice, where he lived for four years and got to know painters such as Titian and Tintoretto. As an ambitious young artist, El Greco was in need of wealthy collectors and patrons, and his search for patronage led him to move to Rome. Giulio Clovio, a celebrated painter of miniatures, introduced him to Cardinal Alessandro Farnese, and El Greco was subsequently invited to live in the Farnese Palace, where he became part of the cardinal's artistic entourage. During his years in Rome (1570–77), he painted works for the Farnese family, as well as other patrons. El Greco could be quite difficult and had a history of falling out with patrons. After just a few years, he was expelled from the Farnese household. He remained in Rome, however, and set up an independent workshop. The Frick portrait is one of very few full-length portraits by El Greco and one of only four or five known portraits that he painted in Rome.

Vincenzo Anastagi was a minor noble from Perugia. In 1563, together with his brother Marcello, he was made a Knight of Malta. Anastagi was an expert in fortifications, and in 1565, during the famous Turkish siege, he defended the city of Valletta in Malta. He became *sergente maggiore* (sergeant major) of Castel Sant'Angelo, the main fortification in Rome, defending the area of the Vatican along the Tiber. At some point, he returned to Malta, where he died sometime between 1585 and 1587. It was reported that he died in a fight with two other Knights of Malta.

We know little about Anastagi's interest in the arts or why he commissioned the portrait from El Greco. The painting portrays him in a way usually reserved for rulers—full-length and wearing a suit of armor. It is a grand statement on the part of both Anastagi and El Greco. El Greco's portrait of

Anastagi is part of a tradition of depicting figures in armor, especially popular in sixteenth-century Venice with artists such as Titian. Only a few decades later, between 1607 and 1608, Caravaggio was to portray the Grand Master of the Knights of Malta, Alof de Wignacourt (Louvre, Paris), in a similar way to Anastagi. I have often wondered if Caravaggio ever saw the El Greco portrait, in Rome or in Malta.

—X.S.

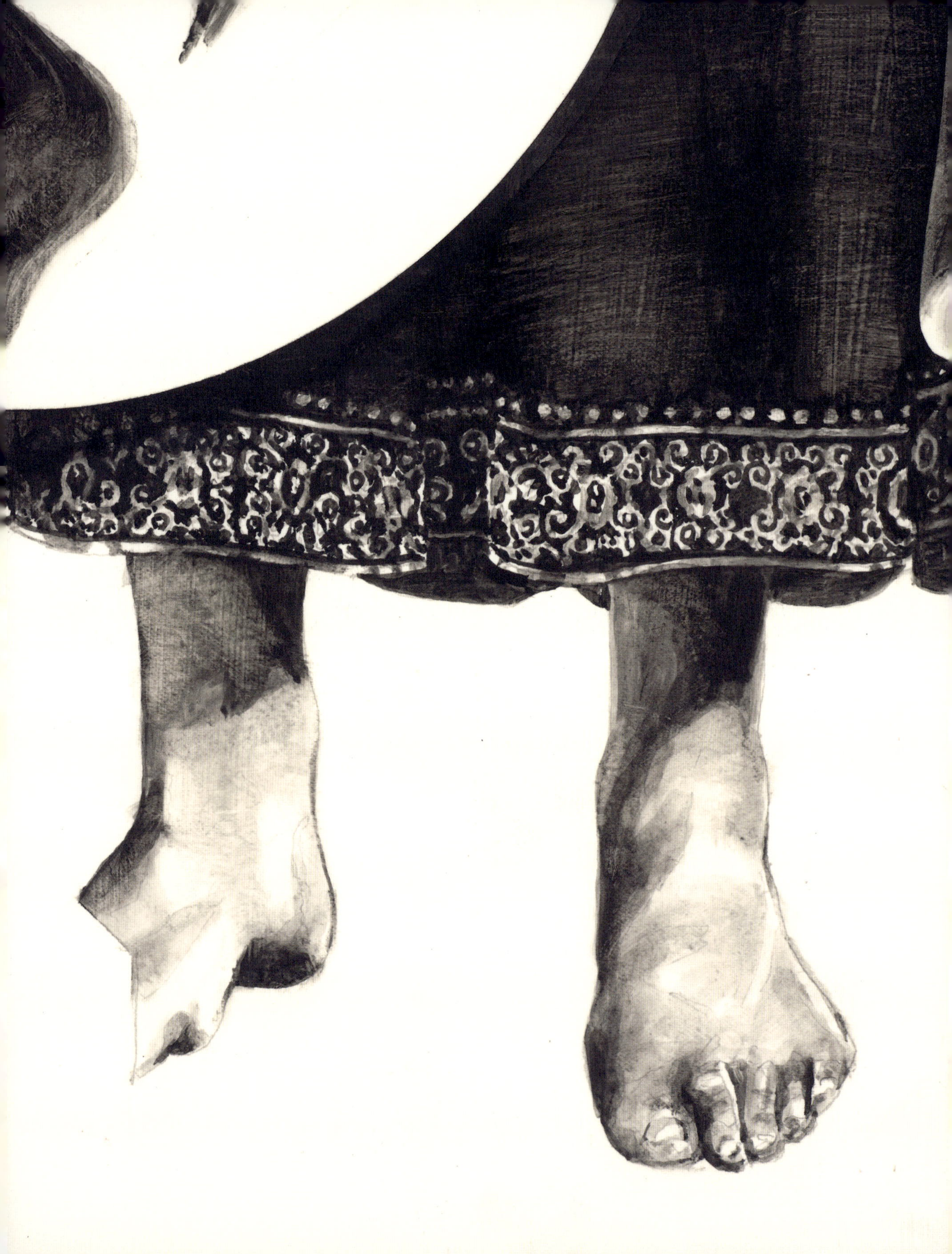

PIERO DELLA FRANCESCA

The Borgo San Sepolcro Polyptych

1454–69

The Saint

1½ OZ. BOURBON

½ OZ. LILLET BLANC

¼ OZ. GRAPEFRUIT JUICE

¾ OZ. LEMON JUICE

¼ OZ. GINGER SUGAR SYRUP

Serve chilled in a cocktail glass and
garnish with grapefruit peel

This cocktail alludes to the four full-length images of saints that originally made up The Borgo San Sepolcro Polyptych.

Enveloped in a dark red cloak, over a green tunic with a bejeweled hem, a single, monumental figure is set against the blue sky, with a marble balustrade behind him. St. John the Evangelist is here absorbed in reading a book. This painting was once part of a group of paintings that came from an altarpiece known as *The Borgo San Sepolcro Polyptych.* The altarpiece, three other pieces of which are also owned by the Frick, was dismantled probably at some point in the sixteenth century.

The Frick is one of only four museums in the United States that own works by Piero della Francesca. The Clark Art Institute in Williamstown has a *Virgin and Child with Four Angels,* a very late work; the Isabella Stewart Gardner Museum in Boston has the fragment of a fresco showing the mythological figure of Hercules; and the National Gallery in Washington has a *St. Apollonia,* which came from *The Borgo San Sepolcro Polyptych.* Of the four American museums with works by Piero, the Frick, with its four paintings, is the only one to own more than one.

Piero della Francesca (ca. 1415–1492) was born in the small town of Borgo San Sepolcro in the Tiber valley. He worked on a number of altarpieces and fresco cycles, one of which, *The Stories of the True Cross* in the church of San Francesco in Arezzo, survives almost intact. His *Resurrection* in Borgo San Sepolcro, frescoed on a wall in the city hall of his birthplace, is an iconic work of fifteenth-century Italian art. Piero traveled extensively around Italy and visited many of the courts of the peninsula. He is documented in all the great artistic centers of Italy: in Rome, working for the pope, as well as in Florence, Ancona, Ferrara, and Naples. Many of his works produced for these cities, unfortunately, do not survive.

Piero produced a number of polyptychs that typically show a central image of the Virgin, flanked by images of saints. On the sides are smaller saints painted on the pilasters, and there are more saints and religious figures above. Each altarpiece is topped by a *cimasa,* a panel above the main scene crowning the altarpiece, and placed atop a predella, which is usually decorated with small narrative scenes.

The Frick's four Piero paintings are part of an altarpiece commissioned from the artist for the high altar of the church of Sant'Agostino in Borgo San Sepolcro. Piero received the commission from Angelo di Giovanni di Simone, whose brother Simone and sister-in-law Giovanna had sponsored the construction of the church's high altar. Piero was given the assignment on October 4, 1454, but did not get under way until 1468, as he was busy with other work. The church has a complicated history. It was ceded by the Augustinian Order to the Poor Clares in 1555, at which point it became the church of Santa Chiara. It changed hands a number of times and today is no longer a functioning church.

Apart from the labor of the painter and the pigments and the gold, one of the costliest aspects of a polyptych was the carpentry required to create the frame. For the *Borgo San Sepolcro Polyptych,* they were able to reuse the carpentry intended for an altar in the Franciscan church of San Sepolcro after it was replaced by another altarpiece by the painter Stefano di Giovanni, known as Sassetta. So the old carpentry became available for Piero.

On the main tier of the polyptych, Piero depicted four freestanding saints. At the extreme left was *St. Augustine* (Museu de Arte Antiga, Lisbon), the patron saint of the church and of the Augustinian Order. Next to him was the *Archangel Michael* (National Gallery, London), the patron saint of the man who commissioned the altarpiece—Angelo. To the right of the central panel was the Frick's *St. John the Evangelist*. The writer of one of the four Gospels and of the Apocalypse, St. John is shown in the polyptych as both the patron saint of Borgo San Sepolcro and a saint connected to the patron, Angelo di Giovanni, whose father was called Giovanni. To the extreme right was *St. Nicholas of Tolentino* (Museo Poldi Pezzoli, Milan), a recent Augustinian saint. On the pilasters of the polyptych, a number of bust-length saints were depicted, only three of which survive: *St. Monica* (the mother of St. Augustine) and the *Blessed Angelo Scarpetti* (a local religious figure who was buried in Sant'Agostino in San Sepolcro) both now at the Frick, and *St. Apollonia* (National Gallery, Washington, DC).

The predella most likely depicted scenes from the Passion of Christ. *The Crucifixion* at the Frick is the only one surviving. The others are lost, but we know from early seventeenth-century descriptions that there were at least three other panels that showed the Flagellation, the Deposition, and the Resurrection of Christ, respectively. The exact form of the predella and its iconography remains problematic, as does the issue of what was represented in the missing central panel of the polyptych. The most reasonable suggestion is that it may have been a Coronation of the Virgin.

The altarpiece still has many missing parts. Less than a century after it was painted, about 1555, after the church was transferred to the Poor Clares, Piero's altarpiece was dismantled. Its parts were dispersed and not all survive. This reminds us that so many of these polyptychs and altarpieces would have gone out of fashion and would have been cut to pieces and sold as independent works of art. This is how a single altarpiece by Piero for San Sepolcro is now divided up among Portugal, the United States, Italy, and the United Kingdom. The art historical work on this altarpiece continues, and it is hoped that more parts of it will surface. It is also a long-standing dream to be able to reunite all the surviving fragments in one museum. Something to hope for.

—X.S.

CLAUDE LORRAIN

Jacob, Rachel, and Leah at the Well

1666

Furio Biondo

2 OZ. DRY VERMOUTH

½ OZ. DRY GIN

ADD PROSECCO AND SOME LIME JUICE

Serve chilled in a cocktail glass
and garnish with a rosemary sprig

This cocktail was invented by a friend of mine in honor of his husband. It has become a popular drink among scholars working on Old Master drawings.

The Frick Collection has a small but very fine collection of drawings, most of which were assembled after the death of Henry Clay Frick. Among them are three wonderful drawings by the seventeenth-century French painter Claude Lorrain. We also have a painting by Claude—*The Sermon on the Mount,* made for François Bosquet, the Bishop of Montpellier.

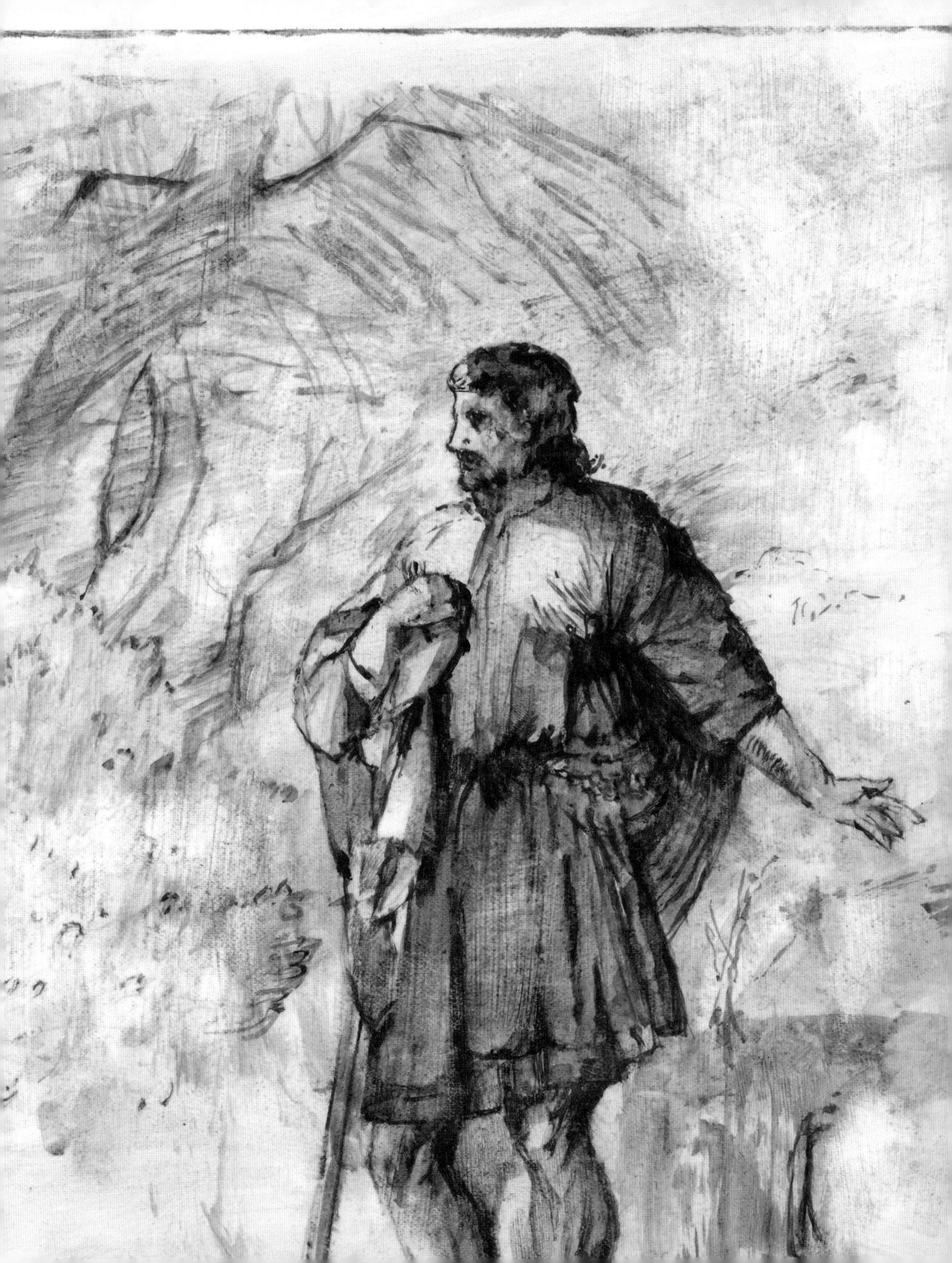

Claude Gellée (1604–1682) was born in Lorraine—hence his sobriquet. Like Nicolas Poussin, he was born in France but chose to spend his life in Rome. Curiously enough, he first moved to Rome to work as a pastry chef. Subsequently, he studied painting in Naples and Rome with Goffredo Wals and with Agostino Tassi. In the early 1620s, he returned to his native Lorraine but, in 1627, moved back to Rome, where he spent the rest of his life. Collected and beloved not only in the seventeenth century but also later on, especially in the eighteenth and early nineteenth centuries in England, Claude's landscapes became the prototypes for landscape painting in Europe and were an influence on artists such as Turner and Constable.

When Claude died, he left a number of albums and boxes of drawings in his workshop. Today there are more than a thousand surviving drawings by Claude. Purchased in 1982, the Frick's Claude drawings came from an important album that originally numbered more than eighty drawings and was likely assembled after his death, probably in the early eighteenth century. The album appears for the first time in 1713 in the inventory of Prince Livio Odescalchi, a Roman aristocrat who had a fine collection of paintings and drawings. The album surfaced on the market in 1957, and in 1960, it was acquired by the art dealer Georges Wildenstein. It became known as the Wildenstein Album. By the time the album reached Wildenstein, it included only sixty drawings, and we do not know what happened to the others. The drawings were pasted into the album in a very haphazard manner, and there was no rhyme or reason as to why they were assembled in this album. It was acquired in 1968 by the great Californian collector Norton Simon, and a few years later, in 1970, Simon dismantled it because the album had conservation issues. After exhibiting the drawings in the 1970s, Norton Simon decided to sell the drawings individually. He kept seven of them and in 1980 put the others on the market. The Frick acquired three of them.

One of the three drawings depicts the complicated love story of Jacob, Rachel, and Leah at the well, from the Book of Genesis. Looking for work, young Jacob travels to the land of Haran to visit his uncle, Laban. On his journey, he comes upon a well in the desert and there sees Rachel approaching.

> *And it came to pass when Jacob saw Rachel, the daughter of Laban, his mother's brother, and the sheep of Laban, his mother's brother, that Jacob went near and rolled the stone from the well's mouth and watered the flock of Laban, his mother's brother. And Jacob kissed Rachel and lifted up his voice and wept.*

This is a story of love at first sight. Jacob falls in love with Rachel and helps her water the sheep.

And Laban had two daughters. The name of the elder was Leah and the name of the younger, Rachel. Leah was tender eyed, but Rachel was beautiful and well favored. And Jacob loved Rachel and said, "I will serve thee seven years for Rachel, thy younger daughter." And Laban said, "It is better that I give her to thee than I should give her to another man. Abide with me." And Jacob served seven years for Rachel, and they seemed unto him but a few days, for the love he had to her. And Jacob said unto Laban, "Give me my wife, for my days are fulfilled, that I may go in unto her." And Laban gathered together all the men of the place and made a feast. And it came to pass in the evening that he took Leah, his daughter, and brought her to him, and he went in unto her. And Laban gave unto his daughter, Leah, his maid Zilpah for a handmaid. And it came to pass that in the morning, behold, it was Leah. And he said to Laban, "What is this thou hast done unto me? Did not I serve thee for Rachel? Wherefore then hast thou beguiled me?" And Laban said, "It must not be so done in our country, to give the younger before the firstborn. Fulfill her week, and we will give thee this also for the service which thou shalt serve with me yet seven other years." And Jacob did so and fulfilled her week, and he gave him Rachel, his daughter, to wife also.

Laban agrees to allow Jacob to marry Rachel but tricks him into marrying Leah, his elder daughter, instead. Jacob only realizes it is Leah the morning after the wedding. He works for Laban for another seven years and finally marries Rachel as well. In this rather peculiar story of bigamy, Jacob, who continues to be in love with Rachel, goes on to father children with Leah, with two maids, and with a number of other women. So this moment of encounter between Jacob and Rachel at the well is the beginning of a very complex story. Because it is not easy to represent the story visually, most painters show both Leah and Rachel at the well.

The Frick drawing is preparatory for a painting now at the Hermitage Museum in Saint Petersburg that was made for a patron in Antwerp in 1666. The subject of Jacob, Leah, and Rachel was painted by Claude a number of times. The comparison between Leah and Rachel was often seen as the contrast between different ways of life. In Michelangelo's tomb of Pope Julius II, for example, the two female statues flanking Moses depict Leah and Rachel.

—X.S.

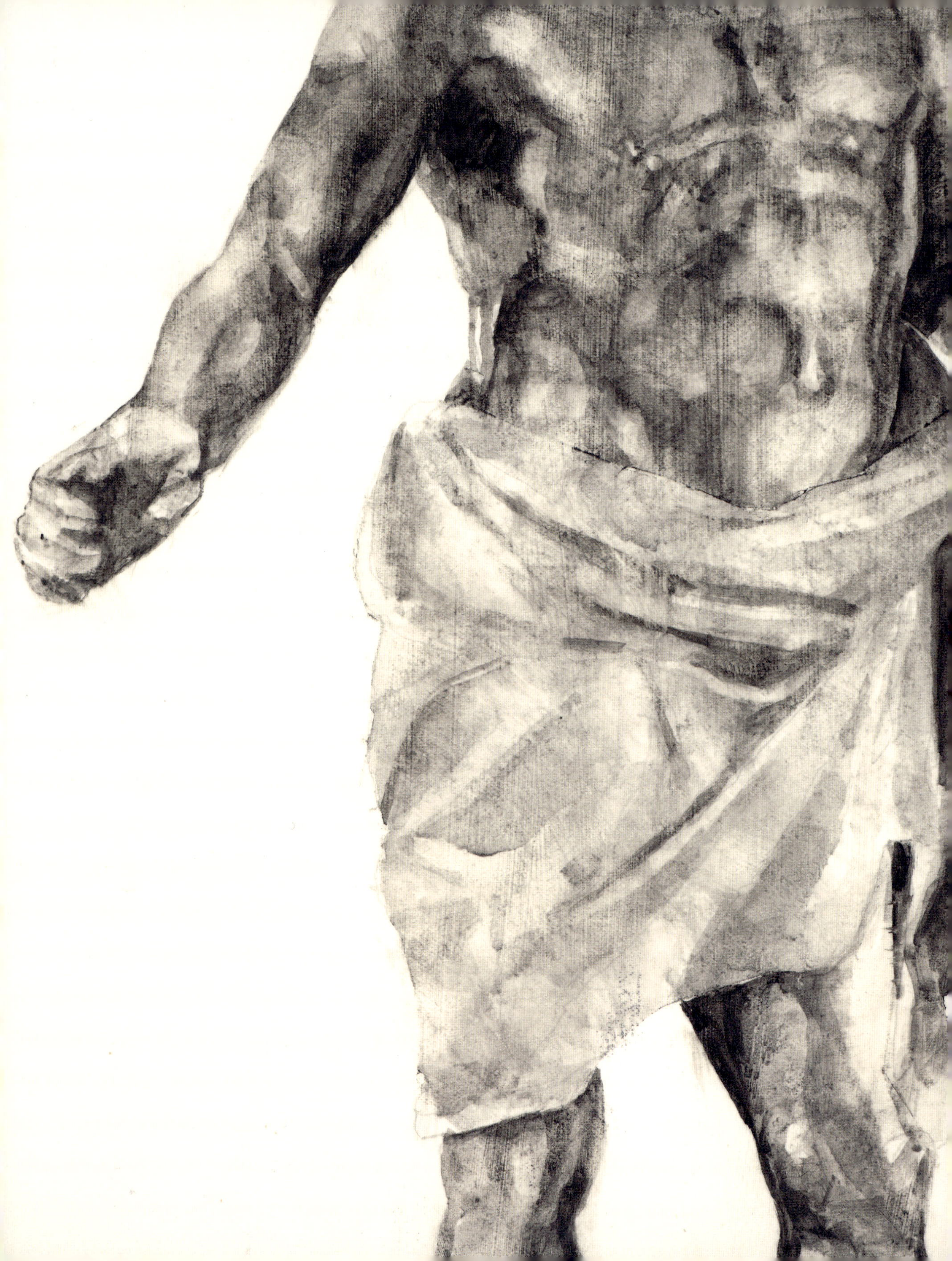

ANTICO

Hercules

PROBABLY 1499

Malvasia Wine

Serve in a wine glass

Antico's main patrons, the Gonzaga family from Mantua, were particularly fond of this sweet white wine. It is said that Isabella d'Este, wife of Francesco II Gonzaga, liked it so much that she drank it at breakfast.

The subject: Hercules, one of the best-known heroes in classical mythology. The demigod was said to be so strong that he could defeat any kind of enemy, as he did in deeds known as the Twelve Labors.

The artist: Pier Jacopo Alari Bonacolsi, also known as Antico (meaning "antique"). The son of a Mantovan butcher, Antico (ca. 1460–1528) became one of the most celebrated artists of his time.

The place: Mantua, a small town halfway between Venice and Milan that, from the fourteenth to the eighteenth century, was ruled by the Gonzaga, a princely Italian family.

In the fifteenth century, the Gonzaga were known for their fascination with Roman antiquities. Mantuan artists like Mantegna and Antico shared this interest, some of them traveling to Rome to see the remains of its grand imperial past. Others drew inspiration solely from drawings. Antico went to Rome at least once, probably several times, and started to make small-scale copies of some of the ancient statues that could be seen there. Other sculptors, such as Filarete or Bertoldo di Giovanni, also tried to cast statuettes after the antique. But none achieved the same level of accuracy in the replication of the details of ancient statuary and the same technical flawlessness as Antico.

While most of Antico's statuettes were made after ancient sculptures, we do not know if that is the case for the Frick *Hercules*. Some scholars believe that a statuette in the Louvre is its ancient prototype, while others argue that it is in fact a later cast after Antico's own statuette.

Whichever the case, Antico would not have lacked sources of inspiration for his *Hercules*: many ancient works share poses, facial types, hairstyles, and body types with the Frick statuette.

But why would Antico make small-scale copies of ancient statues? At the time, antiquity was very much in fashion. After neoclassicism, and after the advent of photography, it is easy to overlook the novelty and originality of the idea of replicating ancient statues. But in the fifteenth century, antiquity was brand new, not least because ancient statues were being unearthed for the first time. Before the end of the fifteenth century, very few antique statues actually survived in Rome. And very few people could travel all the way to Rome. In this context, copying was a creative process. And let us not forget that newly found statues were often missing limbs or attributes, and artists had to complete them. Imitation was truly a creative process at the time.

But the power of Antico's statuettes lies in their combination of the monumentality of ancient full-scale statuary with jewel-like qualities that appealed to the ruling classes of Mantua. Antico's statuettes communicate grandeur while they can be held in one's hand. The small round base of the *Hercules* seems designed to both bestow monumentality and to invite turning in order to appreciate the minute details of the casting: the hairy lion pelt, the gilded locks of hair on the top of the head and the beard, and the silvering of the eyes, lost, somehow, in a dreamlike expression. The dark black tone of the bronze is yet another demonstration of Antico's skill, as he managed to concoct a chemical formula for the patina that would resist oxidation and prevent it from turning green.

There are five different versions of the *Hercules*, with the Frick exemplar, in many ways, being the most accomplished. The fact that Antico could cast five different versions of the same statuette is the ultimate demonstration of his technical ability. Normally, the wax model of a statuette would get lost during the casting process. But Antico applied an innovative technique that allowed him to preserve the wax model and to replicate it over time. Modern viewers may be tempted to think that copies are artistically worthless, that imitation is incompatible with originality. But in Antico's time, the replication of something was a tribute to its importance. Replicability went hand in hand with appreciation—the more something was copied, the more important it was.

We do not know for whom the five different versions were made. Antico worked almost exclusively for the Gonzaga family. He started working for Gianfrancesco Gonzaga di Ròdigo and Antonia del Balzo, but soon bishop-elect Ludovico Gonzaga and Isabella d'Este also became his patrons. Isabella was originally from Ferrara but married Francesco II Gonzaga, thereby becoming Marchioness of Mantua. After her husband's death, she ruled the city for a couple of years as a regent for her underage son. A patron of the arts, she is much celebrated for the cultivated environment that she created around herself. Immensely powerful and shrewd in her politics, she managed to achieve many goals that, as a woman, would normally be denied to her. There is only one surviving work by Antico whose patron can be identified with certainty—and that is Isabella. For all the other works, the descriptions of statuettes in the inventories of the different members of the Gonzaga family are too vague to establish the patron of a given exemplar. It is almost impossible, therefore, to know for whom the Frick *Hercules* was made.

While the fact that Antico did not sign his works makes it more difficult for us to understand what was made for whom, it also reveals the artist's subtle thinking. Had he signed his works with his name, he would have shattered the pretense that they were actual antiques. Only without Antico's signature could they be taken as such.

Statuettes like Antico's, apparently so simple, challenge many of the modern viewer's assumptions about the value of antiquity and prove immensely sophisticated, both from a conceptual and a technical point of view. Together with many other bronzes, the *Hercules* was acquired by Henry Clay Frick in 1916 from John Pierpont Morgan's collection. It cost only $165, while comparable works in bronze from the same sale were valued at about $100,000. Why was this important work so little valued? Did Henry Clay Frick appreciate how wonderful it was? Maybe he did, for he kept it in his private collection. It did not enter the museum's collection until 1970, long after his death, when it was donated to the Frick by his daughter, Helen Clay Frick.

—G.D.

JACQUES-LOUIS DAVID

Alexandrine-Thérèse Nardot, Comtesse Daru

1810

Orange Blossom

1 OZ. GIN

1 OZ. SWEET VERMOUTH

2 OZ. FRESH ORANGE JUICE

Serve chilled in a cocktail glass

This cocktail has been chosen to complement the spectacular headdress worn by the subject of this painting, which seems to be a tiara made of fresh orange blossoms.

Jacques-Louis David, leader of the neoclassical school of painting in France in the late eighteenth and early nineteenth centuries, is best known for monumental classical scenes such as his famous *Oath of the Horatii* (Louvre, Paris). Some associate David with the French Revolution, with the art of Napoleonic culture, and this is accurate; the artist himself was embroiled in the political chaos of this time. Born in Paris in 1748, he was imprisoned during the revolution, and with the fall of Napoleon in 1815, he was exiled from France. He fled to Belgium, where he died in 1825.

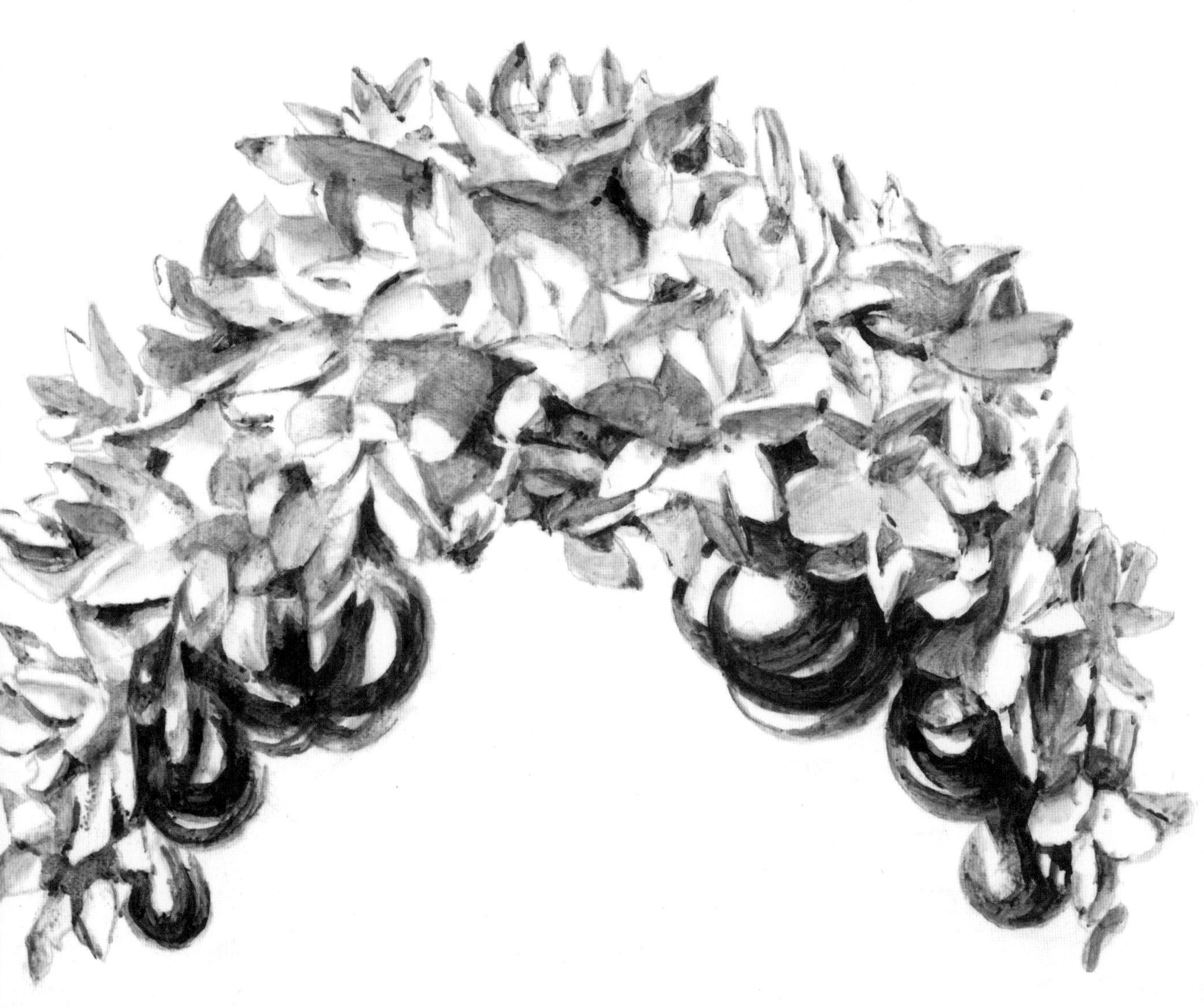

Neoclassicism became the language of the revolution and of Napoleon Bonaparte, who crowned himself emperor of France and appointed David as his First Painter. One of the best known of his many paintings is a monumental depiction of the 1804 crowning of Napoleon and his wife, Josephine, as emperor and empress of France (also at the Louvre). Under David's brush, the event takes on the gravity of a moment of ancient history. David approached each of the many figures in *The Coronation of Napoleon* with almost obsessive attention to detail, some of it embellishment and invention. For example, some people who did not attend the coronation are pictured in the scene—most famously, Napoleon's own mother, who had been angry with Napoleon at the time. Napoleon asked David to paint her into the scene for posterity.

David finished the *Coronation* in 1807 but years later, in 1810, had still not been paid for it. By this time, Napoleon had divorced Josephine and was getting ready to marry his next wife, Marie-Louise. With David's chances of being paid waning, he appealed for help to someone close to Napoleon: Pierre, Comte Daru, who held many positions during Napoleon's regime. One of them was as master of the imperial household; in this capacity, he had the ability to pay debts like that owed to David, who was finally paid for his work, thanks to Daru.

As a way to repay Daru, the artist decided to secretly paint a portrait of the count's wife, Alexandrine, the Comtesse Daru. This is the painting at the Frick. He surprised the count by installing the portrait of his wife in the family's salon for Daru to discover upon his return home one day. (The artist was able to paint her in secret because Daru was away from Paris in the spring of 1810, helping Napoleon with the preparations for his marriage to Marie-Louise.) The Darus were delighted with the portrait. For an artist who was so well known, particularly for historical works—for a kind of Napoleonic propaganda—it was a rare treat to have something so intimate and personal by his hand.

The countess wears a light smile and an almost ridiculous headdress of orange blossoms. Her matching set of earrings and necklace may be jade or green chalcedony. The careful touch of David's brush articulates each stone encircled with diamonds and interspersed with pearls.

Her style of dress, with a high waist directly under the bust, is still today referred to as "Empire waist," in reference to this First Empire of France in the early nineteenth century. It was also meant to evoke Greco-Roman styles. This type of dress called for bare arms, which left women vulnerable to cold, and a necessary accessory was a cashmere shawl like the one she carries. These were imported from the East and were extremely expensive.

The countess sits in a chair that appears to be made of mahogany, a luxury wood harvested in the European colonies in the Caribbean using enslaved labor and imported to Europe at great cost. The chair is decorated on the armrests with gilt-bronze sphinxes. David carefully depicted the reflection of the red pattern of the shawl against the cheek of the gilt-bronze sphinx. Alexandrine's fingertips linger at the handle of a fan, a detail that captures the essence of the whole portrait: relaxed, approachable, intimate—the opposite of the propaganda that David typically painted.

On the left of the canvas is this signature: *L. David, 1810*. The artist wrote that at exactly four o'clock on March, 14, 1810, a detail we know because on that day, at that time, the countess had company, the famous author Marie-Henri Beyle, known by his pen name Stendhal, who recorded the signing in his diary. Stendahl was in love with the countess, although the rumors of them having an affair have not been substantiated. He was a cousin of Comte Daru, and although he did not particularly like his cousin (referring to him many times as "the terrible Daru"), Stendhal came to Paris from his native Grenoble to take advantage of his cousin's position in Napoleon's circle, in order to secure his own. He was eventually successful in doing so, and in the meantime, he fell in love with his cousin's wife.

Stendhal records many things about Alexandrine in his journal. A description he writes around the time of this portrait seems to describe her appearance: "A woman of twenty-seven, rather stout, with dark chestnut hair, black and very thick eyebrows, small, quite sparkling eyes, who likes to be active. Her appearance reveals a warm temperament. Her features reveal a forceful, frank, and jolly character." Notably, he does not describe her as beautiful; there is something else about her that he finds appealing and compelling.

One can get annoyed with Stendhal. In one strange passage, he contemplates whether or not he can "have" Alexandrine (however you want to interpret that word). He debates her qualities and laments that she is not as much fun at balls as she used to be and no longer stays out dancing until four in the morning. By this point, around 1810, when David paints her, she is twenty-seven years old and has had six children. When Stendhal writes these musings about her, she is pregnant again. This is a common enough experience for women throughout history. She dies five years after this portrait is painted, at the age of thirty-one, while giving birth to her twelfth child.

The week after David finished this portrait, the countess wrote him in thanks, saying that she loved it more than anything. Accompanying her letter was a gift. We do not know what it was, but it was of such value and perhaps of such expense that the artist was embarrassed by it. His portrait was supposed to be a gift of thanks, and she gave him something of great value in return. We do not know much more about her; she did not live a long life. But we do know that she loved this portrait.

—A.N.

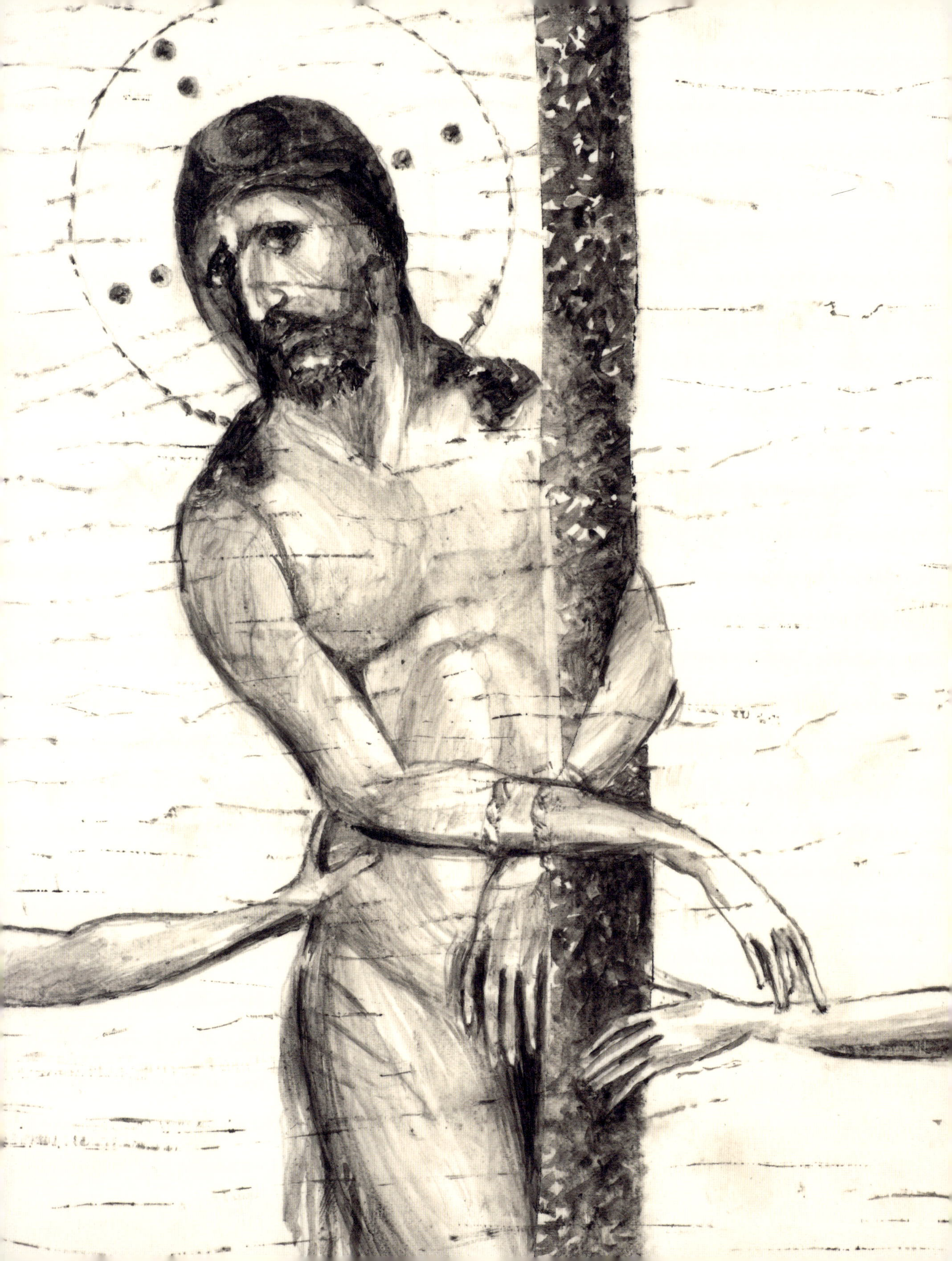

CIMABUE

The Flagellation of Christ

CA. 1280

Gold Rush

2 OZ. BOURBON

1 OZ. HONEY SYRUP

¾ OZ. LEMON JUICE

Serve chilled in a cocktail glass and garnish with a lemon peel

This golden cocktail invented in New York in the 1920s is a nod to the gold ground on which Cimabue's Flagellation *is painted.*

In Dante's *Divine Comedy*, the author visits Hell and Purgatory before ascending to Paradise. Halfway through the book—in the eleventh canto of *Purgatory*, the second of the three *cantiche*—Dante encounters people guilty of the sin of pride. Representing the burden of pride, the proud souls carry, and are crushed by, large stones as they climb up the mountain. On the terrace of pride, Dante encounters Oderisi da Gubbio, a miniature painter active at the end of the thirteenth century in Bologna and one of the very few artists in

The Divine Comedy. While talking to Dante, Oderisi pronounces this judgment: "O empty glorying in human power! How short a day the crown remains in leaf, if it's not followed by a duller age! In painting it was Cimabue's belief he held the field; now Giotto's got the cry and Cimabue's fame is dim." In other words, the great artist Cimabue thought he was the most celebrated artist of this time until Giotto came along, at which point Giotto became more famous than his teacher.

A key figure in the history of Western art, Cimabue (ca. 1240–ca. 1302) is often seen as the painter who transformed what we now call the Byzantine style—the art of the Byzantine Empire, which existed after the fall of Rome, from late antiquity to early in the Middle Ages. The Byzantine tradition of icon paintings on gold grounds, with religious figures that are rather static and follow a tradition based on the repetition of standard imagery of the Virgin Mary or Christ, was challenged by Cimabue and then by his student Giotto and other early Renaissance artists. We do not know much about him, unfortunately. Of the very few of his works that survive, all are religious.

The panel, the only work by Cimabue in a public collection in the United States, depicts the Flagellation of Christ, the moment in the Passion of Christ when Christ is tied to a column and whipped by soldiers before being condemned to death and crucified. The figure of Christ is elegantly attached to a slender column made of marble, with two men whipping him on either side. In the background are buildings that provide a theatrical setting. Cimabue plays with different ideas of space, with the two executioners interacting with the body of Christ in front of these buildings. Perspective as we know it had not yet been invented.

When the Frick acquired the panel in 1950, it was acquired as being by Cimabue. There was, however, disagreement about its authorship. The great art historian Millard Meiss was convinced that the small *Flagellation* was a Sienese picture and that it was by Duccio. On the other hand, the Italian art historian Roberto Longhi defended the attribution of the small painting to Cimabue. The debate continued for about fifty years, during which time the painting was described by the Frick as being from the "Tuscan School."

The scale of this very small devotional work is unlike most of Cimabue's extant works, which are quite large. But in 2000, a painting of the same size and very similar to the Frick painting was discovered in Suffolk, England. It depicts an enthroned Virgin and Child with two angels and is unmistakably the work of Cimabue. Dillian Gordon, one of the greatest curators in the history of the National Gallery in London, brilliantly observed that the punching and the treatment of the gold and the way in which the figures are painted were exactly the same as the Frick painting. The small *Virgin and Child with Two Angels* was purchased by the National Gallery in London, and Gordon proved beyond a doubt that the two works were part of a much larger ensemble. Studies undertaken at the time showed that these two panels are painted on the same type of wood and were originally part of the same work.

The original work must have been a diptych, showing different religious scenes on each of its two panels, probably for a total of eight. For unknown reasons, this work was cut down and the scenes dispersed. Both the Frick piece and the National Gallery one seem to have a provenance from France, so the likelihood is that this diptych in its entirety, or at least a large part of it, reached France before the nineteenth century and then was cut down.

Many pieces of this ensemble—apart from the Frick and National Gallery scenes—are missing. A third panel was discovered in a house in France in the summer of 2019. Acquired by a private collector at an auction at the end of 2019, the newly discovered panel shows another scene from the Passion of Christ—the Mocking of Christ—and the painting is in the same style as the Frick panel. We now know, thanks to technical analysis, that the National Gallery painting would have been at top left, with the *Mocking of Christ* below it and the *Flagellation* to the side. This means that there is a missing scene—possibly a representation of the Kiss of Judas—on this left panel. We do not have any surviving scenes from the right panel, and it may have been damaged or destroyed. Nonetheless, the survival of three pieces of the left panel gives us some hope that the fourth piece may still be somewhere in France. The discovery and rediscovery of the ensemble's constituents, and their examination by curators, scholars, and conservators, advances our knowledge of these works of art in significant ways. And we hope that one day these three paintings by Cimabue—and maybe more—can be reunited and seen together.

—X.S.

JEAN-ANTOINE HOUDON

Élisabeth-Suzanne de Jaucourt, Comtesse du Cayla

1777

Frosé

1 BOTTLE ROSÉ
8 OZ. STRAWBERRIES, HULLED AND QUARTERED
½ CUP SUGAR
JUICE OF ONE LEMON

Freeze rosé overnight in deep pan
Mix strawberries and sugar, let sit for 30 minutes
Combine frozen rosé (which now has a slushy consistency) with sugary strawberries and lemon juice
Puree in blender
Serve in a coupe glass

This refreshing cocktail evokes summers in the south of France, where Madame du Cayla's family owned vast wine-producing estates.

When this small marble portrait bust of Élisabeth-Suzanne de Jaucourt, Comtesse du Cayla, was carved, in 1777, Élisabeth was just a girl of twenty. Jean-Antoine Houdon (1741–1828) was already a celebrated artist, on his way to becoming something resembling the official sculpture portraitist of the main

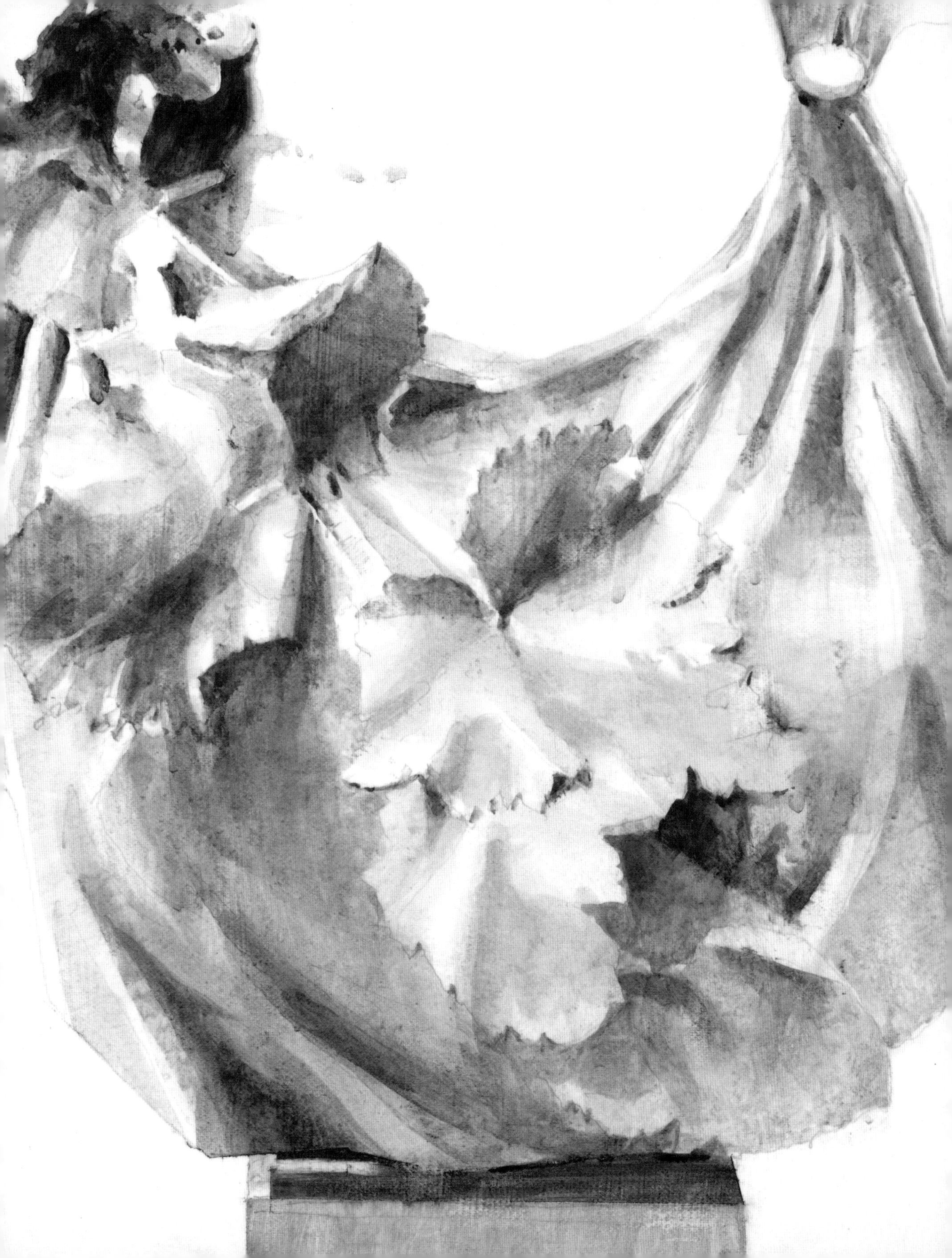

protagonists of eighteenth- and early nineteenth-century France—the Age of Enlightenment and the French Revolution.

But Houdon was as important in the United States—where he traveled in the 1780s on the invitation of Thomas Jefferson and Benjamin Franklin to carry out a major commission of a full-length marble statue of George Washington—as he was in France. He met with Washington, took a life mask of his face, and made several portrait busts of him that are now scattered across America and the globe, thereby contributing to the creation of an official iconography of the first president of the United States.

But I want to talk not about Houdon's portraits of great men but rather about his portrait of this little-known eighteenth-century woman, Élisabeth-Suzanne de Jaucourt. In many ways, Houdon's *Comtesse du Cayla* surpasses and outshines most of Houdon's portraits of men. Maybe because this is the portrait of a woman, for whom it was not necessary to create an official iconography, there is more intimacy in this portrait than there is in any bust by Houdon of the grand male protagonists of his time. We feel we have access to a moment in this woman's private life—she looks surprised yet delighted to see us, the viewers.

The bust is a wonderful example of Houdon's virtuoso carving of marble. It goes from very smooth, polished surfaces for the skin to rougher, coarser surfaces for the hair; from thin veils of marble for the grape leaves across Madame's chest—and imagine how difficult it is to carve this marble so thin—to thicker masses of marble for the hair strewn with flowers. The hair is a true miracle of marble carving. Here, Houdon manages to sculpt not just marble but also light. By carving areas of deep shadow next to thick waves of marble, he was able to articulate the volumes of the cascading hair of the countess in a wondrous way.

There is one detail in the bust that is puzzling—that is, the spray of grape leaves. Why is it there? There are two different hypotheses, not mutually exclusive. The first is that it's a reference to the surname of the countess's husband, Hercule-Étienne-Philippe de Baschi (who was also her cousin). "Baschi" chimes with the name Bacchus, the god of wine, and a branch of grape leaves also features in the coat of arms of the Baschi family. This is not surprising: the Baschi family owned vast estates in southern France, in Languedoc, which produced huge amounts of wine; so the grape leaves might be a reference to one of the main sources of income for the family.

The second possibility is that the countess is portrayed here as a bacchante, a votary of Bacchus, an interpretation that is validated by the response of eighteenth-century viewers. When this was first shown at the Paris Salon in 1777, one critic wrote admiringly in his diaries: "We see in madame la comtesse du Cayla the sweet drunkenness, the lively gaiety, the frivolous abandonment of a bacchante at the beginning of an orgy, during the first moments of pleasure." He might have gone a step too far with his interpretation of this bust, but portraits of aristocratic women as bacchantes were far from uncommon at the time.

By turning her head slightly, Houdon prompts the viewer to discover different perspectives from which to appreciate the bust. As we move to the side, we realize that the countess is caught in the act of running. We see her hair and the cloak floating in the wind behind her. Not only did Houdon defy the hard texture of marble, but he also found a way to challenge the portrait bust as a type—usually the most static, rigid kind of representation. He catches this woman in movement, thus pushing bust portraiture to its structural and conceptual limits. Moving away from bust portraiture as a celebration of perpetual grandeur, Houdon instead seeks to freeze an instant in stone forever.

Henry Clay Frick was so fond of this bust that when he commissioned a portrait of his daughter, Helen Clay Frick, he asked the American sculptor Malvina Cornell Hoffman to "do my daughter in the eighteenth-century manner" following Houdon's example. And yet, this is the only bust by the French sculptor that he managed to purchase. Since its founder's death in 1919, the Frick has acquired several additional pieces by this virtuoso and beguiling sculptor.

—G.D.

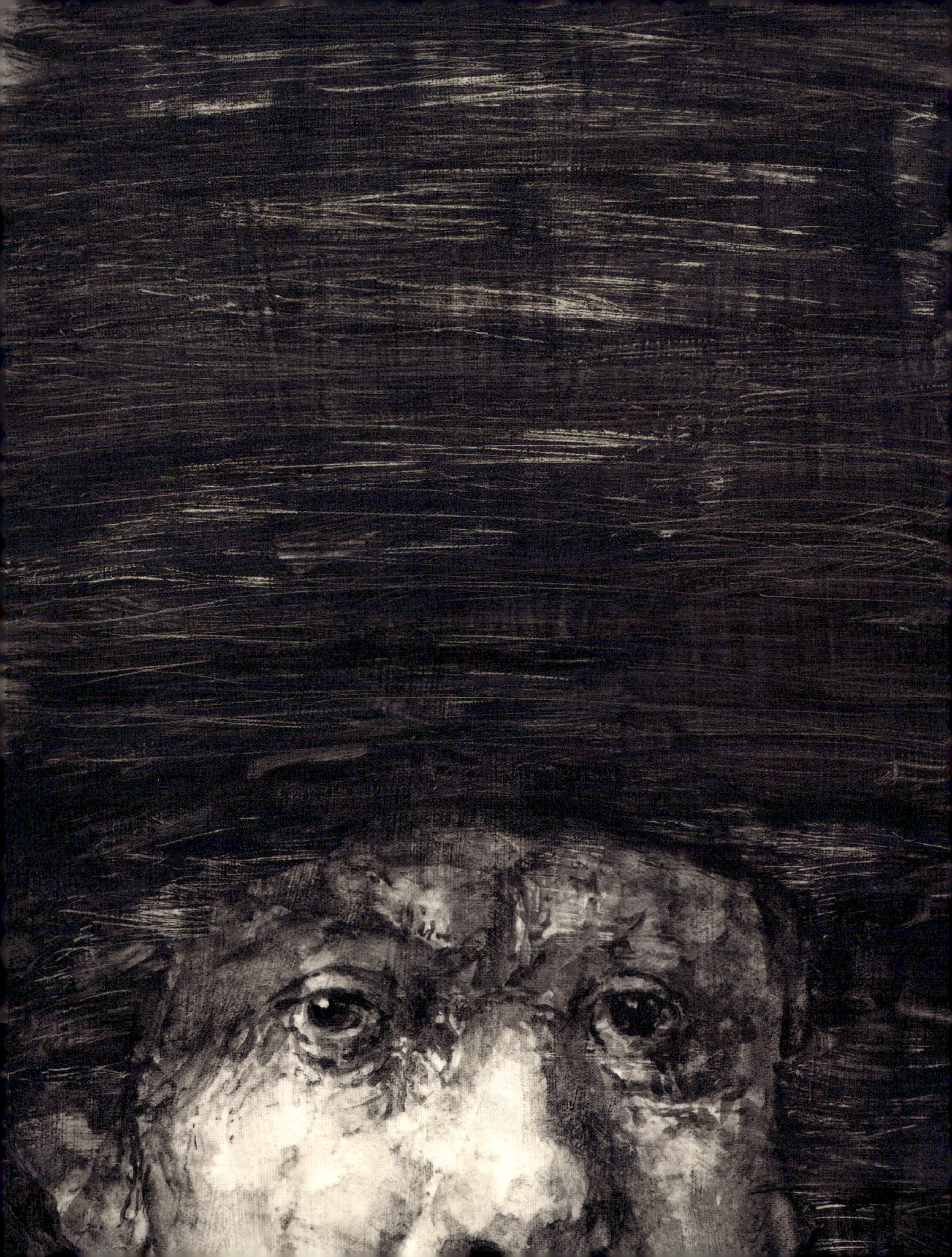

REMBRANDT HARMENSZ. VAN RIJN

Self-Portrait

1658

Whiskey Sour

2 OZ. WHISKEY

¾ OZ. SIMPLE SYRUP

¾ OZ. LEMON JUICE

Serve chilled in a cocktail glass

This self-portrait was painted at the time of Rembrandt's bankruptcy. No doubt, this would have left a most sour taste in his mouth, hence my choice of cocktail.

Rembrandt explored and recorded his own image more than any other artist in the European canon. Between paintings and works on paper, drawings and etchings, it has been calculated that he created more than fifty self-portraits—on average, probably at least one every year of his career. This self-portrait, painted in 1658, is the largest of them. We do not know for whom it was painted or who owned it to begin with. It first appeared in the nineteenth century, and through most of the century, it resided at Melbury House in Dorset, belonging to multiple generations of the Earls of Ilchester. And it was from the Earls of Ilchester that, in 1906, Henry Clay Frick acquired the painting and brought it to New York.

We do not know what the market was for the Rembrandt self-portraits, but clearly they promoted the image of the artist. Rembrandt was fascinated by his own image and his body's transformation as he aged. Interestingly enough, most of the self-portraits do not show him as a painter. Rembrandt often depicted himself in costume, as a historical or religious figure from the past. Those that do show him in the act of working are an exception.

Born in Leiden, Rembrandt (1606–1669) moved to Amsterdam in the early 1630s. The very early self-portraits by him are from around 1628–30, just before he moved. He looked at himself in a mirror with different expressions of his face, but also different and very dramatic effects of light. Rembrandt had a very successful career in Amsterdam. By May of 1639, he had amassed so considerable a fortune that he was able to buy a grand house and establish a large workshop in it. For the next twenty years, he lived with his family in this house, which is now the Rembrandt House Museum. Rembrandt never left the Netherlands, but he avidly collected objects from America, Asia, and a number of European countries. This collecting passion also extended to artworks, and Rembrandt amassed a large collection in the house.

Rembrandt was a poor manager of his finances and his business, and in July 1656 he went bankrupt. Over the next two years, he was forced to sell his art, as well as his collection of curiosities, at auction. These objects, however, did not sell for what Rembrandt was hoping for, and in February 1658, he had to sell the house. He moved to a much more modest dwelling, where he spent the rest of his life. With his financial problems and the death of all of his family members, these last years of Rembrandt's life were tragic. He died a pauper and was buried in an unmarked grave.

Dated 1658, the Frick's self-portrait would have been painted around the time the artist had to auction off his belongings, sell his house, and move to a much poorer district. You cannot, however, sense this misfortune from the painting. Remarkably, he still presents a grand vision of himself. I find it fascinating that he is painting the largest self-portrait of himself at such a low point in his life. You get the feeling that Rembrandt is resilient, that he keeps working, and that it is art that sustains him.

The artist shows himself in an extraordinary costume and almost enthroned. Looking at this portrait, you would never guess that this is a bankrupt painter having to sell off his belongings. This is a very rich outfit with details in gold, with a grand red sash and cloak. He holds, in his left hand, a walking cane capped in silver, which he clasps almost as if holding a scepter. This type of walking stick, with this silver capping, was common in eastern Asia. It is probably something that Rembrandt owned or had in his studio. In a contemporaneous Rembrandt painting showing King Saul being consoled by David playing the harp (Mauritshuis, The Hague), the biblical king wears a grand turban and crown and an outfit similar to the one in the Frick self-portrait.

The way this is painted is absolutely extraordinary: the bright whites over brown and gold and yellow, with little touches of red and black. And of course, Rembrandt's own powerful hands. He was actually a very small man, very modest in stature and look. But he presents himself as a much grander figure. I love the way his hands project out toward us. It is always worth remembering that the hands are, for a painter, the tools of his trade. The face in the self-portrait is, of course, the most powerful part: Rembrandt stares at us. There is this wonderful conceit where the beret casts a shadow over Rembrandt's eyes down to his nose, and the lower part of the face instead emerges from the shade.

Is this a poignant, sad image of a man who is confronting failure? Or is this a defiant image, an image of rebirth, of a new beginning after a difficulty in life? The American painter and critic Kenyon Cox wrote a beautiful description of the painting in 1909: "It is the head of an old lion at bay, worn and melancholy, yet conscious of his strength, determined and a little defiant."

—X.S.

ROSALBA CARRIERA

Portrait of a Man in Pilgrim's Costume and *Portrait of a Woman*

1730S

Vesper Martini

3 OZ. DRY GIN

1 OZ. VODKA

1½ OZ. LILLET BLANC

Serve ice-cold in a martini glass and garnish with a lemon peel

This cocktail, my all-time favorite, was invented by Ian Fleming for the 1953 James Bond novel Casino Royale. *Bond's international adventures make this a fitting cocktail for a woman whose international fame in the eighteenth century rivaled that of 007 today.*

Rosalba Carriera (1673–1757) was so celebrated and well known in Italy that she was referred to simply by her first name: Signora Rosalba. Born in Venice, she had two siblings, her sisters Giovanna and Angela, and they all trained as painters. Their father was a lawyer and their mother a lacemaker. By the early 1700s, Rosalba was working in Venice for an international market. She also

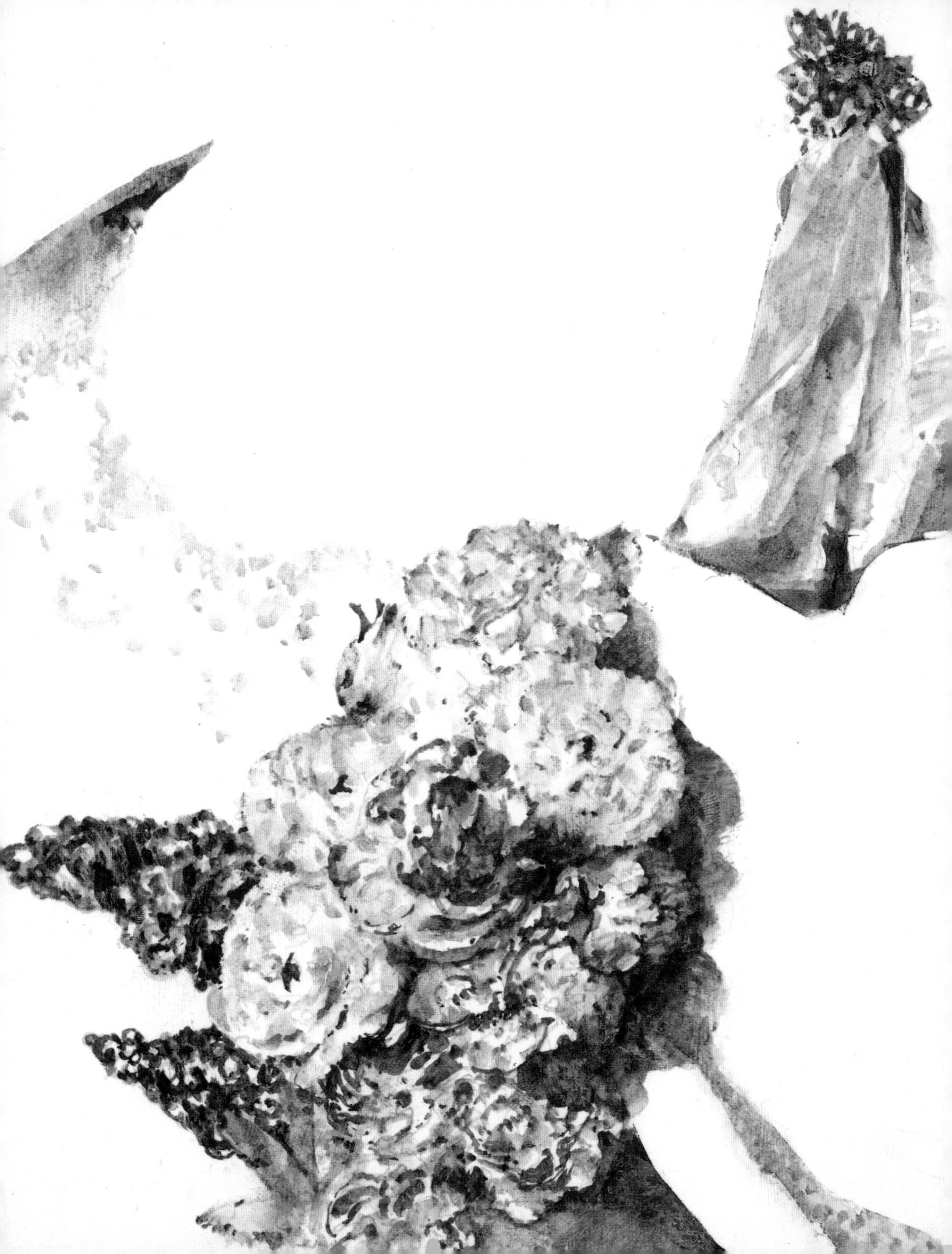

ran her father's business, and after his death she ran the household with her mother and her sisters. The works that initially made her famous were miniatures, but she subsequently began to produce pastel portraits, becoming the preeminent artist in the field in Europe. Countless French, German, and British travelers to Venice made a stop at Rosalba's house and studio to sit for her and bring home a pastel portrait. Rosalba was a member of some of the most distinguished academies in Italy—the Accademia di San Luca in Rome, the Accademia Clementina in Bologna—as well as the Académie in Paris. The men who ran the academies seldom allowed females to join, so it was a rare occurrence when a female colleague was granted membership. Rosalba never married and lived in Venice for most of her life in a house on the Grand Canal, next to what is today the Peggy Guggenheim Collection.

In 1720, Rosalba went to France at the invitation of Pierre Crozat, a great collector who was at the center of Parisian culture. At the time, it would have been very unusual for a female artist to travel across Europe and be invited to work in a different country. Through Crozat, Rosalba met Antoine Watteau, with whom she became good friends. She portrayed him and later owned drawings by him. While in Paris, she also portrayed the young king, Louis XV. We have many of Rosalba's letters and diaries—more than most any other Venetian painter at the time. We know from them that she went to the opera and the ballet with her sisters and her mother and also that she worked ceaselessly. The French diary also gives us some fun snippets about what was happening at court at the time. For example, on January 28, 1721: "The duc de Noailles, brother of Madame de Louvois, and captain of the Royal Guard, had a terror of cats. The King, knowing this, scratched him from behind, imitating a cat. The duc fainted and hurt himself, and the King cried." There are also entries that provide a glimpse into the struggles of the artist, whom we know suffered from bouts of depression. The entry of October 14, 1720, reads: "It is a sad day for me."

Two gorgeous pastel portraits by Rosalba were bequeathed to the Frick in 2020 by the collector Alexis Gregory. We do not know who either of the sitters is. Despite what might be one's immediate impression, it is unlikely that they were husband and wife or that the pastels were designed to be pendants. The female portrait is typical of Rosalba's images of women. It depicts an elegant woman, provocatively attired in a rather low-cut dress decorated with jewels and flowers. The attire of the male sitter is rather unusual. Over a blue jacket embroidered with flowers and a lace cravat, he sports a black cape, hat, and staff that are all directly related to the images of pilgrims at the time. Is the man really a pilgrim? Another possibility is that the sitter is Rosalba's brother-in-law, the painter Giovanni Antonio Pellegrini, and the pilgrim attire a play on his surname, which means "pilgrim" in Italian. However, we know from other portraits that Pellegrini did not look like the man in the pastel. There were also noble families named Pellegrini in Italy. And it could also relate to the name of a foreigner: Pilgrim, Pèlerin, or Pilger. Or do the clothes allude to French fashion? Rosalba's friend Watteau had created an entire iconography around the notion of pilgrimages of love. In his *fêtes galantes*, men and women are often dressed as pilgrims. And finally, could the outfit simply be a costume for the annual Carnival of Venice? The tricorn hat is usually associated with Venetian costume during the carnival. Rosalba painted a number of sitters dressed up for the carnival.

When it was examined recently, the male portrait disclosed a fascinating surprise. Tucked behind the stretcher was a small piece of paper, what is known in Italian as a *santino*, with an image of a medallion with the Virgin and Child and the three Magi, as well as a dedication to the three saints. The brief text states that "the three Magi of Cologne, for the grace of God, would preserve travelers from the bad hours of travel, headaches, epilepsy, fever, witchcraft, and any sort of malefice and sudden death." We have evidence that Rosalba did this on a number of occasions. In a letter from Pier Caterino Zeno to Anton Francesco Marmi in Florence, written in December 1729, he writes about Rosalba's

> *distinct devotion to the Three Kings, who brought themselves to the adoration of the baby Jesus at the grotto in Bethlehem. Once she gave me a certain portrait to send to my brother in Vienna. And she gave me a little card of the three aforementioned adoring Magi and said to these she entrusted the safe outward journey of the portrait, adding that whenever such little images had accompanied her pictures, they had always arrived safely.*

It was incredibly moving for me to be able to touch this piece of paper, which was probably last placed behind the stretcher by Rosalba herself. And I like to imagine what she might think if she knew that this very same pastel ended up in New York.

Rosalba's career ended tragically. She lost her sister Giovanna in the 1730s, followed by their mother. By the 1740s, Rosalba had started to lose her sight from cataracts. She underwent at least three very painful operations, which only worsened the condition. By the early 1750s, she was totally blind. She spent the last seven years of her life in absolute darkness in her house. She was buried in the little parish of San Vio.

—X.S.

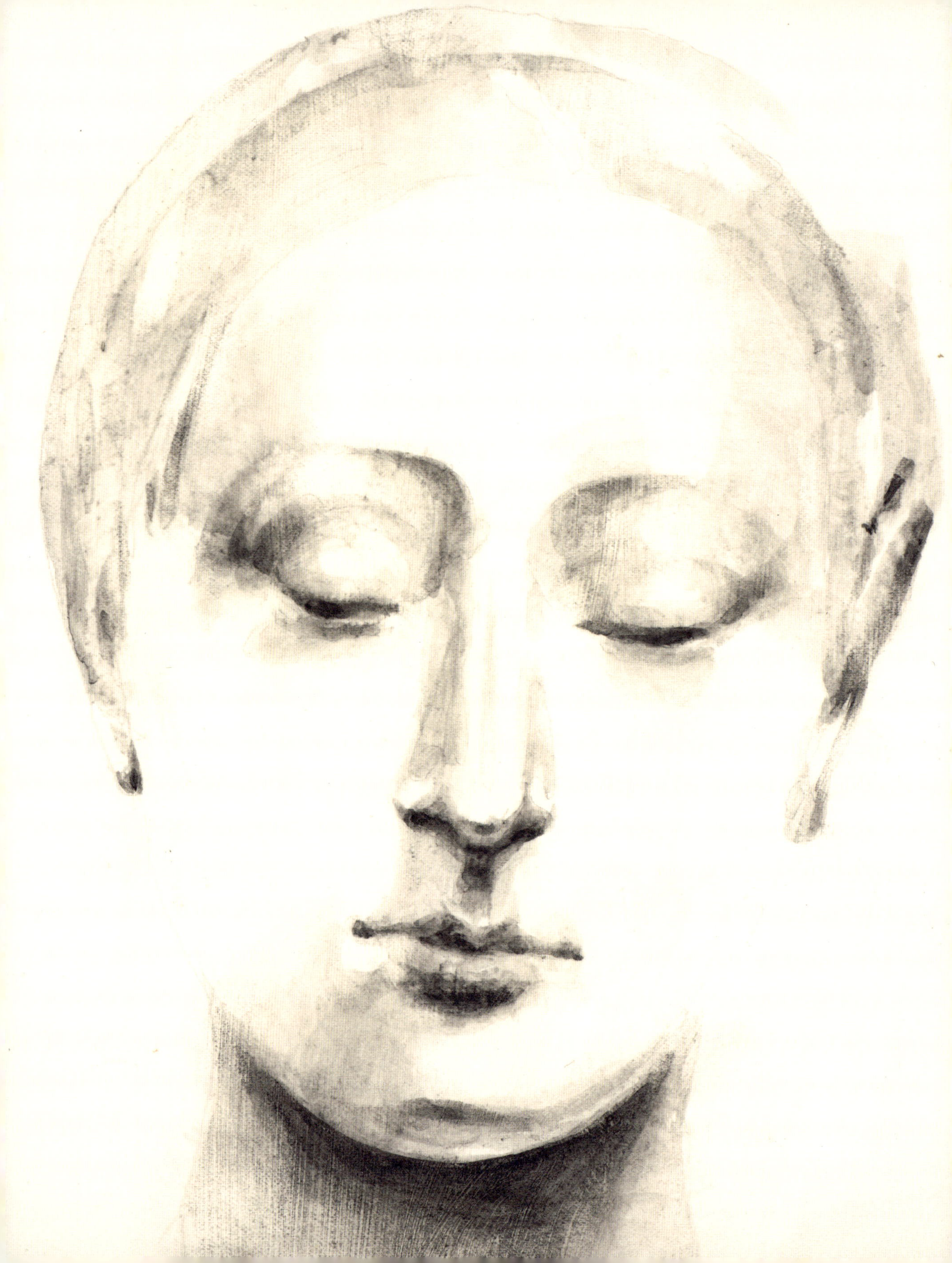

FRANCESCO LAURANA

Bust of a Woman

CA. 1470S

Dalmatian

1½ OZ. VODKA
3 OZ. GRAPEFRUIT JUICE
1½ OZ. BLACK-PEPPER SIMPLE SYRUP

Combine with ice in a cocktail shaker, shake vigorously, and strain into an ice-filled tumbler

FOR THE BLACK-PEPPER SIMPLE SYRUP (MAKES 1½ CUPS):
¼ CUP CRUSHED PEPPERCORNS
1 CUP WATER
1 CUP SUGAR

Combine in a small pot
Bring to a boil, stirring occasionally, until sugar is dissolved
Remove from heat
For a more robust flavor, allow mixture to steep for a few minutes
Strain and chill

This strong pepper-infused cocktail is a tribute to Laurana's birthplace, Vrana, in Dalmatia (modern-day Croatia).

This Carrara marble bust is one of the Frick's most prized Italian sculptures. However, Francesco Laurana (ca. 1420/30–ca. 1502) was not an Italian sculptor. First of all, Italy didn't become a state until the 1860s. Before then, the Italian peninsula was made up of many small states, usually at war with each other, though admittedly there was a sense that, because of a shared heritage and a shared language, there was a shared nation, Italy. The borders of this nation actually extended beyond the borders of modern-day Italy to include the coast of modern-day Croatia, where Laurana was originally from. He was born Frane Vranjanin, meaning "Francis from Vrana." Vrana is a town close to the ancient city of Zadar on the Dalmatian coast. In Italian, the artist's name became "Francesco de la Vrana"; because *u* and *v* were not distinct letters in fifteenth-century Italian, he became known as Francesco de Laurana. Nothing is known about Francesco before 1453—when we find him at work in Naples for the Castel Nuovo (New Castle) with a number of other sculptors—and very little is known about the rest of his life. At some point, he moved to Sicily, where he worked extensively, and in the last part of his life, he was in southern France, where some of his works survive in the area around Avignon.

The Frick example is one of three similar busts. One is at the National Gallery in Washington, DC, and the other was mostly destroyed in the bombing of Berlin during World War II and survives in a fragmentary state, with the head in Berlin and the bust in Moscow. The two pieces have never been reunited, but both have been completed with a cast of the missing parts. Scholars have engaged in a long debate over the originality of the busts, and some have speculated that at least one of them is a nineteenth-century forgery.

The Frick bust, however, cannot be a nineteenth-century forgery. It was found in the port of Marseille, in the south of France, as early as the early eighteenth century. Initially believed to be an antique bust of Agrippina, the little-known bust remained in France until it was acquired in 1914 by the art dealer Duveen, who bought it from Princess Suzanne d'Orange, Marchioness of Mailly-Nesle. Henry Clay Frick bought it two years later, in 1916.

The fact that the bust was found in Marseille suggests that this may be a French woman for whom Laurana worked during his stay in southern France. But, if all three busts are original—as seems to be the growing consensus—the sheer number of her surviving portraits suggests that this was a woman of the highest lineage, possibly a member of the Aragonese dynasty.

Traditionally, the bust is identified either as the wife of King Alfonso II of Naples, Ippolita Maria Sforza, of Milanese origins, or as Ippolita's daughter, Isabella d'Aragona, who married her own cousin, Gian Galeazzo Sforza, Duke of Milan. A few years after the wedding, Gian Galeazzo was killed by his legal guardian, Ludovico il Moro, leading to a very unhappy and precarious widowhood for Isabella. She used to sign her letters dramatically as "Isabella, unique in misfortune." But after the French invasion of Italy in 1499, Isabella—aged about thirty—was granted the title of Duchess of Bari, in Apulia, where she led a splendid court life for the rest of her days.

Unfortunately, no one has ever been able to identify the scenes of the classicizing reliefs on the base of the bust, which might have provided another clue as to the identity of the woman. However, they all seem to show scenes of female heroism against male violence and male threat—a story befitting Isabella's. No convincing explanation has yet been found for the inscription, DMS, on the base of a column depicted in the reliefs. It's possible that it is the dedicatory inscription that can be found on many Roman monuments—DIS MANIBUS SACRUM (to the God Manes)—that is, the Gods of the Underworld in care of deceased loved ones.

The back of the Frick bust is flat, and the sitter is tilting her head slightly downward, which probably means that this bust was placed in a niche high up on a wall. Its function remains mysterious. We know that at least one female bust by Laurana was used as a funerary monument, that of Eleanor of Aragon (now at Palazzo Abatellis in Palermo). However, Eleanor died in 1405, some twenty-five years before Laurana was even born. This means that the Frick bust could also be funerary, and it could even portray someone who had died long before Laurana started to carve it. So really, who knows the identity of the sitter? It's a million-dollar question.

Because of the difficulty of identifying the sitters of Laurana's portrait busts, some have thought they are portraits of ideal feminine beauty, not of any actual woman. While such portraits of women were made later in the sixteenth century following the canon of beauty as institutionalized by Petrarchan poetry, it seems a bit too early for these portrait busts to be similar experiments in idealized portraiture. But there is definitely some kind of abstraction, or idealization, going on here. You do not see any wrinkles in this woman's face; you do not see any defects; you do not feel you can touch the flesh of her face. Instead, you realize that the bust is designed as a composite of perfectly interlocking geometrical shapes (an approach that would be replicated by early twentieth-century modernist sculptors). But, looking at the faces of Laurana's many statues of the Virgin and Child, so similar to those of the portrait busts, it becomes clear that, yes, the busts may be idealized, but in the sense that they are Madonna-like representations of real women, probably associating the sitter's virtue—or a notion of virtue aligned with Christian values—with the Virgin's.

Nowadays, Laurana's busts are totally white. But it was only after Michelangelo and neoclassicism prescribed whiteness for marble statues that busts such as these were stripped of their original polychromy, which was deemed vulgar and primitive. Some of them still retain their original colors, giving us a sense of how much closer to life these works originally looked. When it comes to female portraiture of the fifteenth century, we are not able to judge the balance between naturalism and abstraction, not least because these objects have suffered from the shifting conceptions of what female beauty (and good sculpture) should look like.

—G.D.

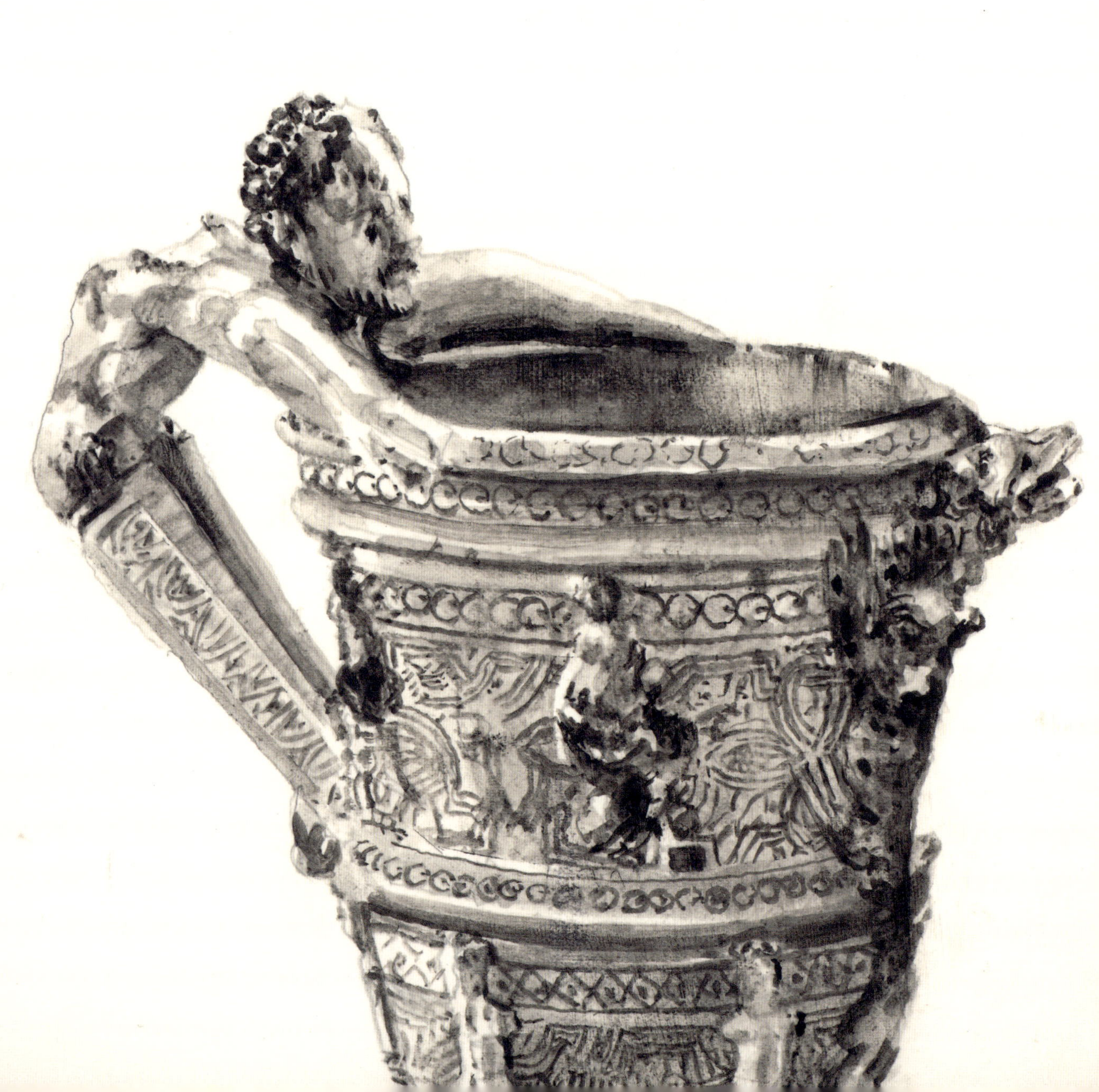

SAINT-PORCHAIRE WARE

Ewers

MID-16TH CENTURY

Boulevardier

1 OZ. BOURBON

1 OZ. SWEET VERMOUTH

1 OZ. CAMPARI

Serve on the rocks in a tumbler
and garnish with an orange peel

The quintessential American–French cocktail, the Boulevardier was created to celebrate the 1927 launch in Paris of The Boulevardier, *a literary magazine founded by the American writer Erskine Gwynne.*

The Frick owns three pieces of Saint-Porchaire ware, a type of glazed earthenware produced in France in the sixteenth century, probably between the 1540s and the 1560s. There are only between sixty and seventy of these objects, and each is unique in shape and decoration. The decoration often includes human figures, animals, shells, and other natural elements. This is very much part of a decorative tradition going back to Italian models such as the *grotteschi* and decorative elements brought to France by Italian artists working at the courts of Francis I and Henry II, the so-called School of Fontainebleau. Even though they were made with fairly simple materials, the objects were all clearly luxury objects created for decorative purposes for the royal family and other aristocrats at the time.

The shapes of these objects are based on metalwork, and scholars have studied the numerous links between their form and decoration and bookbinding, architecture, painted decoration, engravings, and a number of other arts.

The very intricate decoration covering Saint-Porchaire ware was made over a type of particularly white clay, and the brown, black, and reddish lines—which one might assume are painted on the clay before the object is glazed and fired—are in fact inlaid. The white clay was pressed in with stamps, and then clays of different colors, usually brown, black, or red, were inserted into the incised lines to create these extraordinary decorations. Over them, three-dimensional reliefs in the shapes of small animals were applied, colored, and then glazed and fired. This is an extraordinarily complicated technique that we still do not fully understand.

Why is it called Saint-Porchaire? In the 1890s, French scholars identified sixteenth-century references to ceramics produced at the time as made of "terre de Saint-Porchaire" (Saint-Porchaire earth) or in the "façon de Saint-Porchaire" (the manner of Saint-Porchaire). The town of Saint-Porchaire—in the southwest of France, north of Bordeaux—is known for the pure white clay, rich in kaolin, indigenous to the area. Were these ceramics created in Saint-Porchaire itself and then brought to Paris and other important cities in France? Or were they created in Paris with clay coming from Saint-Porchaire? Were they created by an individual or a single workshop? Or were they created by a number of different workshops, which were active either in Saint-Porchaire or in Paris, or even possibly somewhere else in France?

Saint-Porchaire ware was much sought after by collectors in the nineteenth and early twentieth centuries. A number of Rothschild family members owned some pieces, as did, for example, Sir Richard Wallace and other collectors like John Pierpont Morgan. Henry Clay Frick acquired the first of the three Saint-Porchaire ewers in the museum. The other two are more recent acquisitions—one acquired in 2015, as a gift from Sidney R. Knafel, the third bequeathed in 2020 by Alexis Gregory.

One big question focuses on the nature of the relationship between Saint-Porchaire ware and the work of Bernard Palissy (1509–1590), a venerated French ceramic artist in the Renaissance. Palissy came from a Huguenot background and was caught in the middle of the Wars of Religion that divided France at the time. He died while imprisoned in the Bastille. He is famous for creating dishes and ewers with casts, taken from life, of shells and small animals. These objects are covered in small ceramic insects, frogs, reptiles, and fish. Was Palissy involved in any way with the production at Saint-Porchaire? One of the great creations by Palissy was a grotto, entirely covered with ceramic shells and animals, that he made for Queen Catherine de' Medici, in the Tuileries Palace. The grotto was destroyed, but in the nineteenth century and then again in the 1980s, excavations near the Louvre unearthed fragments of it. The excavations also uncovered a number of the molds that were used to create the decoration, the patterns, on Palissy's ceramics.

Both the Frick's curator of decorative arts and our conservator noticed that the lizard in one of these molds matches that on the spout of the ewer given to the museum by Sidney Knafel. This may mean that our ewer was created by Palissy in the style of Saint-Porchaire. Did Palissy, therefore, work on some of the Saint-Porchaire objects? Was this part of his early career, something that he did as a young man, or did he inherit—and then reuse—some of the molds that were used by the people who made Saint-Porchaire ware? How did Palissy come into possession of the mold? These questions remain unanswered. Small decorative art objects like these, in fact, are very exciting objects in terms of research and the questions they raise.

—X.S.

FRANCESCO DA SANGALLO

St. John Baptizing

CA. 1534–38

Negroni Bianco

I OZ. GIN

I OZ. LILLET BLANC

I OZ. SUZE

Serve on the rocks in a tumbler
and garnish with an orange peel

This is one of the numerous variations on the famous Florentine cocktail invented by Count Negroni. It includes Suze, a liqueur made from the root of gentian—an aromatic herb that grows in the Alps—and invented in France in 1889. For me, this herbal take on the Negroni evokes the wilderness where the Baptist lived.

It can be quite challenging for a curator to try to bring into a museum something of the original context of a work of art. Until relatively recently, art was not created with a museum destination in mind. Everything we display at the Frick originally came from a house—a grand palace or villa—or from a church. In a museum, away from these contexts, it can be difficult to

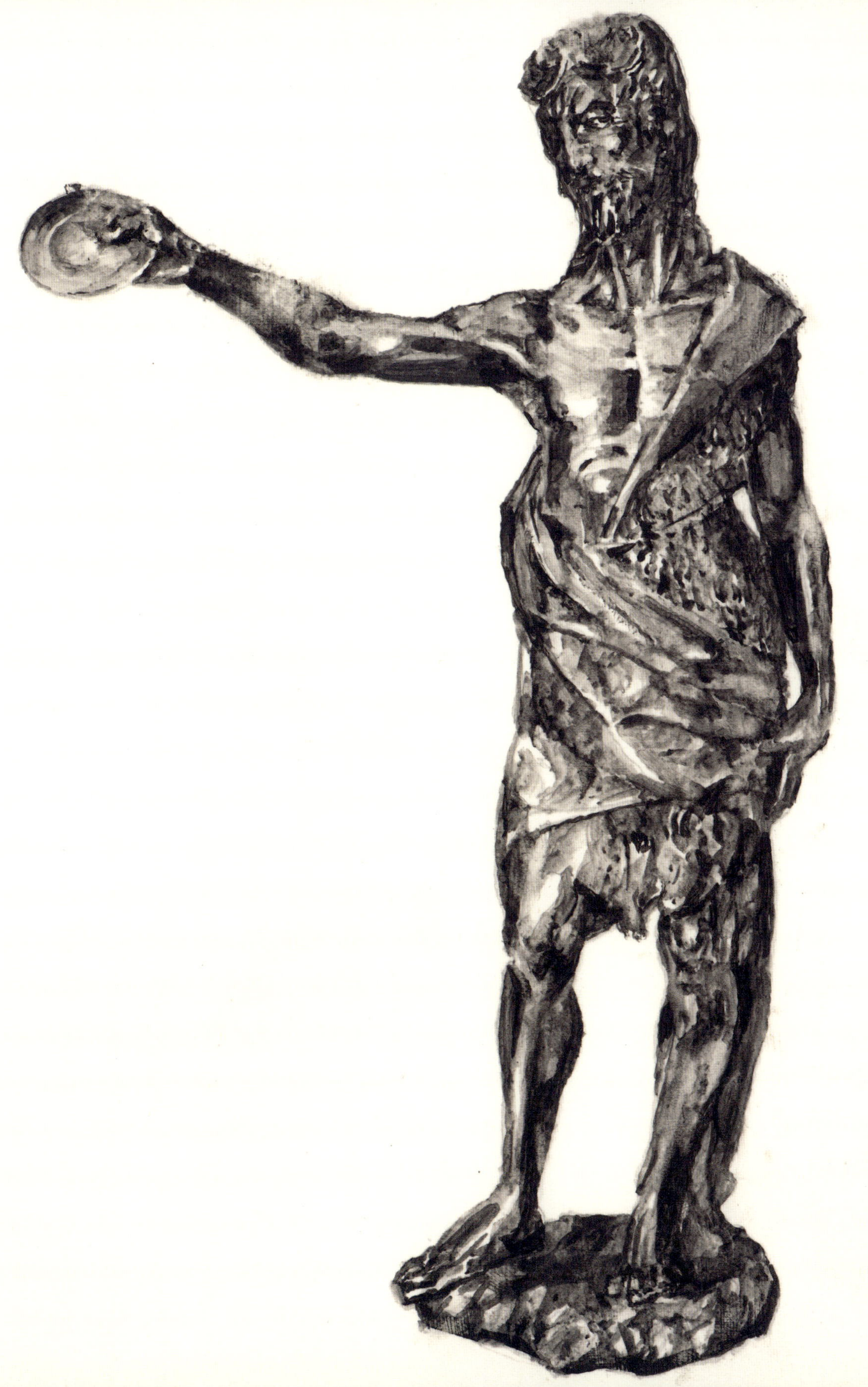

fully understand a particular work of art. This is particularly true of this bronze statuette by the Tuscan Renaissance sculptor Francesco da Sangallo (1494–1576).

Francesco came from a family of artists. His father was the great architect Giuliano da Sangallo, and his uncle and cousins were also architects and artists. Sangallo himself was both an architect and a sculptor. He worked mostly in marble, but this statuette of the Baptist in the act of baptizing is cast in solid bronze. He holds a shallow bowl in his right hand, and with it he is in the act of pouring water. John inhabited the desert near the River Jordan and is often depicted dressed in rough clothes. As an object in itself, the statuette looks complete on its pedestal on a table at the Frick, where it is one of our most important sculptural works. When John Pope-Hennessy wrote the catalogue of sculptures of the Frick, the Italian volume had an image of the Sangallo statue on the cover.

The statuette—the artist's only signed work in bronze—was created for the church of Santa Maria delle Carceri in the city of Prato, northwest of Florence. The church is named after the prisons—the *carceri*—of the city that once stood where the church is now. In 1484, a young boy from Prato had a vision there; he saw a fresco of the Virgin and Child on the walls of the prisons coming to life. A church was commissioned to commemorate the miracle. It was paid for in great part by Lorenzo de' Medici and was designed by Giuliano da Sangallo, Francesco's father. Centrally planned with a dome, the church was left unfinished by Sangallo, and its facade is still incomplete.

On March 22, 1534—almost fifty years after the church was built—the *ortolani* (vegetable sellers) and the *poponai* (melon sellers) of Prato collected thirty *scudi* to pay a stone carver, Giovan Francesco Pagni, to make a holy water font—an *acquasantiera* or *pila*—to be placed at the entrance of the church so that people could cross themselves with blessed water as they walked in and out. Apparently, the vegetable and fruit sellers were not entirely happy with the final result, and four years later, in August 1538, they commissioned Francesco da Sangallo to enhance the *acquasantiera* with a statue. Sangallo added a little column decorated with leaves and the bronze sculpture on top of St. John in the act of baptizing.

The work remained in the church until the late nineteenth century, when the bronze sculpture was sold. It went through the Florentine dealer, Stefano Bardini, to a German collection, then to John Pierpont Morgan, and eventually to Frick, who acquired it together with a large selection of the Morgan bronzes, in 1916. In 1902, an exact copy in bronze of the John the Baptist was commissioned for the church in Prato and placed over the *acquasantiera*. To this day, one can see the original marble *acquasantiera* in the church with a modern copy of the Sangallo sculpture above it.

At the Frick, this statuette is set on a small base that is usually on a large table in the West Gallery. In early 2021, when the museum temporarily moved to Frick Madison, the idea came about of bringing some of the statue's original context into the temporary space. Working with the Factum Arte studio in Madrid, as well as with the church of Santa Maria delle Carceri, we commissioned the fabrication of an exact facsimile of the holy water font for the original John the Baptist to be placed on top of—effectively the reverse of what was done in the church in Prato.

For the first time in more than a hundred years, the sculpture on the top of the facsimile can be seen at the right height—from below, not from above, and in the right position in space. It is not a sculpture that is meant to be seen from above, sitting on a table, but something that should be seen from below. Suddenly, the proportions of the sculpture and the elegant gesture of the Baptist pouring water become more natural. A reconstruction of this kind, though, cannot entirely reconstruct a context but can only evoke it. For instance, the basin of the *acquasantiera* would have originally contained water, but this cannot be replicated, for conservation reasons, in the museum. Also, we now know from documents that the St. John was originally gilded. We can only imagine the interior of the church, candlelit, with this gold sculpture's reflection glimmering in the water below.

—X.S.

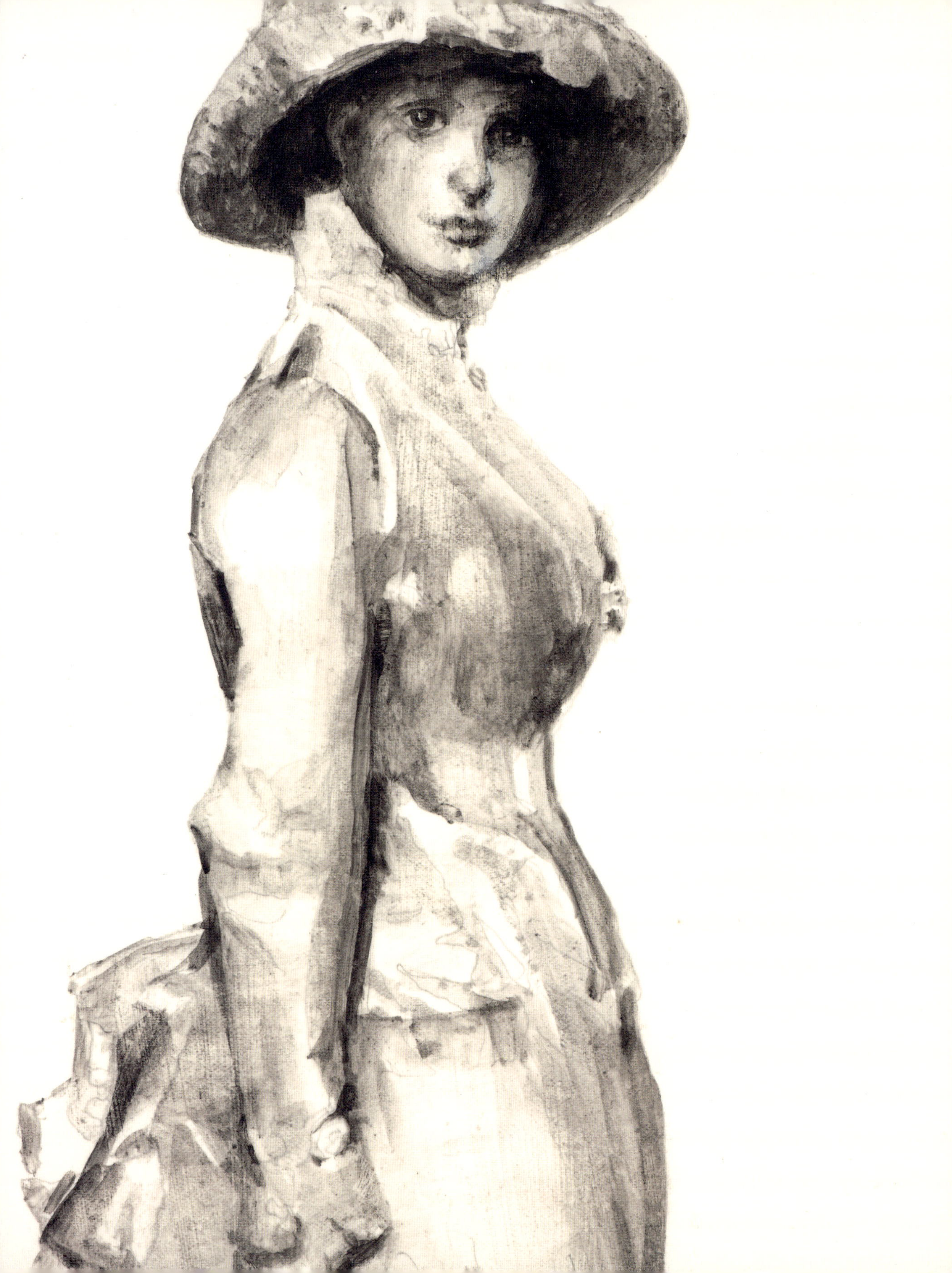

JAMES McNEILL WHISTLER

Harmony in Pink and Grey: Portrait of Lady Meux

1881–82

The Mummy

2 OZ. VODKA

1 OZ. TRIPLE SEC

1 TBSP. LEMON JUICE

Pour over ice in a highball glass and top with sparkling water

This cocktail pays tribute to Lady Meux's activities as an avid collector of Egyptian and Assyrian antiquities, including a famous mummy.

American-born painter James McNeill Whistler (1834–1903) was a celebrated society portraitist in London until his public conflict with the art critic John Ruskin. He sued Ruskin for libel, and though he won the case, he bankrupted himself in the process and left London under a cloud of scandal. After a sojourn in Venice, Whistler returned to London at the end of 1880, but his old clientele would not come near him. One observer suggested that the only people who would patronize Whistler at this point were people "with no class to lose." That is how some contemporaries might have described Lady Meux.

Lady Meux was a notorious society figure. Gossip columns were preoccupied with her modest (and, according to rumor, scandalous) beginnings. She was reputed to have been a bartender, an actress, possibly a prostitute. One newspaper referred to her as a former "bareback rider at a circus." She eventually met and married the extremely wealthy Sir Henry Bruce Meux (pronounced "Mews"), heir to a brewery fortune who inherited a baronetcy soon after they married, in 1878. The press attacked him too, calling him a lunatic and mentally incapacitated for marrying someone like her, whose previous names were Valerie Susan Langdon and Val Reece, the latter possibly taken from a man who had previously supported her. (The press continues to treat her this way; when her gun was sold at auction in December 2020, the BBC referred to her as a "banjo-playing Victorian prostitute." The gun sold for three times its estimate.)

Lady Meux was the first to patronize Whistler after his return to London. She commissioned at least three portraits. The first, showing her in a black dress, white fur, and diamond jewelry, is today in the Honolulu Museum of Art. The second, at The Frick Collection, is the subject of this episode. A third, *Harmony in Crimson and Brown,* which shows her in furs, was destroyed, purportedly by the artist after a heated encounter with Lady Meux. (Whistler was known to be difficult, as was Lady Meux.) There was talk of a fourth portrait of her in riding attire, but it was apparently never begun. It is amazing to think about a room of full-length portraits by Whistler of Lady Meux in different modes.

In the Frick picture, her hat casts a shadow on her face. Upon seeing this portrait, Henry James remarked that her hat does not fit. The hat seems to play more of a compositional role than a sartorial one and may not represent contemporary fashion. To complete the composition, Whistler added his butterfly monogram, which was inspired by Japanese prints and included in many of his works.

One has to wonder about the difference between what the artist has conveyed in paint and what the sitter was really like. A quick look at the extant photographs of Lady Meux indicates that Whistler edited, making her painted figure appear slenderer and more petite. A drawing in the Davison Art Center at Wesleyan University seems to show Whistler experimenting with this composition—the hat is much broader in the drawing; he includes a framing structure behind her; and he moves the location of his monogram, which appears in the drawing to her left and in the painting to her right. Underneath the drawing is an inscription with what appears to have been the painting's original title. Many of Whistler's portraits use musical terminology: arrangements, nocturnes, harmonies. The drawing gives the title *Harmony in Flesh Colour and Pink.* Very little of her flesh is pictured, but of course the "flesh colour" in the title is not referring specifically to her flesh. We do not need to belabor the point that flesh color in Whistler's context is referring generically to the white European flesh tone that would conventionally be seen in

European art history. For whatever reason, he changed the title to pinks and grays, and the painting plays with the subtleties of those hues and values.

Lady Meux was eccentric, engaging in activities that made her an easy target for public ridicule. She traveled in a carriage pulled by zebras, or zebra-horse hybrids, which she bred on her estate at Theobalds Park. This extraordinary complex (today a hotel) boasted a swimming pool, a roller skating rink, and a museum for her collection of some eighteen hundred Egyptian and Assyrian antiquities. Perhaps the most famous of these is the mummy case and mummy of Nesmin, which were associated with a curse on anyone who tried to remove the mummy from its burial site. The man through whom Lady Meux acquired the mummy, Walter Ingram, was killed a few years after he brokered the acquisition of the mummy, by an elephant during an elephant-hunting trip. A *Pittsburgh Press* newspaper article published in 1911, shortly after Lady Meux's death, suggested that the true reason why the British Museum did not accept her bequest of her collection was because of the curse. The mummy and case are now in the collection of the museum at the Rhode Island School of Design.

Lady Meux had to read terrible things about herself in the press, especially after her husband left her his entire fortune when he died in 1900. News about her and how she spent her late husband's fortune was discussed in newspapers in such far-flung places as Calgary, Alberta; Pittsburgh; St. Louis; and along the East Coast of the United States. One of her late husband's relatives was quoted as saying that she would rather "starve" than be associated with Lady Meux, who became more and more a social pariah. Lady Meux eventually chose an heir with no connection to her or to her husband's family: Sir Hedworth Lambton, considered by British contemporaries a military hero after his participation in the Boer War in South Africa, a devastating conflict to which she had contributed thousands of dollars. He and his wife lived nearby, but they were not close friends. Stories told in the papers recounted that she met him at a horse race at which no one spoke to her but him, out of politeness. Her only requirement of him in order to inherit her fortune was that he take the Meux name, which he did. She wrote in her will a message to her husband's family: she did not leave the money to them because they had treated her so poorly. There is sadness in her revenge. With no children, she sought to create her own legacy, to identify a deserving beneficiary. She had spent many years being treated like an outcast.

Portraits often present a veneer of power and fashion that hides the vulnerabilities and challenges of the individual who is depicted. Knowing her story—even the events of the decades after this portrait was made in the early 1880s—shines a light on the young woman behind those dark brown eyes, looking out pensively and also hopefully from beneath that ill-fitting hat.

—A.N.

JOSEPH CHINARD

Étienne Vincent de Margnolas

1809

Napoleon

2 OZ. GIN

½ OZ. BRANDY-BASED ORANGE LIQUEUR

½ OZ. DUBONNET ROUGE

Serve in a cocktail glass

This simple drink is a tribute to Joseph Chinard's greatest benefactor.

Born in Lyon, in the south of France, Joseph Chinard (1756–1813) is best known for his portraits of Napoleon and his family. But his path to becoming the official portraitist of Napoleon's family was long and tortuous. Like many contemporary French artists, he spent time in Rome studying the remains of the ancient past. During his time there (1784–86), he was arrested and put on trial for a variety of transgressions. According to a neighbor, he and his roommate had

> *meetings with naked women with whom they dance obscenely, as the gardener will tell you. They* [Chinard and his roommate] *say that it is high time to kill the pope, and after that, it will be easy to subjugate the cardinals and*

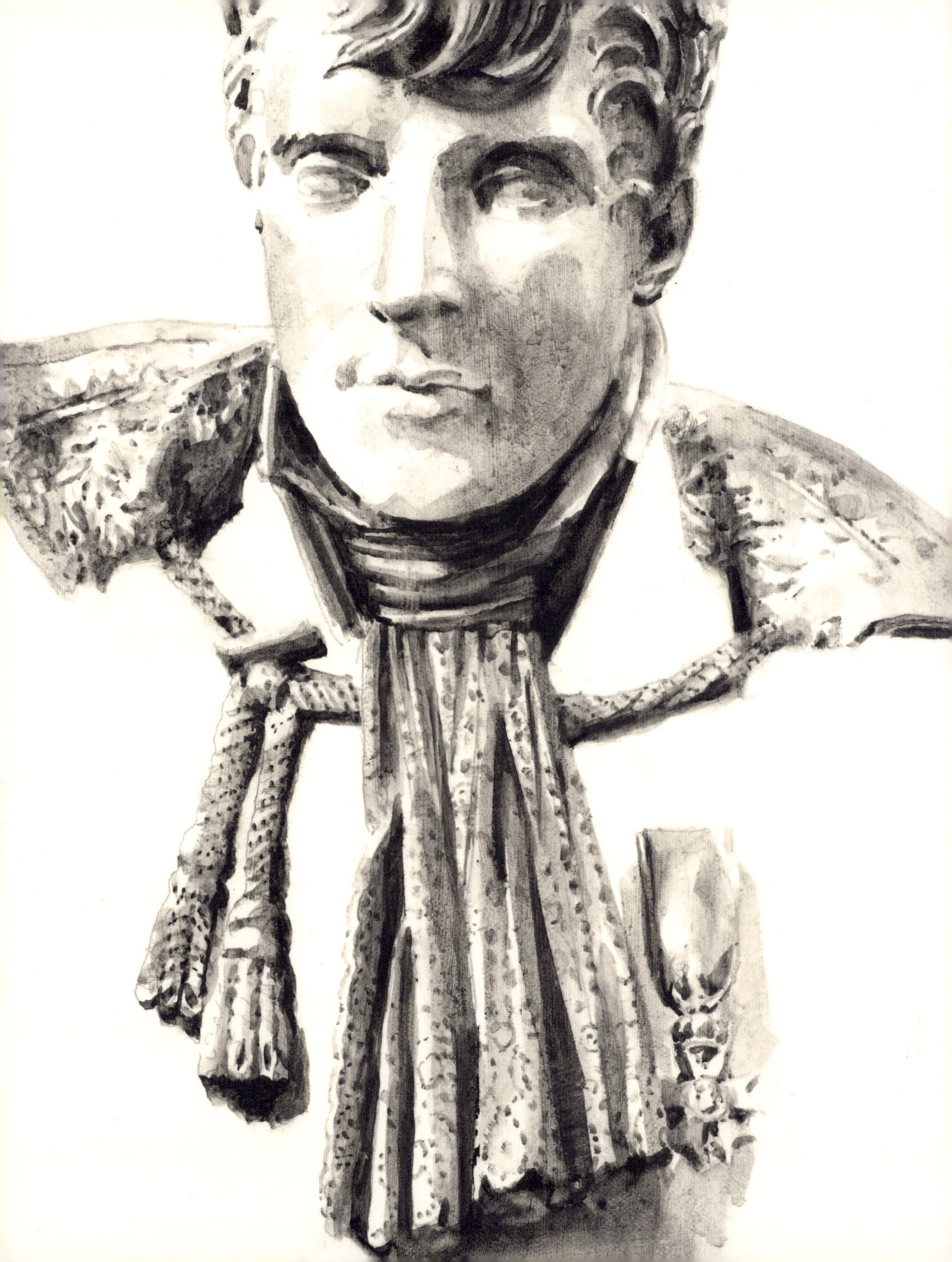

establish the same freedom in Rome as there is in France now. They deny both Paradise and Hell. They say it's a lot of nonsense. And they eat poultry and meat when it is forbidden and thereby ridicule the Catholic faith. And what's worse? They invite young men and women from Rome to join their school.

The trial was something of an international scandal and ended in a stalemate, mostly due to the intervention of Cardinal de Bernis, a longtime friend and counselor of Madame de Pompadour (Louis XV's mistress). Although Chinard was banned from the Papal States, he was allowed to return home with his possessions. Back in France, he was hailed as a revolutionary hero. But this did not last long because very soon his sculptures—some of which had been central to the trial condemning him as a revolutionary—were deemed not revolutionary enough by the Jacobins under the Terror. Accused of betraying the revolutionary cause, Chinard was convicted for a second time in France!

While serving his time in the French prisons, Chinard was allowed to work. His stylistic choices changed dramatically, shifting toward increasingly heroic, static, and rigid figures. Interestingly, he also adopted the habit of covering his statues and statuettes with inscriptions to clarify their meaning. Can we blame him? After all, he had paid a heavy price for the misunderstandings surrounding his works. But these incidents, and Chinard's decision to cover his statues in inscriptions, also tell us about a crucial problem for artists of Chinard's generation—the difficulty of negotiating the tension between new "revolutionary" iconography and old forms appealing to an audience whose taste was formed during the ancien régime.

After his release from prison, Chinard understood that he needed a network of powerful people to protect him during those turbulent times. So he sought the patronage of a very powerful and rich couple from his hometown, Lyon: Jacques-Rose and Juliette Récamier. Juliette hosted one of the most celebrated salons in Paris and was a renowned beauty who became the muse of many neoclassical artists. Thanks to her, Chinard realized, he could aspire to the patronage of Napoleon himself. In 1797, he was bold enough to write a letter to Napoleon asking him to make him useful to the revolutionary cause, and Napoleon did so, commissioning several sculptures from him.

With Napoleon's own commissions came a wealth of commissions from his closest friends and advisors. Among them was Étienne Vincent de Margnolas, who, like Chinard and the Récamiers, was from Lyon. Margnolas climbed the ranks of Napoleon's regime with extraordinary speed. In 1807, he was awarded the newly established Légion d'Honneur, which you can see in the bust, pinned on his chest (with Napoleon's head in profile). The next year, he became prefect of the Po region, in northern Italy. Less than two years later, in February 1809, he was appointed a councillor of state. Not yet thirty, he was among the highest-ranking dignitaries of the empire.

Margnolas is shown wearing the uniform of a councillor of state, so the portrait bust must have been made after February 1809. The stillness of his face is undercut by the sweeping movement of the cloak, which seems on the verge of falling down, were it not for the rope holding it up. There is also another jarring contrast between the very polished surface of the skin and the small details encrusted on the cloak—look at the tassels, the rope, the lace, and also the oak leaves pattern. Only a material as flexible as clay would allow for the variations in texture that make this bust so beguiling and arresting.

Made after February 1809, the bust was probably commissioned before Margnolas's sudden death of pneumonia in October of that year. Some think that the bust may be commemorative of Margnolas's death, which would explain his somewhat impassive face, which could have been taken from a death mask. In any case, the bust was exhibited at the Salon in Paris the following year, and after the death of Margnolas's son, it passed to the family of Margnolas's cousin, who kept it at the Château de Launay until 1997. It was then sold at auction, to be acquired a few years later by the Frick.

—G.D.

PAOLO VENEZIANO with GIOVANNI VENEZIANO
The Coronation of the Virgin

1358

Mint Julep

2 OZ. BOURBON

2 TSP. WATER

1 TSP. BROWN SUGAR

4 CRUSHED MINT LEAVES

Serve on the rocks in a silver cup and garnish with a mint sprig

The Mint Julep is one of the oldest American cocktails, invented in the South in the eighteenth century. The silver or pewter cup in which it is traditionally served is a nod to the precious metals Paolo Veneziano incorporated so magnificently into his paintings.

Paolo Veneziano (ca. 1295–1362) is considered the father of Venetian painting. The son of a painter and the father of painters, he ran the most important workshop in Venice at the time and produced many religious works—from small, portable devotional works to grand altarpieces. He worked for those at the highest levels of Venetian society—for the doge and the most

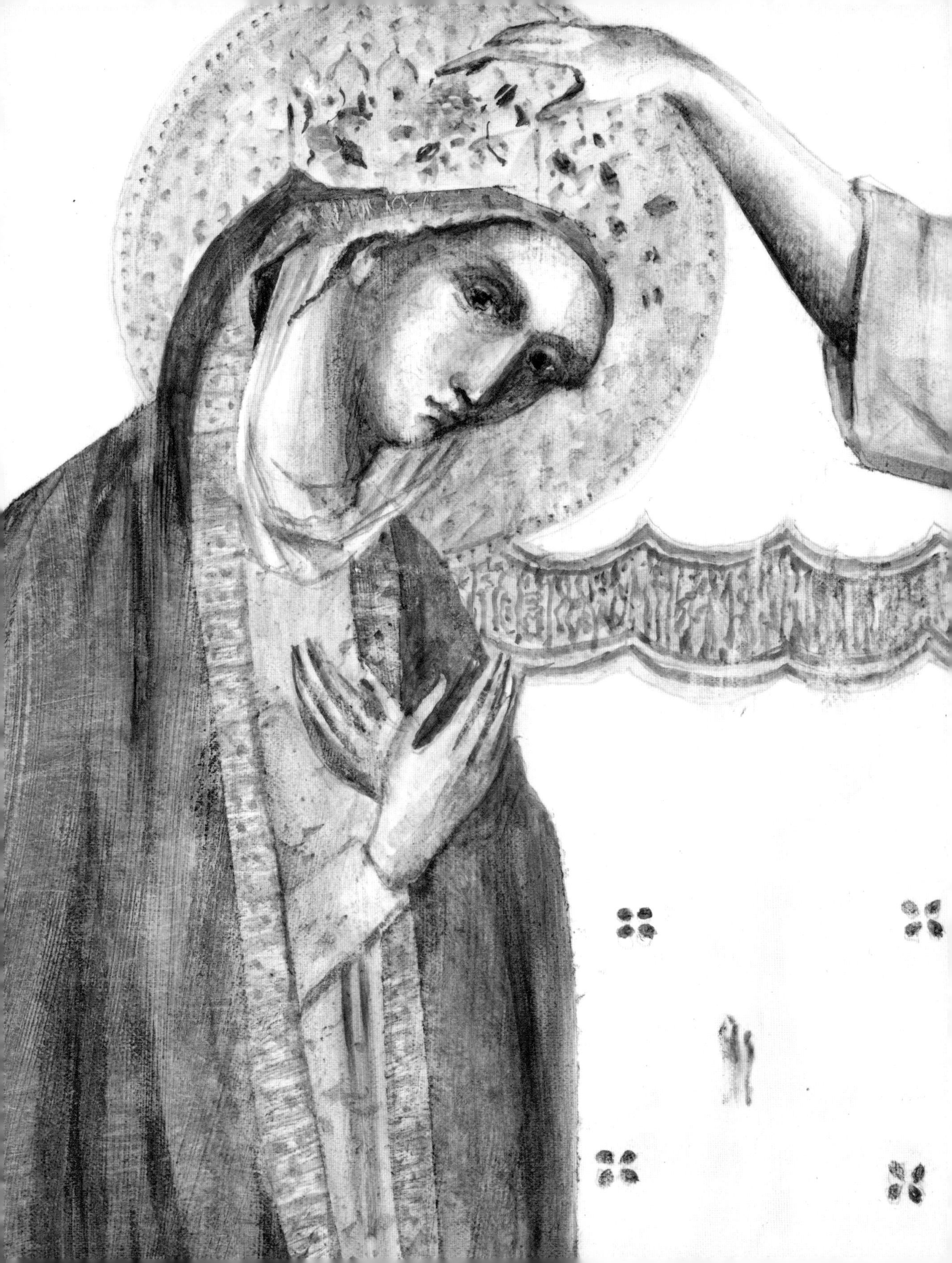

prominent ecclesiastical institutions of the day—but his clientele extended well beyond the confines of the city. The relationship between Venice and the Adriatic coast was very strong, and there are works by Paolo Veneziano on both sides of the Adriatic, in Dalmatia (today's Croatia) and in the Marche.

The fourteenth century was a very important time in Venice. A number of the main buildings in the city were rebuilt or redecorated, the Doge's Palace being one of them. As head of Venice's most esteemed workshop, Paolo played a key role during this period. In 1345, he signed and dated a series of panels made to decorate the high altar of the Basilica of San Marco.

Paolo's *Coronation of the Virgin* is the most important work by the artist outside of Europe. It is also his last signed and dated work. The subject is taken from an apocryphal episode that does not appear in the Gospels. The figures of Christ and the Virgin are enthroned, surrounded by a glory, or choir, of angels; Christ is in the act of crowning his mother. According to Christian tradition, after the death of the Virgin and her bodily assumption to heaven, Christ crowned her as the Queen of Heaven. The iconography of Mary as the Queen of Heaven was very popular in Italy during the late Middle Ages and Renaissance.

Paolo includes many precious materials in the Frick painting. Gold is applied using a range of techniques to decorate the halos, crowns, and jewels, as well as the clothes of both Christ and the Virgin. The blue mantles of Christ and Mary are decorated with silver that would originally have glittered but has tarnished over time. The two figures have set their feet on representations of the sun, in gold, and the moon, in silver. The association of Christ with the sun and the Virgin Mary with the moon is a very old, traditional one. The gold inscription over blue, at bottom, is from a religious text celebrating the Queen of Heaven, while the gold text on green presents the signatures of the artists—Paolo Veneziano, together with his son Giovanni, described as Giovannino (the young Giovanni)—and the date, 1358. Paolo Veneziano painted this work toward the end of his life; he is documented a short time later, in 1362, as being already dead.

On the sides of the main figures are two extraordinary, almost identical angels holding portable organs. Above the architectural throne is a wonderful group of richly dressed angels playing different musical instruments, including lutes, harps, trumpets, and tambourines. The pairing of the Coronation of the Virgin with a music-making angelic choir and orchestra is very much in keeping with the traditional depiction of this event.

The Coronation of the Virgin is first documented in Palazzo Bacinetti in Ravenna. In the early 1870s, through a German dealer, the painting reached the Castle of Sigmaringen, in southern Germany, where it belonged to a minor branch of the Hohenzollern family. The painting was there between the 1870s and 1928, when much of the collection was dispersed. It arrived at the Frick in 1930.

In 1925, just a few years before the *Coronation* was acquired, Helen Clay, Frick's daughter, traveled to central Italy. She kept a scrapbook in which she pasted photographs of great works of art she had seen. One of the things she included in her notebook was a set of full-length figures of saints, on two tiers, by Paolo Veneziano, which she saw at the Pinacoteca of San Severino Marche. At the time, they were believed to be by another Venetian painter, Lorenzo Veneziano. In 1977, the German art historian Hanna Kiel suggested that the Frick *Coronation* and the saints in San Severino were originally part of the same polyptych.

The Paolo Veneziano panels in San Severino are documented in the 1820s in the church of Santa Maria del Glorioso, just outside the city, but they probably originally came from the church of Santa Maria del Mercato, now renamed San Domenico, which was the main Dominican church in San Severino. Many of the saints in the polyptych are Dominican saints associated with this church. The building was entirely refurbished in the sixteenth century and again during the following two centuries. It is likely that the *Coronation* was originally the central component of a very significant polyptych made by Paolo for San Severino Marche. The polyptych can be reconstructed virtually, but there are still a number of parts missing. There are at least two half-length figures on the second tier of the altarpiece that are no longer there, and the upper part (the *cimasa*) that was above the *Coronation* is lost. This altarpiece is not documented, but it is likely to have been commissioned by the Dominicans in San Severino.

We do not know how or when the *Coronation* was separated from the San Severino panels. Perhaps one day it will be possible to temporarily unite them, hopefully in both New York and San Severino.

—X.S.

VECCHIETTA

The Resurrection

1472

Vin Santo and Cantucci

Serve Vin Santo in a wine glass
Pair with almond *cantucci* biscuits

Among the famous wines of Siena, Vecchietta's birthplace, is Vin Santo (Holy Wine). According to some, it was given this name because it was used during mass. Others say it was used to heal the sick during the plague of 1348 and deemed miraculous. Today, this sweet wine is typically drunk in Tuscany with cantucci *(or biscotti). Let them soak in Vin Santo—eat and drink!*

This relief of the Resurrection—the only signed work by Vecchietta outside of Italy—is very close to my heart because Vecchietta was the subject of my Ph.D. research. Born in Siena (in lower Tuscany), Vecchietta (1410–1480) traveled a bit as a youth but spent most of his career in his hometown, becoming its most important artist. He was a sculptor, a painter, and an architect, spanning all possible media.

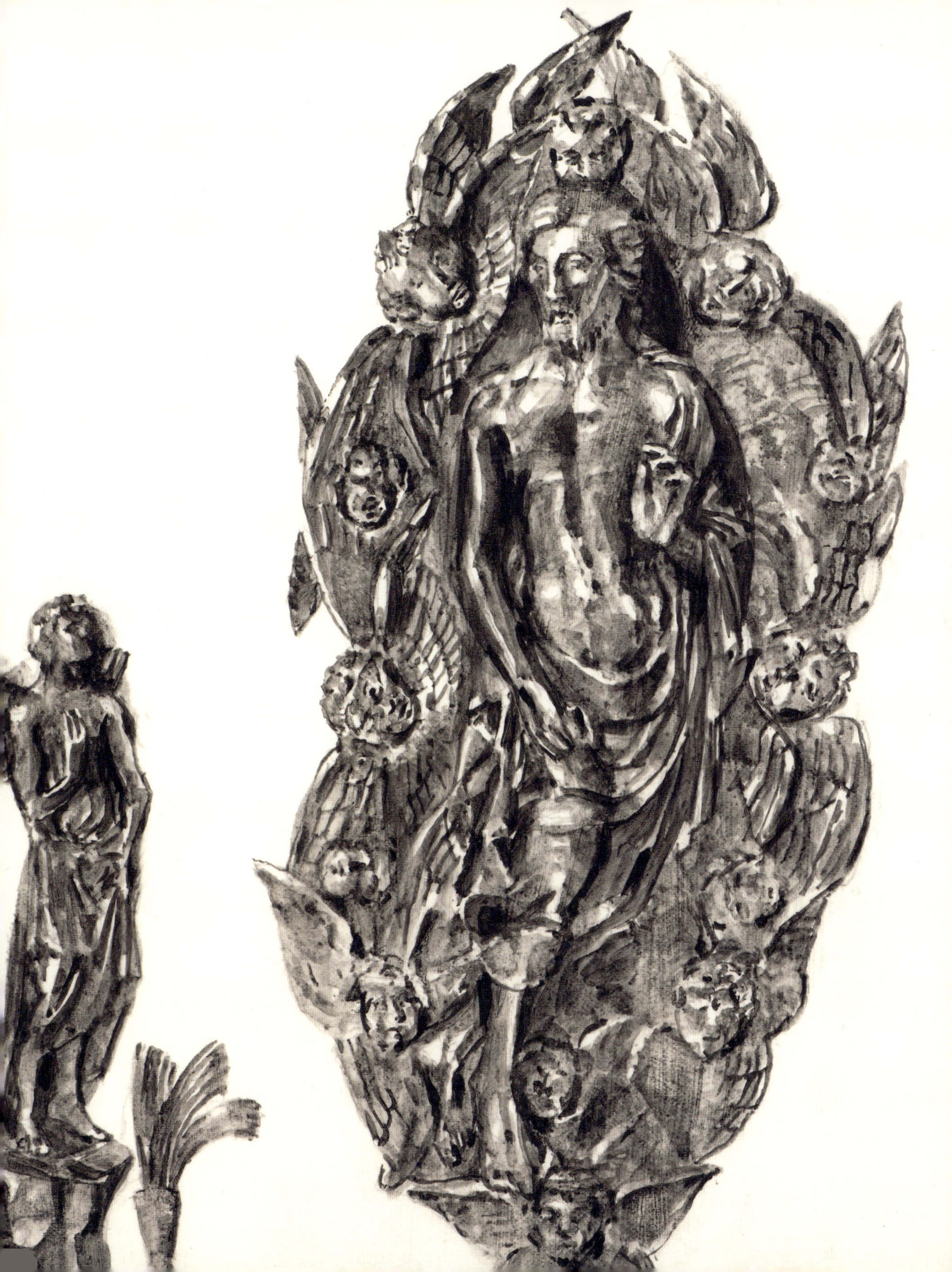

The decade of the 1470s was very important for Vecchietta because that is when he completed a number of commissions in bronze, a medium in which he does not seem to have previously worked. The *Resurrection* relief sits at the early stages of this series of works. It is signed and dated 1472 but has a rather strange inscription. It reads: "The work of Lorenzo di Pietro, the painter, also known as Vecchietta, from Siena, 1472." Why would Vecchietta sign a sculpture as a painter? There is no definitive answer to this question, although we know that he signed his sculptures as a painter many times and vice versa. Some say it was a shrewd tactic to advertise his ability to work in different materials. In other words, "You are looking at a sculpture, but if you need a painting, I'm still your guy." But it is important to note that the all-encompassing word *artist* that we use today was not available to Vecchietta. He would never have called himself an artist—that is a much later category. At the time, the profession of artist did not exist as such, and being a painter was very different from being a sculptor. They were two different career paths regulated by two different guilds, and in order to work both as a painter and a sculptor Vecchietta had to enroll in both guilds. By calling himself a painter on a sculpture, he was taking a huge step in challenging the system of guild regulations and moving toward the modern conception of sculpting and painting as the work of an artist.

Not only was Vecchietta purposeful about his image, but he also gave a lot of thought to the subject of this work, the Resurrection. What captivates me about this relief is the way in which you cannot really make sense of its space rationally. And that is mainly because Vecchietta combines two different perspectives. We see Christ at eye level, but the soldiers are seen as if from below. And also, the sepulcher occupies an awkward space in relation to the little mountains on the sides and the soldiers themselves, one of whom is leaning against it. Christ himself is in such high relief that he seems to have been pulled out from the background of the panel, as if he were coming toward the foreground of the scene—toward us, the viewers. And yet, the small angel head under his feet still has its wings within the sepulcher! How is that possible? It simply is not. In fact, Vecchietta is probably telling us that whatever happened during the Resurrection cannot be represented according to the laws of perspective. The Resurrection is the ultimate miracle, and as such, it happens in a space that is not rational and so eschews the limits of representation by the human hand.

But what was the function of this sophisticated work in bronze? Nobody actually knows. Nor do we know for whom it was made. But we do know that in Siena there was a tradition of *quadri di bronzo,* bronze paintings that would hang in people's homes. There are seals on the back of *The Resurrection* that tell us that by the seventeenth century it belonged to Cardinal Flavio Chigi, the cardinal-nephew of Pope Alexander VII. The Chigi were a prominent family of Sienese bankers and art patrons, but it is unknown if they ever had contact with Vecchietta. The relief was kept in the family palazzo in Rome until the early twentieth century, when it was bought by John Pierpont Morgan and later sold to Henry Clay Frick together with many other bronzes from Morgan's collection, in 1916.

—G.D.

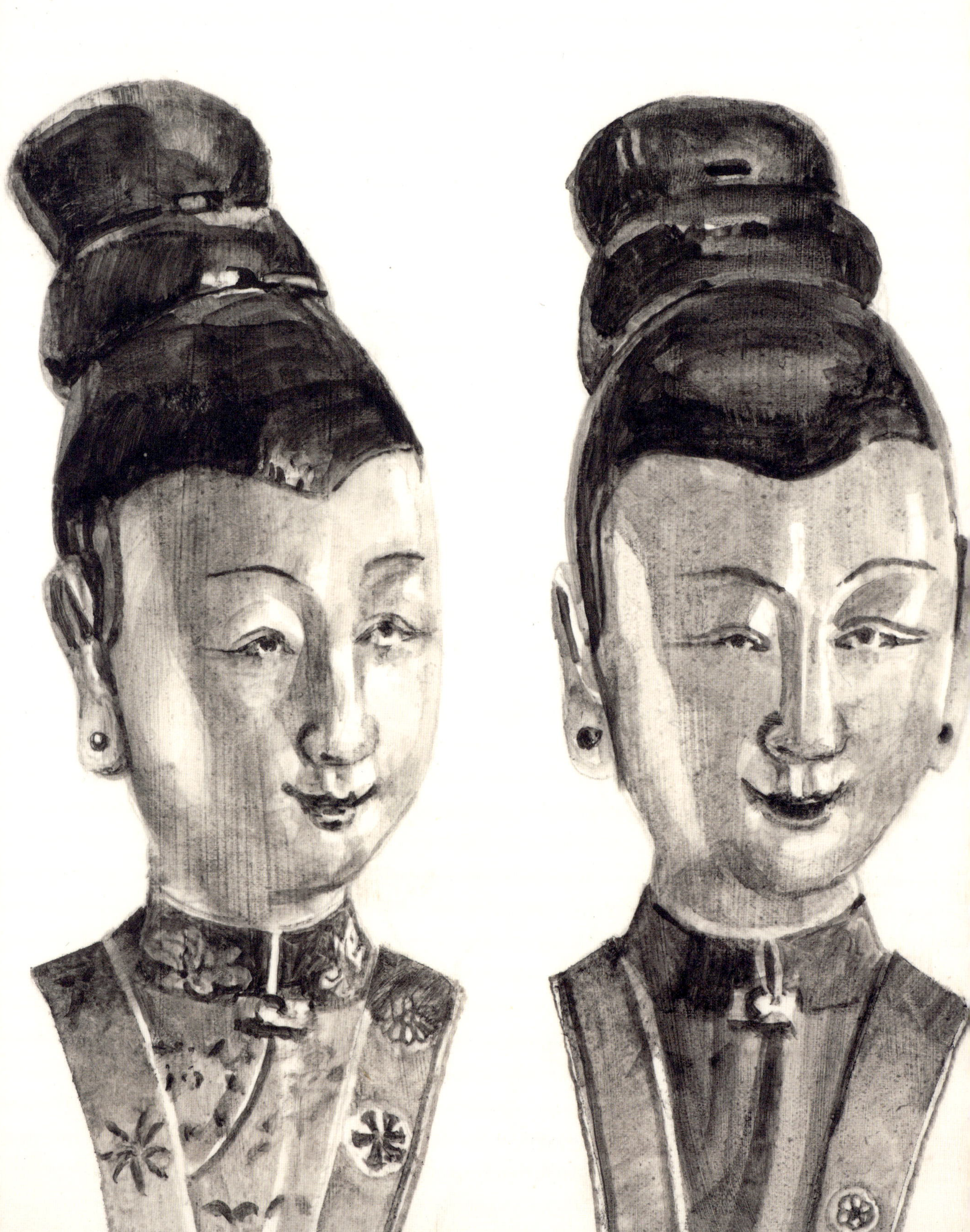

CHINESE, QING DYNASTY

Two Figures of Ladies on Stands

18TH CENTURY

Chrysanthemum

2 OZ. DRY VERMOUTH

1 OZ. BÉNÉDICTINE

3 DASHES OF ABSINTHE

Shake and strain over ice in a cocktail glass

This cocktail's floral name makes it the perfect companion to the porcelain ladies, whose clothing is decorated with designs of chrysanthemum flowers. Native to China and known in many varieties, chrysanthemums are an auspicious symbol in Chinese culture, signifying good fortune and prosperity.

These two hard-paste porcelain ladies are more than three feet tall. They are not portraits but rather represent idealized female figures. Made during the centuries-long Qing dynasty, which lasted from 1644 to 1911, they were produced under the Kangxi Emperor (r. 1662–1722), who was the longest-ruling emperor in Chinese history. When we think of the late seventeenth and early eighteenth centuries, we might think of Vermeer, who was active in

Delft about the time the Kangxi Emperor ascended to the throne, or of Antoine Watteau and the beginnings of the rococo style, which coincided with the end of his reign. But China in this period was a complex place with limited interaction with Europe. Art, artists, and authorship functioned and were perceived somewhat differently than in Europe.

Like most Chinese porcelain, these figures were made in the city of Jingdezhen, in southern China. The highest-quality porcelain produced in the Jingdezhen kilns, the most spectacular pieces, were reserved for the imperial court. A limited number of pieces was made for export to Europe. This pair of porcelain ladies may be two such pieces; they are of very high quality and would have been difficult to make.

They exemplify ideals of female beauty celebrated in this culture at the time. Note, for instance, the elegant shapes of the eyes, which are punctured at the center to create an illusion of dark pupils. The ears are pierced and would have been adorned with earrings. The delicate form of the lips; the slender nose; the very thin, arched eyebrows; the widow's peak of the hairline; and, of course, the luminous, light porcelain skin—all these details testify to the ladies' beauty. In this culture, as in so many, ideals of feminine beauty were linked to social class. Here, the whiteness of the skin distances these figures from the idea of labor and toiling outside under the sun, doing hard work. The idea of not being out in the sun, of leading a life of privilege, was part of this ideal feminine beauty.

The figures may also have conveyed generosity, welcoming, kindness, perhaps even a sense of hospitable subservience. Their small, delicate hands, dramatically framed by double-hanging sleeves, may once have held or extended little gifts, perhaps fruits or flowers. Their sharply pointed fingernails are very different from the manicures seen in depictions of women in eighteenth-century Europe. These may seem strange to some audiences today, but I have recently seen people wearing nails like this on the streets of New York, in the year 2021. It is interesting the way that some styles go in and out of fashion in various cultures.

The two figures are differentiated by the color and pattern of their clothing, which is painted with precision in overglaze. One of my favorite details is the way their jackets open slightly at the bottom to show the linings. One of the skirts features a circular design of flying storks, heightened with gold; the other bears chrysanthemum flowers. At the very bottoms of the skirts, the pointed toes of the shoes peek out, a charming detail that reminds us of the bodies underneath these flowing fabrics.

Both are perched on stands decorated with the Buddhist symbol of good fortune, the *wan*. They reinforce the auspicious symbolism that characterizes these figures. In addition to being beautiful porcelain objects, they would have been seen as harbingers of good fortune and prosperity.

When one looks at the figures from the side, in profile, it can be seen that they stand differently—one bends forward much more than the other. And while that might suggest she is bowing, it is probably the result of a flaw in the firing of the porcelain—another indication of the difficulty of making porcelain at this scale. The similarity between their forms indicates that molds were used for various components of the figures, which were then assembled by hand to be fired. This type of porcelain has a charming name: biscuit ware, so called because the porcelain is fired without a glaze and the "biscuit" (the fired porcelain) is then painted with an overglaze. Because of the green overglaze, they belong to the *famille verte* categorization. The fact that the classification has a French name gives a sense of the desire in Europe, and particularly in France, to collect, amass, and classify these objects of Asian porcelain.

Objects of this size and shape—as opposed to stackable porcelain bowls and plates—would have been extremely difficult and costly to ship from Asia to Europe. It is believed that very few figures of this kind made it to Europe.

The earliest record of ownership of these two Chinese figures puts them in London with George Salting, an avid collector of Asian porcelains. In 1903, they passed to the collection of the American financier and collector John Pierpont Morgan, who had estates in London and New York. When Morgan acquired them, he had them sent, as he usually did with the porcelain he acquired, to the Metropolitan Museum of Art, where his enormous collection of porcelains was on view. It is notable that when these large quantities of Chinese objects, including the Frick's two Chinese ladies, came to America, the vast majority of Chinese people were barred from immigrating to the United States due to the Chinese Exclusion Act of 1882. The act was repealed in 1943.

After Morgan's death in 1913, Frick acquired a number of items from his collection, among them, the two Chinese porcelain ladies. The dealer Duveen, who had encouraged the purchase, characterized them as among the most important porcelain pieces that Frick could get his hands on. Frick acquired them in 1918. The comparative value of some of Frick's Old Master paintings versus the Kangxi figures may surprise some viewers today. For example, Frick acquired Giovanni Bellini's *St. Francis in the Desert* for $170,000, while Duveen asked $130,000 for the porcelain figures. (Frick ended up paying about $117,000 for them.) That was a lot more than the $14,000 Morgan had spent on them just fifteen years prior. While Bellini's picture has been referred to by some critics as the most beautiful painting in America, the two Chinese figures are not nearly as well known to the public. Nonetheless, they remain among the most important—and to me, spectacular—porcelain pieces at the Frick.

—A.N.

FRANCESCO GUARDI

Regatta in Venice and *View of the Cannaregio Canal in Venice*

CA. 1770

Sgroppino

½ OZ. VODKA

1 OZ. PROSECCO

2 SCOOPS OF LEMON SORBET

Serve in a flute glass and garnish with a mint sprig

With lemon sorbet, vodka, and prosecco, this drink is a modern take on the Sgroppino, which dates to sixteenth-century Venice. The name derives from the Venetian dialect word sgropin *(sorbet). It is frequently drunk in Venice in the summer, at the end of a meal, but is sometimes also served between courses as a palate cleanser, which is also the way it was used in banquets.*

This pair of Venetian *vedute,* or view paintings, show different sites in Venice. Francesco Guardi (1712–1793), the last great Venetian view painter, followed in the footsteps of artists like Luca Carlevarijs and two of the most famous producers of *vedute,* Canaletto and his nephew Bernardo Bellotto. He worked mostly for the international market of tourists traveling to Venice who wanted to

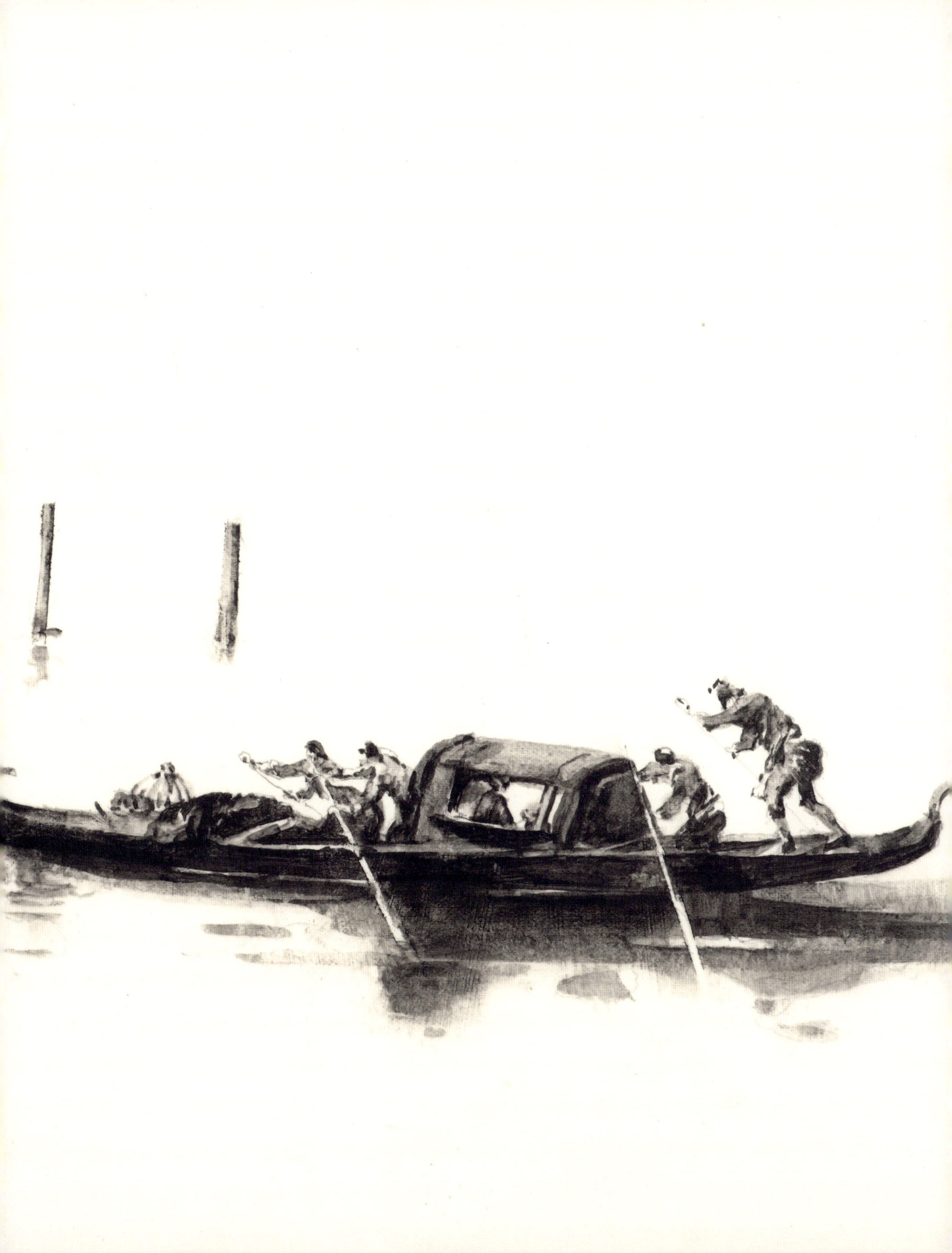

return home to England, France, or other places in Europe with views of Venice. While Guardi's predecessors spent time abroad—most famously, Canaletto spent a decade in England, and Bellotto traveled extensively in central and eastern Europe, mostly Saxony and Poland—Guardi was firmly based in Venice.

The first of the two paintings depicts the Grand Canal, at the heart of Venice, looking north, toward the Rialto Bridge, with grand palazzos framing the canal on each side. A regatta is taking place with different types of boats, some single-occupancy, others with couples or groups of people. These boats would have been decorated in very lavish ways. In the painting, one-man *gondolette,* small gondolas, are racing surrounded by larger *bissone* and *peote* watching the race. These are elegantly ornamented in blue, gold, and pink, and one is Chinese in style.

The view shown has not changed much since the eighteenth century. On the left is Ca' Balbi, and immediately to its left, a decorated structure, built between the palazzo and the neighboring one, Ca' Foscari. The area was called the Volta di Canal—the "curve of the canal." There, for the regattas, a *macchina* would be built, a temporary structure of wood and papier-mâché that provided seating for important people watching the regatta. This was also where prizes were given out to the winners of the race. Regattas would be held for the visits to Venice of important people. We do not know the precise occasion of the regatta depicted in Guardi's painting.

The other *veduta* shows the second-largest canal in Venice after the Grand Canal: the Cannaregio Canal, which goes up from the Grand Canal, north toward the open lagoon. The view looks toward another bridge, the Ponte dei Tre Archi. The canal runs along the Fondamenta of Cannaregio, a pavement area with people walking alongside the waterway. Behind it are small houses with their residents putting laundry out to dry. Boats also populate this canal: gondolas transporting people up and down the canal, fishermen on a small boat, and a wonderful boat near the *fondamenta* that has been loaded with boxes and crates. On one of the crates, the initials of the artist, *F.G.*, and *P.* (for PINXIT, "painted this") can be seen.

At the center of the composition is Ca' Surian Bellotto, a large palazzo built in the seventeenth century for the Surian, a family of Armenian origins. At the end of the eighteenth century, it was taken over by the Bellotto family (no relation to Canaletto's nephew). In Guardi's painting, there is a large coat of arms over the door of the palazzo, and a group of people who are richly dressed in livery and are welcoming someone into the palace. In the eighteenth century, Ca' Surian Bellotto was the French embassy in Venice. The painting probably depicts the arrival of an important guest of the ambassador or of the French government. The embassy building is also known for having been the place where, for about a year, in 1743–44, the great Swiss philosopher Jean-Jacques Rousseau worked as a secretary to the French ambassador in Venice.

In the eighteenth century, only three countries had fixed ambassadors to Venice: Spain, France, and Britain. The arrival of a new ambassador was an occasion for great festivities. Among Canaletto's best paintings, for example, are two pairs of large canvases depicting the arrivals of the French ambassador (now divided between the Hermitage Museum in Saint Petersburg and the Pushkin Museum in Moscow) and of the Imperial one (Crespi Collection, Milan). Britain sent ambassadors only on special occasions but did maintain a permanent "resident," an individual with no diplomatic role who was mostly a commercial representative. Surprisingly, the two Frick paintings were painted for the British resident and not for the French ambassador.

John Strange, the British resident in Venice from 1773 to 1788, was a scholar, an archeologist, a literary figure, and a great patron of the arts. He purchased a number of Guardi views and commissioned others. For example, he asked the painter to create a set of four views of the Veneto countryside, two of which represented Villa Loredan at Paese, which was rented by Strange and his wife as their summer residence outside of Venice.

In 1788, Strange returned to London, and he died there without ever returning to Venice. His wife, Sarah, had died in 1783 in Venice, and the couple did not have any children. Strange left instructions for his entire collection to be sold, and over a number of sales at Christie's, and through some donations, the whole of it—made up of archeological artifacts, paintings, drawings, prints, books, and natural curiosities—was dispersed.

—X.S.

LEONE LEONI

Andrea Doria

CA. 1541

Grog

1 OZ. LIME (OR LEMON) JUICE
1 OZ. BROWN SUGAR
1 OZ. DARK RUM
4 OZ. WATER

A CINNAMON STICK (OPTIONAL)

Serve in a tumbler

The basic components of this most traditional drink of sailors are always rum and water, but because it was drunk on fleets from all over the world, there are countless recipes for it. This is our very special Frick version.

This very small yet important sixteenth-century medal of the Genoese seafaring admiral Andrea Doria has a fascinating story. On the obverse (the front of the medal) is the effigy of Doria, identified by an inscription ending with P.P., which stands for PATER PATRIAE (Father of the Homeland). For a long time, the Dorias had been one of Genoa's most powerful families, but in 1528,

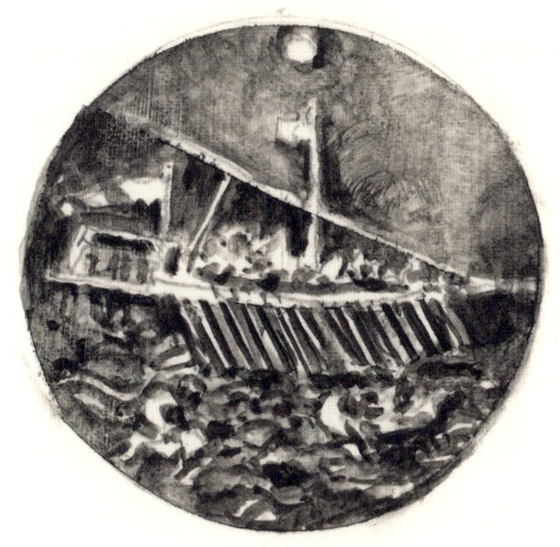

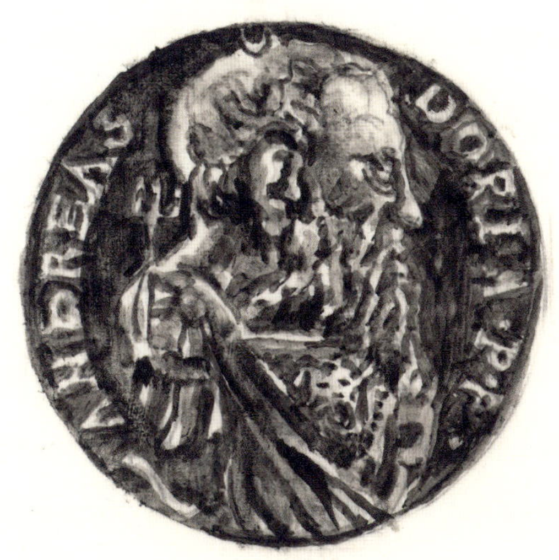
ANDREAS DORIA P P

thanks to an alliance with the Holy Roman Emperor Charles V, Andrea became the de facto ruler of the city, which was then one of Europe's most prosperous. From Genoa, Doria's personally owned fleet of galleys was able to control western European waters and keep them free from pirates, which is why he was revered and celebrated all over Europe.

But this medal is also important for the artist who cast it, Leone Leoni (1509–1590). Leoni was probably born in Arezzo, in Tuscany, because he was often called Leone "Aretino." In 1537, he moved to Rome, where he became one of the leading artists at the court of Pope Paul III. Three years later, his temper got the better of him, and he stabbed a papal goldsmith, Pellegrino di Leuti, who had accused him of making forgeries (many years later Leoni also stabbed Titian's son, Orazio). Leoni was sentenced to having his hand cut off—imagine what a tragedy that was for a sculptor—but the pope commuted his sentence into service on the galleys, the long, slender, shallow ships that were propelled mainly by oars and typically used slaves or convicts for the rowing. The galleys on which Leoni was to serve his sentence were owned and commanded by Andrea Doria, and that is how their lives intersected.

Considering Doria's role as a shipowner, it is not surprising to find one of his galleys on the reverse of this medal. But there may be more to the story behind this object. Some scholars have speculated that the scene, with a smaller boat next to the bigger galley, represents the moment when Leoni was freed by Doria from his imprisonment and led to the admiral's court at the magnificent Villa del Principe in Genoa, where he was allowed to work for some months. During this period, Leoni is believed to have cast this medal as a token of gratitude, together with several other works for Doria.

After being appointed superintendent of the mint in Milan and then nearby Piacenza, Leoni established himself in Milan, where his success allowed him to build a magnificent house for himself, the so-called Casa degli Omenoni, which took several decades to build. With Leoni's prestige growing, he was finally introduced to Charles V in 1548, and from then on, he worked for the emperor. He had to travel to his court several times, but he never enjoyed those travels. During his first trip, while he was staying in Brussels, he wrote a letter to Ferrante Gonzaga, governor of Milan, in which he protested that "these inhuman countries are as different in their customs from ours [Italy] as butter is from the beer which these people swallow so brutally."

Despite such complaints, Leoni was receiving the patronage of the most powerful man on the continent and started to work on countless commissions for the emperor, applying many of the skills he had acquired in Genoa. In the burgeoning artistic environment of Doria's court, Leoni had learned how to combine ancient mythology with classicizing motifs in order to celebrate a military commander. Doria and Genoa changed Leone's life forever, and it is Leone himself who tells us so, in another version of the medal at the Frick, where on the reverse, instead of the galley, is an image of Leoni himself, surrounded by the broken chains of his imprisonment. Quite literally, Leone Leoni and Andrea Doria are two sides of the same coin.

—G.D.

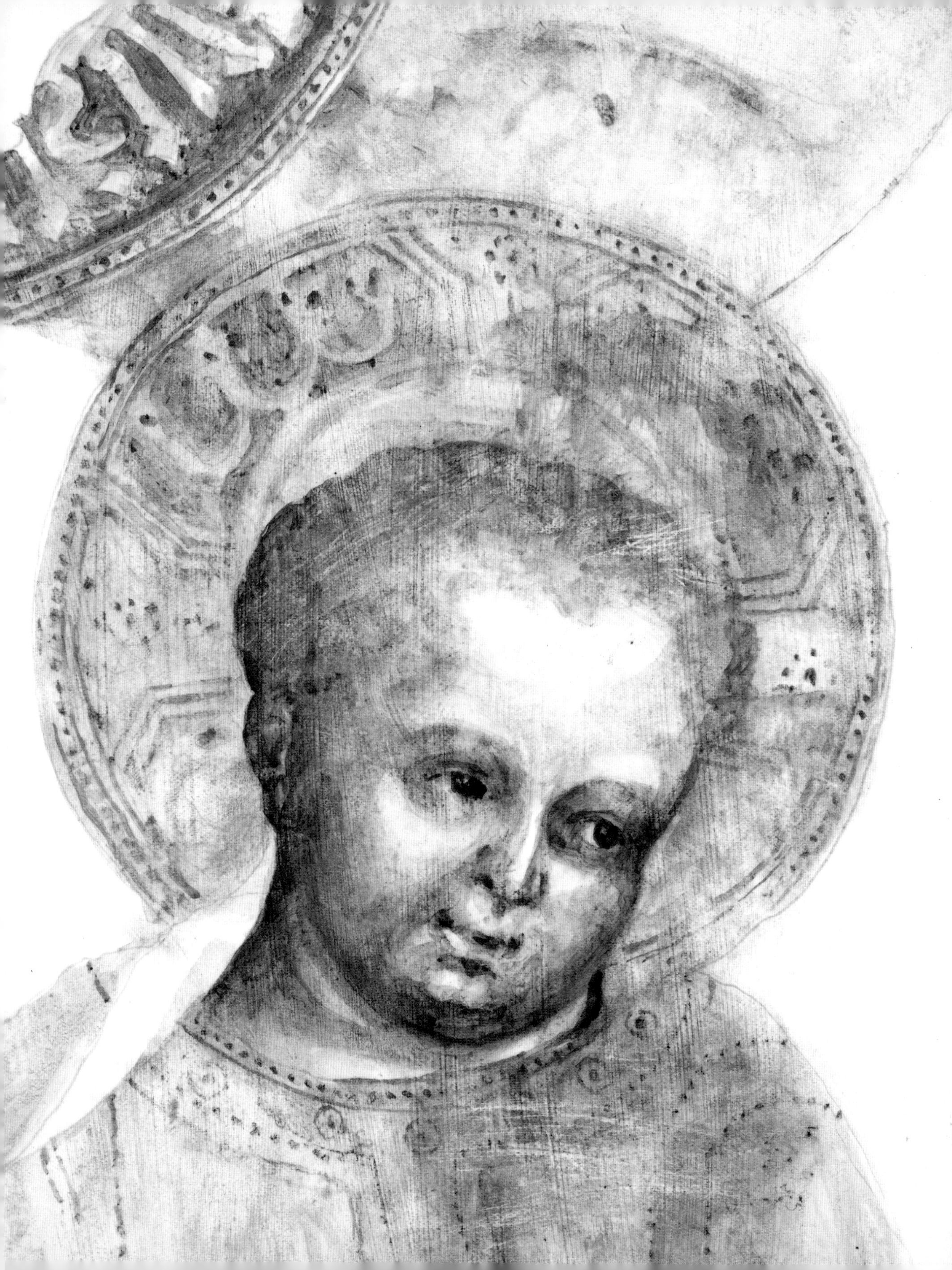

GENTILE DA FABRIANO

Madonna and Child, with Saints Lawrence and Julian

1423–25

Cosmopolitan

1 OZ. VODKA

½ OZ. TRIPLE SEC

1 OZ. CRANBERRY JUICE

½ OZ. LEMON JUICE

Serve chilled in a cocktail glass and garnish with a lemon peel

This classic cocktail seems appropriate for Gentile da Fabriano, an artist who was truly a cosmopolitan by the standards of fifteenth-century Italy.

This panel painting from the early 1420s is one of the very few works at the Frick that still has its original frame. A few parts are later replacements, but the main structure is original, and at the very bottom is the signature of the artist: Gentile da Fabriano. The painting is beautifully described by the great scholar Keith Christiansen in his 1982 monography on Gentile:

Combined with an insistent corporeality are the livelier, less poignant expressions of the Virgin and Child, set off by the fervent devotion of saints in the flower of youth. The way the Child's attention is diverted by the captive bird, symbol of Christ's Passion, is a particularly felicitous idea. No less ingenious is the way space is defined by the painted ledge, by arbitrarily cropping off the foreground figures, and by carefully describing the planes of the throne. The subtle displacement of the halos in order to free a profile again indicates Gentile's concerns.

Gentile da Fabriano (ca. 1370–1427) came, as the name suggests, from Fabriano, a small town in the Marche region in central Italy. He grew up and was probably trained there but traveled across the whole of the Italian peninsula throughout most of his thirty-year career, working in Florence, Venice, Rome, Siena, Orvieto, and a number of other Italian cities. We first hear of him in the early 1400s in Venice.

The most famous extant work of Gentile's is no doubt the glorious *Adoration of the Magi*, in the Uffizi in Florence, a wonderfully composed scene with elegant figures, incredible textiles, details in gold and silver, and also the extensive use of *pastiglia*, gilded raised gesso that gives a three-dimensional effect to some of the decorations. At the end of his life, Gentile worked in Rome, frescoing San Giovanni in Laterano—one of the four main basilicas—following in the footsteps of another great painter, Pisanello, who had left his fresco cycle unfinished. Unfortunately, all we have of this fresco cycle is a seventeenth-century drawing that records part of the cycle before it was entirely destroyed when the basilica was extensively refurbished by the architect Francesco Borromini.

Gentile is categorized today as having worked in the International Gothic style, a term coined in the late nineteenth century that describes the artistic currents and exchanges that took place between the end of the fourteenth and the early fifteenth century across Europe, starting in Burgundy in France but reaching England, Bohemia, and Italy. Many artists who, like Gentile, traveled extensively looked at works that had arrived in the courts of Italy.

The painting at the Frick represents the Virgin enthroned. The two saints that accompany the central group are clearly identifiable through their attributes and in part through the inscriptions at the bottom of the frame, which very handily tell us who they are. On the left is St. Lawrence (LAURENTIUS), a third-century early Christian deacon, saint, and martyr. He was famously put to death by being burned alive on a gridiron. In the painting, he holds, just toward the edge of the frame, his metal gridiron.

The other saint, on the right, is identified by two symbols, a sword and a palm, which is usually a symbol of martyrdom. Again, he is named on the frame, St. Julian (IULIANUS). Julian the Hospitaller is a fourth-century saint whose romantic but tragic story is first recounted in Jacobus da Varagine's *Golden Legend* and later taken up by other writers. Most famously, in 1877, Gustave Flaubert's *Three Tales* includes the story of St. Julian, a legend that echoes classical tragedy, especially the story of Oedipus Rex. Julian came from a wealthy family. As a young man, it was prophesized that he would kill his parents. Terrified by this, Julian fled his parents' house and moved far away. Years later, returning from a hunt, he reached his house earlier than expected, only to surprise his wife in bed with another man. Overcome with anger, he killed them both on the spot. Leaving the house, he was shocked to see his wife outside talking to friends. She told him that his parents had come to visit, and as they were tired, she had given them their bed to sleep in. The prophecy had proved true. Julian abandoned his family and led a saintly life as a penance for his crime.

The representation of Julian in Gentile's painting, however, is problematic. The sword is a typical symbol of Julian, linking him to the murder of his parents, but the palm of martyrdom does not really apply to Julian the Hospitaller because he was not a martyred saint. So why does he sport this second attribute? This incongruity may reflect some confusion on Gentile's part between St. Julian the Hospitaller and St. Julian of Antioch, a martyred fourth-century saint also known as St. Julian the Martyr. He was put in a sack full of scorpions and vipers and thrown into the sea by the pagans.

We do not know for whom the painting was created or where it was painted. Was it created in Fabriano, the hometown of Gentile? Or was it painted for a patron in Florence? Both Lawrence and Julian are common saints in Tuscany. Both names are most likely linked to the patronage of the work. Perhaps it was two brothers—a Lorenzo and a Giuliano—or a father and son who commissioned it.

The painting is not recorded before 1846, when it belonged to Albert, Duc de Broglie, collector as well as twice prime minister of France. This provenance has a very curious link to another painting in the collection. The duke was the brother of the Comtesse d'Haussonville, who is represented in the famous portrait by Ingres, one of the iconic works at the Frick. I imagine that the Comtesse d'Haussonville must have known this painting well because it was in the collection of her brother.

—X.S.

DU PAQUIER PORCELAIN MANUFACTORY

Elephant-Shaped Wine Dispenser

1740

Tokaji Wine

Serve slightly chilled in a tulip glass

Tokaji wine—from an area in Hungary famous for its production of sweet white wines—was often used as a diplomatic gift. Both Louis XIV and Louis XV of France were known to be fond of it. Emperor Franz Joseph sent Queen Victoria a bottle of Tokaji for every month of her life on each of her birthdays.

Active for three decades, from the mid-1710s to the mid-1740s, the Du Paquier Porcelain Manufactory in Vienna was the second porcelain manufactory to be established in Europe. European porcelain was invented at the Meissen Porcelain Manufactory, and the formula was a closely guarded secret, with workers at the manufactory effectively confined to the fortress at Meissen. However, due to leaks and industrial espionage, Claudius Innocentius du Paquier—a Dutchman about whom we know very

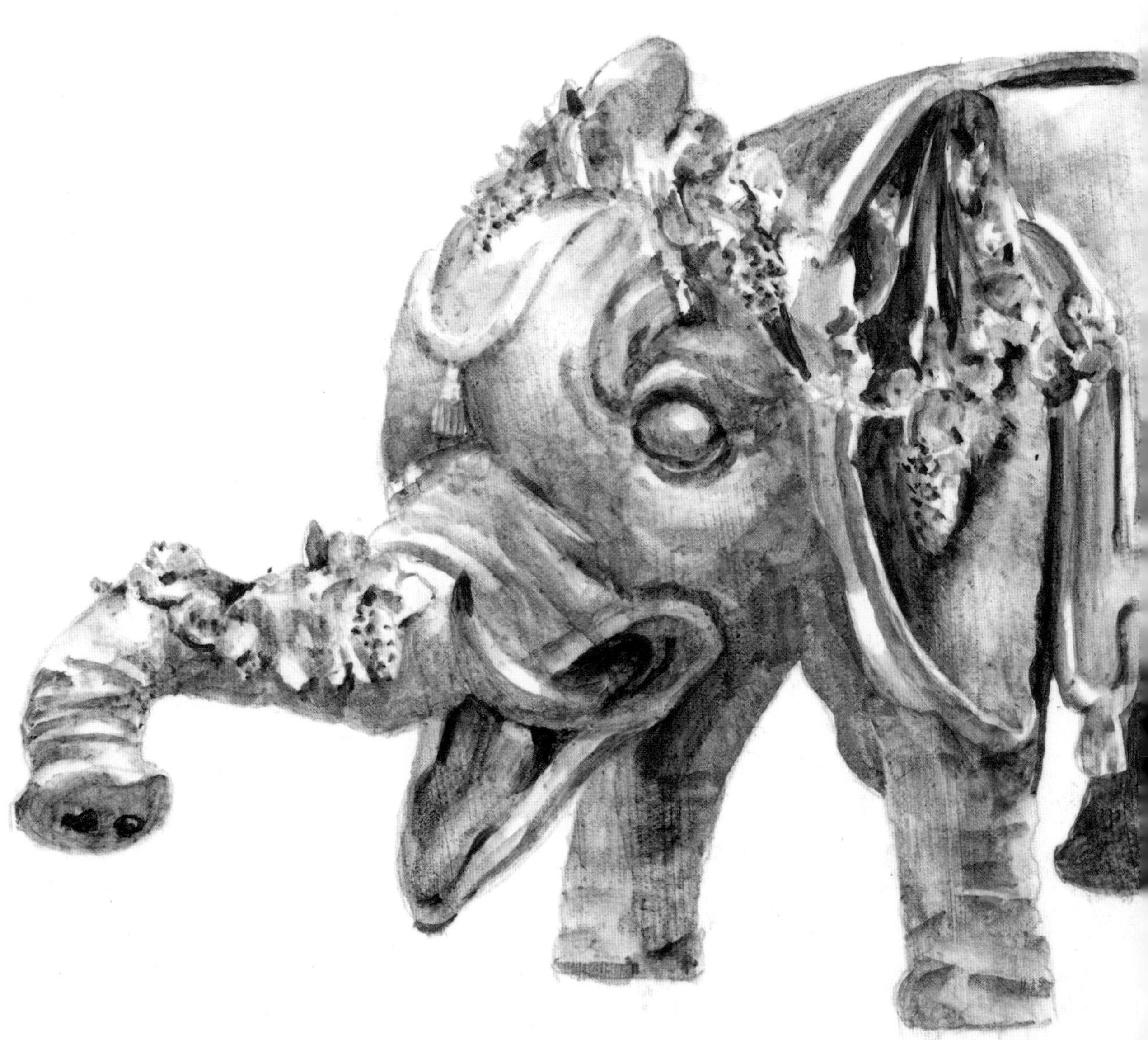

little—managed to lure some Saxon workers to Vienna along with the recipe and was able to start making porcelain at the manufactory that he created.

The Du Paquier manufactory was broadly under imperial patronage, and many of the commissions came from the emperor and the imperial family and sometimes from foreign rulers and aristocrats. Among the unique characteristics of the porcelain are its reddish-pink decorations and unusual forms and designs. Thanks to the generosity of Melinda and Paul Sullivan, a significant group of Du Paquier objects entered the Frick's collection in 2016. The porcelain elephant at the Frick is a rather curious piece, as no one working at the Du Paquier factory was likely to have had exposure to elephants. This object was probably based on visual records such as prints and drawings.

The fashion among the elites in the seventeenth and eighteenth centuries for installing porcelain rooms in their homes is exemplified by an extraordinary room fashioned for the Dubsky Palace in Brno, the capital of Moravia and one of the largest cities of the Austrian Empire, together with Vienna and Budapest. One of the earliest such porcelain rooms, the Dubsky room includes vases, plates, and sconces all made of Du Paquier porcelain. The decoration of the furniture, the mantelpiece, and the chandeliers are also by Du Paquier. The room was removed from the palace but has been reconstructed at the Museum of Applied Arts in Vienna.

Many Du Paquier objects traveled outside of the empire, typically as diplomatic gifts. A series of such gifts were exchanged between Vienna and Saint Petersburg. Between 1730 and 1740, when Anna Ivanovna, the niece of Peter the Great, was the empress of Russia, the alliance with Austria was particularly strong, bolstered by their joint battles against the Turks. Austria and Russia were also allied at the time in the War of the Polish Succession. A cruel tyrant known for her ruthlessness, Ivanovna was also rather eccentric. During Russia's particularly frigid winter of 1739–40, the empress commissioned the construction of an ice palace in Saint Petersburg. The palace was supposedly up to sixty-five feet tall and had a number of rooms, each decorated with furnishings, mantelpieces, mirrors, sofas, beds, and tables made of ice. Surrounding the palace was a garden with ice trees with ice birds on them and a number of ice animals, including a life-size ice elephant. The empress had been given an elephant by the ruler of Persia in 1736.

The gifts exchanged between Austria and Russia included a large service made for the empress by the Du Paquier Porcelain Manufactory. One of its tureens, which bears the Romanov coat of arms with the crowned double-headed eagle, is at the Frick, part of the Sullivan gift. The most extraordinary piece made by Du Paquier for Anna Ivanovna is a large object made of porcelain pieces and silver (now at the Hermitage Museum in Saint

Petersburg). It comprises a large silver tray with a moving ring on which are placed a number of small porcelain figures, holding little porcelain cups, that can be rotated around the central part. At its center is a porcelain elephant decorated with grapes and leaves and surmounted by a figure of Bacchus. The elephant would have been filled with sweet Tokaji wine, which could be dispensed in the cups around the tray below. The figure of Bacchus serves as a lid over the hole into which the wine is poured. And halfway down the trunk of the elephant is another little figure, which served as a tap allowing the wine to come out of the trunk of the elephant. This unusual object seems like something the creator of the ice palace would have liked very much. And of course, Anna Ivanovna's taste was well known in the courts of Europe at the time.

How does the Frick's elephant relate to the empress's elephant in Saint Petersburg? While the Russian set is profusely colored, the Frick piece is white. The Frick elephant is also hollow and has holes, as does the Saint Petersburg one. It has been proposed that the New York elephant had been made as a spare. Du Paquier might have produced a finished elephant for the empress but kept a second white porcelain one in case the imperial elephant broke and needed to be replaced. We do, however, know, thanks to technical analysis, that the Frick elephant was also originally polychromed, and tiny traces of color remain on it. We still do not know for certain why this second elephant was produced. It may have been made by Du Paquier for another patron or with the intention of selling it to another patron.

The Du Paquier Porcelain Manufactory did not last very long. In 1744, Du Paquier sold it to the Austrian government, and it became the Imperial Porcelain Manufactory.

—X.S.

PIETER BRUEGEL THE ELDER

Three Soldiers

1568

Radler

EQUAL PARTS OF:

LAGER

LEMONADE

Serve slightly chilled in a beer glass

Apparently invented for a group of cyclists, this popular German drink— radler *is German for "cyclist"—is known in Italy as a Bicicletta (bicycle) and in Britain as a Shandy. It is typically a combination of lager beer and lemonade, but the beer can also be mixed with a soft drink. The ratio of beer to lemonade is a matter of taste. I usually drink half and half. No doubt, Bruegel's soldiers would have drunk a lot of beer—most likely, however, without the lemonade.*

One of the few works by Pieter Bruegel the Elder in American collections, this small painting is a grisaille, or monochrome painting—in this case, only black, brown, and white are used. The signature and date (1568) at the bottom left indicate that it was made just a year before the artist died.

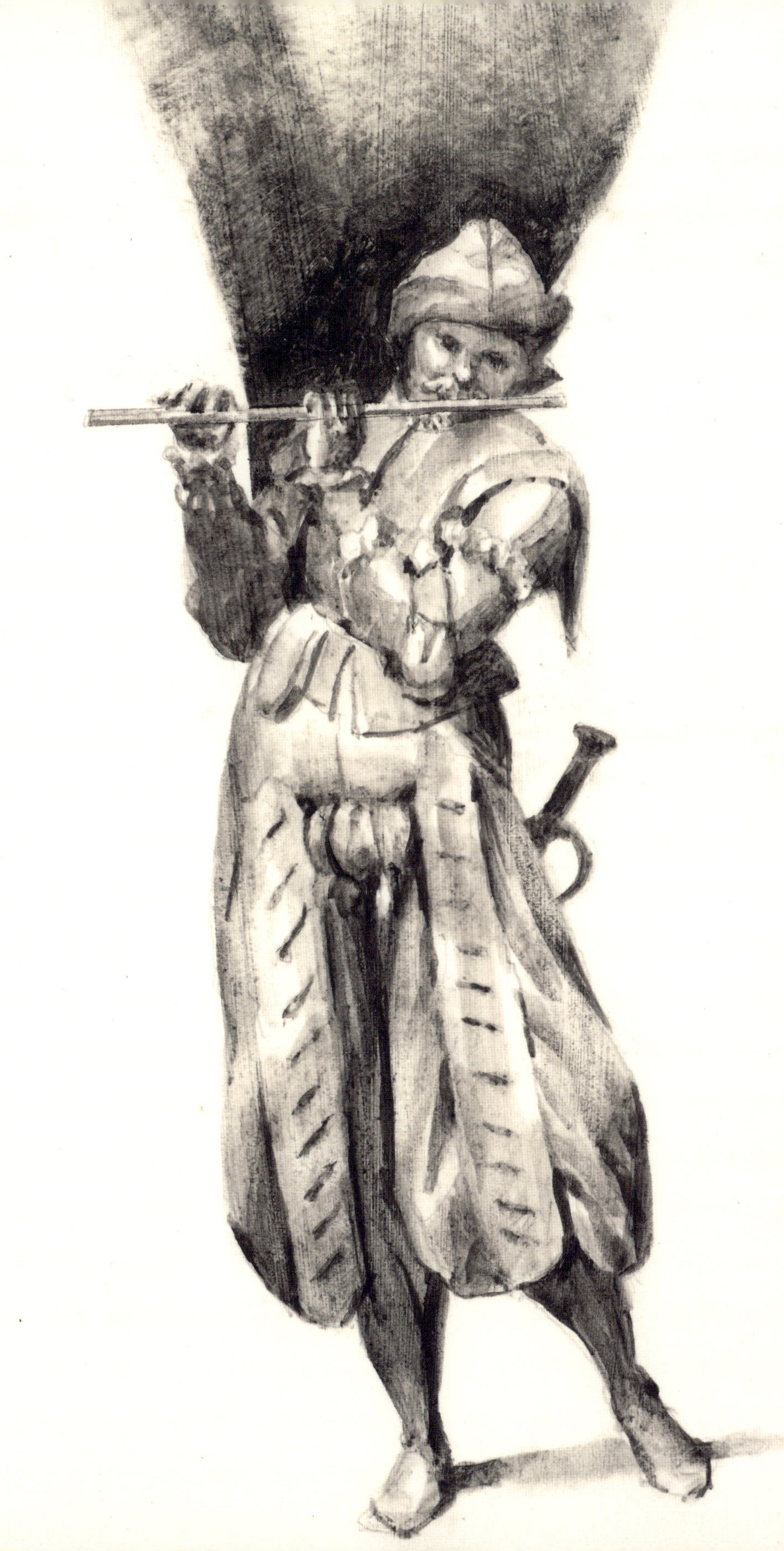

This painting, which entered the Frick's collection in 1965, originally came from King Charles I of England, who had one of the most important collections in Europe in the seventeenth century. In his inventory of 1639, the painting is recorded in his main royal residence, Whitehall Palace. On the back of the panel is a mark with the initials *C.P.*, which were used by Charles when he was Prince of Wales, before he became king. The painting remained in the royal collection until the eighteenth century but not without some interruptions. In 1653, during the Civil War, the Bruegel was sold at the Commonwealth sale to a private individual, only to be later bought back by Charles II. It was moved to Kensington Palace and was later inventoried as being in storage, a reflection of Bruegel's waning fame in the eighteenth century. It seems that the painting then belonged to a royal secretary and, having passed through a number of collections in England, reappeared on the market in Wingham, near Canterbury, in 1960, and was bought by a dealer from Ramsgate and subsequently, through the dealer Agnew's, acquired by the Frick.

One of the most important painters active north of the Alps in the sixteenth century, Pieter Bruegel the Elder (ca. 1525–1569) spent the better part of his career between the cities of Antwerp and Brussels in Flanders. In the early 1550s, he traveled south to Italy, spending time in Rome with the intention of going to Sicily. A number of drawings record some of the sights that Bruegel saw on this trip.

Bruegel is best known today for his depictions of peasants in scenes that are richly detailed, often humorous, and imbued with allegorical or moral significance. He also depicted religious subjects. Arguably Bruegel's finest work is his series of paintings, five of which survive today, of the times of the year. It is unclear if there were originally twelve paintings in the series or just six, with each panel meant to be identified with two months of the year. Three are in the Kunsthistorisches Museum in Vienna, one is in the Lobkowicz Collection in Prague, and a fourth—*The Harvesters*—one of the most important Old Master paintings in New York, is at the Metropolitan Museum of Art.

Bruegel was also an extraordinary draftsman and very involved in printmaking. One of my favorite drawings by him is of a group of strangely dressed figures with hoods and nets protecting their faces and holding large baskets. They are beekeepers. The Frick's painting relates to the world of Bruegel's drawings and prints, not just because of its monochromatic palette but also because of its size and subject.

The costumes of the three figures in the Frick painting are very similar. The man on the left, seen from the back, is playing a drum. The central one is holding a standard. The one on the right is playing a flute. These figures would have been recognized as *landsknechts*, a type of German mercenary foot soldier. The word *landsknecht* means "servant of the land." Mercenary armies existed in Europe all the way back to the Middle Ages; they were usually Swiss mercenaries but later on, also German. They were paid by whichever ruler needed an army. In the sixteenth century, the *landsknechts* were mainly used by the Holy Roman Emperor Charles V. They were known for their fierce fighting. They become infamous in the sixteenth century for the Sack of Rome in 1527. Charles V unleashed his mercenary army on Rome, allowing them to pillage the city. While mercenary armies were very much part of European life until fairly modern times, only one of these armies still exists: the papal Swiss Guard.

Landsknechts were headed by a standard-bearer, who, after the captain, was one of the most important figures of the militia. The standard-bearer was accompanied by two musicians, a drummer and a fifer, whose purpose was to enliven the march of the soldiers and encourage them to fight in battle. Representations of *landsknechts* in the sixteenth and seventeenth centuries often show this group of three figures. Bruegel probably took inspiration from contemporaneous prints by artists such as Lucas van Leyden and Jakob Binck.

As far as we know, Bruegel made only three grisaille paintings. The other two are religious scenes: *Christ and the Woman Taken in Adultery* at the Courtauld Gallery, London, and *The Death of the Virgin* at Upton House in Warwickshire. The three grisailles are clearly not a series as they are dissimilar in subject matter and format.

Does the Frick's little Bruegel have an allegorical meaning? Or is it just a depiction of *landsknechts*? Or is it a more dramatic moment: the beginning of a battle? The standard-bearer is raising the flag as the others incite the army to fight. More likely, this is a genre scene, a scene of everyday life—three soldiers, whom Bruegel would have observed in Flanders, purposefully marching through the countryside.

—X.S.

JOSHUA REYNOLDS

Selina, Lady Skipwith

1787

Asparagus Fizz

1 ASPARAGUS STALK, MUDDLED

1½ OZ. GIN

½ OZ. FRESH LEMON JUICE

Stir with ice and strain
Top with champagne
Serve in a tall glass and garnish with an asparagus spear

This cocktail is inspired by a journal entry written by the subject of the portrait on November 30, 1828, in which she records that she has tasted asparagus for the first time.

Tucked into Selina's neckerchief is a nosegay, a fragrant bouquet of flowers that was a common accessory of women at the time. It offers a touch of color to the array of whites of her dress, skin, and hair. Her left hand drapes limply over the armrest of the bench, which is rendered in such broad strokes that it appears almost unfinished. In comparison, much care has been paid to the articulation of her face.

Though today gray hair is generally associated with older age, the fashion for British women in elite society at the time, even for young women, was to style their hair or wigs with high volume, powdered

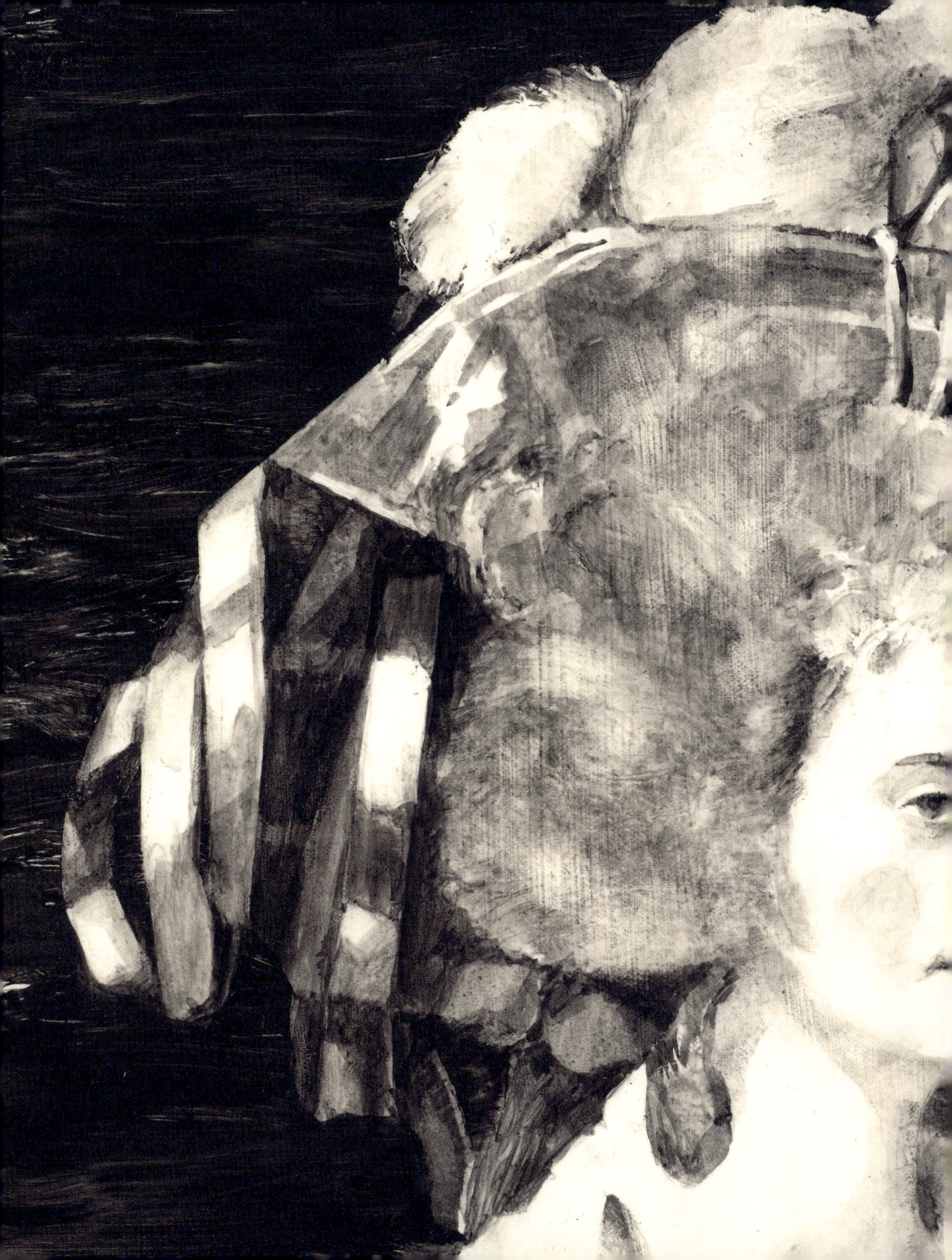

white or gray. Lady Skipwith was thirty-five years old when she sat for this portrait. The whiteness of her skin represents an ideal of feminine beauty that was tied to class and race and which was exaggerated by the application of makeup, often containing deadly lead white. A bright, almost feverish red blotch on her cheek also reflects this ideal of feminine beauty, conveying youth and also modesty: a modest woman would blush if something untoward was said to her, while an immodest one might not.

People sometimes ask, "Why does she look so sad?" She looks to some modern viewers almost sickly, as if she will soon die of consumption. This may be what art historians refer to as "period eye." How, in the year 2021, can viewers with diverse perspectives understand the expression she is meant to convey to audiences in eighteenth-century Britain? Given the primary functions of female portraiture in that culture—to promote the sitter's beauty, lineage, and other qualities—this was meant to be a positive depiction of her in which she appears demure, modest, and complacent.

However, we know from her letters and diary that she was sad. Her father had forbidden her to marry the man she loved, Sir George Shuckburgh. Just a few years before her portrait by Reynolds (1723–1792), she had become the last unmarried sister in her household despite being the eldest. In a letter, she wrote of her heartbreak at not being allowed to marry Shuckburgh and the difficulty of being the last sister at home. Sir Thomas Skipwith, an older friend of her father's, proposed and was rejected a number of times until she finally accepted in 1785. They became engaged in July and married a few months later. About a year and a half into her marriage, in May of 1787, she sat for this portrait.

She began a journal when she was fifteen years old, and her entries are generally cursory, recording the comings and goings of her family, the horse races they attended, their travels among their several residences. On the day she became engaged, she did not write about it, recording only that "Miss S"— short for Miss Shirley, her unmarried surname, referring to herself in the third person—"went for a ride in Bushy Park." Nor did she mention her upcoming marriage or preparations for it. Curiously, just before her marriage, she either stopped writing, with a hiatus of some fifteen years, or the section of her journal was lost soon after her death. Instead, in the gap in her journal entries from just before her marriage until 1800 are transcriptions of poems and other writings. The first is a poem by Frances Greville called "A Prayer for Indifference," which is a plea for an end to emotional feeling. It can be tempting to project her biography onto it.

Three years after Reynolds painted her, she was widowed. Strangely, it is only after her husband's death that she appears in Reynolds's account book as having paid for the portrait. This invites the question of when the portrait ended up with her: Did she and Skipwith live with it as a married couple? Did it remain in Reynolds's studio until she paid for it? The early history and who actually commissioned it are unknown.

When her husband died, she had been married four and a half years and was childless at age thirty-eight. One of her relations referred to Skipwith as an unworthy husband. Nonetheless, he was praised for leaving her his family estate, which showed respect for his wife. This was not always the case in such situations; sometimes the estate bypassed a widow for a male relative in his line. But he left the Skipwith estate to her until the end of her life, at which point it would pass to a male heir. Before his death, he had selected as his heir Grey Skipwith, a boy from a distant American branch of the Skipwith family, which ran the plantation in Prestwould, Virginia, that today is the site of some of the earliest slave dwellings in the United States. As a young boy, Grey was sent to England to be raised as Thomas Skipwith's heir.

Some forty years after Reynolds's portrait, at the age of seventy-six, Lady Skipwith was depicted by another leading artist of British painting of the time, Thomas Lawrence. Lady Skipwith was friends with Lawrence's sister, Anne Bloxam. As a gesture of thanks for the kindness that Lady Skipwith had shown to his sister, Lawrence painted her portrait. However, Lady Skipwith did not want to be given a gift, so she paid Anne Bloxam the £350 that she would have given to the artist. Thus she became the patron of the portrait, rare in her time for a widow of her age.

Her journal after the year 1800 (at which point she was forty-eight years old) describes the life of what seems like an entirely different person. Her writing is different—more florid, with more details (like tasting asparagus for the first time), telling of her active social life and her health. She writes in the first person, describing how she feels and what she does. She became a mother, in a sense, by adopting her first child at age fifty-two. She adopted one of Grey Skipwith's twenty children as her own daughter, and a second child after that first child was married, at which point Lady Skipwith was in her seventies.

A memoir written by her great-nephew conveys that she was a strict, formidable, and vivacious woman. She rode horses well into her seventies and was able to dismount without assistance. Correspondingly, she looks out from her portrait by Lawrence with a cheerful, forthright demeanor.

She left the earlier portrait by Reynolds with the Skipwith family. The older, happier portrait she sent to her Shirley family relations. Whether or not this separation reflects a difference in the way she felt about the two portraits is unknown. The Reynolds portrait remained with the Skipwith family for some decades until being sold toward the end of the nineteenth century to Henry Clay Frick. The Lawrence portrait remains with the Shirley family today.

—A.N.

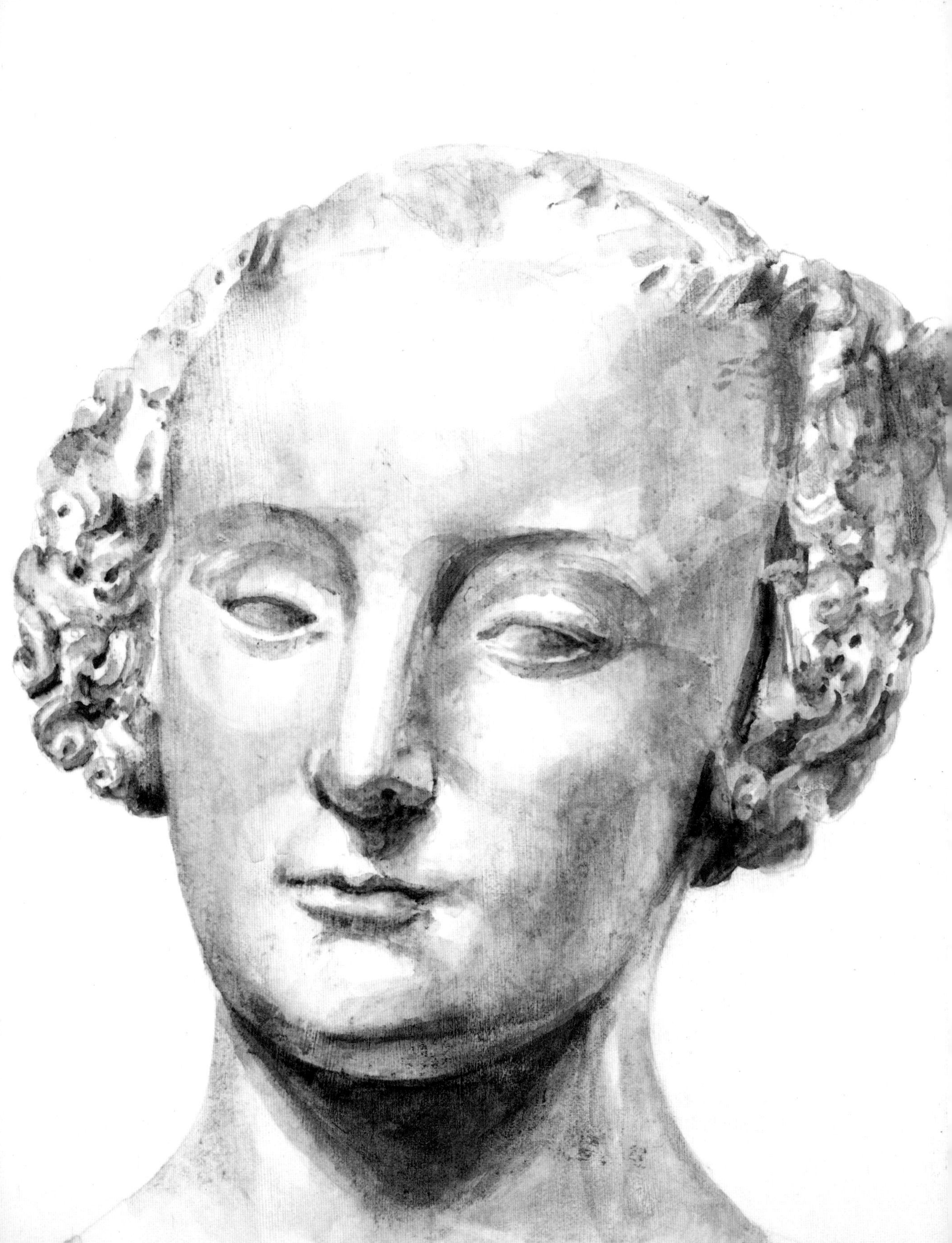

ANDREA DEL VERROCCHIO

Bust of a Woman

CA. 1460–70

Alchermes

Serve in a liqueur glass

This bright red, almost scarlet Florentine liqueur derives its name from what in Arabic was called al-qirmiz, *an insect-based extract. It was very popular in fifteenth-century Florence. The Medici family was so fond of it that it came to be known in France as the "Medici liqueur." Nowadays, it is used mostly as an ingredient in dessert recipes.*

The subject of this amazing bust is unknown, but its artist is very famous. Andrea del Verrocchio (1435–1488) was both a sculptor and a painter, but his primary claim to fame may be that he was the teacher of an even more famous artist: Leonardo da Vinci. Scholars have pointed out that the woman's hairstyle is one that became fashionable during the 1470s, so that is probably when—quite early in Verrocchio's career—the bust was carved.

The bust itself is quite extraordinary. When you look at the different layers of clothing and their subtle interplay, you immediately understand Verrocchio's great skill as a marble carver. As you spend more time looking at the bust, you begin to get the sense that this woman has just disengaged from your gaze. The turning of her head, the slight asymmetry of the shoulders, and the separation of the arms from the body indicate a figure in motion. If you look at her from the side, you see that she is leaning slightly backward as if to convey surprise at seeing the viewer. The sense of movement is enhanced by the slight pull of the garment against the shoulders and the way her outer garment falls to one side, away from her body, at the bottom right.

The bust has an early twentieth-century base on which the sitter is identified as Ginevra de' Benci, whose portrait Leonardo painted (now at the National Gallery of Art in Washington, DC). This speculative identification sheds light on something quite important, which is that in the fifteenth century busts of women were rarely inscribed with the names of their sitters. That probably has a lot to do with women's subordinated social status at the time, but it also has to do with the idea, then widespread, that a woman's beauty, more than her name, was the most distinctive marker of her identity.

If she is not Ginevra de' Benci, who is this woman? For a long time, she has been identified as a member of the Colleoni, a prominent family from Bergamo, a city close to Milan in northern Italy. In particular, scholars postulated that the sitter was Medea Colleoni, who died in 1470, aged only eighteen. The association between a Florentine sculptor and a family from Bergamo stems in part from the fact that Verrocchio had traveled to Venice to make a bronze monument to Bartolomeo Colleoni, one of the most important condottieri of his time. Scholars believed they were on the right track because they identified the seven small shapes within the pomegranate motif on the damask sleeve of the Frick bust as testicles, which the Colleoni had adopted as their heraldic device. "Colleoni" rhymes quite well with *coglioni* (a colloquial way to designate testicles in vernacular Italian), whereby the Colleoni wanted to signal the manliness of their military men. When you look closely at these small shapes, however, you realize that they look neither like testicles nor like any of the testicle-shaped devices adopted by the family. Most importantly, countless fifteenth-century textiles that survive in museums today actually feature that same element. And they cannot all come from the Colleoni family collection.

Although it seems unlikely that the identity of its sitter will be revealed any time soon, every time I look at the bust, I appreciate the wide range of emotions that Verrocchio manages to condense in this woman's gaze and posture.

First proposed as a possible acquisition in 1930, the bust entered the Frick's collection in 1961 as part of Trustee John D. Rockefeller Jr.'s bequest. Like other works from the same bequest, however, the bust would not be on view at the Frick for another twenty-five years out of respect for Helen Clay Frick, who had voted against the acquisition of Rockefeller's bequest, possibly because she believed that gifts as important as that one could outshine the legacy of her father. In 1986—two years after the death of Helen Clay and after a more than twenty-year-long loan to the Princeton University Art Museum—the bust returned to the Frick. As it was in Rockefeller's collection, the bust is complemented by an early twentieth-century base.

—G.D.

JAMES McNEILL WHISTLER

Arrangement in Black and Gold: Comte Robert de Montesquiou-Fezensac

1891–92

Black Manhattan

2 OZ. RYE WHISKEY

1 OZ. AMARO

DASH OF ANGOSTURA BITTERS

Serve chilled in a cocktail glass and garnish with a maraschino cherry

I would like to finish this book as it began, with a Manhattan. This variation of the classic Manhattan, allegedly invented by a man by the name of "Black," alludes to the color in Whistler's extraordinary Arrangement in Black and Gold.

The works of art in the Frick's collection date from about 1280, with Cimabue's small *Flagellation of Christ,* to 1891–92, with this portrait by the American artist James McNeill Whistler (1834–1903). Whistler is in fact the best represented artist in the collection, with more than twenty paintings, pastels, and etchings. All five paintings by Whistler—four full-length portraits and

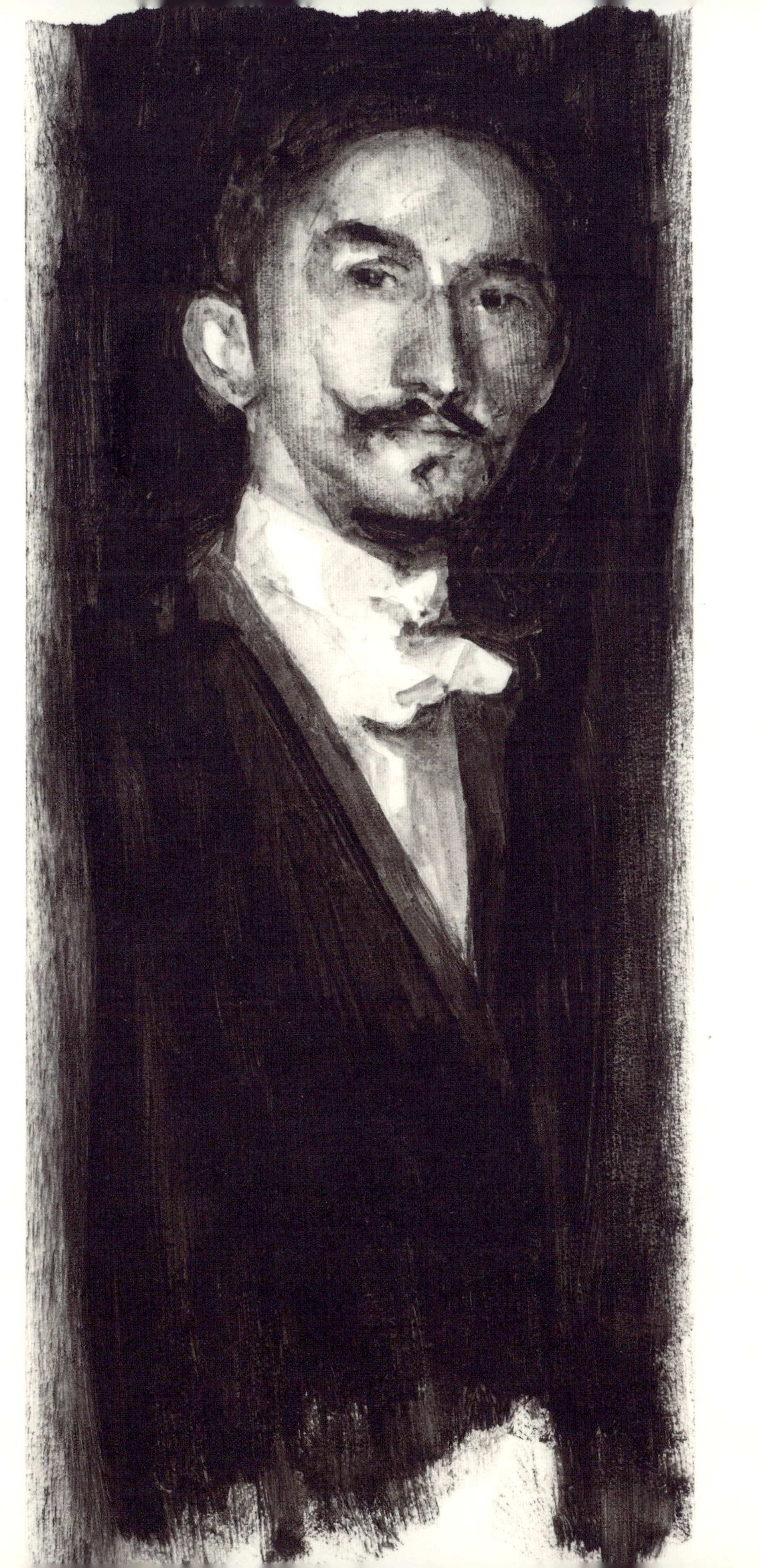

a seascape—still have their original frames, which were designed by the artist himself. Though born in the United States, Whistler spent nearly his entire life in Europe, between London and Paris.

Comte Robert de Montesquiou-Fezensac (1855–1921) was a man of letters, an aesthete, and an arbiter of taste in Paris at the turn of the century. He came from a prominent French noble family that claimed descent from a dynasty that went all the way back to the Merovingian period. Among his famous ancestors was D'Artagnan, the hero of Alexandre Dumas's *Three Musketeers*. Another ancestor was the governess of the king of Rome, Napoleon's son. Montesquiou came from a large family, but by 1883, his mother and all his older brothers had died. As a result, he inherited the title, and this led to a very difficult relationship with his father. As a young man, Montesquiou became well known in Paris for his poetry but also for his unusual attire and many other eccentricities. Through the substantial fortune he had inherited, he led a lavish life, but his extravagance was such that he was frequently short on funds.

In 1885, Montesquiou met a young Argentinian, Gabriel Yturri; the two would be together for twenty years, until 1905, when Yturri died. Montesquiou survived Yturri by more than a decade. Officially, Yturri was Montesquiou's secretary, but everyone knew that they were a couple. They were buried together in the cemetery at Versailles.

On July 3, 1885, around the time he met Yturri, Montesquiou met Whistler—at the Reform Club, a gentlemen's club in London—through an introduction arranged by Henry James. Whistler was more than twenty years older than Montesquiou and already very famous. The two became friends, and Montesquiou started collecting works by Whistler, especially etchings and drawings. It was not until 1891, however, that Montesquiou sat for a portrait by Whistler. Montesquiou sat for the painter on a number of occasions—first in London in 1891, and subsequently in Paris. The portrait was exhibited in 1894 in Paris.

The count is shown looking straight at the viewer, even though both the count and the count's cousin, Countess Greffulhe, a great society figure at the time, suggested to Whistler that the portrait should have been in profile. He is shown holding a cane in his right hand, and with a gray cape over his left arm. The cape is a chinchilla fur coat that Greffulhe lent to Montesquiou for one of the sittings to add a different color to the arrangement of blacks that Whistler was painting. The fur coat was apparently rather heavy, and Montesquiou got tired of holding it.

The painting was displayed in Montesquiou's residence. He was famous for his lavish houses, which he decorated with works of art from Europe and Asia. Whistler planned to paint a second portrait of Montesquiou, in gray. We know that it was started, but it seems that Whistler was not happy with it and ended up either painting over it or, more likely, destroying it. It was only a few years later, still in the 1890s, that another painter of the time, the Italian Giovanni Boldini, portrayed Montesquiou in gray (Musée d'Orsay, Paris).

In 1902, Montesquiou sold the painting to an American, Richard Canfield. Canfield was the wealthy owner of gambling houses on the East Coast. He became interested in Whistler and started collecting works by him, assembling the second-largest collection of works by the artist at the time. The sale of the portrait to Canfield infuriated Whistler. Montesquiou had promised Whistler that he was going to bequeath the portrait after his death to the Louvre. Whistler wrote a scathing letter to Montesquiou, and the two did not meet again.

Just a few months before Canfield died, after a fall in the New York subway stop at 14th Street, he sold a number of his Whistlers to the art dealer Knoedler, for a considerable amount of money. Henry Clay Frick bought three of them: two portraits—those of Rosa Corder and of Montesquiou—and a seascape painted by Whistler in Chile in 1866. This was the start of Frick's collection of Whistler works. He displayed works by the artist on the second floor of the house, near his bedroom, and on the first floor in his office, a room demolished in the 1930s to make space for what is today's Oval Room.

One of the great scholars of Whistler, and especially of the Montesquiou portrait, was Edgar Munhall, the Frick's first chief curator. So much of what we do today at the Frick is indebted to the foundation laid by Edgar. He oversaw the first scholarly catalogues of the collection in the 1960s, and remained an active figure at the museum until his death in 2016. Between 1995 and 1996, he curated a marvelous exhibition around the Montesquiou portrait, bringing together a number of portraits of Montesquiou—he was supposedly portrayed more than fifty-five times—and documents and objects that belonged to him. It is thanks to the research of previous curators, starting with Edgar, that we can now present so many stories and so much information on works of art at the Frick. Many questions remain, and because of lingering mysteries and the complexities of history, research remains of vital importance for us at the Frick, and in the museum world.

—X.S.

THE WORKS

Artworks are listed alphabetically by the artist's last name or by the name or sobriquet by which the artist is best known. Multiple works by the same artist are listed chronologically. The red numbers refer to page numbers.

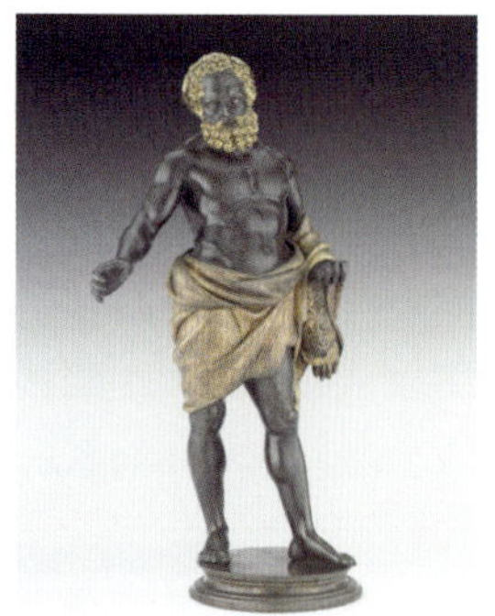

Antico
Hercules, probably 1499
191

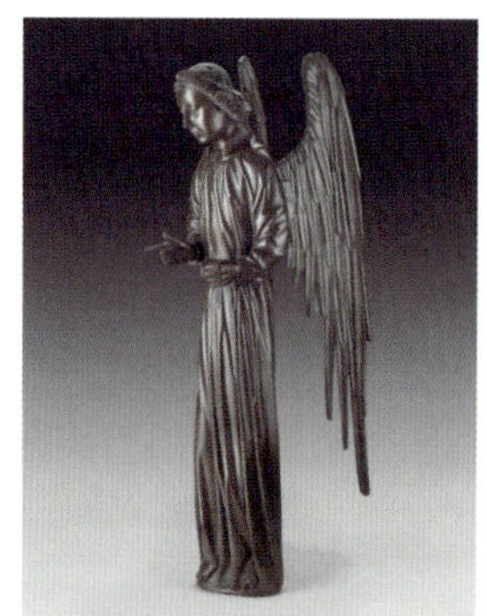

Jean Barbet
Angel, 1475
46

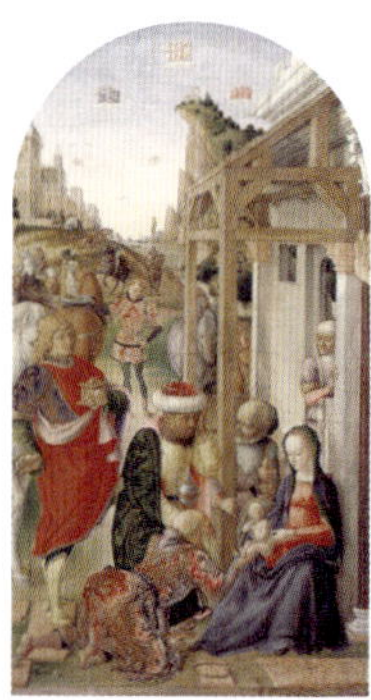

Lazzaro Bastiani
Adoration of the Magi, 1470s
159

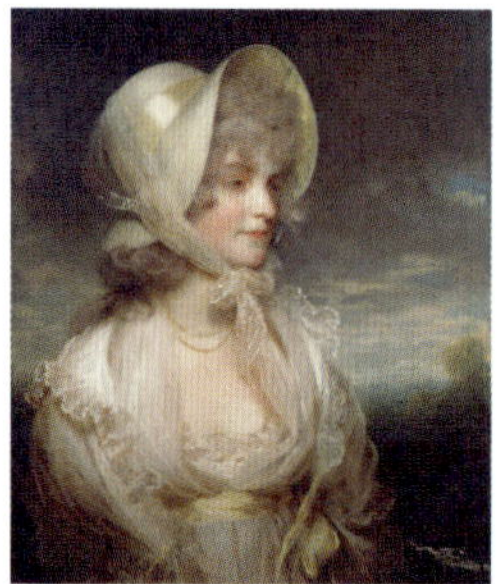

William Beechey
Elizabeth Sophia Baillie (née de Visme), 1795
103

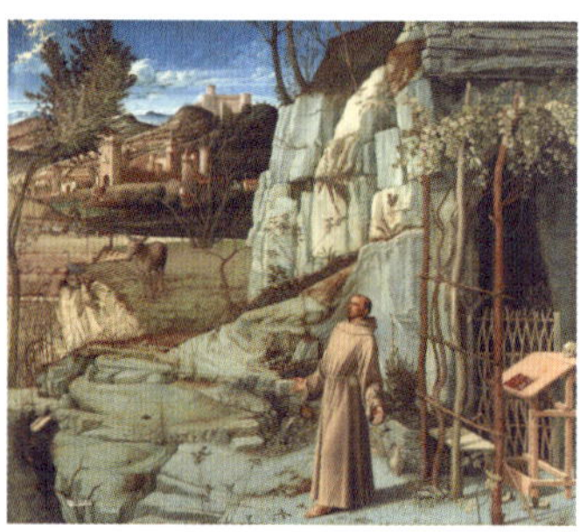

Giovanni Bellini
St. Francis in the Desert, ca. 1476–78
19

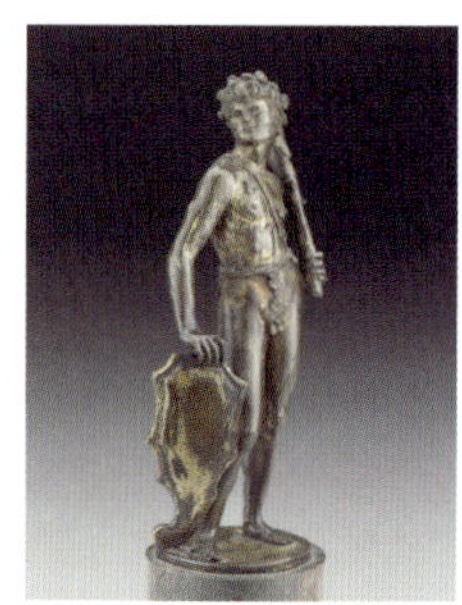

Bertoldo di Giovanni
Shield Bearer, ca. 1470–80
83

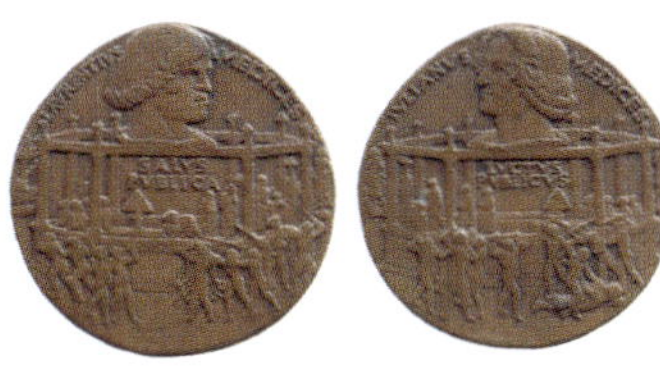

Bertoldo di Giovanni
The Pazzi Conspiracy Medal, 1478
122

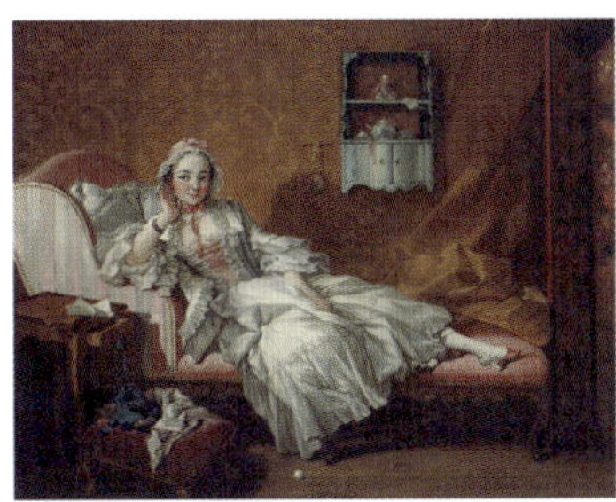

François Boucher
A Lady on Her Day Bed, 1743
38

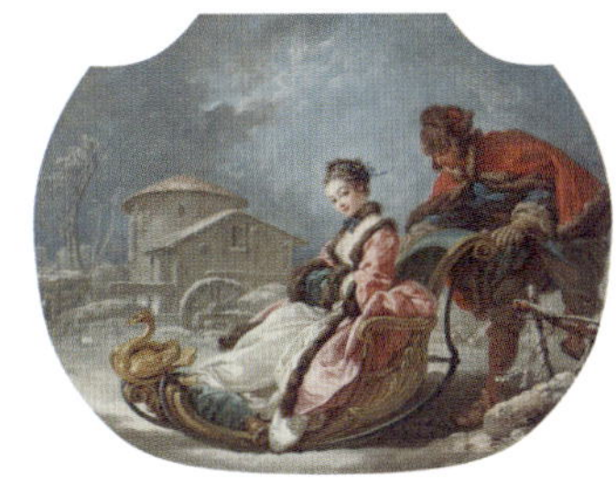

François Boucher
The Four Seasons: Winter, 1755
171

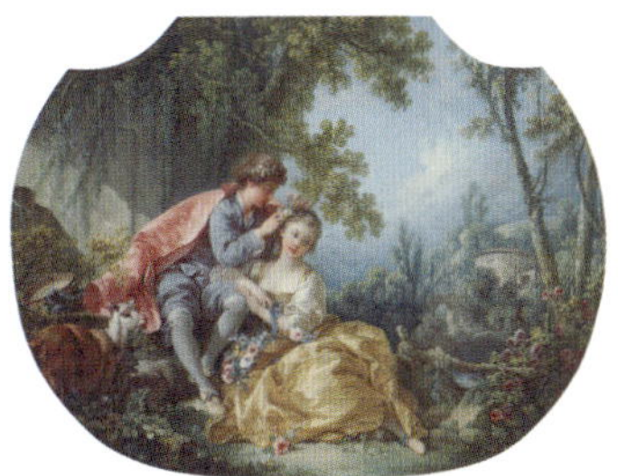

François Boucher
The Four Seasons: Spring, 1755
171

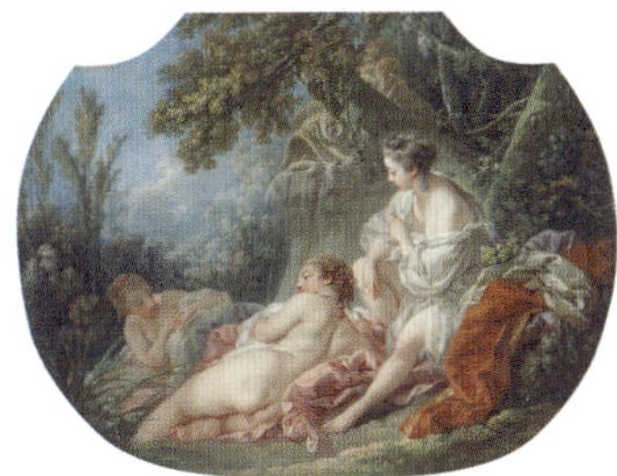

François Boucher
The Four Seasons: Summer, 1755
171

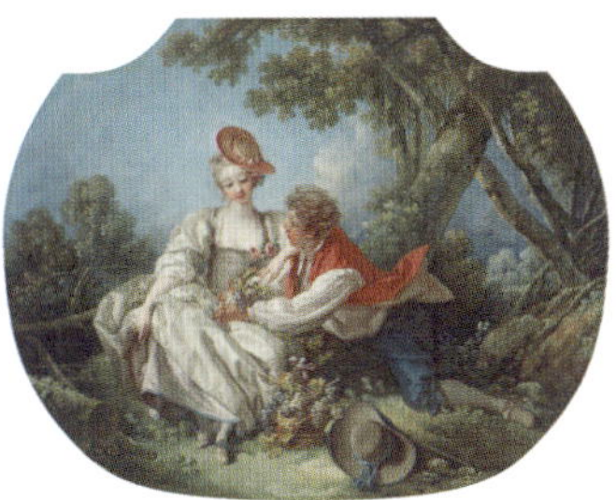

François Boucher
The Four Seasons: Autumn, 1755
171

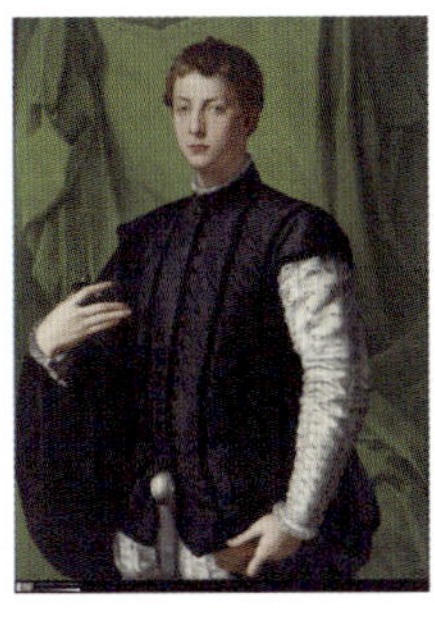

Agnolo Bronzino
Lodovico Capponi, ca. 1550–55
114

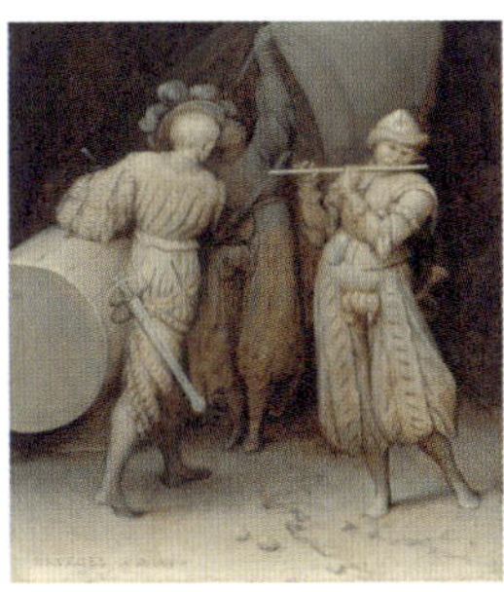

Pieter Bruegel the Elder
Three Soldiers, 1568
262

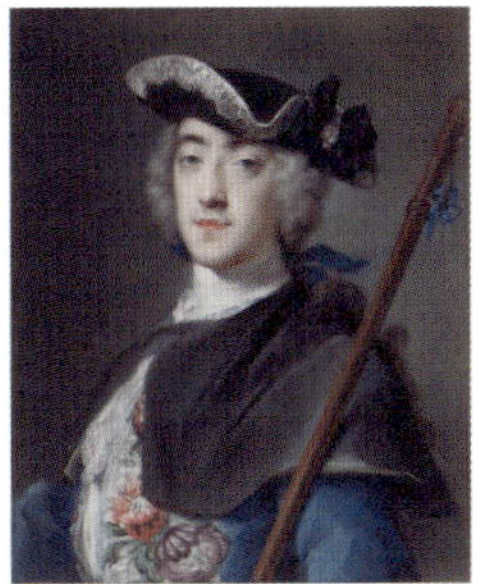

Rosalba Carriera
Portrait of a Man in Pilgrim's Costume, 1730s
210

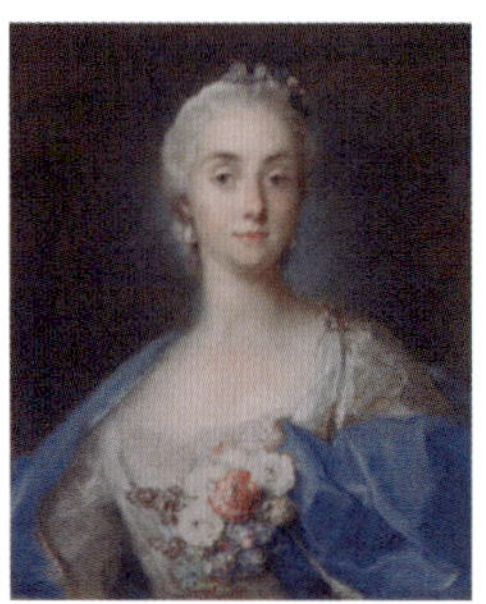

Rosalba Carriera
Portrait of a Woman, 1730s
210

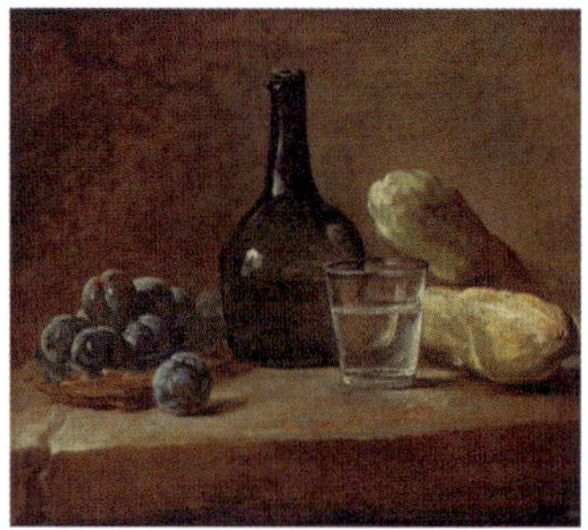

Jean-Siméon Chardin
Still Life with Plums, ca. 1730
131

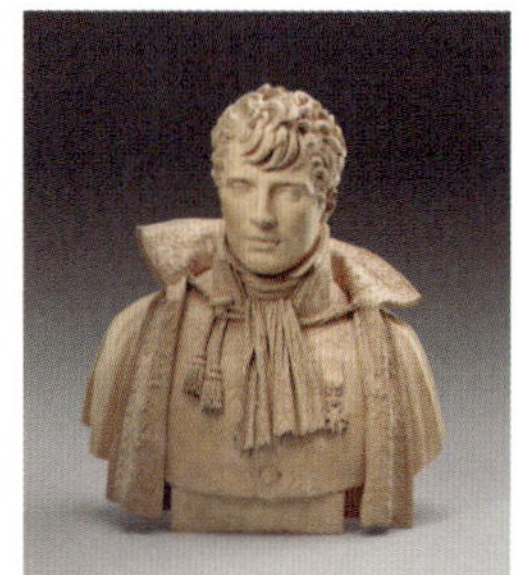

Joseph Chinard
Étienne Vincent de Margnolas, 1809
230

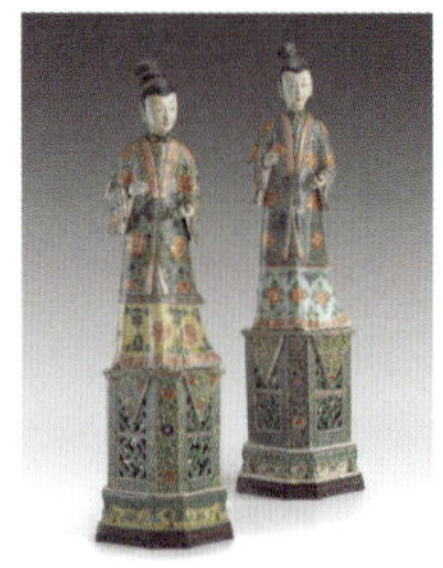

Chinese, Qing Dynasty
Two Figures of Ladies on Stands, 18th century
243

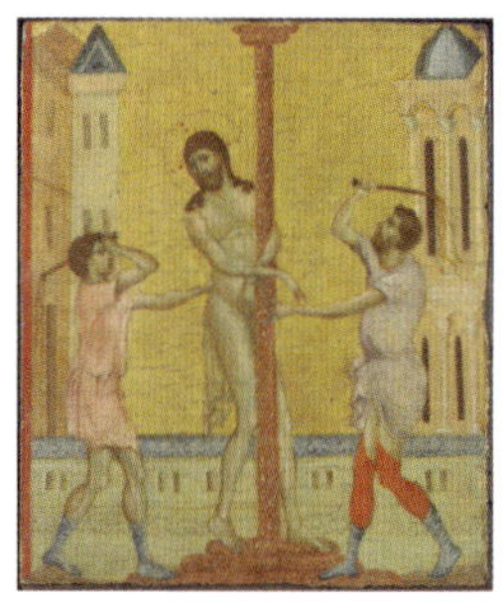

Cimabue
The Flagellation of Christ, ca. 1280
199

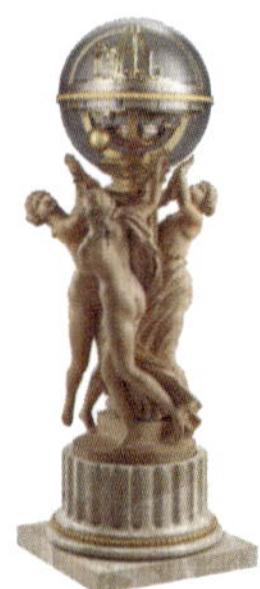

Clodion and Jean-Baptiste Lepaute
The Dance of Time: Three Nymphs Supporting a Clock, 1788
162

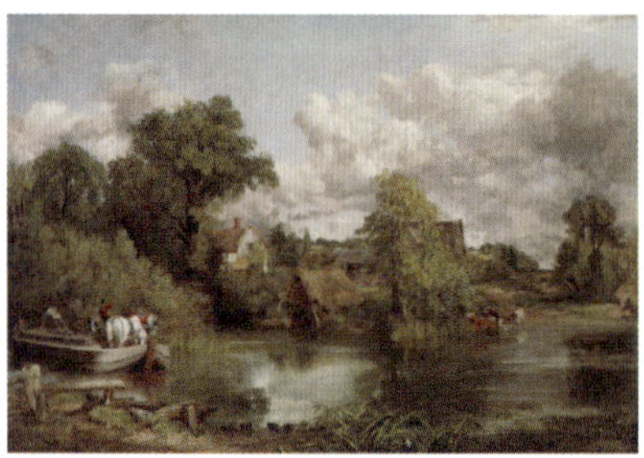

John Constable
The White Horse, 1819
30

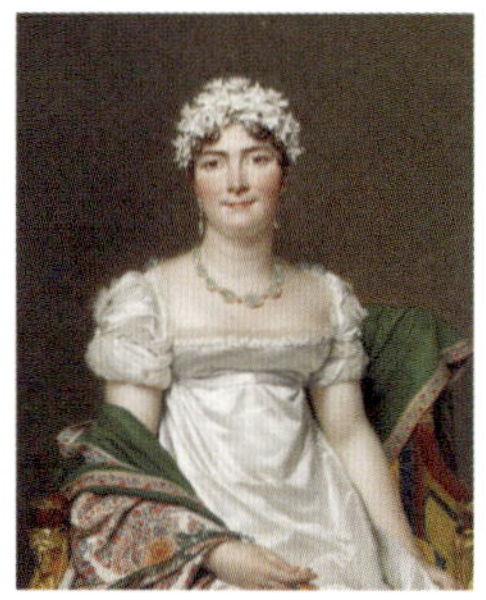

Jacques-Louis David
Alexandrine-Thérèse Nardot, Comtesse Daru, 1810
194

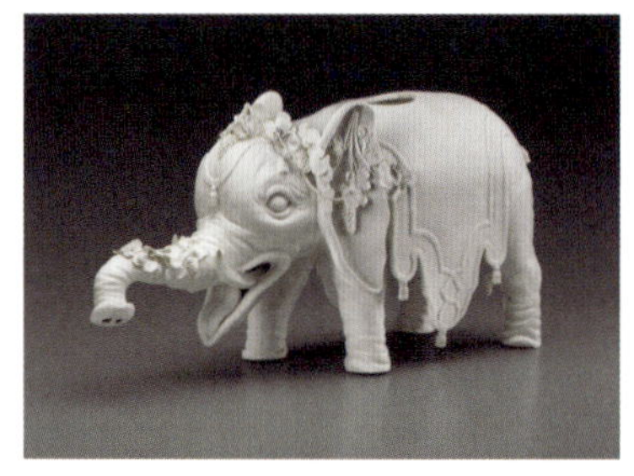

Du Paquier Porcelain Manufactory
Elephant-Shaped Wine Dispenser, 1740
258

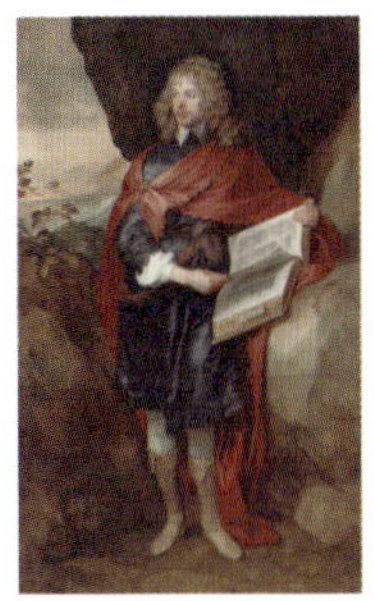

Anthony van Dyck
Sir John Suckling, ca. 1638
26

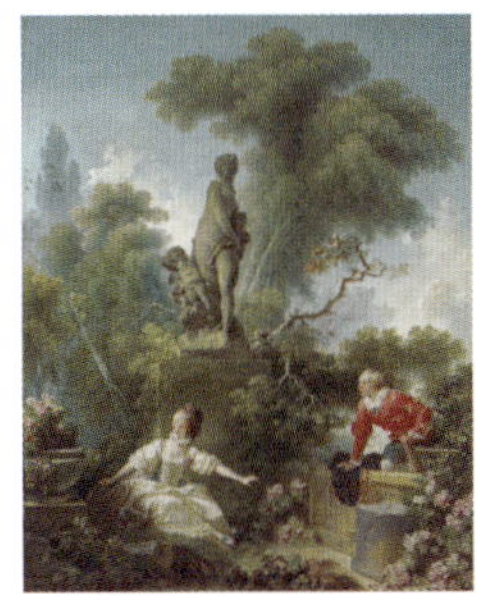

Jean-Honoré Fragonard
The Progress of Love: The Meeting, 1771–72
107

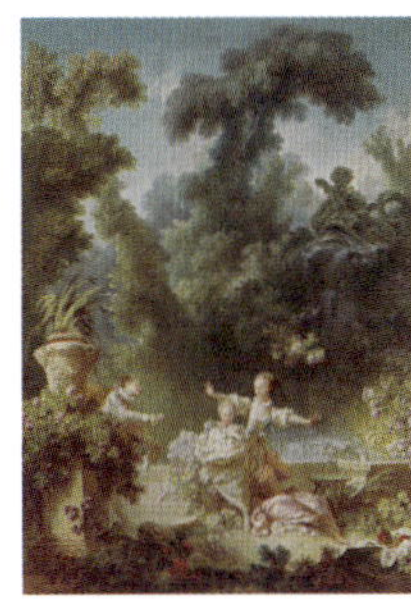

Jean-Honoré Fragonard
The Progress of Love: The Pursuit, 1771–72
107

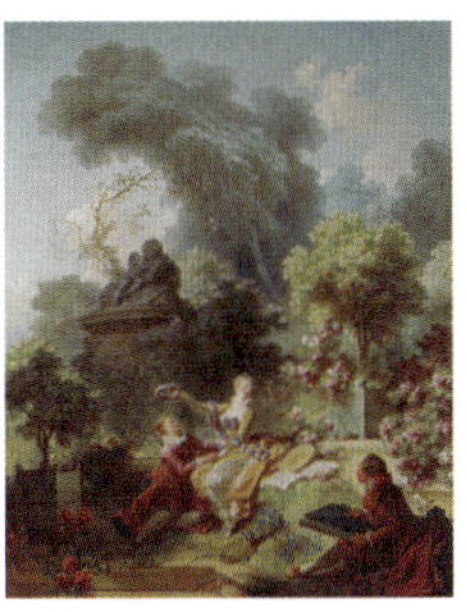

Jean-Honoré Fragonard
The Progress of Love: The Lover Crowned, 1771–72
107

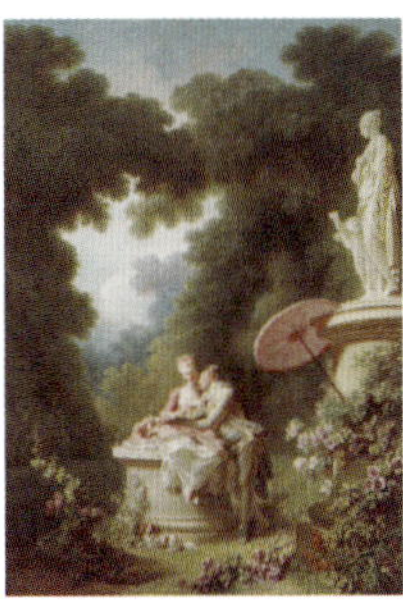

Jean-Honoré Fragonard
The Progress of Love: Love Letters, 1771–72
107

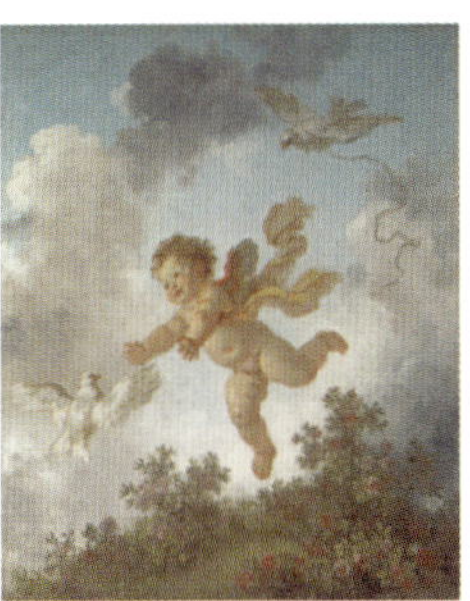

Jean-Honoré Fragonard
The Progress of Love: Love Pursuing a Dove, ca. 1790–91
111

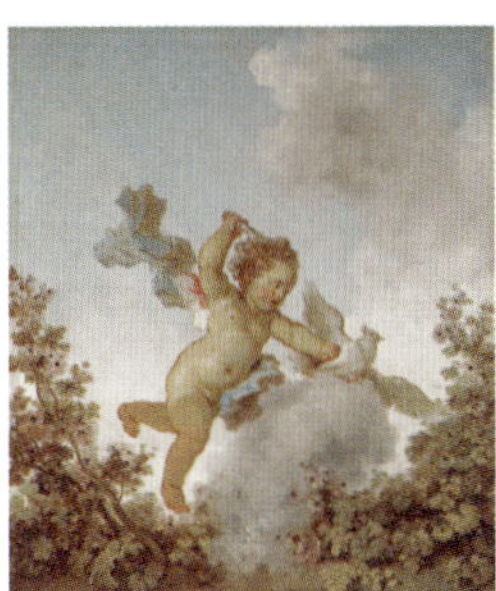

Jean-Honoré Fragonard
The Progress of Love: Love the Avenger, ca. 1790–91
111

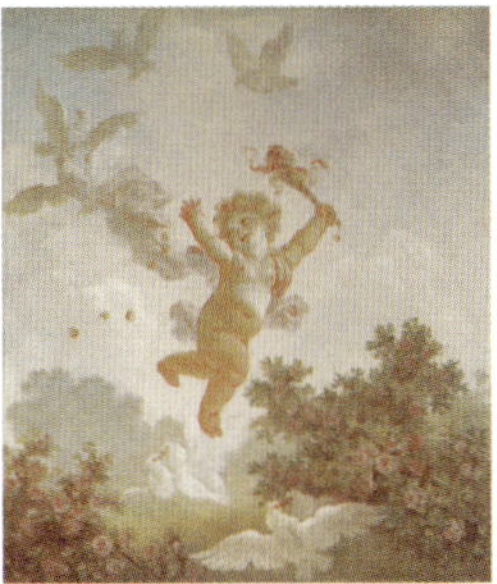

Jean-Honoré Fragonard
The Progress of Love: Love the Jester, ca. 1790–91
111

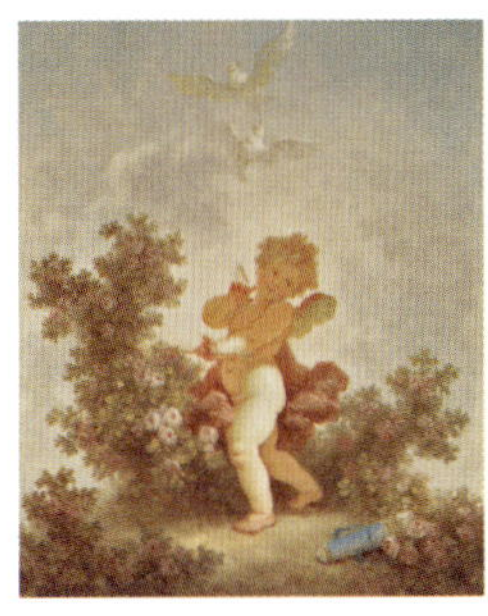

Jean-Honoré Fragonard
The Progress of Love: Love the Sentinel, ca. 1790–91
111

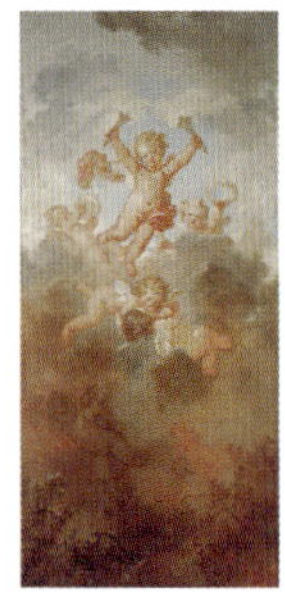

Jean-Honoré Fragonard
The Progress of Love: Love Triumphant, ca. 1790–91
111

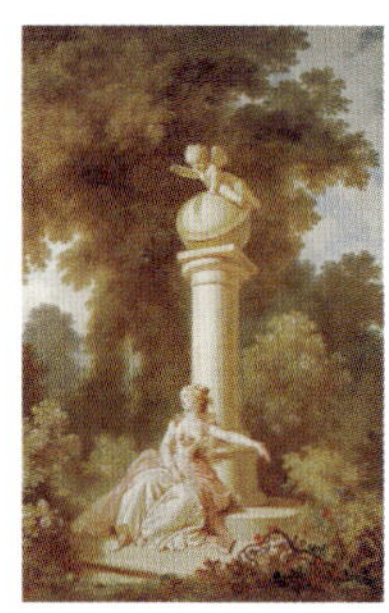

Jean-Honoré Fragonard
The Progress of Love: Reverie, ca. 1790–91
111

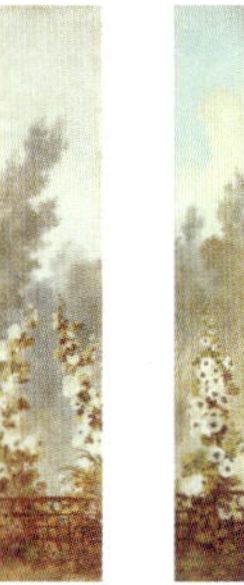
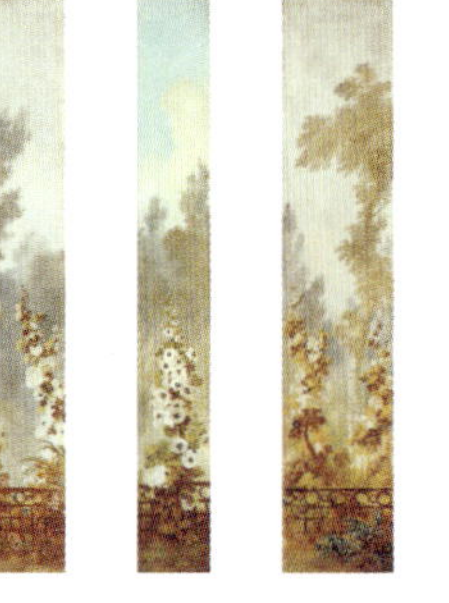

Jean-Honoré Fragonard
The Progress of Love: Hollyhocks, ca. 1790–91
111

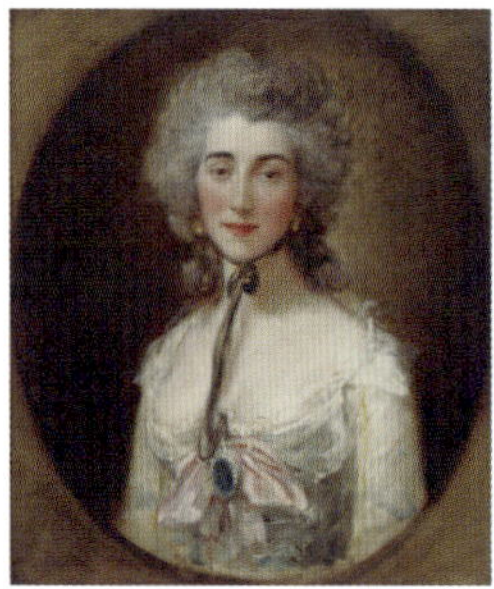

Thomas Gainsborough
Grace Dalrymple Elliott, ca. 1782
55

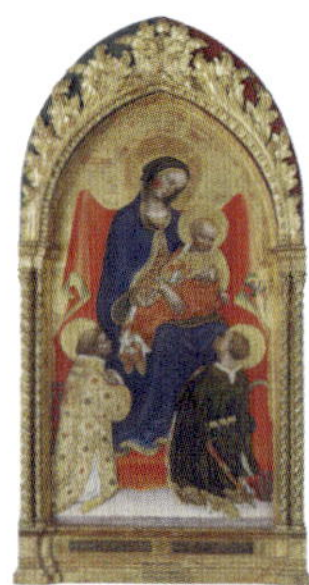

Gentile da Fabriano
Madonna and Child, with Saints Lawrence and Julian, 1423–25
255

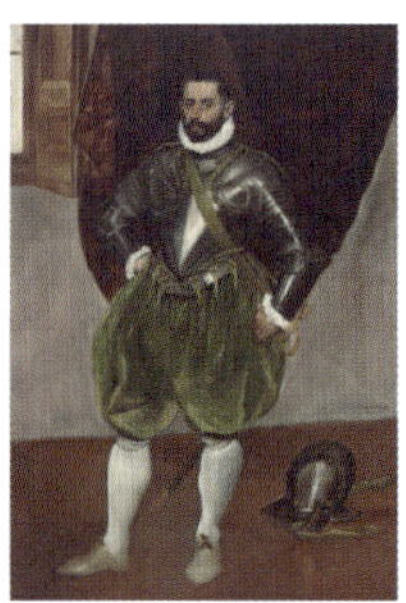

El Greco
Vincenzo Anastagi, ca. 1575
178

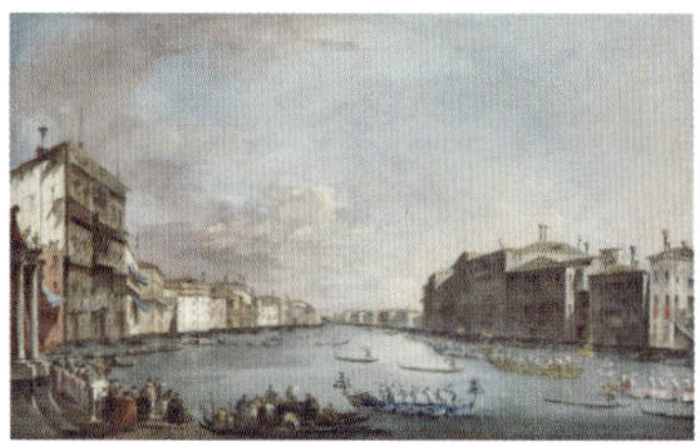

Francesco Guardi
Regatta in Venice, ca. 1770
246

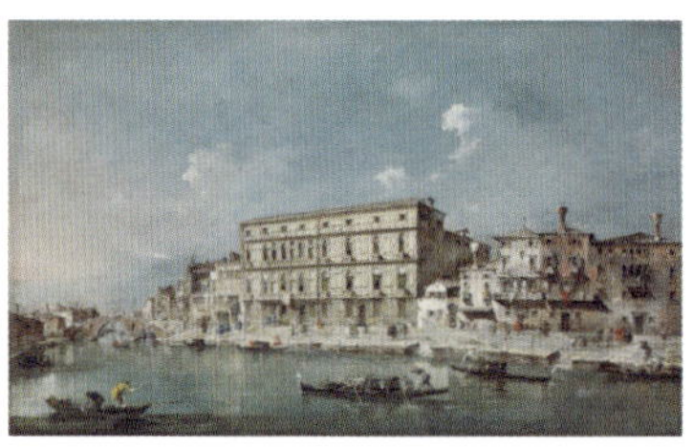

Francesco Guardi
View of the Cannaregio Canal in Venice, ca. 1770
246

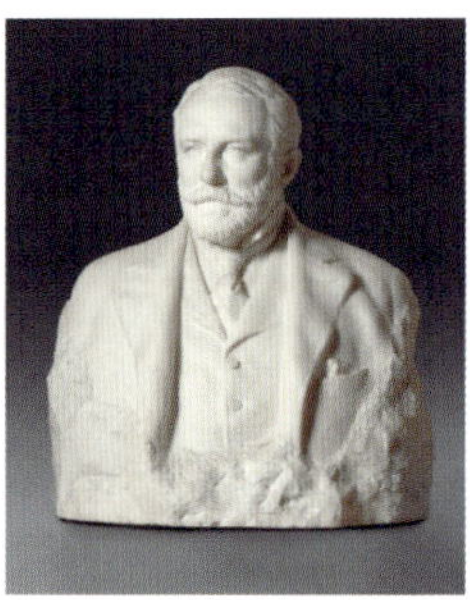

Malvina Cornell Hoffman
Henry Clay Frick, 1922
154

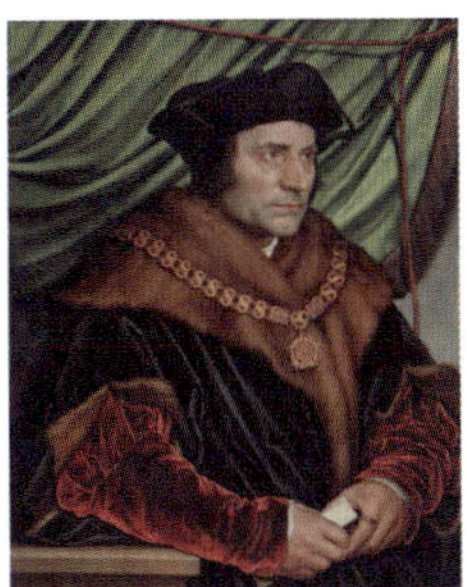

Hans Holbein the Younger
Sir Thomas More, 1527
63

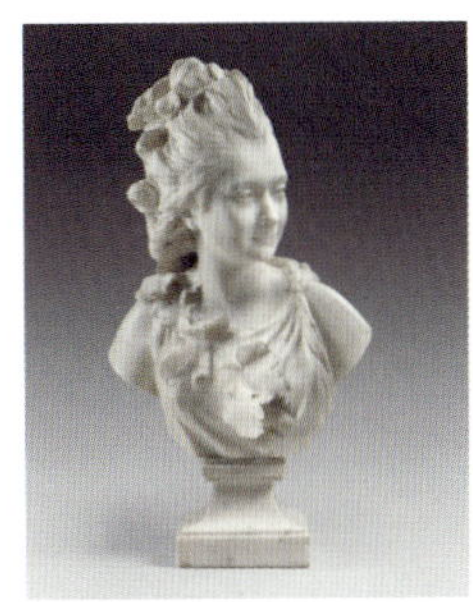

Jean-Antoine Houdon
Élisabeth-Suzanne de Jaucourt, Comtesse du Cayla, 1777
202

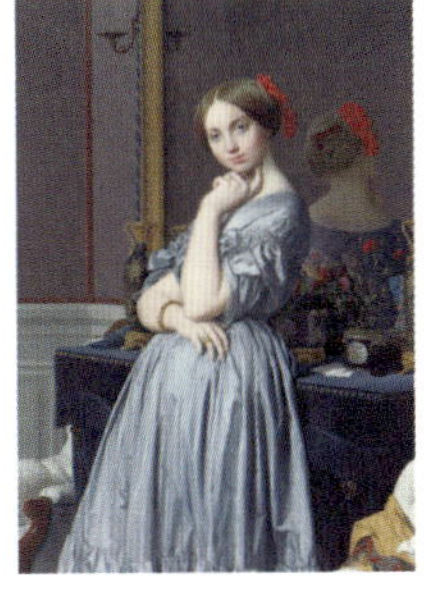

Jean-Auguste-Dominique Ingres
Louise, Princesse de Broglie, Later the Comtesse d'Haussonville, 1845
95

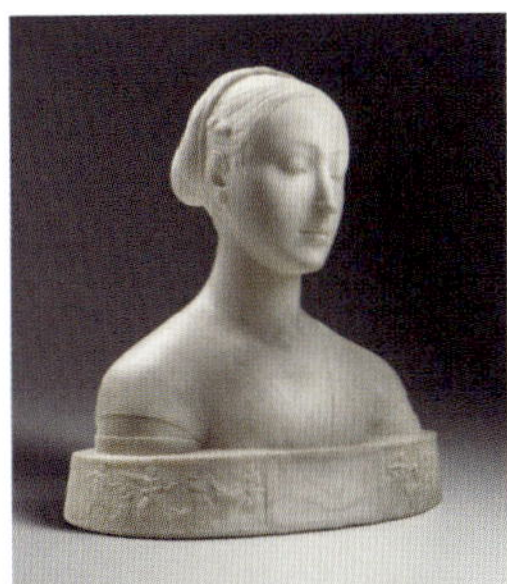

Francesco Laurana
Bust of a Woman, ca. 1470s
215

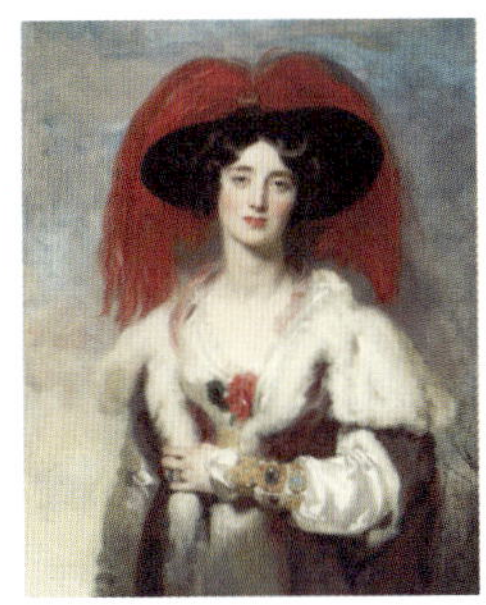

Thomas Lawrence
Julia, Lady Peel, 1827
147

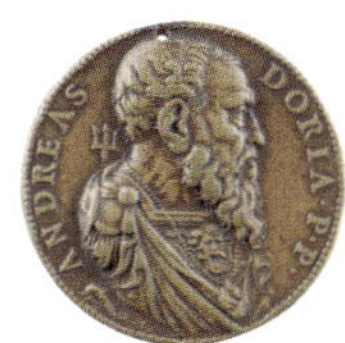

Leone Leoni
Andrea Doria, ca. 1541
250

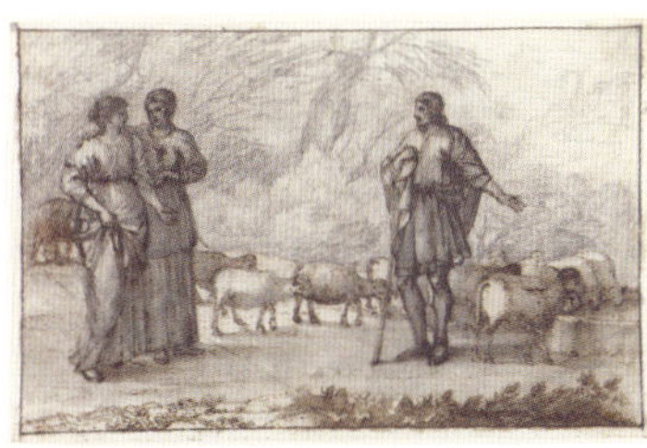

Claude Lorrain
Jacob, Rachel, and Leah at the Well, 1666
186

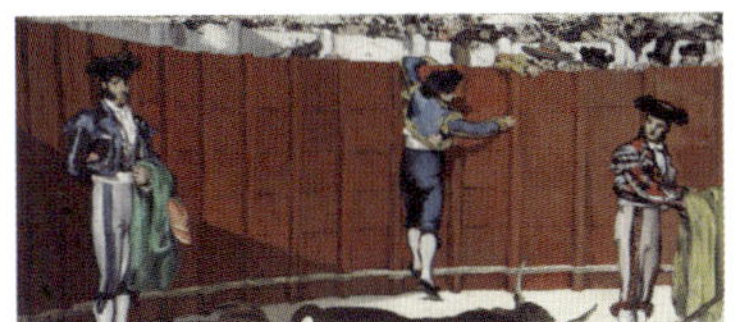

Édouard Manet
The Bullfight, 1864
175

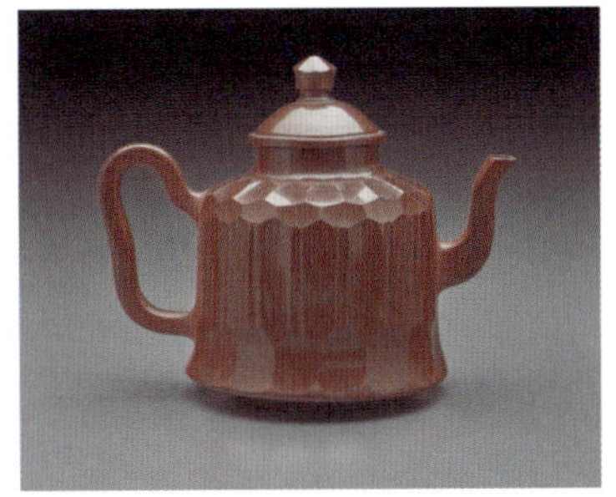

Meissen Porcelain Manufactory
Teapot, ca. 1710–13
99

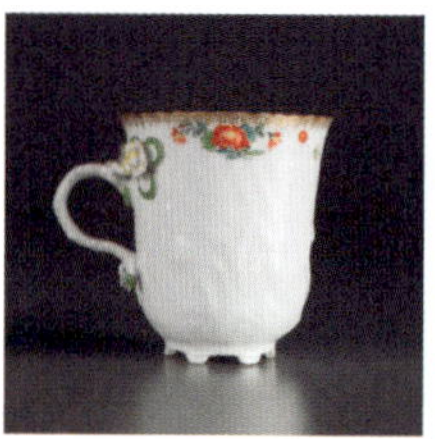
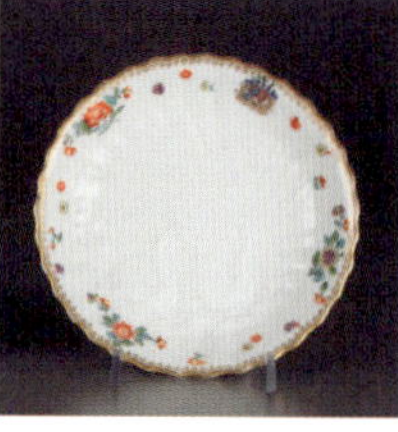

Meissen Porcelain Manufactory
Cup and Saucer from the "Swan" Service,
ca. 1737–40
167

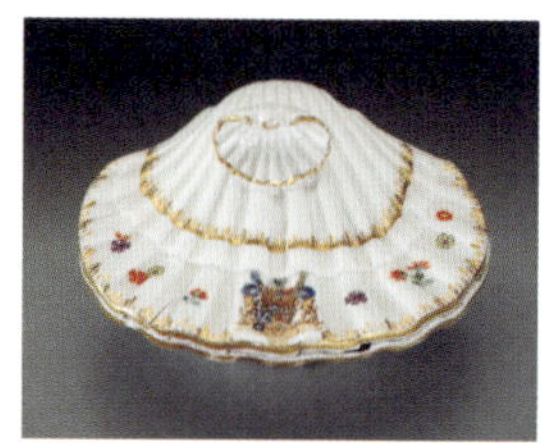

Meissen Porcelain Manufactory
Spicebox from the "Swan" Service,
ca. 1737–41
167

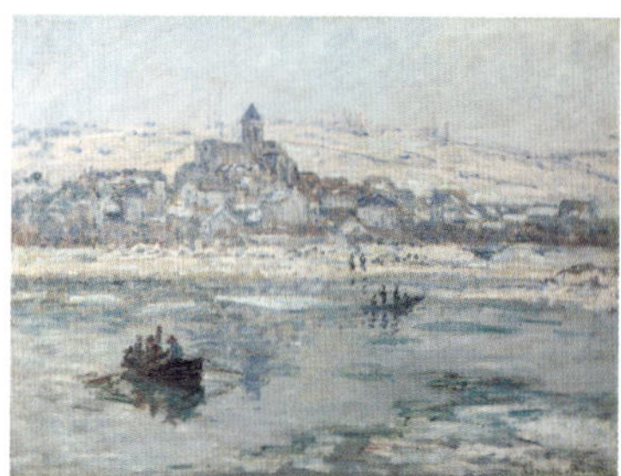

Claude Monet
Vétheuil in Winter, 1878–79
139

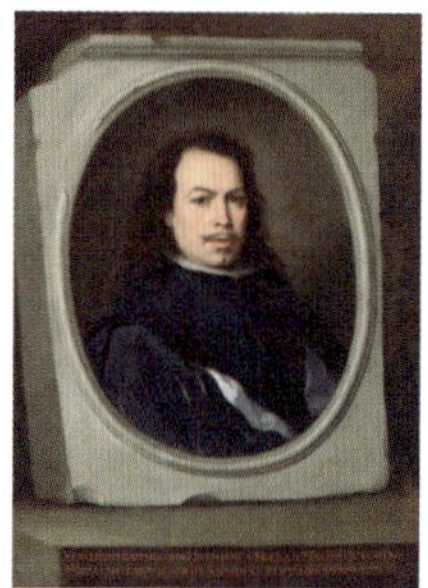

Bartolomé Estebán Murillo
Self-Portrait, ca. 1650–55
143

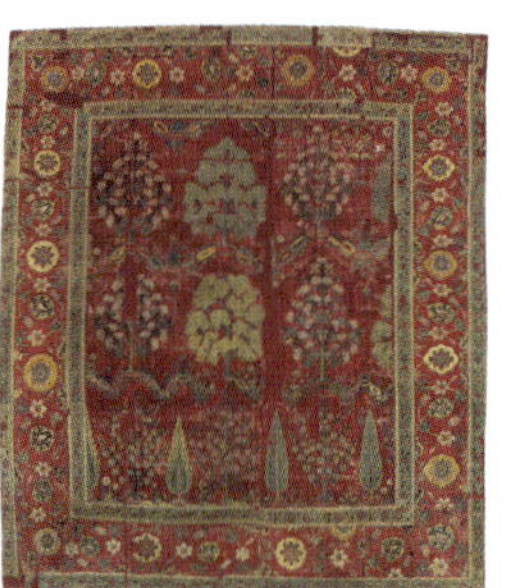

Northern Indian
Carpet with Trees, ca. 1630
119

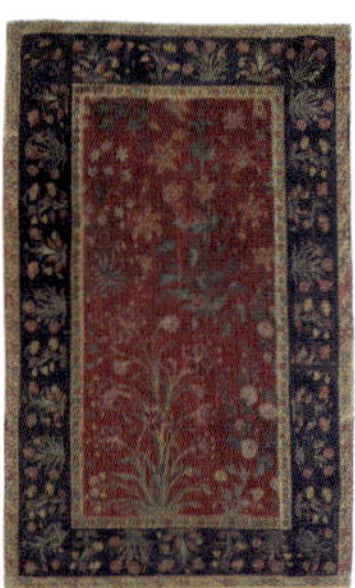

Northern Indian
Carpet with Flowers, ca. 1650
119

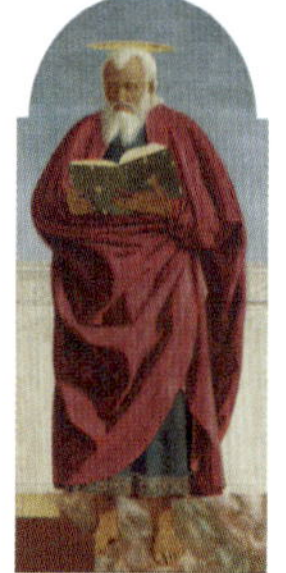

Piero della Francesca
St. John the Evangelist, 1454–69
183

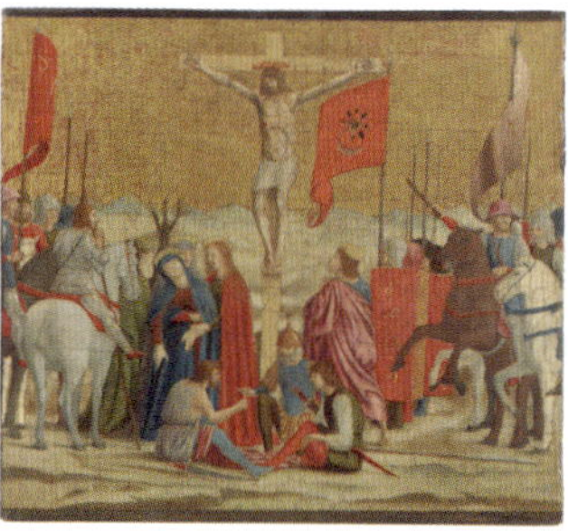

Piero della Francesca
The Crucifixion, 1454–69
183

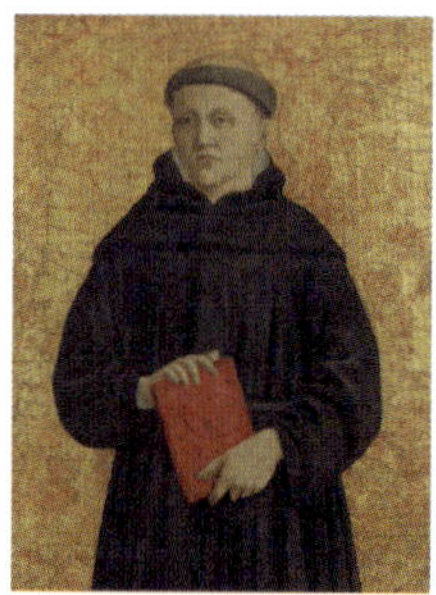

Piero della Francesca
St. Leonard (?), 1454–69
183

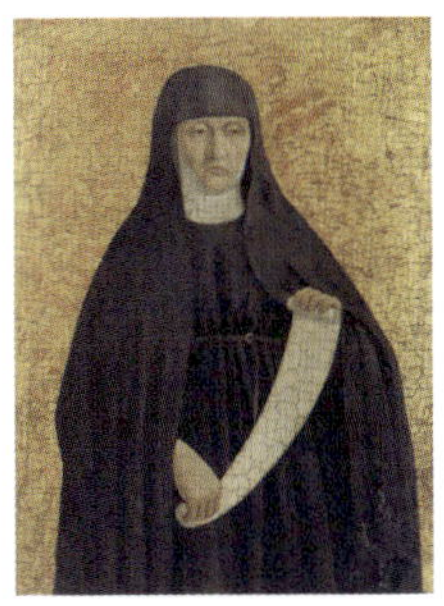

Piero della Francesca
St. Monica, 1454–69
183

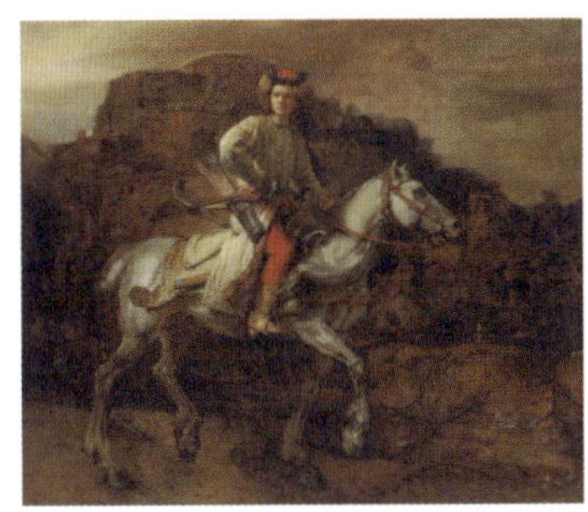

Rembrandt Harmensz. van Rijn
The Polish Rider, ca. 1655
23

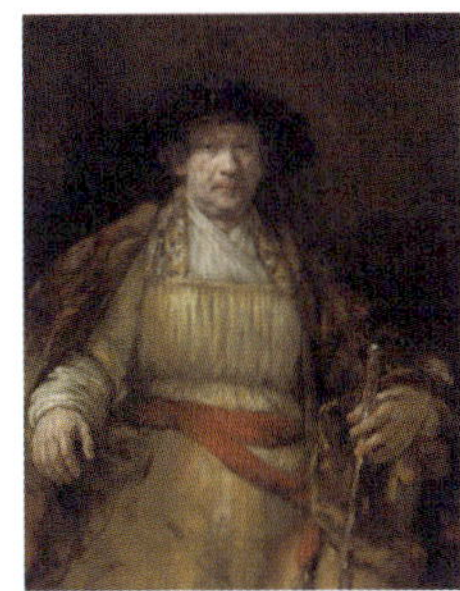

Rembrandt Harmensz. van Rijn
Self-Portrait, 1658
207

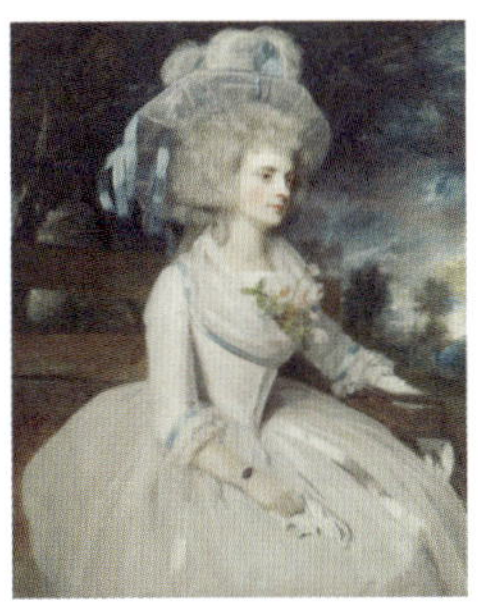

Joshua Reynolds
Selina, Lady Skipwith, 1787
266

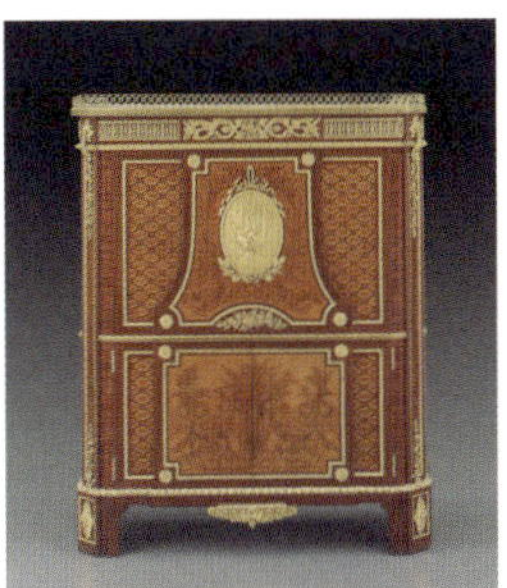

Jean-Henri Riesener
Secretaire, ca. 1780 and ca. 1790
66

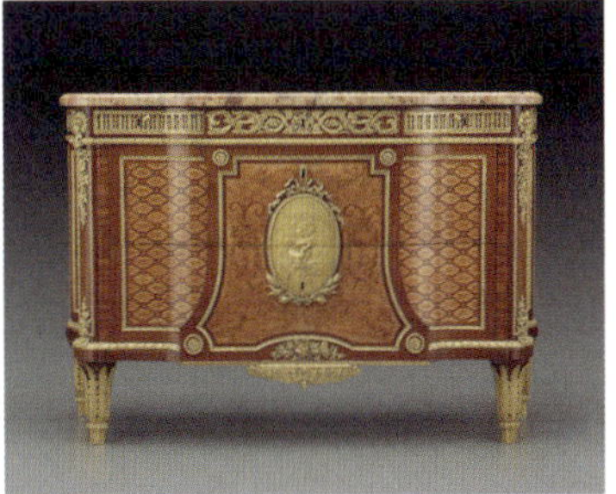

Jean-Henri Riesener
Commode, ca. 1780 and ca. 1790
66

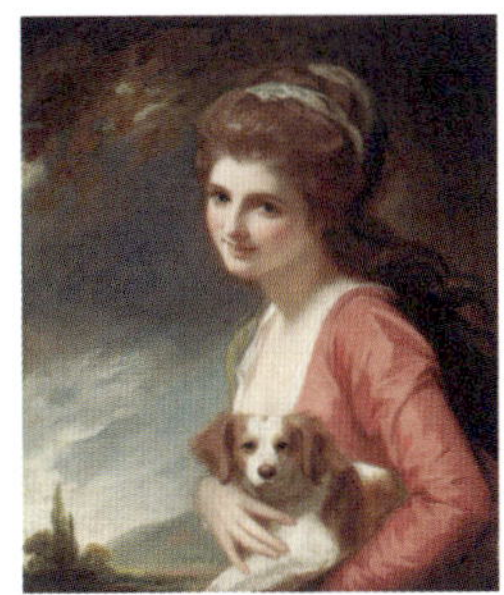

George Romney
Lady Hamilton as "Nature," 1782
127

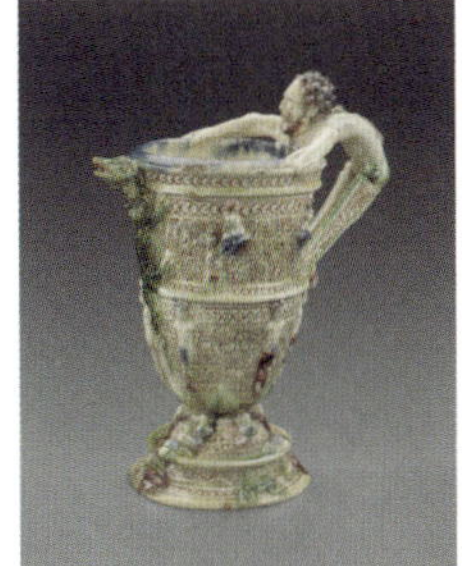

Saint-Porchaire Ware,
attributed to Bernard Palissy
Ewer, mid-16th century
219

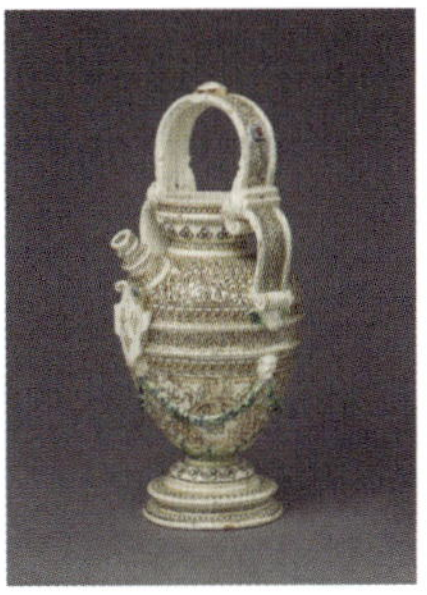

Saint-Porchaire Ware
Ewer, mid-16th century
219

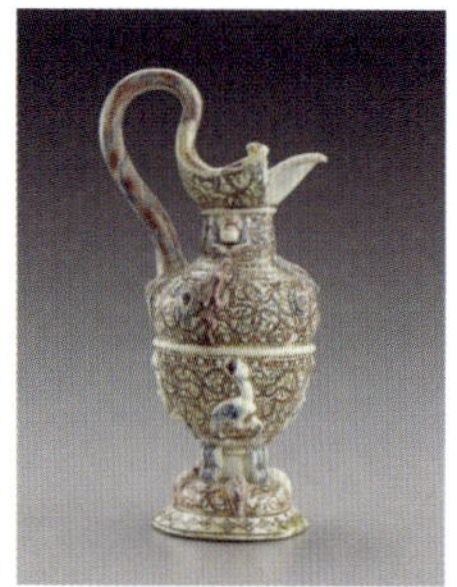

Saint-Porchaire Ware
Ewer, mid-16th century
219

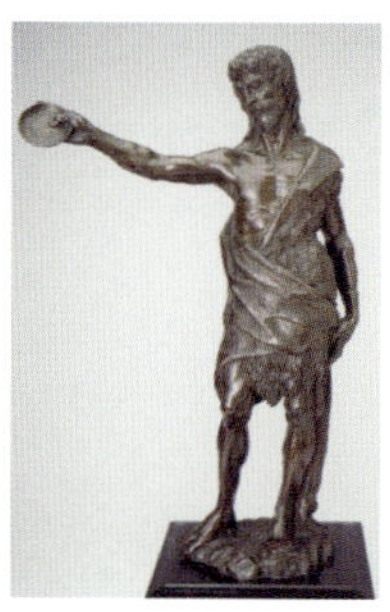

Francesco da Sangallo
St. John Baptizing, ca. 1534–38
222

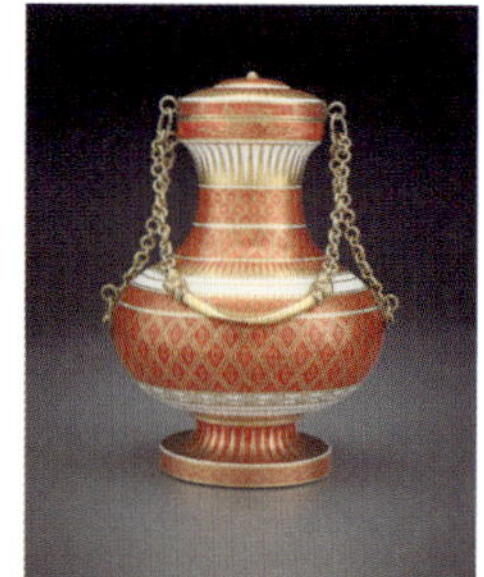

Sèvres Porcelain Manufactory
Vase Japon, 1774
86

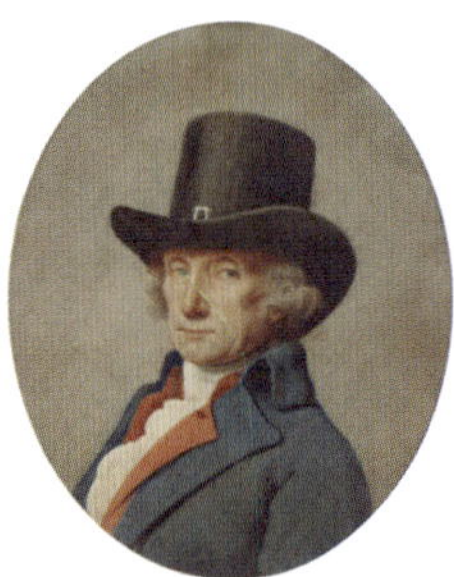

George Stubbs
Warren Hastings, ca. 1791
59

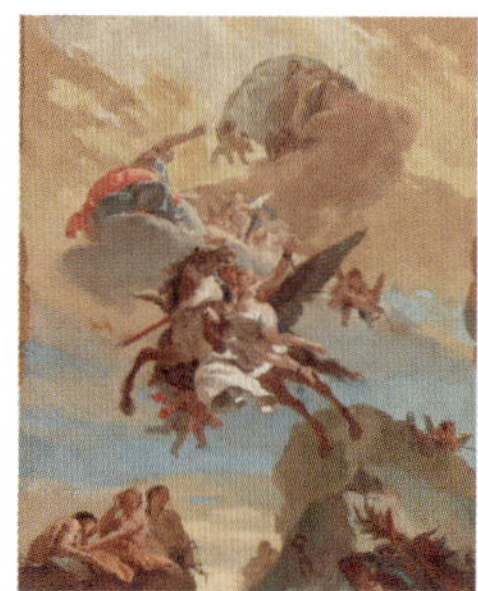

Giambattista Tiepolo
Perseus and Andromeda, 1730
134

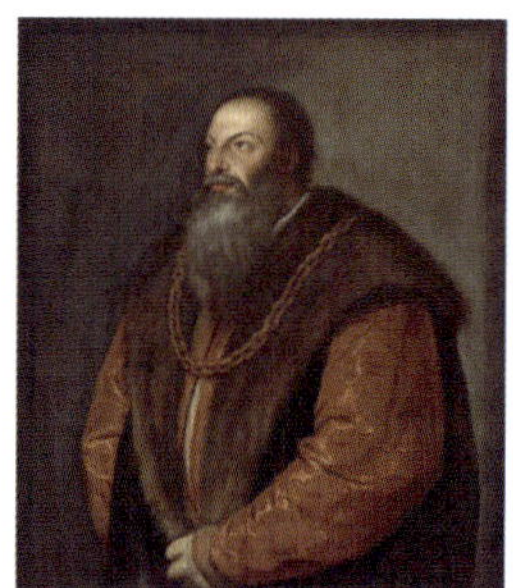

Titian
Pietro Aretino, ca. 1537
91

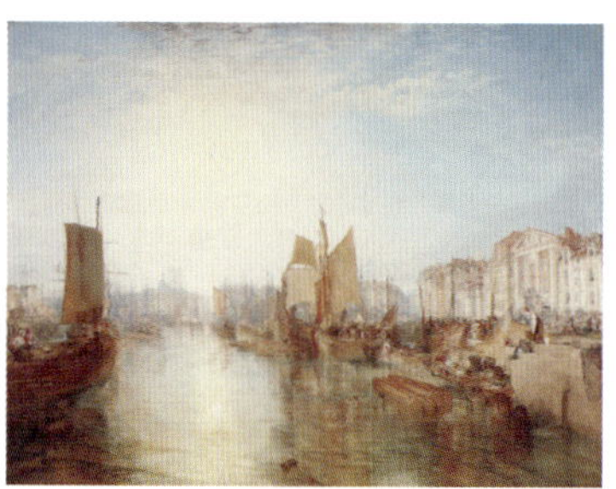

Joseph Mallord William Turner
Harbor of Dieppe: Changement de Domicile, 1826
35

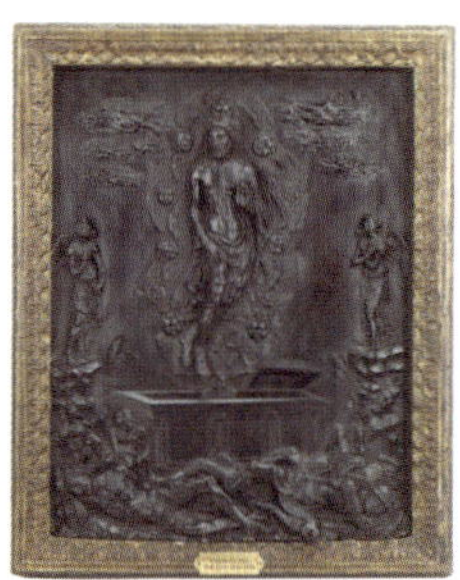

Vecchietta
The Resurrection, 1472
238

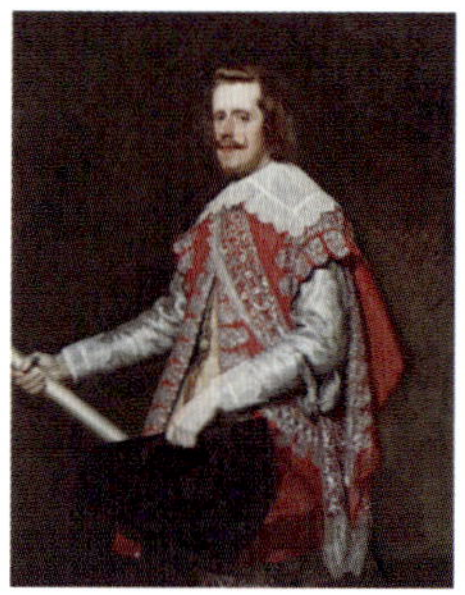

Diego Rodríguez de Silva y Velázquez
King Philip IV of Spain, 1644
43

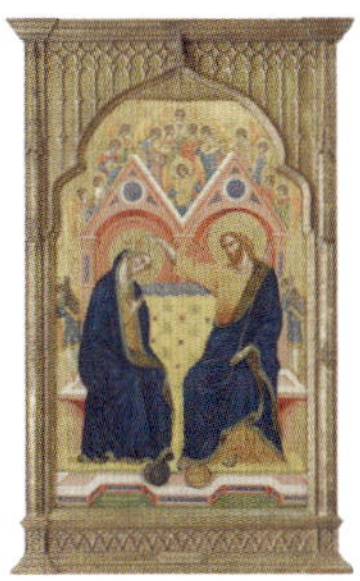

Paolo Veneziano with
Giovanni Veneziano
The Coronation of the Virgin, 1358
234

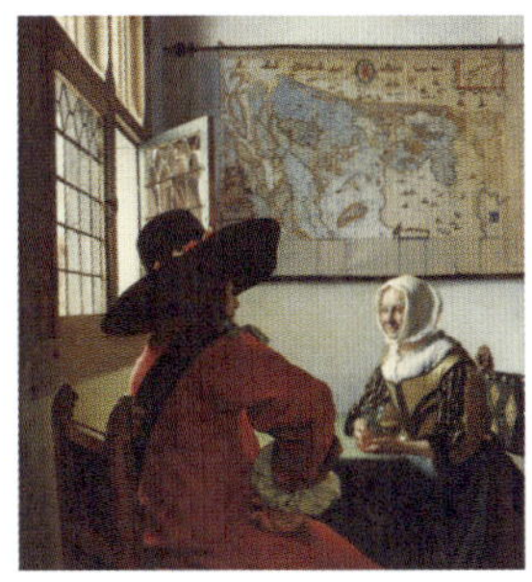

Johannes Vermeer
Officer and Laughing Girl, ca. 1657
71

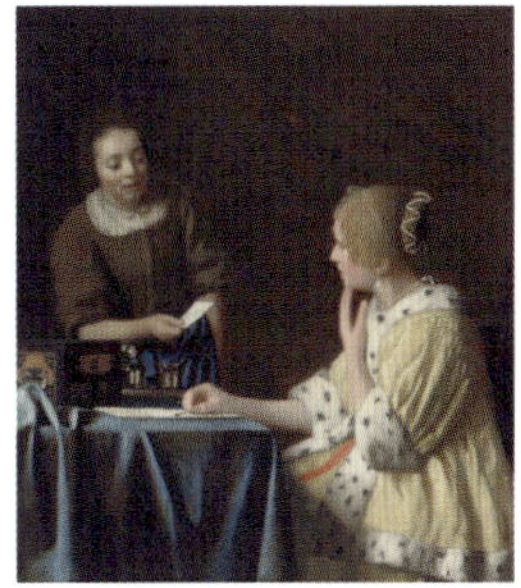

Johannes Vermeer
Mistress and Maid, 1666–68
150

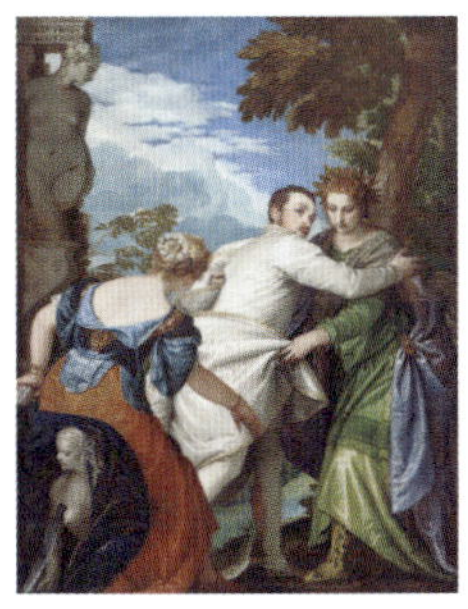

Paolo Veronese
The Choice Between Virtue and Vice,
ca. 1565
78

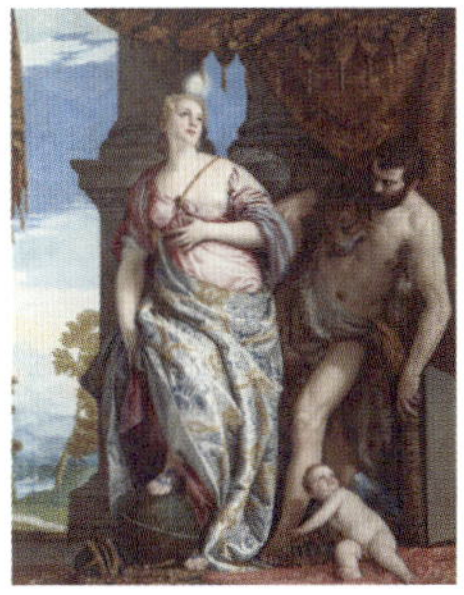

Paolo Veronese
Wisdom and Strength, ca. 1565
75

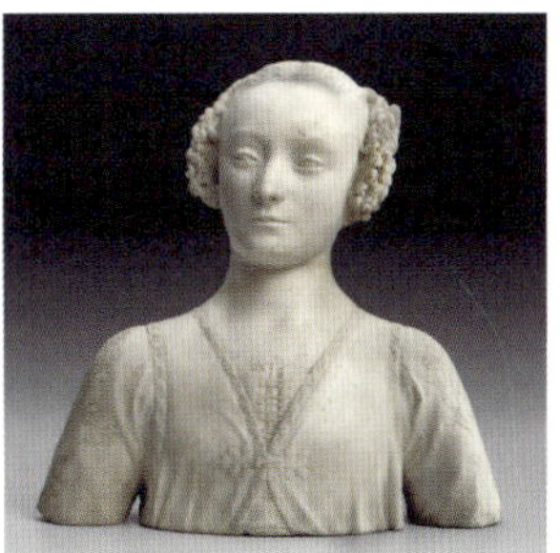

Andrea del Verrocchio
Bust of a Woman, ca. 1460–70
271

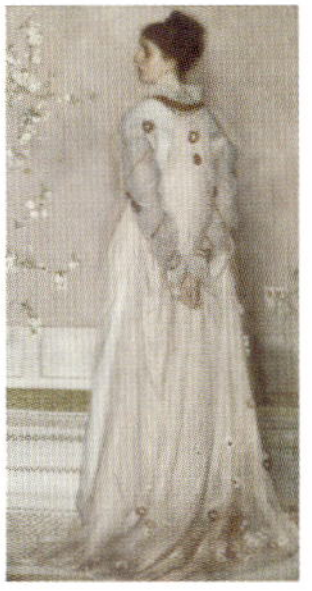

James McNeill Whistler
Symphony in Flesh Colour and Pink: Portrait of Mrs. Frances Leyland, 1871–74
51

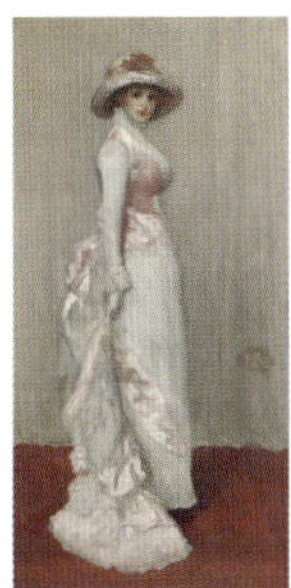

James McNeill Whistler
Harmony in Pink and Grey: Portrait of Lady Meux, 1881–82
227

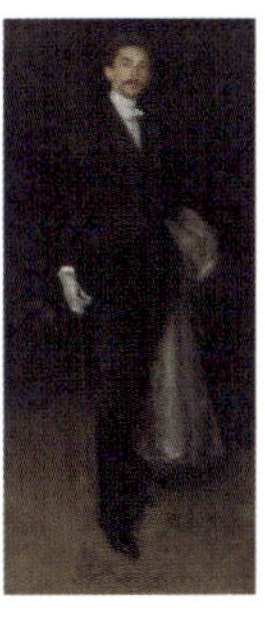

James McNeill Whistler
Arrangement in Black and Gold: Comte Robert de Montesquiou-Fezensac, 1891–92
274

This publication is made possible by Virginia and Randall Barbato.

First published in the United States of America in 2022 by
Rizzoli Electa
A division of Rizzoli International Publications, Inc.
300 Park Avenue South
New York, New York 10010
rizzoliusa.com

Publisher: CHARLES MIERS
Associate Publisher: MARGARET CHACE
Senior Editor: PHILIP REESER
Production Manager: ALYN EVANS
Design Coordinator: OLIVIA RUSSIN
Copy Editor: ELIZABETH SMITH
Proofreader: CLAUDIA BAUER
Managing Editor: LYNN SCRABIS

in association with

The Frick Collection
1 East 70th Street
New York, New York 10021
frick.org

Editor in Chief: MICHAELYN MITCHELL
Assistant Editor: CHRISTOPHER SNOW HOPKINS

Designer: SARAH GIFFORD

All Serrano drawings are oil monochrome on cardboard and were painted in 2020–21.

The Dalmatian cocktail (page 215) was developed by *Saveur*'s Helen Rosner.

ISBN: 978-0-8478-7246-6
Library of Congress Control Number: 2022934935

2022 2023 2024 2025 / 10 9 8 7 6 5 4 3 2 1

PRINTED IN CHINA

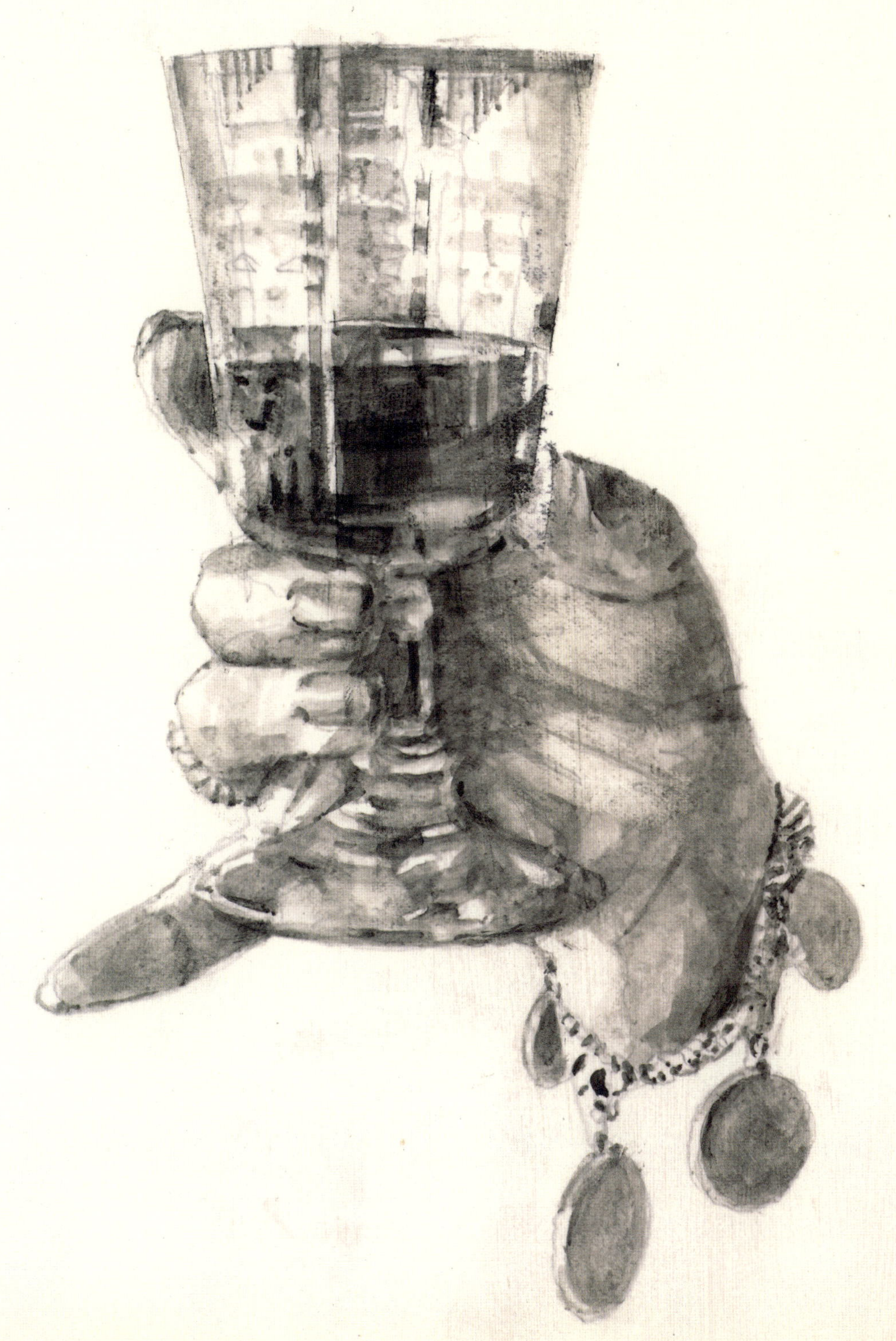